INTRODUCTION TO PSYCHOTHERAPY

Randolph B. PIPES

Auburn University

Donna S. DAVENPORT

Texas A & M University

INTRODUCTION TO PSYCHOTHERAPY

Common Clinical Wisdom

PRENTICE HALL, Englewood Cliffs, New Jersey 07632

Library of Congress Cataloging-in-Publication Data

PIPES, RANDOLPH BERLIN.
    Introduction to psychotherapy : common clinical wisdom / Randolph
B. Pipes, Donna S. Davenport.
        p. cm.
    Includes bibliographical references.
    ISBN 0-13-493578-0
    1. Psychotherapy. I. Davenport, Donna S. II. Title.
    [DNLM: 1. Physician-Patient Relations. 2. Psychotherapy. WM 420
P665i]
RC480.P48 1990
616.89′1—dc20
DNLM/DLC
for Library of Congress   89-23183

Editorial/production supervision: *Edith Riker/DebraAnn Thompson*
Interior design: *DebraAnn Thompson*
Cover design: *Miriam Recio*
Manufacturing buyer: *Robert Anderson*

 © 1990 by Prentice-Hall, Inc.
A Division of Simon & Schuster
Englewood Cliffs, New Jersey 07632

Printed in the United States of America

10 9 8 7 6 5 4 3

ISBN 0-13-493578-0

Prentice-Hall International (UK) Limited, *London*
Prentice-Hall of Australia Pty. Limited, *Sydney*
Prentice-Hall Canada Inc., *Toronto*
Prentice-Hall Hispanoamericana, S.A., *Mexico*
Prentice-Hall of India Private Limited, *New Delhi*
Prentice-Hall of Japan, Inc., *Tokyo*
Simon & Schuster Asia Pte. Ltd., *Singapore*
Editora Prentice-Hall do Brasil, Ltda., *Rio de Janeiro*

To Anne whose support made it possible
and
To Ollie and Earl with gratitude and love

CONTENTS

Preface   *xiii*

ONE
INTRODUCTION: A VIEW OF PSYCHOTHERAPY   *1*

Focus on Therapy: The Person or the Environment   *2*
Limits of Psychotherapy   *2*
Assumptions of the Book   *4*
Summary   *10*

TWO
QUESTIONS BEGINNING THERAPISTS ASK   *12*

Boundary/Management Issues   *13*
Personal Inquiries/Emotional Issues   *21*
General Therapeutic Issues   *30*
Supervisory Issues   *39*
Summary   *42*
Appendix: Index of Questions   *43*

THREE
THERAPIST FEARS/CONCERNS

The Fear of Clients Getting Too Close   *46*
The Fear of "Making a Fool of Oneself"   *48*
The Fear of Not Being Competent to Help   *53*
The Fear of Making the Client Worse   *54*
The Fear of Not Liking the Client   *55*
Concern about the Client Not Liking the Therapist   *56*
Concern about Losing Control of the Session   *57*
Concern about Losing Control of Emotions   *60*
Concern about Making a Difference   *61*
Concern about the Supervisor's Evaluation   *61*
Summary   *62*

FOUR
CLIENT FEARS

How Will I Be Treated?   *65*
How Will I Be Viewed as a Client in Psychotherapy?   *76*
Will I Like the Effects of Being in Therapy?   *85*
Summary   *88*

FIVE
INTAKE INTERVIEWING

Overview of the First Session   *90*
Philosophy of the Intake Session   *95*
Conducting the Intake Interview   *102*
Mental Status Exam   *105*
Formal Intake Interview   *109*
The Suicidal Client   *113*
Optional Questions   *117*
Dimensions of Interest to Therapists   *118*
Tests   *120*
Summary   *122*
Appendix A To Chapter 5: Outline of an
    Intake Interview   *123*
Appendix B To Chapter 5: Outline for Assessing
    Suicidal Risk   *124*

SIX
THE THERAPEUTIC STANCE

The Therapeutic Relationship *126*
Therapist Responsibilities *128*
Client Responsibilities *131*
Guidelines for Early Sessions *132*
Summary *136*

SEVEN
LISTENING

Signals of Poor Listening *140*
Levels of Listening *144*
Summary *150*

EIGHT
TRANSFERENCE/COUNTERTRANSFERENCE

Transference *151*
Countertransference *161*
Summary Comments on Transference *161*
Summary Comments on Countertransference *166*

NINE
RESISTANCE

Resistance *168*
Reluctance *170*
Transference Resistance *172*
Resistant or Reluctant Behaviors *173*
Summary *177*

TEN
TERMINATION

Guidelines for Termination *180*
Summary *187*

ELEVEN
MISTAKES THERAPISTS MAKE   *188*

Mistakes and Theoretical Orientation   *189*
Common Mistakes   *189*
Summary   *207*

TWELVE
ETHICAL AND LEGAL ISSUES   *208*

Ethics   *208*
Record Keeping and Legal Issues   *218*
Summary   *221*
Appendix: Sample Client Information Form   *223*

THIRTEEN
RESPONSIBILITY   *227*

Theoretical Contributions   *228*
Responsibility, Newly Defined   *230*
Therapeutic Distinctions   *234*
Therapeutic Considerations   *239*
Summary   *241*

FOURTEEN
RELATIONSHIPS   *242*

Basic Assumptions about Relationships   *242*
Dysfunctional Styles   *248*
Relationship Skills   *250*
Therapeutic Considerations   *253*
Summary   *255*

REFERENCES AND SELECTED RECOMMENDED READING   *257*

SELECTED BIBLIOGRAPHY ON SHORT-TERM/TIME-
LIMITED PSYCHOTHERAPY (BOOKS AND ARTICLES
PUBLISHED IN 1980 AND AFTERWARD)   *268*

SELECTED BIBLIOGRAPHY OF BOOKS
ABOUT PSYCHOTHERAPY   *272*

THE AUTHORS   *277*

NAME INDEX   *279*

SUBJECT INDEX   *285*

PREFACE

This book is designed as an introductory text for psychotherapy and counseling practica in graduate training programs. The primary emphasis in the book is on what might be called common clinical wisdom—ideas which are typically endorsed by a diversity of experienced counselors and psychotherapists. By using the phrase in the title of the book, we have obviously underscored our belief that there is such a thing as "common clinical wisdom."

Books about psychotherapy inevitably raise the hopes and expectations of prospective readers. On the one hand, we hope some of your expectations *will* be met. On the other hand, even if we accomplished all we set out to do (a dim prospect at best), there are always more topics which "should" have been covered, different emphases which "should" have been placed here or there, etc. We will say more in the Introduction about the perspective we have tried to take in this book. At this point, however, we will say a few things about what we are *not* attempting to do in the book.

This book is about individual counseling and psychotherapy. We make no attempt to discuss other models such as group therapy or family therapy. We also do not attempt to address in any comprehensive way specific disorders such as alcoholism, depression, panic disorders, etc. Furthermore, as much as we support the idea of specialized courses and practica dealing with diverse populations, this book does not attempt, except in very brief ways, to address psychotherapeutic services to such populations. In our view, beginning psychotherapists can profit greatly by widely reading the literature of diverse populations, especially those concerning ethnic and racial minorities, women, gay men, and lesbians. The multicultural nature of our society simply demands therapists who are culturally sensitive, aware of gender issues, and informed about the interplay between culture and personality.

Although some scholarly work is cited, this book is not designed to survey the empirical literature about psychotherapy. Books which readers might find helpful in this regard include Beutler (1983), Garfield and Bergin (1986), and Weiner (1975).

In the book we do not attempt to discuss theory at great length. We assume some familiarity with theories of counseling and psychotherapy. We do make some theoretical assumptions (discussed in the Introduction), but perhaps our first assumption is that *psychotherapy generally does produce positive change* (e.g., Howard, Kopta, Krause, & Orlinsky, 1986; Shapiro & Shapiro, 1982; Smith, Glass, & Miller, 1980).

A number of chapters in this book are developed around issues traditional to the introductory text: Listening, Resistance, Termination, etc. We have also added other material not generally found in introductory texts. After the Introduction, we begin with a lengthy chapter which attempts to address in practical and straightforward terms many of the questions beginning therapists ask. Second, we include two chapters, "Responsibility" and "Relationships," which we hope will give students an example of how experienced therapists actually think about therapeutic issues. (An "interpersonal" perspective, broadly speaking, is taken in these chapters and throughout the book.) Third, chapters on "Client Fears," "Therapist Fears," and "Mistakes Therapists Make" are included. Typically, book chapters have not been devoted to these important areas. Fourth, we include bibliographies both on short-term therapy and on other resource books students may find helpful. We have used as classroom texts (for practicum) several of these resource books. Our students have found a number of them helpful, including those by Weiner (1975) and Teyber (1988). If our book proves not to be your cup of tea, perhaps one of the books in the resource bibliography will be of help.

This book is not about how to provide a primarily educational experience (e.g., assertion training) for the client nor is it focused on very short-term psychotherapy, although some of what we say is undoubtedly applicable to these situations. We recognize some of the financial and philosophical pressures pushing therapists toward short-term interventions (e.g., Cummings, 1988). For this reason, as we said above, we provide (at the end of the book) the reader with a selected bibliography of books and articles related to short-term therapy.

We have tried to write the book the way we do supervision. In part, this means that some issues are emphasized in more than one chapter. Although some may call this redundancy, our experience has been that ideas used in the supervision of psychotherapy are closely intertwined and refuse to be cut cleanly as if there were predetermined fault lines. Also consistent with our supervisory style, we attempt to have an ongoing, informal mix of specific practical ideas and somewhat eclectic conceptualization having primary roots in interpersonal and existential theory.

There is debate, much of it cultural and political in our view, as to the difference (if there is one) between counseling and psychotherapy. We use the terms more or less interchangeably in the book despite potential drawbacks to this approach. Although in popular parlance, counseling may be seen as less intensive or less deep than psychotherapy, we have known people who call themselves counselors who help people make profound changes in their lives, and we have known people who call themselves psychotherapists who perform a helping service perhaps no better than a sympathetic bartender. One is tempted to fall under Freud's influence and entitle any book on the subject, *The Talking Cure*.

We hope we have avoided discriminatory language—words do make a difference. We have included some *quotes* which contain sexist language. Although we are embarrassed for the authors of these quotes, we hope the reader will not be offended by the inclusions.

The examples we give are a mixture of actual cases and constructed ones containing elements of several different cases. Any actual cases involving sensitive, identifiable elements have been altered by setting, gender, etc., to ensure anonymity.

We have tried, as we suppose most authors do, to write with what one might call intellectual integrity. This means a number of things to us, including being clear when something is our opinion rather than a fact. It also means that we try, within the constraints of our format, to include opinions differing from, and evidence raising questions about, our positions.

ACKNOWLEDGMENTS

RBP: I would like to express my appreciation to my parents for their love; Gene Meadows for helping to provide a departmental environment in which a book could be written; my former supervisors, including Ollie Bown and Earl Koile, who greatly and positively influenced my thinking about psychotherapy; my supervisees for good questions; students and staff (especially Kim Hilton, Joy Bowden, and Bettye Campbell) who have been extremely helpful in preparing the manuscript; Carol Wada, our editor at Prentice Hall; reviewers (including Phil Lewis, John Westefeld, and Gene Meadows) who read part or all of the manuscript and offered many helpful suggestions; and to any of my friends (including Ollie and Earl) whose ideas may have ended up in this book without credit.

DSD: In addition to echoing the above thanks to our editor and reviewers, I would like to acknowledge the assistance and contributions of several individuals. Two of my internship supervisors—Tom Lowry and Coystal Stone—

challenged me conceptually, offered me considerable encouragement to use myself therapeutically, and served as excellent role models. Similarly, a number of my past and present students have offered that same combination of challenge and support as they force me to clarify my theoretical assumptions and enhance my clinical skills. They don't let me get by with much, and I'm grateful.

I would also like to thank friends and colleagues from the past, especially Carol Lou Treat and Don Garris, for important contributions to my professional and personal growth. Additional thanks are extended to Wade Birch, for ensuring that I had time to write while working at the Student Counseling Service, and to Carole Pierce and Fred Dorn for their continued encouragement to write down what I knew.

Finally, I want to express my gratitude to members of my family for their longstanding support and for offering me the values that I associate with being a helping professional. Who would I be without you?

1

INTRODUCTION: A VIEW OF PSYCHOTHERAPY

In J. R. R. Tolkien's *Lord of the Rings* (1965), the following interchange takes place:

> Frodo: "Now I am wondering what can have happened. Should I wait for him?"
> Gildor was silent for a moment. "I do not like this news," he said at last. . . .
> "The choice is yours: to go or wait."
> "And it is also said," answered Frodo, "go not to the Elves for counsel, for they will answer both no and yes."
> "Is it indeed," laughed Gildor. "Elves seldom give unguarded advice, for advice is a dangerous gift, even from the wise to the wise, and all courses may run ill. But what would you? You have not told me all concerning yourself; and how then shall I choose better than you?" (p. 123)

Tolkien understood one of the central dialectics which run through Western psychotherapy. On the one hand is the urge to instruct clients in some better way of living their lives, the inclination to point out how clients can better fit some external reality, and/or improve their rationality. On the other hand is a set of more ambiguous inclinations centered on some sort of trust in the client to achieve satisfaction within a reality created by the client and nurtured by the therapist. Most typically in this view, clients are fundamentally seen as participating in and profiting from an *interpersonal experience* more than from receiving information or being persuaded about something.

1

In his imperfect way, Gildor may be said to represent the latter part of the dialectic. Gildor is reluctant to point out pitfalls or issue warnings right away. Despite the potential drawbacks of his position, the view of psychotherapy endorsed in this book is quite sympathetic to the philosophy expressed by Gildor.

FOCUS ON THERAPY: THE PERSON OR THE ENVIRONMENT

Presumably, one of the characteristics of all human cultures is that within the culture there are certain people, at certain times, who exhibit and/or report an undesirable (to them) state of affairs in terms of their perceptions, thoughts, behavior, or emotions, or some combination thereof. These may be or may not be undesirable to others. Presumably, it is also a characteristic of each culture that certain processes, procedures, and structures are both made available to and at times imposed upon the individual to deal with these perceived problems. This book is about one such process—we call it psychotherapy or counseling.

Although there are various ways by which people may achieve satisfaction with regard to these perceptions, thoughts, feelings, and behavior, one can identify two broad paths which seem more or less inclusive: (a) individuals can make changes in themselves, or (b) individuals can alter their environments.

As we see it, psychotherapy is concerned with each of these categories both individually and in interaction. In practice, psychotherapy is almost always some interaction between these two categories chiefly for three reasons: (a) In outpatient psychotherapy, the therapist has access to the client's environment only through the client (an obvious exception is the client-therapist relationship itself, with the therapist *being* a part of the environment in that case); (b) We assume that individuals and their environments are involved in reciprocal determinism (Bandura, 1978); and (c) Complex problems typically require intervention at more than one level.

The psychotherapy we describe in this book is aimed first and foremost at enabling individuals to change themselves. This does not mean that we hold the environment to be of little consequence in terms of people's "good mental health." In part it reflects our belief that many individuals who come for therapy cannot initially make the kinds of changes that would be needed in their environment to facilitate maximally their mental health without first making some changes in how they view and experience themselves in relationship to their world. This process takes time, and it is not simple.

LIMITS OF PSYCHOTHERAPY

Human beings have always (at least for a very long time) been faced with the task of solving their psychological problems. Perhaps our first lesson as a psychotherapist should be that individuals solved problems related to their mental health long before we came on the scene. We are part of the great universe of potentially helpful resources, but like other methods, the processes we use to help people have their limits. We must and should share the stage with other helpers (for example, friends, relatives, rabbis, priests, ministers, hairdressers, divorce lawyers, industrial supervisors, and bartenders (Cowen, 1982).

Psychotherapy is limited in a number of ways: by the fact that it seems to need cultural sanction, by clients' genetic endowment, by their childhood experiences, by the current environment in which they live, by our own expertise, and by chance. When we say that psychotherapy has limits, we are echoing the ideas of a diverse group of psychotherapists. (In fact, the idea that psychotherapy has limits is a good example of common clinical wisdom.) For example, Freud clearly recognized some of these limitations when he said that psychoanalysis was designed to turn neurosis into ordinary misery. The existential psychotherapists have also recognized the limits of psychotherapy by emphasizing the centrality of experiences which have powerful influences on us but which we cannot escape (e.g., death and freedom).

In our view, it is important to remember that change may be activated or enhanced by unpredictable and uncontrollable events. For example, one's economic circumstances may be greatly altered by a stock market collapse; one's child may contract a terminal illness; a lucrative position may become available just as one begins searching for a job; a tennis game between strangers may lead to a lasting friendship; or an individual may have the good fortune to be referred to an excellent psychotherapist. Such events as the ones just described obviously have profound effects upon people. In a similar vein, Bandura (1982) argued that chance encounters "play a prominent role in shaping the course of human lives" (p. 747). Against such a backdrop, we should promise neither our clients nor ourselves more than may be possible. We must accept, not with resignation but with humility, that chance may play a part in our clients' lives which is far larger than our own contributions. We believe that, in general, good psychotherapists have an appreciation for the unpredictable and the uncontrollable—that they have a view of life which "incorporates tragic, ironic, romantic, and comic visions of reality. . . ." (Messer and Winokur, 1980. p. 818). Clearly, we have a deep investment in the relationship between the unpredictability and limits of life on the one hand and the intentions, choices, and actions of our clients on the other. This richly complex perspective on life can only be dimly illuminated in graduate school. It probably has more to do with great literature than it does with theories of psychotherapy. Weinberg (1984) has well expressed a part of the limitation from which many of us suffer:

> Therapists as a group tend to intellectualize too much; they find it hard to acknowledge that much of life is primitive, that love may burst forth in unexpected places, as between homosexuals or people very different in age; they spend years trying to repair relationships where love does not exist, where it never existed, as if fixing up lines of communication, interpreting one person to another can result in anything comparable to the magic that simply appears at times. (p. 7)

Thus, the potential limitations of psychotherapy include, in addition to the ones described earlier, the limited perspective therapists often have on what human nature is and is not.

ASSUMPTIONS OF THE BOOK

We make a number of assumptions in this book. Implicit, though not discussed, are the following two assumptions: (a) Human beings are to some extent free, and their behavior is not determined; and (b) Development is a life-long process which alters some, but not all, basic personality structures. We also make a number of other assumptions, each of which we will comment on briefly in this Introduction. These assumptions include the following: (a) There is such a thing as common clinical wisdom; (b) There are common curative factors in all psychotherapies; (c) Affect plays a central role in psychotherapy; (d) The construct of the self is an important one in psychotherapy; (e) Early experience has a profound and lasting impact on personality development; (f) Toxic interpersonal experiences are generally the foundation of pathology; (g) The interpersonal aspect of psychotherapy is the key to its power; and (h) The culture and the family play a central role in mental health or the lack thereof.

Common Clinical Wisdom.   Perhaps the most important assumption in the book is that there is such a thing as common clinical wisdom. As we will say in more than one place, certainly one's theoretical orientation determines to some extent what one does, what one sees as important, and what one sees as mistakes. Despite this fact, we believe that good psychotherapists, whatever their theoretical orientation, use many of the same techniques and even conceptualizations. These range from almost universally accepted conceptualizations (for example, the observation that anger may "cover" low self-esteem) to principles of intervention (such as noting that allowing clients to talk mainly about others rather than about themselves rarely leads to behavior change). Most good therapists we know do not, at the end of the first session, mutter something such as, "This all looks rather bad, and I'm not sure there is much hope for you." Another example of common clinical wisdom is well expressed by Eagle (1987):

> In any case, common sense and common wisdom alone, without any more rigorous data on therapeutic process and outcome, would dictate that, other things being equal, a more empathic, soothing, and accepting response is generally likely to be more therapeutic than haughtiness, aloofness, and coldness. (p. 182)

An idea related to common clinical wisdom is that psychotherapists *as a group* struggle with common problems or dilemmas (e.g., Dryden, 1987). These include questions such as, "To what extent should my values affect my clients' values?" "What should I do about a client who keeps coming to therapy but seems to be making no progress?" "When (if ever) should I allow my clients' problems to take precedence over my personal life?" "What action (if any) should I take if I know that my adult client is being physically abused?" In this book we attempt to grapple with some of the issues which seem to arise inevitably for psychotherapists.

Common Elements of Psychotherapy. Generally speaking, research seems to suggest that differential effectiveness, while at times claimed by some schools of theory, has yet to be established. Stiles, Shapiro, and Elliott (1986) write:

> Despite the plethora of purportedly distinct psychotherapeutic treatments (Parloff, 1976, 1984), influential reviews of comparative outcome research (Luborsky, Singer, & Luborsky, 1975; Smith, Glass, & Miller, 1980) together with frequently cited studies (e.g., Sloane, Staples, Cristol, Yorkson, & Whipple, 1975) appear to support the conclusion that outcomes of diverse therapies are generally similar. . . . No . . . consensus exists concerning the relative effectiveness of diverse therapies (e.g., DeLeon, VandenBos, & Cummings, 1983; Kiesler, 1985; Office of Technology Assessment, 1980). (p. 165)

Further support for this position can be found in Snyder and Wills (1989), Glass and Kliegl (1983), and Gurman, Kniskern, and Pinsof (1986).

One of the explanations offered for this similarity of outcome is that all psychotherapies contain "common elements." Various authors (e.g., Frank, 1985; Garfield, 1980; Goldfried, 1980; Hobbs, 1962) have suggested what these common elements might be. We are in general agreement that common elements are important. Following the above writers, we suggest the existence of four such elements:

1. An emotionally charged relationship—which by providing an optimum balance of challenge, support, and involvement offers an opportunity for development or restoration of the self in a more or less healthy interpersonal environment.
2. A new way of looking at the problem (including a rationale for it) and potential solutions in relationship to the self.
3. Encouragement to try new and more adaptive behavior.
4. An influential person (the therapist) who models and encourages self-acceptance and courage.

These four processes frequently overlap and complement each other. Obviously, however, different client problems draw differentially on these common elements. For example, individuals with a personality disorder are perhaps most heavily influenced by the first process, a client whose spouse has died may be heavily influenced by the second process, clients with phobias probably chiefly respond to the third element above, and people who feel guilty about something may be heavily influenced by the fourth process.

The role of affect.   We believe that affect is something to be focused on in psychotherapy. Affect plays a number of key roles in the therapeutic process. It can help motivate clients to seek and make changes; it helps clients signal to their therapist when they are overwhelmed; it can help clients and therapists better identify what is of central importance to the client; it helps clients and therapists identify areas in need of development and change; and it helps give access to clients' self-system—their deepest beliefs, assumptions, perceptions, etc., thereby making change more likely. Its expression, in appropriate form, is seen as part of being mentally healthy. In many cases catharsis, especially if accompanied by insight, seems to provide some relief for clients. (Of course, we do not really know whether such emotional expression actually has healing properties or only signals an important change in the self-system.) Although cognitive therapies have greatly influenced psychotherapy in the United States, only recently have we begun to see fresh attempts to deal with the conceptualization of affect (e.g., Buck, 1985; Greenberg and Safran, 1987, 1989). Even if it seems a bit simplistic, we think it important to underscore that a problem with affect is why, in the eyes of most clients, they come seeking psychotherapy.

Centrality of the self.   The self is seen as having or lacking such key properties as attachment, autonomy, sense of efficacy, and openness to immediate experience. We find especially helpful many of the ideas of Kohut (e.g., 1977, 1984), who focused on the "self" and the relationship between the self and the therapist. Thus, the reader will find us using the word *self* in this book, suggesting its heuristic value for conceptualizing disturbance. Mahoney (1985) has described well the idea that symptoms are less something to be altered than an expression of a self-configuration:

> My own experiences as a therapist have led me to agree cautiously that a vast amount of personal energy seems to be chambered into the avoidance of certain changes. For example, several of my clients seemed to have identified with their problems to the point that symptomatic improvements were frightening assaults on identity. When I asked one chronically depressed man what he thought it would take for him to change, he answered, "I guess I would have to be somebody else." (p. 33)

Poor interpersonal relationships produce pathology.   We believe that the great majority of client problems are related to interpersonal experiences. We are influenced by writers of the "interpersonal" school such as Kiesler (1982) who drew on the work of Harry Stack Sullivan and by the Stone Center's "self in relation" theory (e.g., Surrey, 1986.). Thus, the general orientation of the book is "interpersonal," with less emphasis on drive theory, conflict theory, behavioral theory, or cognitive theory. On the other hand, as we will say repeatedly, many therapeutic situations, in our opinion, seem to be addressed similarly by divergent theory systems. For example, most therapists would probably agree, even if they might describe the process somewhat differently, that a primary issue for all human beings is grappling with our limits when faced with situations over which we have little or no control.

Importance of early interpersonal experiences. We assume that many of the experiences of central importance to a client's current functioning are those occurring in the long dependency (roughly 15 years) of childhood common to each of us. That is to say, the difficult problems which bring clients to therapy most often have contributing factors in childhood or adolescence. There are two reasons why we believe that this assumption makes sense. The first is that the tens of thousands of interactions between parent and child provide the ideal setting for learning. Second, the inherent and powerful attachment/dependency structure of the learning environment is believed to result in beliefs, assumptions, and expectations which are both highly resistant to change and which are fully integrated into a self-system which uses these not as appendages, but as fundamental building blocks of identity.

Some readers may not believe that all problems originate in childhood. Others will argue that even if they do there is no practical implication. We are not proposing a trauma theory of neuroses. That is, we believe that only a very small percentage of clients come to therapy primarily because of one traumatic event in their childhood. Even Freud abandoned this position as too simplistic early in his work. On the other hand, we do believe that severe disturbances in personality are most often the result of the repeated failure of the environment to provide an optimum balance of consistent and safe structure and empathy for the child.

We also realize that there are certain developmental (for example, the aging process) and situational (for example, death of a spouse) problems which bring clients to therapy and perhaps which do not have as their linchpin childhood experiences. These types of problems, if they do not involve the self-system developed during childhood and adolescence, will, in our view, prove to be very responsive to psychotherapy. This is not to suggest that such problems are simple or that they will be easily resolved. For example, being raped or having one's spouse die may take many months or years of painful adjustment. On the other hand, when progress is not forthcoming (and assuming that the therapist is reasonably skilled and is providing a warm, caring environment), there is an increased possibility that longstanding behavior patterns are contributing to the delay in adjustment. We believe that in actuality it would be rather puzzling for the sense of self developed in our first 15 years *not* to affect how we cope and struggle with the problems we now face. Certainly, many have in a sense transformed the self they were, but the deep structures created in the powerful early learning environment are never destroyed; as a minimum they affect the type of transformation which has taken place. Guidano and Liotti (1985) expressed this idea well:

> Moreover, from the beginning the gradual structuring of self-knowledge is constantly biasing—within the possibilities of slow cognitive growth—the child's

> ongoing perception of incoming information through the selection of specific domains of exchange in his interaction with experience. (p. 109)

Guidano and Liotti tie who we are directly to childhood experience and particularly to attachment theory:

> As a logical consequence of the assumption that human knowledge is imbued with interactive-reflective properties, a crucial role is attributed to interpersonal and relational domains in the development of self-knowledge. We therefore agree with Ainsworth et al. (1978) in connecting attachment theory (cf. Bowlby, 1969, 1973, 1980) as a fact of explanatory theory supplying a structured framework for understanding and organizing observational and experimental data already available, that is, a new integrating paradigm of human development that gives us an inclusive and organized vision of all factors that contribute to the structuring of self-knowledge.
> . . . the quality of attachment itself becomes even more complex and articulated in the course of development: From mere physical attachment in early infancy it evolves toward a structured relationship, intensely charged with emotions, that becomes one of the essential media for the shaping of self-conceptions. . . . Hence, attachment becomes, in the course of development, a highly structured vehicle through which increasingly complex and unlimited information about oneself and the surrounding reality becomes available. (pp. 108–110)

Those readers unfamiliar with Guidano and Liotti may be surprised to learn that the material quoted above comes neither from a book on neoanalytic psychotherapy nor from one on developmental psychology, but rather from a book entitled *Cognition and Psychotherapy* (Mahoney and Freeman, 1985). Thus, we believe that our broad theoretical perspective, which for want of perhaps a better term we label *interpersonal,* shares common assumptions with other perspectives, such as some cognitive ones. Furthermore, we assume that some focus on the childhood learning environment provides the therapist with a potentially emotionally charged, workable route to the sense of self-identity which shapes and controls our reactions to the environment and other purposeful activity.

Importance of the therapeutic relationship.   We assume that the relationship between the client and therapist is of critical importance in whether the client will make good progress in psychotherapy. Theorists as diverse as Rogers (e.g., 1951) and Glasser (1965) have emphasized the important role of relationships in the healing process.

Although there are multiple uses of the term *therapeutic alliance* (Roth, 1987), we believe that this term captures the essence of a key ingredient in therapy—the idea that the client and therapist work together in *alliance* toward solving a common goal, which is typically the reduction of psychological suffering, the restoration of hope, and an enhanced sense of meaning and satisfaction in life for the client. Like any alliance, the therapeutic one is subject to the vicissitudes of human emotion—both that of the client and of the therapist. Certainly, clients may become angry with therapists and vice versa; either or both parties may at times retreat from the relationship, etc. But the fundamental stance which is taken by the therapist is that the client is someone to be supported and understood and that the therapist will not turn mean or demanding if the client is having trouble in the relationship. If we can do this as therapists, can be consistently empathic, and if we can for the most part avoid using the client for our own neurotic needs, we have thereby laid the foundation for change. Put another way, clients' perceptions of our having their best interests as an unambiguous goal to which we are actively committed, coupled with our capacity to communicate to clients, on an ongoing basis, our deep understanding of what it is like to be them, is probably enough to ensure psychotherapeutic gain for some individuals. Additionally, it forms the basis for therapeutic gain in other cases which may call on additional skills and activities of the therapist.

In our view, if progress is not seen in psychotherapy, the first "suspect" is the relationship between client and therapist. Even if there are other issues involved (for example, the personality structure of the client or the environment), these other issues often interact with aspects of the relationship to retard progress. So we urge the therapist to keep as a central and ongoing focus the following question: "What kind of relationship am I offering the client and how is the relationship affecting the client's progress or lack thereof?"

Impact of culture and the social environment.   Although we recognize that the client's environment often plays a central role in causing and maintaining the client's difficulties, as we said earlier, we do not emphasize an analysis of the environment herein. In our view, strong conceptualizations of the environment which do justice to the complexity of external reality and internal perception have yet to be developed. This is particularly true when one confronts the dilemma of the extent to which one chooses (or does not choose) one's environments. This issue of there not being satisfactory conceptualizations of the environment is a good example of the fact that there are fundamental issues bearing on therapeutic practice that have not yet been satisfactorily addressed by the discipline (P. Lewis, personal communication, April 1989).

We should also note, however, that researchers and theorists have indeed provided us with *some* helpful perspectives (e.g., Claiborn and Lichtenburg, 1989; Magnusson, 1981; Stewart and Healy, 1989). (For an interesting article addressing the implications of seeing "personhood" as centralized [separate from the environment], see Sampson, 1985.)

Behavior therapists, family therapists, feminist therapists, and cross cultural researchers have all made contributions to our understanding of how the environment affects the individual. Many of these contributions are consistent with the "common clinical wisdom" perspective which we take in this book. For example, we are in full agreement with feminist psychotherapists (e.g., Gilbert, 1980; Rosewater, 1984; Rosewater and Walker, 1985) who have argued that the sexist nature of society places women at greater risk for conflicts and psychological "difficulties." This idea is not just some abstract political theory but rather has immediate and real consequences for how we as therapists view the difficulties of our clients. For example, when a woman reports being upset due to sexual harassment at the office, most therapists (we hope) are likely to start with the assumption that office environments often do include sexual harassment, that such processes are damaging to women's mental health, and that this damage occurs at least in part because the woman is a human being and not, for example, because she is afraid of her sexuality, is lacking in maturity, or is suffering from some other personality deficit.

Although therapeutic orientations vary widely in terms of the importance attached to the environment as an ongoing cause of behavioral and emotional difficulties and although current conceptualizations of the environment seem incomplete, common clinical wisdom would suggest that therapists should routinely remind themselves that clients live in a social, cultural, and family context which exerts an ever-present, powerful influence on clients' lives. All the observations and suggestions we make in this book we hope will be understood as being consistent with, and supportive of, the above idea.

SUMMARY

Psychotherapy is a form of help which shares the "helping stage" with other cultural structures and other formal and informal helping professions. Like other forms of helping, psychotherapy has its limits.

A key assumption of the book is that many psychotherapists share similar ideas about what is good therapeutic practice in a wide variety of situations. Research suggests that psychotherapy helps the majority of people who seek it, but there is little evidence that one form is better than another. There are assumed to be common elements (e.g., a rationale for what has caused the problem) in the various schools of psychotherapy.

This book is written from what might be called an "interpersonal perspective" (e.g., Teyber, 1988), which emphasizes the importance of interpersonal relationships in the development of both psychological suffering and psychological health. Psychotherapy should include a focus on affect in general, and in particular on the affect associated with interpersonal relationships, including the therapeutic one.

We view childhood and adolescent experiences as frequently being important in the development of psychological difficulties; however, psychotherapy is not typically the search for some childhood trauma. The sense of "self in relationship to the world" developed by repeated experience in our interpersonal family environment has a lasting influence on how we process experience, feel about ourselves, select environments, and react to current interpersonal relationships.

Despite our "interpersonal" orientation, however, our chief aim is to identify and comment on ideas, techniques, and clinical wisdom cutting across many theoretical lines. For example, some client difficulties are seen by us and many other therapists as being greatly exacerbated (or even primarily caused) by environmental forces. As a second example, many therapists, whatever they call it, and whether they do it to a greater or lesser extent, probably try in part to help clients see problems from a different perspective (e.g., Conoley and Garber, 1985). Although we stop short of calling ourselves eclectic, we share some foundation with those who draw systematically from various perspectives (e.g., Howard, Nance, and Meyers, 1986; Norcross, 1986.).

Like many people who have written about psychotherapy, we strongly emphasize the importance of the relationship between client and therapist. We emphasize the therapeutic relationship for at least two reasons. First, clients are not likely to be influenced in a strongly positive way by therapists with whom they have a poor relationship. Second, past and present relationships have such an impact on how people feel about themselves, it seems reasonable to assume that the relationship between client and therapist is an important variable in the therapeutic process. We assume that clients frequently seek therapy as a direct result of the deleterious effect on their self-system of one or more past or present poor relationships. The therapeutic relationship thus offers the client the opportunity to develop or restore this self-system.

2

QUESTIONS BEGINNING THERAPISTS ASK

> In the great crises of life, in the supreme moments when to be or not to be is the question, little tricks of suggestion do not help. Then the doctor's whole being is challenged.
>
> —C. G. Jung

For very good reasons, one might question the utility of including this chapter in a book on learning to do psychotherapy. In fact, if you view what we write in this chapter as answering the questions we pose, we will have failed in our purpose. Although we do know from experience what many of the questions are which beginning therapists ask, *we also know that in most cases the questions are difficult to answer outside of a context and that any given question reflects various concerns depending on who has asked the question.* We cannot emphasize too strongly the limitations of addressing complex questions in a brief fashion. We also know, however, that when you are just starting out to be a therapist there are a great many unknowns and many things about which to be worried. Because we believe that therapy is seldom effective when the therapist is being overwhelmed by anxiety and because we believe that having at least a little information about unknown areas reduces anxiety, we will in this chapter pose a number of questions which over the years our students have raised.

We will discuss each question briefly, outlining some ideas we have about the issue being addressed. In many cases we will tell you what we might do. As we imply above, we do not think of our comments as being definitive answers but rather as the starting point for you to provide your own answers.

We emphasize strongly that when we place possible therapists' responses in quotes, we are *not* telling you to say those exact words (in fact we would seldom say those exact words ourselves) but are giving you some ideas about ways to approach the problem. At times you may believe that our suggestions are "off base"; we hope you will think critically about how our ideas are different from yours. Our greatest hope is that these questions will be used by you individually and in supervision or class in such a way as to stimulate your thinking on the subject. We caution that there is tremendous variation among agencies in terms of their policies about some of these issues and that the answers to some questions will vary according to local norms and client ethnicity. Furthermore, different supervisors will answer the questions in different ways, and you are particularly encouraged to discuss with your supervisor any comments which trouble you. Despite the above cautions, we hope and believe that you will find a number of specific suggestions which will be helpful to you. We also hope that this chapter will be a kind of second "introduction" to the book by giving you a flavor for how we think about some of the challenges faced by counselors and psychotherapists. See the appendix to this chapter for a complete list of the questions discussed in the chapter. For an additional list of questions (with comments), see chapter 62 of Lewis Wolberg's *The Technique of Psychotherapy* (1988). For organizational purposes, we have divided the questions into four categories: Boundary/Management Issues, Personal Inquiries/Emotional Issues, General Therapeutic Issues, and Supervisory Issues.

BOUNDARY/MANAGEMENT ISSUES

1. *How should I introduce myself?* Some settings, hospitals more often, have a norm which suggests using forms of addresses (Mr., Ms., Mrs., Dr.). The authors prefer the use of the given and last name without titles if there is no specific norm. Even when there is a norm, there are usually a few intrepid souls who use whatever form they find most comfortable. Some inpatient facilities may want you to use a specific form of address in order to help maintain boundary conditions. Except under such circumstances, we encourage you to introduce yourself the way you feel most comfortable. There really is no right or wrong answer to this question.

2. *If I am a student in training, should I inform clients of this fact?* Yes. Clients have a right to know that you are delivering services as a part of a class or as part of your responsibility as a practicum student.

3. *How should I bring up the issue of audio or video recording?* Most training programs require that you audio or video record your counseling sessions. Furthermore, the vast majority of agencies require that you obtain written permis-

sion to record these sessions. Certainly, you should never record a session without the client's being aware of the recording. Perhaps the easiest way to handle this issue is, following introductions, to say something like this: "Before we get started, I'd like to mention a couple of things. I'm a student in the graduate program, and as a matter of routine I tape-record my sessions. This is helpful to me since I, and at times my supervisor, can go back over the tape to listen for how I might have been more helpful to you. So, if it's all right with you, I'd like to ask you to sign the form that we ask everyone to sign, and then I'll record the session." We strongly advise against long explanations. If you present taping in a short, straightforward and positive manner, you will find that over 90 percent of your clients will readily agree to taping. If a client expresses reservations, you might say something like this: "Of course, the choice is yours. Since recording the sessions is so helpful to me, I wonder if we could just give it a try, and then if you feel too anxious, we can always cut it off. How does that sound?" If the client still refuses to be taped, we recommend that you discontinue, for the time being, the discussion. Of course, refusal on the part of the client is almost always very diagnostic. Sometimes you will find that clients have a very simple question about taping and that after you answer it, taping will be no problem. For example, they may want to know when the tapes will be erased (a good release form should contain this information anyway) or whether certain people (for example, their instructors if they are college students) will have access to the tape. The issue of taping cannot be separated from the issue of confidentiality (see next question).

   4.   What should I tell clients about confidentiality? You should know that experienced therapists have wide differences among themselves in how they address with clients the issue of confidentiality. Some like to give the client, in the first session, some information on this important subject. Others wait for the client to raise the issue or may bring it up selectively depending on the client's dynamics. Legally, you may find yourself in trouble if you do not break confidentiality under certain circumstances. These circumstances vary from state to state but usually include situations where the client is a danger to self or others or in the case of child abuse. The law may also require you to report other criminal acts (whether they were committed in the past or have been threatened) in which the client is involved. Similarly, you may be compelled, under threat of contempt of court, to testify or release information about your client. In fact, if you are a student (or are otherwise not licensed), you may be especially vulnerable to such court orders since what is called "privileged communication" often extends only to licensed professionals. Although it has been argued that clients deserve information about the legal limits of confidentiality and privileged communication, in actual practice the majority of psychotherapists probably give limited information until specifically asked by the client. You may find that one of the forms used by the agency where you are working gives the client some information about confidentiality. The usual practice of the authors is to describe confidentiality and privileged communication in the first session. More discussion may be necessary if the client is particularly concerned about the issue. If you believe that confidentiality must be broken, you should, of course, first consult with your supervisor. Alternatives to breaking confidentiality should be explored fully. Furthermore, the client should be informed of your impending actions. The entire process should be used therapeutically in every way possible. When you give the client some information about the issue, you are encouraged to be somewhat brief and nonapologetic. For example, you might say something like, "Even though there are a few extreme instances in which I might have to tell someone what you've said, as an example when you are a danger to yourself, in fact this type of situation rarely occurs. So even though it's theoretically possible that I could tell someone what you have told me, it is not at all likely and would be a very extreme situation." If you do say something like this to the client, it is very important that you give the client a chance to respond, ask questions, and express feelings.

You will find additional discussion concerning this issue in the chapter "Client Fears," as well as in the chapter "Ethical and Legal Issues."

5.   *Should I give clients my home phone number?* In most cases there is little reason to do this. Probably the majority of therapists do give clients in acute crises their phone number. Two reasons are most often cited for not giving out your phone number: (a) It may encourage excessive dependency on the part of the client; or/and (b) It may confuse the client about boundaries. A third and more personal reason may be, "I don't want my dinner interrupted." Arguments often cited to support giving out a phone number include the following: (a) The client feels cared for; (b) You may be legally responsible if you don't make provision for emergencies; and (c) You may want clients to call if they are "desperate." If your phone number is listed, clients can, of course, call you even if you don't give them your number. Nonetheless, giving your phone number is, of course, much more than merely providing information. Our policy is to give our telephone number to clients who are suicidal or who are in acute distress. When the "privilege" is abused, this development is processed in therapy. You will find that most clients will not abuse the privilege of calling you in a crisis. We believe that most clients want to be independent. If you are getting, from several clients, what you consider to be too many calls, consider the possibility that you may actually want clients to be dependent on you in this way. As a practical matter, if clients need your phone number, they most certainly need the number for the local crisis center. After all, you are not at home 24 hours of each day.

6.   *Do I need liability insurance?* Increasingly, the answer to this question is yes. You may or may not be required by your training program to carry such insurance. Professional organizations such as the American Psychological Association and the American Association for Counseling and Development offer student policies as do several private companies. If you take out a policy, be sure to get one that protects from any suit arising from seeing a client during the policy even if the suit is brought after the policy expires.

7.   *Should I keep personal notes on my clients?* At times it may be helpful to keep brief, unofficial notes on clients. The critical point is that such notes be

safeguarded and written in such a way so that loss will not compromise confidentiality. We should point out that some agencies may have policies forbidding the keeping of personal notes. Furthermore, published articles concerning dual records seem to be mixed as to the advisability of this procedure (Soisson, VandeCreek, and Knapp, 1987). One problem with such notes is that if there is a crisis and you are unavailable, the official notes, not your personal ones, will of course be the basis of treatment. Make sure that important, relevant information is in the official notes. Additional comments concerning record keeping are found in the chapter "Ethical and Legal Issues," as well as below.

8.   *Should I take notes during therapy sessions?* We believe that it is best not to take notes during the session perhaps excepting intake interviews. Allow yourself a little time after each session so that you can make notes in the chart and/or write your personal notes. Many clients are "put off" by note taking, and the process seems to put a barrier between client and therapist. It is also true, however, that many therapists *do* take notes.

9.   *What should I write in progress notes?* Most agencies have a format which is required for use in progress notes. The most widely used (or some variant thereof) is the Subjective-Observed-Assessment-Plan (SOAP) system. (SOAP is actually a part of a comprehensive system labeled Problem Oriented Medical Record [Weed, 1968].) *Subjective* refers to the client's self-report—for example, "I feel depressed," or "I have been shouting at my wife lately." *Observed* refers to what the therapist actually sees during therapy—for example, "Client was dressed shabbily," or "Client cried throughout the session." *Assessment* refers to your analysis of what produced the client's current symptoms—for example, "The client's inability to express his feelings toward his wife has resulted in depression," or "The client's anger appears to be a result of his low self-esteem." *Plan* refers to the action which the therapist and client anticipate taking to alleviate symptoms—for example, "will continue desensitization," or "will continue discussing the client's feelings of insecurity." As you can see, the SOAP system is somewhat behavioral in its philosophical underpinnings. Agencies receiving state or federal money tend to use this or a similar system. Other agencies (for example, many university counseling centers) require only a brief summary of the session. As an alternative to SOAP (if you have a choice), you might consider using the Individual Psychotherapy Session Note (Presser and Pfost, 1985).

From a legal standpoint, you should always record any threat to self or others, together with action taken as a result. For example: "Client threatened suicide. Made assessment of danger; no specific plan, no immediate means, good family support. Discussed with Drs. Smith and Jones. Joint decision—no immediate threat. Gave client my phone number and number of crisis center." In general, if there is a legal issue involved, you should make entries in the record which will help protect you from a suit. It is unfortunate that progress notes have become a legal battleground, but the fact is that they have. Twenty years ago it might have been fine to just do your best; today you must do your best *and* record *how* you have done your best (Soisson, VandeCreek, and Knapp, 1987).

In general, labels should be avoided when writing in progress notes. For example, because of the prejudice against individuals who are gay or lesbian, many therapists, including the authors, are reluctant to use words such as *homosexual* or *gay* in progress notes and prefer instead to talk about "sexual preference issues." Naturally, if the client is gay but does not present with this issue, no entry about sexual preference would be made.

Additional comments concerning record keeping may be found in the chapter "Ethical and Legal Issues."

10. When should I deviate from the usual session frequency? For most outpatient agencies, clients are seen once a week. Since there is almost a cultural expectation for this frequency, psychotherapists usually follow it unless there is an unusual circumstance. One such unusual circumstance would be clients in acute crisis who are often seen twice each week. Special forms of therapy (e.g., biofeedback, relaxation, desensitization) are exceptions to the rule, and you should obtain specific supervision on such techniques. Orthodox psychoanalysis, of course, involves more than one contact per week since the client's defenses are assumed to solidify too easily over the period of an entire week.

For a variety of reasons, some clients may ask to be seen every other week or once a month. This is especially true in rural areas and in cases involving follow-up at VA hospitals. Our inclination is to allow clients to be seen at the interval they request. Obviously, clients who want to be seen only once per month are making a statement about the level of involvement they want in this enterprise of psychotherapy. Clients who are terminating may, toward the very end of therapy, be seen every two weeks, and then even this length of time might be extended to once a month. The most important thing is that clients have a good sense of what they can count on. Do not encourage "dropping by" or the setting of extra appointments. Naturally, there will be times when clients are in a crisis, will come by, and will need to be seen, or they may call while in crisis and request an extra appointment. When this happens, you should certainly agree to see them if there seems to be a pressing concern of a critical nature. Alternatively, talking with them at that time for a few minutes on the phone may be intervention enough until their regularly scheduled appointment. Another option would be to ask them to call you at the office at a particular time before their next appointment. Or you might simply leave open the option of their calling again should the need arise. Often just knowing that you *would* be available in a crisis helps prevent the crisis. The decision as to which of these alternatives is most appropriate should be made jointly with the client.

11. Should I allow clients to switch appointment times? Generally speaking, we discourage this procedure. If you start moving appointment times around, you will find that clients often have more and more special circumstances requiring them to move their appointment. If you reinforce behavior, do not be surprised when it increases in frequency. Clients need the stability and reassurance that comes with having a specific time for therapy. For example, if the two of you have agreed to meet on Thursdays at 10:00 A.M., try to stick to this schedule rather than allowing little problems to dictate meeting at 9:00 A.M. one week, 1:00 P.M. the next week, and back to 10:00 A.M. the following week. One of the ways in which the client shows dedication to therapy is to make a commitment about the time set aside for therapy. If little problems keep arising which seem to call for rescheduling the time you are to meet, you should rightly wonder how serious the client is about therapy. These comments do not apply if you work in an agency where clients do not receive an unchanging time slot. Furthermore, although a stable "time slot" for a client is desirable, this goal does not mean that the therapist should be rigid or unreasonable. There are actually wide differences among therapists about this issue, which probably suggests that whether you tend to be more flexible or less flexible about it, you will be able to find support for your position. Finally, make sure that *you* do not find yourself needing to change the client's appointment time.

12. *Should I allow clients to start early if they are in the waiting room and I am available?* Later (#37) we will discuss the importance of stopping on time. The same principle applies to starting early. Clients will show up early and may ask if you are free. The answer is no unless there is a crisis.

13. *What should I say if a client wants to tape-record the session?* Therapists differ widely as to whether they object or not to the client's recording of the session. Some therapists encourage their clients to do so; other therapists believe that such a procedure tends to dilute therapy or foster intellectualizing. Our advice is to be cautious about permitting this but not to arbitrarily rule it out. The most important question is not whether you should or should not but rather in what way the request is related to the client's dynamics. For example, individuals who are extremely paranoid should not be encouraged to record the sessions, nor should individuals who are in legal difficulty. Our comments concerning this question also apply if the client asks to borrow *your* recording of the session.

14. *What should I say if a client wants to bring a friend or parent to meet me?* We discourage this practice except near the end of therapy. It is most important to try to understand why clients want to do it. At times, they may have been maneuvered into suggesting it by an individual who feels threatened by what is happening in therapy and wants to "check you out." Other times, they may be motivated to show you off—"this is the person who has helped me so much." In such instances, dependency is a prime candidate for the motivating dynamic. Near the end of therapy, however, clients may be using the introduction as one of their ways to end the therapy experience. In such cases, it may be part of a positive termination. We say this realizing that when the client introduces the therapist to a friend or relative during the termination phase of therapy, there may be a fantasy that the therapist will be reborn in the person with whom the client *will* have an ongoing relationship.

15. *What kind of clothes should I wear as a therapist?* Naturally, it depends on the agency. Ties are usually not required for males nor are dresses for females. Shorts and cutoffs are generally not appropriate. If you are a student, when you

go for an interview it is appropriate to ask about the clothes therapists typically wear at that particular agency. A good example of a personal appearance issue is that of males wearing an earring. In some agencies males are quite free to wear an earring. In other agencies directors may be hesitant about allowing such a procedure if the client population is extremely conservative. In general, your appearance, whether it concerns clothes, hair, earrings, or whatever, should not do violence to the cultural norms and expectations of the population with which you will be working. Strong (1968) articulated a model of counseling which gives theoretical reasons for the therapist to be considered an "expert," "trustworthy," and "socially attractive" by the client. If the client is uncomfortable with your appearance, any or all of these variables may be affected.

16. *What should I do when clients call me at home when they are in crisis?* Frequently, agencies have some guidelines to assist you in such a situation, so be sure to check to see if this is true in your case. Outcomes to this sort of crisis fall into three categories. One possibility is that the client, after talking with you for a few minutes, will decide that he or she can make it until the next appointment, or at least until you can see them the next day on an emergency basis. A second possibility may be that some arrangement for family or friends may be made to assist in the crisis. These sorts of arrangements must be made with the cooperation of the client since in some circumstances the *worst* thing to do would be to involve family or friends. If you believe on the basis of the telephone conversation and your previous contact with the client that the client is an imminent danger to self or others, you will need to make arrangements to hospitalize the client. Do not go to the client's house and especially not alone. Under most circumstances the first choice is to have clients go to the emergency room (either driving themselves or having a friend drive them). Depending on the situation, you or another on-call therapist may meet them there to assist them in being admitted. Depending on the agency you work for and the rules of the local hospital, you will need either a staff psychologist or consulting psychiatrist to approve the admission. This can usually be accomplished by your calling the person with authority to admit, explaining the situation to them, and asking them to call the hospital. In an extreme emergency, clients can go to any hospital emergency room, but the treatment received at such rooms varies widely and will be much better if a mental health professional has at least called to explain the situation. As we said above, be sure to talk with your on-site supervisor about this issue. If you know what to do before the problem arises, the problem will be much less difficult to handle.

17. *Should I visit a client who has been admitted to the hospital?* If your client has been admitted to a local psychiatric hospital, the answer is almost always yes. What form of treatment you should be delivering, how often you should go, etc., is something which will need to be discussed between you and the psychologist or psychiatrist who is supervising the client's case in the hospital. Remember that except in emergencies, a "release of information" from the client is needed before you can talk to the hospital staff about your client. It is generally advisable

to talk to your client and the hospital's supervising psychologist expeditiously to ensure that the client is receiving what you view as appropriate treatment. If your client is to be discharged into the care of parents or will be leaving the city upon discharge, it is very important that you help ensure continuity of treatment.

If your client is being admitted to an inpatient drug/alcohol treatment program, you will not generally visit them. However, there may be exceptions to this rule if, for example, you have seen the client over a long period of time.

If the client has been admitted to a hospital for medical reasons, we generally do not visit them. The general guideline is to visit clients only when you are seeing them as a part of your professional relationship. This is not to say that if one of your clients is in a bad accident you should never visit her or him in the hospital. The point is that when you are inclined to deviate from the typical therapy session contact, you should be very clear on why you are deviating and the possible drawbacks for changing the usual rules. In all cases, your supervisor should be contacted before you visit a client in the hospital. It is important to remember that some agencies have a very strict policy about seeing clients away from the office (see below).

18.   *Is it all right to schedule a therapy session away from the office?* There are, of course, some behavioral treatment programs which utilize such procedures as a central part of the treatment. If you have taken appropriate precautions and cleared the procedure with your supervisor, there should be no problem in such instances. In more traditional forms of psychotherapy, you should be very cautious about seeing clients outside the office setting. For example, clients with a borderline personality disorder may be very confused about this sort of "boundary violation." Clients who are attracted to you may misread your intentions. If a client were to be injured during the session, there would be the question of liability, and of course confidentiality is much harder to ensure outside an office setting. Furthermore, as we said above, some agencies place severe limitations on the circumstances under which a client can be seen away from the office. For example, under no circumstances should you invite a client to your home for therapy unless you have an office there and have been seeing the client there regularly.

Therapists differ about whether it is ever permissible to have a session "over coffee." We do not believe that it is appropriate even under very favorable conditions. We do recognize, however, that there are probably some therapists who, toward the end of therapy with a few clients, are willing to "have coffee" as a part of the process of ending therapy. We believe that the risks inherent in such a process far outweigh potential gains.

On the other hand, we believe that clients who have been hospitalized, especially adolescents, at times may benefit from walking on the hospital grounds with you during a therapy session. Some therapists would advise strongly against this procedure. As a minimum, in a hospital setting this sort of thing should be discussed with the treatment team.

PERSONAL INQUIRIES/EMOTIONAL ISSUES

19.   *What should I say if a client wants to know my credentials or training?* Of course, a question about training may be an attempt to undercut your power, may be indicative of the client's inability to trust, may reflect the client's ambivalence about being in therapy, or some combination of the above. Psychotherapists are, however, increasingly cognizant of the client's rights as a consumer. Furthermore, the growing number of different types of help-giving specialties inevitably leads to some confusion on the part of clients. The media has also played a part in disseminating information about what therapists do. For example, there are books for the general population describing the differences between approaches such as Gestalt, Psychoanalytic, and Behavioral psychotherapies. Therefore, you can scarcely blame clients for asking about some of these issues even though we may also get a glimpse of their personality when they ask such questions, especially if the point is belabored. If you are sympathetic to the idea that questions about credentials should be handled straightforwardly, you will find an ally in Arnold Lazarus, who in his book *Behavior Therapy and Beyond* (1971) describes an incident in which a client responded well to his nondefensive answers. All these complexities do not, however, change the fact that if you are just starting to be a therapist, and you are asked about your experience, you will probably feel on the spot. If asked, for example, how many clients you have seen, don't "try to be Freud" by saying something like "credentials must be important to you." If you do give such a response, don't be surprised if the client says, "Yes, credentials are important to me when I see someone without them." Clients are seldom stupid, and they react (understandably) quite strongly to anything they perceive as defensive and to therapists trying to be something they are not. When asked about your experience, don't try to defend yourself by listing your course work or your informal experience. Generally, the less explanation, the better. Thus, if asked how many clients you have seen, consider a reply like this, "I'm a graduate student in training. I haven't seen a lot of people in formal counseling sessions. How do you feel about that? If it bothers you, let's talk about it." (The response is more effective if you can look directly at the client and speak in a calm and confident tone—something which may at first be difficult to do.) A response such as the one above models for the client the kind of straightforward honesty you hope will characterize the relationship and shows that you are mature and confident enough to readily acknowledge that you are not Fritz Perls. Nine out of ten clients will appreciate your refreshing candor and will take it as a sign that they don't need to worry too much about your experience. On the other hand, it is perhaps not necessary to say, "You are my third client—I am a rank beginner." While still showing a refreshing (even sprightly) candor, this response gives the client nothing to hold on to. We encourage you to be straightforward but not blunt. Only a very small percentage of clients ever ask about experience. Furthermore, if you tell them up front that you are a student when you are asking permission to tape, you will

almost never get a question about your experience—you will have already have simply and directly addressed the issue.

20.   *Should I tell clients if they make me angry?* The broader question here is the extent to which it is advisable to tell your client what you are feeling. Both of the authors have occasionally found it helpful to share with clients our reaction to them. In general, however, we believe that the special relationship between therapist and client rules out the advisability of routinely communicating your feelings. Whether you like it or not, the relationship is not an equal one, has certain limits set on it, and in the vast majority of cases does not last across time as does a friendship. Furthermore, it seems to us that clients should be able to expect that ultimately the relationship will make them feel better. If you become angry at a client and express your anger, how can you be sure that the results will be therapeutic? The minimum conditions for expressing anger toward the client are that (a) you have a sound reason for believing that it will be therapeutic and that (b) your anger does not appear to be related to countertransference issues. Some therapists take the position that any strong feeling toward the client does represent countertransference. We do not completely agree with this position. For example, if you negotiate with a client, at his request, for an extra session after normal working hours and he fails to show up because he decided to go to a movie instead, we would not view at least some anger as countertransference. In such a case, it *may* be therapeutic to share some of your reactions with the client. We emphasize, however, that what separates the therapeutic relationship from other relationships is that the purpose is to help the client. In the above example, if you were to express some degree of anger, it should be only a small part of the processing done with the client. Ultimately, the processing must focus not on your being upset but rather on the fear, anger, or whatever felt by the client and carried out in the behavioral outcome. Furthermore, if you do express anger, it is vitally important that you not reject clients or implicitly threaten abandonment and that you use your anger to help clients focus on *their* feelings. On the whole, we believe that being angry with and expressing anger toward clients is not particularly helpful to clients. Usually, when you find yourself angry with a client it is time to (a) ask yourself what pain the client seeks to avoid by doing something to make you angry (asking such a question will make it easier for you to identify with clients and make it more likely that you can intervene based on their needs rather than on yours); (b) ask yourself what gain the client may be anticipating by making you angry; (c) ask yourself what you can learn about the client's personality organization and interpersonal style by considering the context in, and process by, which you were provoked; and (d) seek supervision so as to understand better the extent to which your dynamics are being tapped by the client (with resulting anger on your part). One of the purposes of supervision is to help you better and more quickly identify situations which spark responses from you that are founded less on client needs than on your own "trouble spots."

21.   *What should I say to a client who wants "personal" information about me?* Clients ask this sort of question for many reasons including wanting to gain

power and wanting to shift the focus of attention. Questions may include those about age (they may fear that you are too inexperienced to help them); children (they may wonder how you can help them with their parenting problems if you are not a parent yourself); religion (they may wonder if you share their values); marital status (they may have a sexual interest in you). You should not make the mistake of assuming you know why a question about you was asked. For example, there may be cultural factors influencing such questions, or the person may lack certain social skills, or may be simply trying to get to know you a little better in the best way he or she knows how. Our usual procedure is to answer demographic questions straightforwardly with no further comment or question *at that time*. At the same time, we would, of course, make a mental note in the event the theme arises later. An alternative is to say, "Well, I'm certainly willing to answer that question, but I'm wondering why you asked." Some therapists prefer this latter approach.

In addition to demographic issues, you may also be asked things like, "Where do you live? What do you like to read? How do you like living in _____? How long have you been married?" In such cases, our general rule would be, "Let common sense prevail." If the client has been making sexual approaches toward you and then asks, "Where do you live?" you should probably answer by saying something like, "I'm not sure how knowing where I live is going to help you; maybe this would be a good time for us to review what you want from therapy." Later you may want to more directly process the client's attempt to cross the client-therapist boundary. On the other hand, if you are nearing the end of therapy with a couple and they ask how long you have been married, there is probably little reason not to answer the question. In any instance of the client's asking for information about you, the client's dynamics, the context of the question, and recent developments in therapy all must be taken into consideration when considering whether to answer the question. Like any question from the client, questions about you are grist for the therapeutic mill.

22.   *What should I say if a client asks me about my religious beliefs?* Many clients are interested in religion whether or not they bring it up. Thus, it is not uncommon for devoutly religious persons to be concerned about the religion of their therapist. In part this is because religion and psychotherapy share an interest in "the human condition" as well as an interest in transformation (or development), meaning, and purpose. Another way of expressing this is to say that many of the questions and concerns which bring people to psychotherapy often have what some philosophers and psychotherapists might call a spiritual component. We mean this not in any way to invoke the supernatural but rather to emphasize that therapy is often about valuing, about what is of central importance to the "real self." In addition to their personal concerns about the issue, individuals with deep religious beliefs are at times influenced by other religious individuals who have criticized psychotherapy for being too "humanistic."

Despite some criticism of psychotherapists for failing to acknowledge and grapple with the importance of religion in the lives of many (Bergin, 1980),

Worthington (1986), in a review of the literature, concluded that religious clients are diagnosed accurately without systematic bias.

Generally speaking, we advise against your describing to your clients your religious beliefs (or lack thereof) in detail. Especially in the first session or two you need to get a sense of what the client is looking for, what anxieties are operating around this issue. Worthington (1986) concluded:

> Generally, religious clients prefer counselors who share their values. This is true before or just after counseling begins. Usually by the end of one session, clients do not distinguish between religious and secular counseling unless some issue arises that dramatizes religious values, beliefs, or practices. (p. 429)

A client asking about religion presents a sensitive area in that it involves deeply held values. Our own practice is to say something like, "Religion to me is a very personal thing; do you have a particular question or concern about that?" Many clients answer, "No, I just wanted to know a little about you." Others may be looking for, and express that they are looking for, a therapist who professes to be "Christian," or "Born Again," or "devout Catholic," or "of the Jewish faith." If you do not fall within the group in which the client expresses an interest, this issue should be addressed as directly as possible while still giving clients an easy way to change their mind or at least defer judgment about whether they will or will not continue to see you. For example, if a client says, "I am looking for a Christian counselor," and you do not consider yourself one, consider a response of this nature: "I can see that the issue is important to you. I want to be straight-forward and tell you that I do not consider myself to be a Christian counselor. On the other hand, I do share many of the values which Christianity emphasizes, and I've certainly had as clients individuals who spoke of being a Christian. In those cases my clients have seen, as we worked together, that I would respect their values. However, I certainly will be glad to refer you to someone else if you prefer. (Pause) What are your reactions to what I just said?" The typical scenario at this point is for a discussion to ensue, the decision is put off until the end of the first session, and in the end the client elects not to be referred. If the question is asked after the first session, then we would typically not offer referral (although we would, of course, be *willing* to make a referral) since the client is generally not asking for that after the first session.

If, for example, you consider yourself to be a "born-again Christian" and the client initially states a preference for such a counselor, in our view it would perhaps be permissible, although not necessarily advisable, to indicate that you are indeed "a born-again Christian." (Some experienced therapists would say that you should *never* disclose your religious beliefs to a client, so it is a good topic to discuss with your supervisor.) On the other hand, it is important for you to indicate that you are, for example, more than a *Christian* counselor or therapist. With regard to this particular phrase, the words have come to suggest a reliance *exclusively* on what are called biblical principles. This is obviously not what you are in graduate school training to learn, and it is important that clients not be confused by your saying that you are a born-again Christian counselor. Obviously, you do not want to say something which will have the effect of confusing the client or limiting the kinds of interventions you can make or both. Thus, you should emphasize that you deal with the total person and not just with "matters of faith." For example, one therapist we know who is devoutly religious is from time to time asked, "Are you a Christian counselor?" He answers this question by saying something to the effect of, "I am a Christian, but I am not a Christian counselor. I do not rely exclusively on the Bible to understand people."

A somewhat related issue involves very religious people and whether it is ever advisable to quote the Bible (or Koran or whatever) to them. Many therapists do know some Bible stories or verses and may be inclined to quote one of them to a religious client who, for example, keeps talking about "sin" but never about "love" or "forgiveness." In general, we advise against quoting religious books because the client may easily confuse your role as therapist with that of a spiritual adviser. On the other hand, these books do contain some very powerful stories which may on occasion be used effectively. The important things to remember are that you should not confuse the client about your role, and you should not allow yourself to become an interpreter of religion for the client. It can be quite easy to allow yourself to be put in the role of moral authority. Clients can view you this way no matter what you do, and they certainly do not need your assistance. Worthington (1988) has outlined a model designed to help psychotherapists understand the religious client.

It is helpful to know therapists in your area who are of several religious persuasions since you will certainly be asked to make referrals on this basis from time to time. If you work for a public agency, the issue of religion will not usually be an issue since clients generally assume, or are told if they call and ask, that, for example, Christian counseling is not done at the agency.

23. What should I say if the client says, "You don't really care—this is just your job?" Clients occasionally make this statement. Perhaps it is most frequently made in intake sessions when a client is suicidal. It may also be made later in therapy when the client feels misunderstood. Even though its absolute frequency is not great, when said to a beginning therapist it may be very disconcerting. If you have just started with the client and the client is in crisis, perhaps the most important thing to remember is not to get into a power struggle with the client and not to imply that there is a deep relationship between the two of you. There is obviously little relationship yet, and in our view, you do your clients a disservice trying to convince them otherwise. Avoid the trap of saying something like, "Life is very important to me—so are you." Such a response is overly abstract ("life is important to me") as well as being presumptuous ("so are you"). A very positive part of what the client has said ("you don't care") is that there is an implied challenge in it—"prove me wrong." Thus, although the statement is indeed somewhat hostile, it also has the quality of approaching you and implicitly of asking you for help. This positive but hostile approach usually means that something more than just reflecting feelings will be required from you, although acknowledging feelings will certainly be a part of any good response. After saying such a thing, the client expects to be told, "You are wrong." It is helpful to say in essence, "You are right," thereby disarming a part of the hostility. How do you do this? One way is to say something like this: "Well, you are right. Sitting down with people who are searching for a better life, maybe even a reason to live, is my job. It's a job I've chosen because I like being able to invest myself with other people as they struggle for something better. I like the relationships that come out of that. I know that right now you are wondering if you should invest with me—you're not sure how it will turn out, and I surely don't blame you for being skeptical when others have let you down." Certainly, we are not suggesting that you repeat verbatim what we have written. Nothing could be worse than memorizing a line to deliver at such a critical point in therapy. Your greatest asset as a therapist is your humanness—your ability to make real contact with persons who, for whatever reason, have had great difficulty in doing that with others. We are emphasizing that when clients say, in essence, you are a "hired gun," you might as well acknowledge that you do indeed get paid for it. Once clients realize that you are not interested in defending yourself, that you have no reason to argue with them, they will be able to listen to you. They will be able to hear that you have some understanding of their conflicted feelings, their fears, and the felt constraints under which they labor. They will be able to hear that you are reaching out and that you recognize their reaching out. In the client's eyes, the odds now shift, if only slightly, toward an outcome in which the two of you can meet and she or he can be cared for. This was what the question was about. If the question occurs later in therapy, it may signal either a failure on the part of the therapist to make the client feel understood or it may reflect client dynamics; for example, "No one can love me," or "The good mother should be perfect," or even "I (the client) need to abandon you (the therapist) before you abandon me."

A good supervisor can help you understand whether the sentence arises primarily from a shortcoming on your part or from transference issues on the part of the client. Certainly, you should look very carefully at your own feelings about clients in such circumstances. For example, do you dislike in particular some things about them? Do they remind you of yourself? Have you been subtly withdrawing from the client? The general rule is to consider first your own role in blocking client progress and then to look at client dynamics. Otherwise, it is all too easy to "blame the client" for lack of progress, and you thereby risk losing important insights about yourself—insights which will help make you a better therapist.

24. *How should I talk about sex?* It is important not to dance around the issue of sex. If a male client speaks of "my sex organ," you should make a point of asking a question which includes the word *penis*. The client will then realize that it is just fine for him to label whatever he needs to label. Or, to give another example, suppose a client says, "And then he had his way with me." We ask, "What actually happened?" She replies, "I said no, but he went ahead anyway."

We say, "He had intercourse with you—it sounds like rape." And then she realizes that we are not afraid of emotionally dangerous situations and difficult words. We are strong enough to be her therapist. Of course, in the example just cited, we would remember for future processing the difficulty the client had in approaching the subject. Our point here is that the client will be less afraid of talking when we demonstrate that we are fearless (though sensitive) in approaching subjects which society frequently avoids. When in doubt, ask, and call things by their real names rather than using euphemisms.

25.   *What should I say to a client who says, "Do you like me?"* Some of the comments we made earlier concerning the client who says, "This is just your job," are applicable here. That is, clients who have a great fear of rejection may ask this question in order to be reassured or in order to play out a fantasy in which they become your special client. On the other hand, they may be asking this question in response to some behavior on your part (more generally rejecting, but at times behavior suggesting positive countertransference). Clients, perhaps better than nonclients, can pick up on subtle rejections by other individuals, in this case the therapist. If you really do not like a client, he or she will figure that out sooner or later. Furthermore, most therapists find that they do not make particularly good progress with clients they dislike. The point here is that if you really don't like a client, you should consider referring them. An alternative is to seek supervision on the case so you can work through some of the countertransference issues. But, of course, there may be times when you are on the verge of seeking supervision because you find yourself disliking a client, and the client "beats you to the punch" by asking the above question. There are essentially three schools of thought on such a situation. Many therapists (influenced by psychodynamic theory) believe that the client must deal with these issues and that your thoughts or feelings about the client have no place in a response. If you agree with this philosophy, you might say, "What is it that you need from me that you are not getting?" An alternative might be, "That's hard, isn't it, wanting me to approve of you, yet I don't seem to from where *you* stand." At the other end of the continuum is the acknowledgment that you *don't* like certain things about the client: "You're right; there are some parts of you that I find hard to work with. I don't like the way you box me out, the way you block me out and then complain I don't give enough." A more middle-of-the-road approach attempts to validate, at least in part, the client's perceptions without focusing extensively on the therapist: "That's a good question. I think it's fair to say that I've not always been able to see your pain—and maybe my frustration seems like 'not liking you.' Maybe I haven't seen your pain because you can't let me see it just yet or because I'm a little blind at times, or both. In any event, I think it's been hard for us to always connect in a way that makes you feel understood and valued. How are you feeling about all this?" The authors prefer something similar to the latter, although there are good therapists using each of the approaches. If you are asked the question and you do like the client and have no reason to believe that you have not been accepting of the client, we might say, "Yes I do. Have you been

wondering about that?" We realize that many therapists would leave off the "Yes I do." We have no quarrel with them; we are simply telling you what we might say. As you might expect, this question is sometimes asked when clients are sexually attracted to their therapists.

26.   *What should I say if a client compliments me?* Compliments might be viewed as a mild form of the client's giving you a present. One of the first things you will want to consider is the context of the compliment. For example, did it follow a tense time in therapy? Was it embedded in a discussion of how a parent never gave to the client? Did it follow a discussion of the client's inability to express negative feelings? Your response to a compliment, therefore, must be based in part on how it registers in terms of the dynamics of the situation. In a more general sense, if the client says, for example, "I like your dress," we are prone to say simply, "I'm glad you like it." If the client says something directly about therapy such as, "I really appreciate the way you've supported me while I struggled with my child's operation," we might say, "I *have* felt very much a part of your struggle. I'm glad to have been a positive part of that." We might add, after a pause and depending on the circumstances, "Has it been hard for you to let me close at such a difficult time?" We recommend a middle road with regard to compliments. To paraphrase Freud, "Sometimes a compliment is just a compliment." On the other hand, it can be much more. For example, a client might say, "You have a beautiful dress," and be thinking, "When I was a child, I never had nice things." Or clients might say, "You understand me so much better than I'd ever hoped when I came to therapy," and be feeling that you have been intrusive or that you know *too much* about them. In these last two examples, we point to the ever-present potential that a compliment, like any communication, can have multiple layers of meaning, some of which may not be readily apparent. As a trained therapist, one of your strengths is and will be a certain readiness to hear more than one message when the client speaks. We are particularly underscoring this issue in answering a question about compliments because in our culture compliments take on many meanings. When clients need to communicate something but for whatever reason find it necessary to blunt or cover their real intent, they are perhaps somewhat more prone to use communication styles which have been sanctioned by the culture. Compliments are one such style. Naturally, the *personal* meaning of the compliment is a part of the client's story and must be understood on a person-by-person basis.

27.   *What should I do if a client makes sexual advances toward me?* There are some general rules to follow. First, if the client is making some strong hints along this line, help him/her bring the issue into the open. Therapeutic progress is likely to be very slow or nonexistent if the client is operating on the fantasy that the two of you will one day "be together," that you as the therapist will slowly but surely (or even with dramatic quickness) fall in love with the client. Why do we say that progress will be slow? The answer is quite simple. When clients are completely immersed in a fantasy that the two of you may enter into a sexual relationship, they are very reluctant to damage their chances by revealing the

"bad parts" of themselves. In fact, it will be precisely those parts which the client will seek to cover up.

We understand that a great many clients have fantasies about their therapists and that therapy may progress nicely while these fantasies continue. We are saying that when clients are consciously preoccupied with these fantasies to the point that they are making broad hints, you may expect therapeutic progress to be very slow indeed. Particularly in such cases you must be quite sensitive to the possibility of the client reporting dramatic improvement as a way of winning your love and acceptance. A second guideline is that once the desires have been expressed, clear behavioral limits must be set (it is, of course, unethical to have a sexual relationship with a client). "No, I will not see you outside therapy under any circumstances." "No, even if you terminate therapy, I could never go out with you," etc. Third, once you have been explicit about limits, stand by them. We know one therapist who says something like this: "I will not go out with you, and you can count on that like the Rock of Gibraltar." Such a statement, as we imply above, brings enormous relief to clients since they know they can now let down their guard. They have nothing left to lose, so to speak. Clients sometimes push the issue by asking, "Do you find me attractive?" One response might be: "I think you are very attractive, but under no circumstances will I see you for any reason other than for psychotherapy. I will not have a sexual relationship with you. What are your reactions to what I just said?" Fourth, be sure you do not belittle or demean the client's advances toward you. Although some clients may be what society would call "obnoxious" about this issue, another large group have been very afraid to admit their feelings, even to themselves. At times, you may be the first person they have ever "fallen in love with." They may be ashamed of their attraction to you and unsure of what to do about their feelings. For this group of people, the fact that they are sexually attracted to you is a part of the positive transference. It is a positive sign because it means that they can invest with others in a positive way. It may be their first beginning steps, and it may catch you completely off guard if you had little sense of it. If, for example, you communicate your surprise, this could be very detrimental. So be clear but patient. There are behavioral limits, but the client's fantasies are not bad nor something for them to be ashamed of. They are to be discussed like other feelings. Because therapists are frightened of their own sexual impulses, they may come across to the client as punishing and rejecting. Try to be aware of your own anxiety in this area. Finally, be sure to thoroughly process the client's sexual attraction toward you. For some clients, there may be a very hostile component to the sexual attraction. It may be an attempt to rob you of your power, to punish members of the opposite (or same) sex for an injustice experienced as a child. It may be a continuation of a theme in the client's life which emphasizes an attempt to obtain what is not truly desired, or an attempt to set goals which cannot be achieved. Furthermore, some clients may actually be trying to injure themselves by compromising those individuals (in this case, the therapist) who might assist them. It is most certainly, ultimately, a substitution for what the client wants and needs. But all this will never be discovered if you simply set the limits and assume everything else will fall into place.

GENERAL THERAPEUTIC ISSUES

28.   *Should I contact clients who are "no-shows?"* Check to see if there is an agency policy on this issue. It is a hard question to answer because it generally depends on the client. For example, clients who don't show up for their first appointment are frequently not called, nor are clients who have repeatedly "no-showed" in the past. On the other hand, you would probably call an individual who has never missed a session in 20 visits. (Some therapists believe that any individual who "no-shows" should always be called as a therapeutic technique. From this perspective, clients are treated "as if" they very much wanted to be in therapy but were prevented from doing so. The technique is continued until the client stops "no-showing" or until the client becomes angry because she or he is constantly being contacted, at which point the issue of commitment to therapy is processed.)

In our opinion, it is not advisable to get in the habit of calling individuals who do not show up. Psychotherapy is most often a voluntary endeavor for which individuals must be encouraged to take responsibility. If a client repeatedly "no-shows," this issue *must* be processed in therapy. If a client just stops coming to therapy, you should consider sending him or her a letter which outlines options of either returning to therapy with you or being referred. This type of letter will help protect you against a potential malpractice suit. It also offers the client an opportunity to return to work out his or her reason for leaving. We know that some clients do stop coming with little or no warning; we believe that such a termination procedure generally glosses over important issues. If the client is willing to come for even *one* final session, we would see this as a very positive step.

One very practical issue is what to say to individuals (roommates or relatives) who may answer the telephone if you call. If your client is unavailable, one alternative is to say that since you are difficult to reach, you will call back. A second alternative is to leave the message that you called, requesting that your client return your call. If this alternative is chosen, we recommend that you not leave a telephone number (simply say that the person you are calling has your number) since curious relatives may call back to find out from where you called. If you have left the agency number, the relative then has ascertained that you are in a mental health facility. On the other hand, if you leave your home telephone number, you are asking the client to call you at home, and that is not generally advisable.

Finally, we would note that when you send a letter to a client be sure to use an envelope which includes a return address that does *not* name the mental health facility. Many agencies provide two different types of stationery, one of which will have envelopes using only a post office box number. This ensures confidentiality in that if another person sees your client's mail, that person will not be able to ascertain from the envelope that your client is in counseling.

29. Should I accept presents from clients? From our perspective, this question cannot be answered with a simple yes or no. Some therapists take the position that a present should never be accepted from a client because the present is thought to represent an attempt by the client to erase the dependency felt by the client. In this view, if therapists accept presents, they thereby collude with clients in pretending that dependency is not an issue. There may also be a fantasy on the part of the client that the therapist can be "bought off." In this sense, the client may be asking for forgiveness for a particular shortcoming or may in general be carrying out a theme of seeking the approval of authority figures. Furthermore, the idea of buying off the therapist contains a hostile component related to the dependency issue. That is, individuals who have been "bought" have had their power reduced and are no longer a threat. Particularly if there is monetary payment for the therapy (as in private practice or mental health centers), the proffering of a gift may contain elements of self-punitiveness ("I must pay you over and over for your services since what I offer is of such little importance"). A final caution is that clients may bring gifts when they are sexually attracted to their therapist.

Despite the above considerations, it is our position that it is permissible to accept a present if all of the following conditions are met: (a) The client does not evidence a pattern of responding to authority figures by giving them presents to win their approval; (b) The gift is not unreasonable by cultural standards (e.g., the offering of a small handmade gift is very different than the offer of a new car); (c) Some relationship has developed between the therapist and the client (e.g., it would be unwise to accept a present from a client after he or she had come to see you only once or twice); (d) The offer of a gift does not appear to be related to any recent development in therapy. Whether you choose to accept presents or not, it is most important to remember that when clients offer their therapist a present it is almost always significant. At times you may want to ask something similar to, "What is it like for you to give to me?" We would not normally process the offering of a small present at the termination of therapy. In our view this would be a normal part of the way in which clients can say to themselves and to us, "I appreciate your help; I'm ready to stop taking from you and can now give you something in return." Although some clients may attempt to subvert the therapeutic process with a gift, our own experience has been that these instances are rare. In general, we find that clients who bring gifts do so as an appropriate reflection of their positive attachment to the therapist. Taking into consideration the issues discussed above, we see nothing wrong with this.

30. Is it ever appropriate to give a client a present? To be straightforward in answering the question, let us admit that the authors themselves disagree about the answer. One of us says, "Probably not—I've never done it," and the other says, "Not often—but I have done it on one occasion." The most important question is why you would want to do this. You may be saying, "I have not done a good job of doing therapy; perhaps this present will make up for it." Certainly, if you are a beginning therapist, you will want to think long and hard before giving a client a present. In addition to considering countertransference issues, you must think about how the client will understand your present. For example, you would certainly never give a present to a very immature person or to an individual with a personality disturbance since she or he might be confused by what you had done.

    31.   Is it permissible to touch clients? Most attorneys will tell you not to do this because you could be charged with assault and battery, sexual harassment, or any number of other breaches of duty. Orthodox psychoanalysts strongly recommend against it for theoretical reasons. Many therapists do touch clients from time to time, but we encourage you to be cautious about doing so. If you tend to touch others naturally, you are very likely to touch clients from time to time. We believe that is permissible. In fact, under certain circumstances touching may be therapeutic. It is important to remember that touching means different things to different people, and therefore, until you know a little about your client, touching is a bit risky. Certainly, you should avoid obvious mistakes like touching a same-sex client vulnerable to homosexual panic or hugging an opposite-sex client who is having problems of intimacy with the opposite sex. It should go without saying that touching should involve no sexual intent on the part of the therapist. Handshakes or something like a passing touch on the shoulder are generally quite appropriate. Goodman & Teicher (1988) have addressed the issue and Fisher, Rytting, and Heslin (1976) have discussed some general guidelines about touching. Bacorn and Dixon (1984) noted that research results concerning touching clients were mixed. Their own study found no significant differences between groups on judgments of counselors who did or did not touch. However, some clients did seem to be uncomfortable after having been touched. There is a full range of opinion on this issue among experienced therapists. As we suggest above, we are not opposed to touching when appropriate good judgment is used.

    32.   Is it all right to use expletives? In general, we caution against the therapist's frequent use of expletives. We are not suggesting that you should never use a word like *damn,* but we advise that the frequent use of strong expletives may be counterproductive to therapy. Most clients do not expect therapists to use such words and may be confused as to why such words are being used if they are. Some clients will be offended by them, and the majority of others will wonder why you rely on such words to make your points or may believe you are trying to prove something by your language.

    33.   What should I say if the clients asks, "Do you think I'm gay (or a lesbian)?" First, we note that there have been differences of opinion about how words like *gay, lesbian,* and *homosexual* are to be defined and used (Krajeski, 1986). These are important issues but are beyond the scope of this book. We strongly encourage you to read literature in the area of psychotherapy with gay men and lesbians (e.g., Beane, 1981; Friedman, 1988; Martin, 1982; Stein and Cohen, 1986).

In response to the above question, consider something like the following: "I never try to answer that question for my clients. As I see it, it is very important that something so central to who you are be something *you* decide about. Let's talk some more about the types of feelings you have for men and women." Obviously, clients are expressing anxiety about their sexual orientation if they ask you this question. On the other hand, simply because clients *ask* about whether you think they are gay or not does not mean that they *are* gay. This is especially true of adolescents and young adults who have limited heterosexual experience. Also, some clients may have one or two homosexual *experiences* and then conclude that they are gay or lesbian. It is very important that you as a therapist not jump to any quick conclusions about whether the person is or is not a homosexual. We emphasize that client homosexual experiences, by themselves, do not tell us (or the client) whether the client is gay or lesbian. If the client is concerned about homosexuality, it is important to focus on at least six issues: (1) the client's previous sexual/romantic experiences and how he or she felt about them at the time; (2) the client's sexual/romantic fantasies (that is, do they involve males or females); (3) the client's perceived goals concerning various types of sexual liaisons; (4) the client's feeling about seeking various types of relationships; (5) the client's perception of and fears about how others would react to his or her homosexuality; and (6) the degree to which the person is accepting of his or her own sexual behavior and impulses. We do not believe that homosexuality represents any pathology. We assume that a great majority of experienced psychotherapists would agree. The *Diagnostic and Statistical Manual* (3rd edition, revised) published by the American Psychiatric Association (1987) does not treat homosexuality as psychopathology. If you believe that homosexuality is a psychological problem, we encourage you to discuss the issue with your supervisor. Clients who are conflicted about homosexual urges are typically (though by no means universally) very perceptive about picking up therapist attitudes toward them. If you start with the assumption that homosexuality is bad, you will make it very difficult for conflicted clients to explore their issues. In fact, it is often the case that a therapist is the very first person in whom the client has placed enough trust to talk about the issue of homosexuality. In such a circumstance, it is obviously of great importance that you react with sensitivity and acceptance.

In part because of cultural taboos against homosexuality, clients who are conflicted about this issue often feel isolated, fearful, and lonely. Even for those clients who are gay or lesbian and not conflicted, problems such as a lack of social and family support may make other concerns more difficult to overcome.

Issues of mental health in the gay and lesbian communities have been greatly intensified and made more complicated by the AIDS crisis. There is now an emerging body of writing which can help you become more aware of, and knowledgeable about, the issues involved in seeing clients who either have AIDS or who have tested positive for the virus (Barrows and Halgin, 1988; Nichols, 1986; Price, Omizo, and Hammell, 1986). Slater (1988) described issues involved in working with lesbian and gay youths and provided a bibliography which lists publications of potential value to these youths and their parents. The November

1988 issue of the *American Psychologist* (Volume 43, Number 11) is a special issue with many articles about AIDS.

34.   What should I say if a client wants to write me a letter about something? Although psychotherapy is primarily a verbal endeavor, there are no arbitrary rules about the mechanisms you can or should use to assist clients. If a client is having difficulty expressing feelings, it may help the client to write the feelings down whether in the form of a letter to you, a diary, or whatever. On a few occasions, we have known clients who wanted to write a letter and *mail* it to the therapist. This we strongly discourage—chiefly because it represents a breach of the boundary conditions. Allowing a client to mail you a letter may encourage fantasies of involvement which go beyond the client-therapist relationship. So if clients would like to express their feelings in a letter, that's fine; they should bring the letter to their therapy session and read it to you.

35.   How do I know when a client should be hospitalized? As a beginning therapist, the first rule to follow, of course, is to check with your supervisor if you believe that the client is a candidate for hospitalization. A variety of skills (as well as potential value conflicts) come into play in making judgments about hospitalization; therefore, discussions with your supervisor about the general issue should occur *before* you are faced with it. Generally speaking, you should offer hospitalization when you believe there is a definite possibility that clients might harm themselves or others. Also, offer hospitalization when clients fear they are losing control, if they are out of touch with reality, if they have not slept in two or more days, if they feel manic, or when it appears that they cannot be responsible for themselves. When offered hospitalization, many clients reject it but feel relieved that this form of support is available. As a part of your administrative briefing at your agency, you should ask about hospitalization procedures. Frequently, this will include the client's being examined (interviewed) by a psychiatrist or chief psychologist.

36.   What should I do if I think a client should be hospitalized but the client refuses? In answering this question, we will assume you have tried your best to get the client to consider this option—listened to his or her concerns, reframed the issue, etc.—but the client still says no. One possibility is to set up an appointment each day for the next few days. Another is to contract with the client to call you each day at a certain time. Other options include discussing with the person how to use the crisis line, giving him or her your phone number, and discussing how to use the emergency room. Finally, it may be possible and appropriate in some circumstances to help the person make some arrangements with family or friends. However, if you are moving toward the end of the session and believe that the client would be a strong threat to either his or her own welfare or someone else's once the person leaves the building, we would recommend that you call a supervisor (or another senior person) into the session. This question can rightly be seen as a specific one addressing the larger question of "under what circumstances should I call a supervisor into the session?" In any event, if you are near the end of the session with the client still refusing hospitalization, you might say something like this: "We have been talking for almost an hour now, and although I would like to see you go to the hospital, it seems as if that's not a very good option from where *you* sit. I don't mind telling you that I'm very concerned about your life because you say you want to die, you live alone, you have a loaded gun, and you refuse to give it up. Perhaps there are some alternatives to the hospital which I've overlooked. If you have no serious objection, I'd like to invite another therapist in at this point for the time we have left. I want you to know how important it is to me that we work something out; I think you and I are in agreement that this is a serious time for you." An alternative to bringing someone into the session may be to tell clients that you would like them to see the psychiatrist who is in the building.

Of course you may be asking, what if there is no psychiatrist and no therapist available who is more experienced than I. It is very difficult to say what should be done in such a situation. If you have exhausted all the possibilities outlined above and if the person is both psychotic and dangerous to themselves or others, consider instigating your agency's policy concerning temporary commitment. If the person is not psychotic, you will simply have to make a judgment call about whether to instigate commitment. In fact, this type of dilemma rarely proceeds to this point, yielding rather to one or more of the ideas outlined above. Throughout a crisis of this type, it is very important not to become involved in a power struggle with the client.

37. What should I do about clients who keep talking at the end of the session? These clients fall into three groups: (a) those who do a lot of talking as a matter of routine and merely continue this pattern at the end of the session; (b) those who make a habit of bringing up important issues at the end of sessions; and (c) those who, for any number of reasons, are testing the limits and are asking to be stopped. Clients in the first category quickly learn that when the session is over, it's over. With a small amount of help, they learn to stop themselves (assuming there are no barriers to learning). Clients in the second category are seen not infrequently. They may or may not be aware of their defensive maneuver. When confronted with their pattern, they most frequently respond well and are able to discuss their fear and ambivalence. Clients in the third category tend to be more problematic. As an unconscious ruse, they may become very upset, protesting that they cannot program their feelings and that they don't like fitting into a box. The more they protest, the more you can be sure that they are asking to be stopped—that is, the more they are saying, "I can't stop myself."

Time limits are very important. First, you cannot afford to run past the stopping time when you have another client. If you do, the other client feels cheated, and rightly so. Second, running overtime gives the client a mixed message. Clients want to believe that there is some stability in the world—that they can count on psychotherapy to be consistent when other things aren't. So if you give clients 90 minutes when you promised 60, what are they to think? Are you really strong enough to be their therapist if you can't handle their end-of-session tirades or ramblings? The above comments suggest why you need to hold the line on time. (Incidentally, the rule of sticking to the schedule applies even if you have an "extra" hour following your client session.) But what exactly should you do? First, you can help yourself a great deal by using a clock clearly visible to both you and the client. In fact, two clocks, one which you can easily see and one which the client can easily see, may be helpful. You need to be able to see the clock without interrupting the flow of therapy, and it should also be easy for the client to keep track of time. Second, be clear with clients from the beginning about what time their sessions start and what time they will end. Third, do not open up whole new areas when only five minutes are left. If the client introduces important new material at the last minute, you can say something like this: "Well, that sounds like a very important area. I'm thinking we should begin there next session since we are almost out of time." If the client still continues to talk and shows no sign of stopping, say, "I hate to cut you off, but we really have to stop today." This sentence can be said while you shift and move forward slightly in your chair or, if necessary, stand up. You will find that if you give clients clear, unambiguous messages, they will respond to the clarity. If you give mixed messages, you can expect them to test the limits in order to find out what the rules are.

All therapists must learn (and generally do learn with some practice) to help pace their sessions with clients. If you feel that you have cut a client off abruptly and the client reacts nonverbally, you might make a note and ask about the reaction at the next session. Or, for example, you might say, "Last time I sort of cut you off because we ran out of time, and you seemed a little upset. What were your feelings?" This question may lead into a discussion of the therapy agreement as well as a discussion of the client's difficulty in setting and living by limits.

Be sure that you do not become apologetic for stopping the therapy session on time. Such behavior merely encourages the client to test the limits again. We are not saying that there will never be an emergency requiring you to go over-time. Furthermore, being clear on limits is neither a license nor an excuse for insensitivity. With a little practice, however, you should be going past the agreed stopping time very infrequently. The time you spend with clients is a valuable service you provide. You do not need to give an extra 15 minutes to ensure you have made a contribution. Going overtime is not merely bad for clients; it is also a subtle put-down of your own skills and contributions.

38.   What should I say to a client who says, "Am I crazy?" Clients ask this question for many reasons but most often for one of two reasons. One obvious possibility is that clients may want reassurance that they are not crazy. Since they *feel* so crazy, they believe it would be helpful to be told that they are not. Or perhaps the client is attuned to self-presentation issues and wonders how she or he is coming across. Perhaps others have said, "You are crazy," and the client wants to be told otherwise. A second possibility is that clients may be seeking a very different kind of reassurance—the reassurance that you recognize how serious the problem is. Perhaps they have kept a very tight lid on their pathology, perhaps they successfully hide from others their "crazy" feelings and crazy behavior, and they wonder if you will be insightful enough to see, and brave enough to confront, the crazy part of them. As in so many cases where the client asks a hard-hitting question, our philosophy is to respond briefly with your own thoughts and then gently move the focus back to the client. This means that you have to say more than, "What do *you* think?" For example, to the above question you might answer, "Well, I don't use the word *crazy* because it's not very helpful to me. I do think your problem should be taken seriously. I know it's very disturbing to hear these voices. You know that something is wrong, and you think you may want to do something about it. And I guess that's where I come in—helping you work on that part of you you call crazy."

39.   *What should I do if a client won't say anything?* This issue arises chiefly in four situations. In one, you may be seeing a client who is rather unsophisticated about what psychotherapy is and expects direction from you. A combination of client education together with, where appropriate, your assuming at the first a little more responsibility for the direction of the session will likely have the desired effect. A second situation arises with clients who are socially anxious and who for this reason don't talk very much in the session. With such clients it is necessary to work a little harder at putting them at ease. One can generally proceed by (a) initially making some efforts not to raise their anxiety level higher than it already is and (b) when appropriate, helping them talk about their anxiety in therapy. A third type of situation involves clients who are fairly concrete and who may typically give very short responses, with no elaboration, and then wait for guidance from you. You may need to be a little more active and provide slightly more structure for these clients.

The fourth situation is when you have said something that made a big impact on the client and the client stops talking in the session. This sort of situation may arise at any point in therapy. The first thing to remember is that it takes the client much longer to incorporate what you have said than it took you to say it. So, give the client some time. The second point is that this type of situation involves what can be called a "working silence" (O. Bown, personal communication, 1985). Remember that while clients are silent, they are usually still thinking, reorganizing their thoughts about themselves or the world or perhaps even "pulling themselves together." Thus, silence is not something that needs to be destroyed. Third, remember that the silence may suggest that something important has happened and is happening. Viewed this way, silence should be less likely to raise your anxiety level. Fourth, silence does not mean you have done something wrong. So you need not get busy undoing it. Fifth, clients are rarely as uncomfortable with these working silences as you are. If they become uncomfortable, they will often do something about it.

Perhaps you are still saying, "OK, so now I have a great attitude about silence; I'll try not to get too anxious; I realize they need time to integrate things, etc., etc. But how long should I let them sit there before I say something? And when I do decide to say something, what should it be?" Therapists vary in their answers to these questions, particularly the first one. Part of the answer must lie in the client's nonverbal cues. If the client appears to be deeply absorbed in what he or she is thinking about or is, for example, continuing to cry, you may choose not to interrupt at all. On the other hand, if the client starts to look around and sighs as if to punctuate a thought, it may be time to say something. At the risk of oversimplifying a complex issue, we will say that you should be comfortable with a client being silent for at least ten minutes. This will feel like a very long silence, but occasionally you will see clients who need this much or more time. If you sense that the client might be ready to proceed but doesn't quite know how, you might say something like, "I know you are having some thoughts and feelings. Can you tell me any of them?" Or you might say simply, "I can see these things are very difficult for you to talk about," or "I sense that what I said hit you hard."

We briefly address two other issues involved with silence. First, it may at times be used as a retreat from the therapist. If the silence is more a time of retreat than a time for reorganization (of course, these may be the same to some extent), this issue may need to be processed. Thus, the client may be saying, "Talking with you is so painful I will be quiet." A second point which bears noting is that clients at times refuse to talk if they are angry with the therapist. In this case, silence may take on a punishing function, as expressed in the attitude, "If words are your game, I'm not playing. Now what can you do since I am not talking?" Alternatively, anger followed by silence may suggest that clients fear their anger or, more specifically, fear that it will destroy the therapist. In such a circumstance, the long-term goal is to have the client experience and express this anger in therapy, with a therapist who can withstand this anger without becoming fearful and withdrawing or punishing. These comments are meant to suggest some of the complexities involved in therapeutic silences. The main point is that silence is not something to be eliminated but rather something to be understood in light of the client's dynamics. If you think that you are failing to say things you need to be saying (and thus in your mind contributing to silences), ask your supervisor if he or she agrees. Perhaps you are anxious but doing a good job. On the other hand, if your anxiety is impeding your performance (e.g., preventing you from responding), you need to find out what you are fearful about. On the whole, clients do talk without too much prompting. On the other hand, there are times when they want something from you and wait, whether patiently or impatiently, for you to respond.

40. What if the client doesn't want to be there? Since there are entire books written about the reluctant client and since we devote a chapter in this book to resistance, we will make only brief comments here concerning the issue. Rule number one is that you should avoid power struggles. If they begin by saying that you are a part of the power structure which keeps them down, you are ill-advised to disagree. If they indicate that they have more "street smarts" than you, the first session is no place to talk about how you are on to their game. Rather than being dewy-eyed about all the ways you think you might be able to help such clients with their lives, you need to keep three goals in mind: (a) maintaining the relationship so that you might be able to earn the right to help;

(b) maintaining the relationship so that you will have some opportunity to see whether you can offer anything of interest to the person; and (c) maintaining the relationship since angry people typically haven't had too many good relationships. The redundancy is obviously intentional. If you are working with people who have been incarcerated for a long time, we encourage you to remember that these individuals have a great deal of experience with environments which are punishing, demeaning, and almost never designed for the benefit of the person. Even if these people had entered prison as well-adjusted, caring people, the environment would likely have had deleterious effects on them. Do not expect to be welcomed unambivalently and do not be surprised when you are manipulated—it may be the case of a human being who has learned to survive under brutal conditions.

41. How do I handle clients who always blame someone else? Clients who continually blame other people for their problems represent a challenge for therapists for two reasons. First, it is very difficult for clients to solve problems over which they feel they have no control. Most approaches to (or theories of) therapy include some attention to helping clients assume realistic control over portions of their lives. Second, therapists are sometimes prone to become angry with clients who will not "take responsibility for their behavior." Becoming angry with such clients almost never works, because in their mind there is no connection between what they are doing and your anger. Rather, they tend to think of *you* as out to get them and as lacking in understanding. Actually, there are two broad personality types represented here. Clients who have a narcissistic personality disorder typically have a rather ingrained characterological belief that others are really to blame for all their problems. Significant improvement with these people is very slow—almost always requiring long-term psychotherapy. The second group of people includes the individuals who are much more aware of the fact that they blame others and who are often very aware that they are being defensive when they do this. Self-esteem issues, often rooted in being criticized or judged by significant others, are typically central for these persons.

SUPERVISORY ISSUES

42. What should I expect from supervision? Although there are as many styles of supervision as there are supervisors, you should expect certain things from supervisors: a reasonable amount of support, at least some specific suggestions about how you can improve your therapy skills, sensitivity to your struggles as a beginning therapist, respect for your developing therapeutic style, a willingness to help you confront your shortcomings, and a responsiveness to your expressed needs. From yourself you should expect some time preparing for supervision (listening to tapes, etc.), the courage to bring in cases with which you are having difficulty, a willingness to process with your supervisor difficulties you are having with him/her, responsiveness to suggestions about how to proceed with a case, and the ability to hear both positive and negative feedback about your therapeutic style and interventions. Perhaps the single most important sign that you are having difficulty in supervision is if you find yourself *repeatedly* failing to bring to your supervisor major concerns about your clients or you as a therapist. If you see this sign and fail to take action, you are perhaps depriving yourself of a chance for the experience of good supervision. If you have already had some good psychotherapy supervision, you know what we mean when we say that good supervision is a growth-producing and life-enriching experience. If you have tried repeatedly to work out conflicts with a supervisor and cannot seem to do so, we recommend that you request another supervisor. If the problem is *you,* you will find this out fairly soon. On the other hand, no supervisor is perfect. Identify the good things you can get from a particular supervisor and do everything in your power to benefit from what he or she offers.

One question which often comes up about supervision is whether supervisors should focus on your dynamics as opposed to your specific skills in therapy. Most supervisors agree that supervision is not psychotherapy and that neither supervisee nor supervisor should try to turn supervision into something it is not. Our experience has been that a sizable percentage of supervisors (including ourselves) believe and practice the idea that supervision must at times focus on beliefs and feelings of the supervisee as they hinder the delivery of psychotherapeutic services to the client. Supervisors at university counseling centers are perhaps more likely to have this orientation than are supervisors at mental health centers. Supervisors of a psychoanalytic bent are, of course, quite committed to the idea of focusing on countertransference issues. (Countertransference is discussed in chapter eight of this book.) When you are just getting started as a therapist, you should expect your supervisor to spend a sizable percentage of supervision time helping you focus on what you can *do* to help your clients as opposed to focusing on your dynamics. Friedlander and Ward (1984) speculated that beginning therapists may best profit from "a cognitive-behavioral, highly task oriented supervisor," whereas more advanced students might be better served by a supervisor taking a more psychoanalytic and interpersonal perspective. Nonetheless, Goodyear and Bradley (1983) noted many similarities in how different supervisors viewed supervision.

43.   What should I do if I don't like my supervisor? Most supervisors do supervision not because they are forced to but because they want to, they enjoy it, and they get personal satisfaction out of doing it. They are generally very motivated to do a good job. They want you to benefit from and enjoy supervision. Therefore, in general you will find them to be responsive to your request for more understanding, less advice, more advice, or whatever you think you need to make supervision more effective. Supervisors tend to admire supervisees who can put their cards on the table and articulate their needs. They do not admire supervisees who are discontented with supervision but won't say so. Occasionally, you may get a defensive, inept supervisor. As we said earlier, in such cases make an honest attempt to work it out, and if you fail, request another supervisor.

44.   What should I do if a client brings up a problem I do not know how to treat?

This is a question which does not have a simple answer. Some of the factors to be considered include the following: (a) what you feel comfortable handling; (b) your supervisor's judgment about the case; (c) training you have had that might be relevant; (d) the seriousness of the problem in terms of potential behavioral outcomes; (e) the client's reaction or potential reaction to knowing that you have no experience in the area; (f) availability of potential services from another professional; (g) availability of a referral source which specializes in the problem; (h) client's level of distress; (i) degree to which intensive supervision is available; and (j) the extent to which the problem is recognized as needing a specific kind of treatment. Many times clients who are seeing therapists in training are accepting some sort of trade-off. For example, at a crowded VA hospital, the choice may be between a student therapist and a long wait. At times clients may be aware of such a trade-off, at other times they may not. If there is a clear indication that a more experienced therapist could ideally handle the case but none is available, our belief is that this factor should, in many cases, be discussed with the client. However, not all agencies agree with this procedure. Some prefer to handle such questions internally; then once the decision is made that a therapist in training *can* see the person, the issue is not brought up for discussion with the client.

A distinction should be drawn between problems which you have never had presented to you and problems which you don't have any idea about how to approach. Just because a problem is new to you is, of course, no cause for alarm since in part that is why you are in training. However, even if the presented issue is completely baffling to you initially, this is no cause for alarm. Because psychotherapists use such broad and far-ranging constructs (for example, anger turned inward, lack of trust, etc.), you should be able to conceptualize at least portions of any given problem, particularly after meeting with the person two or three times. For example, if a client says, "I always seem to wake up in the middle of the night and crave food," you may initially have no idea what is going on but probably will start to form some hypotheses after a few sessions.

Perhaps the above sounds like the green light to see any client. Not so. Let us draw a continuum with two extremes using a few of the dimensions listed above. On the one end is a presenting problem you don't know anything about— let's say the person is a veteran who appears to have post-traumatic stress disorder (PTSD). You feel very uncomfortable as the client discusses the situation. The client suggests the possibility of suicide if the issue is not resolved, a doctoral level staff person with expertise in PTSD is available to see the person, you cannot recall having done any reading in the area, and it's never come up in class. Your supervisor doesn't know anything about PTSD, and the client indicates that he is tired of being shifted from student therapist to student therapist since, as he puts it, "They never have any experience." On the other end, a client presents with what seems to be PTSD, but you have a supervisor with much experience in this area. No other person is available right now to see the client, but the client reports only moderately disturbing symptoms with no homicidal or suicidal ideation. The client suggests that he saw a student once before, had a good experience, and is interested in your seeing him. Although you don't know much about PTSD, you have done volunteer work with veterans. In the first case, we would recommend referral. In the second, we would recommend that the student see the client.

Probably the two most critical factors determining whether you should see someone if they have a problem you think you know nothing about is the kind of supervisor available and the apparent seriousness (for example, homicide, suicide, or potential psychotic break) of the symptoms.

45.   How do experienced therapists avoid "taking home" the problems of their clients? Although this is a question we are at times asked, it is very difficult to answer. At the risk of oversimplifying, let us suggest a few things. First, try to spend some time reflecting on your limits as a therapist. "Taking home" problems in part may suggest you think you have more power than you do. Conversely, consider that your clients are getting good treatment from you. You do not need to suffer or put yourself down by worrying. Third, consult frequently. Covering the bases during the day often does reduce worrying at night. Fourth, ask yourself whether you are taking your problems home because your clients are more interesting than your life. If so, do something about your life, not your clients. Fifth, ask yourself whether you are seeing too many clients or too many difficult clients. Sixth, take some solace in the fact that you worry about your clients. All good therapists worry about clients. If you didn't care about the pain others are in, you would not be a therapist. For additional discussion about getting "hooked" by clients' problems, see the chapter "Transference/Countertransference."

Finally, we would perhaps be remiss if we did not say that some stress seems to accompany the mental health profession and that this seems more true for people in training than for experienced therapists (Rodolfa, Kraft, and Reilley, 1988). Medeiros and Prochaska (1988) have identified several coping mechanisms used by psychotherapists to deal with stress including self-evaluation, humor, and seeking social support. Distress among professionals has also been addressed by Kilburg, Nathan, and Thoreson (1986).

SUMMARY

In this chapter we have tried to give you some general ideas, as well as some specific suggestions, for how we think about a number of the ideas with which beginning therapists struggle. As we said at the beginning of the chapter, we encourage you to think about how our ideas differ from yours. We also encourage you to discuss our comments with your supervisor. Psychotherapy is a complex process practiced by a diverse group of people. Although we have tried to stay within what we consider to be the mainstream of ideas about psychotherapy, we recognize that our definition of the mainstream, as well as our specific suggestions, are open to debate.

APPENDIX:
Index of Questions

Boundary/Management Issues

1.	Introducing Yourself	13
2.	Informing Clients of Training Status	13
3.	Discussing Need to Record Sessions	13
4.	Telling Clients about Confidentiality	14
5.	Telling Clients Your Phone Number	15
6.	Liability Insurance	15
7.	Keeping Personal Notes about Clients	15
8.	Taking Notes during the Session	16
9.	What to Write in Progress Notes	16
10.	How Often to See Clients	17
11.	Clients Who Wish to Change Appointments	17
12.	Starting Sessions "Early"	18
13.	Clients Who Want to Tape-Record the Session	18
14.	Clients Who Want to Bring Friends or Relatives	18
15.	What Type of Clothes to Wear	18
16.	Clients Who Call Your Home in Crisis	19
17.	Visiting Clients in the Hospital	19
18.	Scheduling Therapy Away from the Office	20

Personal Inquiries/Emotional Issues

19. Clients' Inquiries About Credentials   21
20. Telling Clients about Your Anger   22
21. Clients Who Request "Personal" Information   22
22. Clients Asking about Your Religious Beliefs   23
23. Clients Who Say That You Are Just Doing Your Job   25
24. Talking about Sex   26
25. Clients Who Say, "Do You Like Me?"   27
26. Clients Complimenting the Therapist   28
27. Clients Who Make Sexual Advances   28

General Therapeutic Issues

28. Contacting Clients Who Are No-Shows   30
29. Accepting Presents from Clients   31
30. Giving Clients Presents   31
31. Touching Clients   32
32. Using Expletives   32
33. Clients Asking Whether They Are Gay (or Lesbian)   32
34. Clients Who Want to Write You a Letter   34
35. When to Hospitalize a Client   34
36. Clients Who Refuse Hospitalization   34
37. Clients Who Keep Talking at the End of the Session   35
38. Clients Who Ask, "Am I Crazy?"   36
39. Clients Who Are Silent   37
40. Reluctant Clients   38
41. Clients Who Blame Someone Else   39

Supervisory Issues

42. What to Expect from Supervision   39
43. Difficulties with Supervisors   40
44. Clients' Problems with Which You Are Unfamiliar   40
45. Avoiding "Taking Home" Client Problems   42

3

THERAPIST FEARS/CONCERNS

A good scare is worth more to a man than good advice

—Ed Howe

In this chapter we want to talk about some of the concerns that beginning therapists have about doing psychotherapy. Some concerns are based in reality, others in misinformation or lack of information, and still others are part of our fantasy life—perhaps symbols of some of our struggles to be loved, to feel good about ourselves. Whatever the source of our concerns, it helps if they are taken seriously by ourselves and our supervisor. On the other hand, one of your tasks as a beginning psychotherapist is not to take *yourself* too seriously. If you must blame yourself (and you undoubtedly will) for making mistakes, try to make it behavioral, rather than characterological self-blame (Janoff-Bulman, 1979). That is, try to view your mistakes (and imagined mistakes) as specific behaviors which you can improve rather than as global personality defects.

As we all know, fear can be constricting. It can limit our creativity, and it is uncomfortable even when it does not seem to limit us. On the other hand, it is important to realize that your fears about being a therapist are also a source of strength for you. Your fears can help alert you to areas to discuss with your supervisor; they are a constant reminder of your ethical and legal responsibilities; they underscore the fact that the person who is your client is a human being to be treated with respect and dignity and who is entitled to the very best you have to offer. Your fears also offer a guide to those parts of you which are candidates for growth and development; they should remind you of the key truth that we all are, and will forever be, limited in some way as a therapist. Even if you find yourself doing that which you fear, you will be amazed at how often you learn something very important about both yourself and the client in such instances. To fear something can easily be the first step toward harnessing and mastering it. In fact, much of mastering begins with a healthy respect (or fear) for that which we do not understand. We will go so far as to say that if you do not have some fears as a therapist, you are probably ill-suited to being one. It was Freud who pointed out that any process which had great healing capacity would naturally also have the power to hurt. If you have no fears about doing therapy, you are either operating out of a dangerous illusion or you are completely convinced that what you do is of no importance. Neither of these positions produces good therapists.

THE FEAR OF CLIENTS GETTING TOO CLOSE

Therapists may be referring to any of several different concerns when expressing a fear about clients getting too close. One such concern is that of fearing how they will be able to handle someone being very dependent on them. In theory most therapists understand that psychotherapy typically involves an element of dependency, especially in the beginning and middle phases. To know this in theory and to work easily with it in practice are, however, two different things. Like others in our culture, psychotherapists often believe, even if secretly so, that dependency is a "dirty" word. Fearing it in ourselves, we subtly discourage it in our clients. That is, just as we fear that our being dependent on someone will take away our power and strip us of our autonomy, so do we fear that another's being dependent on us will ensnare us in an ever-constricting prison. If we view the client's dependency as a phenomenon we must do something about, we may feel forced to intervene in certain ways or to avoid intervening in certain ways. In turn, when we feel *forced* to respond, we lose access to one of our therapeutic strengths—that part of ourselves which is spontaneous and free.

The answer to this dilemma, however, is not to avoid the dependency of our client. A part of the answer lies in a sense of self (*your* self) which does not rely on the actions or feelings of the client for its strength. Such a self can afford to allow another to be dependent. A part of what we mean by this is the lack of a need to defend oneself against the possibility of expressed dependency. For example, one supervisee offered her home phone number to a client in crisis but began by saying, "I don't usually give my home phone number out, but this is my number." Another supervisee suggested to a client that the client could call but that the therapist wouldn't want it to become a pattern. Each of these examples illustrates a case in which the therapist feared that the client might be (or become) dependent. The central point, however, is not that the therapist was aware of potential dependency but that in each case the therapist prematurely (and defensively) assumed that there might be a problem. Such premature assertions about dependency are manifestations of an inner uncertainty about a conflicted area. In part, the solution is to trust oneself to handle dependency issues as they arise rather than taking defensive precautions meant to stop the dependency. Trying to anticipate and prevent the dependency of the client is bad for at least four reasons: (a) It sends the client the wrong message about dependency (i.e., dependency is bad and it should be covered up—"I am weak if I need help"); (b) It frequently makes the client defensive (in the example above about the therapist giving the client the telephone number but doing it inappropriately because of the fear that the client might become excessively dependent, the therapist should not be surprised if the client says, "Don't worry, I won't be calling you"); (c) It fails to help the clients deal with their dependency; and (d) In the end it frequently doesn't prevent even overtly expressed dependency—clients end up, in the example above, calling you at home on numerous occasions.

In addition to the issue of the client's dependency, there may be other fears related to the question of whether a client will "get too close" to us. A central construct here is the idea of boundary. By "boundary" we do not mean a "wall" (with all the pejorative connotations accompanying such a term). Rather, we refer to the characteristics of the relationship along the dimensions of (a) role behavior and (b) identification with the client. Although these two dimensions may be closely related, we separate them here for ease of discussion. (The word *boundary* also involves a number of other administrative and therapeutic issues which will not be discussed here.)

When we speak of boundary issues concerning role behaviors, we are referring to questions such as, "What happens if I suddenly realize that I am acting more like the client's friend than his or her therapist?" First, a word of reassurance. The most critical issue is not whether you do or don't "slip out of role." Beyond such basics as acceptance, involvement, and ethical behavior, it is impossible to say with any degree of completeness what the therapist's role should be for all clients. In fact, one view of therapy is that the roles we play must be somewhat different with the varying needs our clients bring us. Therefore, it is not surprising that we will, from time to time, find ourselves taking a role which allows the client to get close to us in a way that we did not anticipate. If you spend a lot of time worrying about being in or out of role, you are quite likely to end up feeling rather constricted. Furthermore, "slipping out of role" may be precisely to experience and express what Kegan (1982) called "our vulnerability to being recruited to the welfare of another." As Kegan suggests, it is vital that clients be able to recruit their therapists.

We will discuss overidentifying with clients in the chapter "Transference/ Countertransference." Here we mention it only as a concern beginning therapists express when they fear that they might take on the same emotion expressed by the client—say, depression. This sort of fear is frequently expressed by therapists when they say something like, "I really know how this client feels—I feel that way when she describes the situation she's confronting." Again, we emphasize both the legitimacy of this fear (overidentification can certainly lead to poor therapy) but also the advantage which comes with respecting (fearing) your own potential limits. Additionally, we point out that your fear in this area suggests that you very likely do have both the capacity and motivation to resonate with your clients. If you have healthy respect for not doing that in the extreme, you have scarcely damned yourself by saying that you fear being well-tuned to emotional difficulties. Supervisors generally see emotional involvement with (support of) clients as something that is easier to moderate than increase.

Finally, with regard to dependency issues, we want to emphasize that concerns about clients getting too close to you in very short-term therapy may be realistic. That is, you are right to worry about clients becoming too dependent on you if therapy is to last only a few sessions. In such a therapy context, there is not enough time to work through strong dependency. Hence, you should not encourage dependency in very short-term psychotherapy. Although the definition of short-term therapy differs widely, in our own view any therapy lasting (or scheduled to last) less than six months should be considered short-term.

THE FEAR OF "MAKING A FOOL OF ONESELF"

Certainly, it is possible to appear foolish as a therapist—particularly if one takes oneself rather seriously, adopts an unforgiving attitude toward one's mistakes, is determined to defend the importance of one's every utterance, and fails to give clients credit for being the perceptive and forgiving human beings they often are.

One way almost all beginning therapists fear they will look foolish is by saying the obvious. One joke about this issue has a little boy throwing a tantrum in the therapist's office. After 15 minutes of this, the therapist says, "You sound angry." To which the therapy-wise child replies, "Thank you, Dr. Freud."

If by saying you fear that you will say the obvious you mean you fear that a client will *say,* "That's obvious," or "Well, of course," or "I understand that," or even, "Yes, I'd considered that," your *belief* that this may happen is well founded. You will most certainly hear this sort of response from some clients. What the client *says* and what is going on in the interaction are two different things, however. Unfortunately, when clients say something like, "I'd already considered that," our fear of appearing foolish makes us want to accept the client's statement as the end of the discussion. It would seem reasonable that few therapists would welcome the opportunity to continue a discussion in which the client has already anticipated one's interventions. Certainly, you will see clients who really have already given careful consideration to some parts of what you are saying. In fact, on occasions it will become clear to you (and perhaps the client) that the client has thought more deeply about the issue than you have. One's first impulse in such circumstances can range from wanting to change the subject to defensively pointing out that the client is being defensive by discounting your comments. If while feeling foolish you can resist, for a couple of minutes, the temptation to go on the offensive, you may discover that some remarkably powerful therapeutic gains can often be had when the therapist is "caught short," so to speak. In the first place, this is your opportunity to learn more about clients and how they construct the world—more than you obviously knew when you made the remark. Second, if you are nondefensive and simply acknowledge that you were "off base," you give clients a wonderful opportunity to teach you about their world. This acknowledgement, that in a very important way clients know more about their world than you do, places appropriate responsibility on clients for being an active part of the treatment. Your willingness to acknowledge your limitations models for clients a trust in self toward which they are working. Your lack of defensiveness shows clients that you do not need to be protected and hence that they can count on you. By avoiding the temptation to gloss over your imperfection, you paradoxically show that you cannot be exploited, for it is the vulnerability which must be hidden that allows exploitation.

Of course, some clients *do* defend themselves by denigrating the comments of the therapist. If the client repeatedly points to the triteness of your comments, you should "get a second opinion" from your supervisor. The key is to consider the full range of possibilities. If the client is feeling powerless and is seeking to "even the match" by criticizing many of your interventions, certainly you need to address that fact. If the client "goes on the offensive" when the content of the discussion provokes anxiety, certainly that needs attending to. But it may also be that you are holding something back. Perhaps you are "playing safe" because you are afraid of the client; or perhaps you have the (mistaken) view that the client is too vulnerable and fragile to hear anything other than the obvious; or perhaps you are feeling angry or judgmental toward the client and are thus saying things that you *know* won't reflect your true (unacceptable) feelings.

A couple of other points should be made about the issue of appearing foolish by saying obvious things. In fact, much of therapy *does* involve the obvious. First, there is the "obviousness" of discussing the same issue over and over. As we point out in the chapter on therapeutic mistakes, it is important that you do in fact go over and over things in therapy. This repetitiveness is in part how therapy works. Second, it may help to remember that just because *you* think you said something that was overly simplistic does not mean that the client will think the same thing. Although we know of no research to back this idea, we suspect that a great deal of therapeutic gain is achieved when therapists say very simple, obvious things but say them at precisely the right time.

Another aspect of saying the obvious is that therapists sometimes fear that they may repeat stories, metaphors, or favorite one-liners. This is a realistic fear if you are prone to forget whether you have or have not used a story with a particular client. It is not bad to have favorite stories; most therapists over time do accumulate particular ways of expressing powerful "truths." There may be times when repeating an image or metaphor would be very helpful. The key is to remember that you have used it before so that you don't introduce it as if it is a completely new idea. If you are concerned about this issue, consider making a few informal notes after each session. These notes could include how you emphasized key points.

Therapists at times may be concerned about contradicting themselves. For example, you may be challenged by a client who points out that a couple of weeks ago you said that her anger was something she could use constructively—that it was a signal to her that the has a right to go for what she wants. In today's session you suggested that her anger was perhaps a cover for deeper feelings of pain and worthlessness—that anger was not the real issue. At times, in such instances, the client may have misunderstood what you were saying. At other times, it may be very easy for you to resolve the apparent contradiction, or it may be therapeutic for the client to struggle with the issue for a little while. But in some instances it may dawn on you that you do not really understand the phenomenon under discussion. You may feel foolish because you are confused and are not sure how both parts of what you said are true. There are two related issues here. The first is how to deal with a specific and immediate awkward situation. The second is the question of what therapists should do when they "confuse themselves," so to speak. With regard to the first issue, one idea would be to say something which would draw the client out in a way which helps you understand what the client is thinking. Let's continue the example above, with a male therapist and a female client.

CLIENT: So which is it? Is my anger a kind of positive sign that says I'm feeling better about myself; I deserve better treatment, and I intend to get it; or is it just a kind of cop-out–a cover-up that says I don't want you to see my sense of worthlessness. I know things are not just black and white, but those ideas don't seem to be the same. In my view that is a real contradiction.

[Comment: Notice that the client is no longer focusing on her feelings but rather is attuned to the "contradiction." Certainly, the therapist would need to consider how the client's personality structure might result in such a focus. For purposes of this example, however, we will put aside that issue. A second issue, which is very important to consider, is the extent to which the therapist's comments might follow gender stereotypes rather than taking full account of the individual. For example, if this therapist is threatened by strong women who feel good enough about themselves to feel angry on occasion, he may retreat immediately to the explanation that anger is a cover for a sense of worthlessness. However, for the sake of argument, let us assume that gender stereotyping is not a part of the issue here. At this point in the interchange, we simply emphasize that the client seems confused. Let's assume that the therapist also becomes confused and doesn't see an easy way to resolve the contradiction.]

THERAPIST: Well, sometimes I guess I do contradict myself. Does that bother you?

[Comment: While such candor may be helpful at times, here it is defensively motivated. The client is obviously "bothered" by the contradiction or would not have made the statement in the first place. Although it is good that the therapist is somewhat attuned to process issues in cases where clients have legitimate reason for being confused, it may not be helpful to comment on the process. Certainly, there are some clients for whom it would be helpful to struggle with perceived contradictions, and in such instances this last therapist comment might be helpful. However, as we said above, this example is not about the client's personality structure even though we know we can never completely rule out that consideration.]

CLIENT: Yes it does; I don't know how to make sense of my anger. I need some help here.

THERAPIST: Maybe you don't need my help.

[Comment: The therapist is continuing the mistake of implicitly blaming the client. The concerns of the client are not being addressed.]

CLIENT: Well, I think I do, or I wouldn't be in therapy. I'm just trying to figure out what my anger is about.

[Comment: The client feels forced to respond to the provocative comment by the therapist but also "hangs in there," trying again to get closure on the confusing issue of anger. The client needs something from the therapist about anger. The therapist feels unsure and foolish about not being able to resolve the potential contradiction and so is avoiding addressing the issue of anger. The result is that the client is provoked and distracted from a legitimate question. The client is likely not feeling respected.]

THERAPIST: I know you are trying hard to figure out what your *anger* really means. Certainly, there are times when as you talk about it *my* sense of what's going on shifts. I guess that's part of what we're trying to do together—take a look at some of the different ways you express your anger as well as looking at a number of perspectives in terms of what it all means. I think our goal is to arrive at a shared understanding and then maybe go on from there. [Pause] Of the different ways we've talked about your anger, what seems to fit best as you are thinking right now?

[Comment: This is not a bad intervention. It is perhaps a little noncommittal considering that the client was asking what we assumed to be a reasonable question. The therapist *has* acknowledged *his* shifts in understanding without making a big issue of it. We believe that in this case such a balanced response is reasonable.]

CLIENT: There you go again putting it back on me. Why do you always do that?

[Comment: Obviously, the client is still angry—still feels ignored. One now begins to wonder more strongly about how the client's dynamics fit into her being upset about the contradictions.]

THERAPIST: We've been talking about anger. Now it sounds like you *are* angry. [Pause] Perhaps it seems like I've let you down by not answering your question.

[Comment: Since the client continued to be angry, the therapist decided to make a process comment. We believe that such a comment *was* needed since the issue had shifted somewhat from search for understanding to a more immediate powerful emotion. The therapist then turns to one of the possibilities about the meaning of the client's anger to the client. The therapist has no way of knowing for sure what the central meaning of the experience is for the client. However, the therapist chooses an intervention which is perhaps related to the earlier theme of feeling worthless. There are undoubtedly other therapeutic interventions which might prove to be helpful in this circumstance. However, the point we are making here is that our goal is one of helping clients discover and articulate the personal meanings behind their actions and experiences. In the above example, the therapist first became somewhat defensive because he could not resolve in his own mind how *he* actually conceptualized the problem. Toward the end of the example, however, he has made an attempt to help the client to refocus on *her* experience. We believe this later approach is appropriate.]

We said above that there was a second issue—that of how we as therapists view situations in which we have essentially befuddled ourselves. In the above example, we said that, at least initially, we would not "put it back on the client." We realize that some good therapists take the position that it is the client's job to struggle with what the therapist says—that if the therapist is confusing, clients should work through their feelings about this fact. We do not agree that this process always produces the best therapeutic outcome. Nor do we believe that the therapist should in such instances immediately say, "Well, I'm confused myself—I don't think I've thought enough about the construct of anger and how it applies to you." We are advocating a middle ground—one where it is acceptable to acknowledge some limitations including confusion but one which avoids making central to the therapy hour your own shortcomings.

In addition to fearing that they will appear foolish by saying the obvious, therapists also often fear that they will stumble when the client asks them a "tough" question. We discussed some examples of these types of questions (such as, "Do you like me?" or "Do you think I'm crazy?") in the chapter "Questions Beginning Therapists Ask." To fear you may be "put on the spot" by a client is realistic in the sense that therapy, when it is the alive and lively interchange it should be, is marked by spontaneity, unpredictability, and a certain kind of reciprocity. So, if you fear being put on the spot, you might also consider the opposite. That is, how will you enjoy doing therapy if you are successful in constructing a style which prevents clients from "punching through" on occasion? Might it not be the case that this form of vulnerability brings with it both a useful added sensitivity to the interpersonal aspect of psychotherapy as well as an opportunity to experience and confront one's limitations?

THE FEAR OF NOT BEING COMPETENT TO HELP

This is certainly one of the most frequent fears of beginning therapists. We discussed one aspect of this fear in the chapter "Questions Beginning Therapists Ask," under the question about seeing clients who have problems you do not know how to treat. Here, perhaps we can start best by plainly saying the truth: You will undoubtedly see some clients you are not competent to help. We say this for three reasons. First, there is a certain percentage of clients for whom therapy is very unlikely to be of much benefit regardless of the therapist's skills. You will undoubtedly have some of these clients assigned to you from time to time, regardless of the type of screening being used. Second, each of us has weak areas as a psychotherapist. Even the best therapists are not going to be helpful to all "helpable" clients. Third, as a beginning therapist, you may be especially likely to fall (and place yourself) into traps and difficulties that will reduce your effectiveness.

This fear regarding competence is often a persistent, general uneasiness. It may be reflected in anxiety about seeing an intake client about whom you have no information; it may be reflected in questioning whether you should be a therapist; or it may be reflected in your reluctance to discuss what you are doing with your supervisor. This fear may be very difficult for you to deal with because one often believes that others are more self-confident and do not have such fears. Thus, the deep-seated fear that you have little to offer is often not exposed to the very kind of peer discussion which would likely make it much easier to manage. The premium which graduate school places on the appearance of competency seems to foster norms which work against open discussion of *serious* misgivings about one's abilities. At times this problem may intensify with increasing experience, since one's expectations for oneself tend to go up.

As we see it, there are at least two ways of making your unease about your competency more manageable. The first is to try to lower your expectations about the degree to which you should be able to effect "cures." This idea of lowering your expectations carries with it a call to be more tolerant of your mistakes and of poor and questionable therapeutic outcomes. There is an invitation here to suspend judgment of yourself and the outcome of what you do a little longer. You are invited to wonder a little more about the extent to which you can be so sure that what you do is or is not effective. Certainly, your intervention may not have the luster of a master therapist. But we believe that beginning therapists, by holding themselves to very high standards, often overlook many of the crucial roles they play with clients—that of being a caring, respectful, interested person who struggles to understand what the client is trying to express. Second, see if you can identify one or two of your peers who you might be able to talk to about your feelings of incompetence. This sounds like a very simple-minded suggestion—and it is. Nonetheless, it is very easy to overlook the possibility of grappling with this issue with friends. "Bull sessions" may be frequent, but they are often abstract. Even if they are not abstract, they may not include discussion of serious reservations about one's competency. We are not suggesting that "telling all" solves this concern about competency. We are saying that the sense of isolation which often accompanies these concerns may be reduced if you can identify even one peer you think would be willing and able to tell you about his or her struggles as you also relate yours.

THE FEAR OF MAKING THE CLIENT WORSE

There is nothing wrong with starting your career as a psychotherapist by being afraid that you might do damage. As we (and Freud) noted earlier, interventions which are powerful enough to be helpful are also potentially damaging. In our experience, most therapists are not actually afraid that they will *cause* a client to have a psychotic break. (In chapter 5 we will discuss the concern therapists have about causing people to commit suicide.) Rather, what beginning therapists fear is that a client's mental state might "deteriorate" and that this process might not be recognized by the therapist. It is very important that you be concerned if clients show evidence of an impending psychotic break. Such evidence might include, though is not limited to, appearance of delusional-like thought, inability to sleep, feelings of being out of control, highly atypical behavior, and increasingly rigid and ineffective methods of coping with anxiety. It is very important that you keep your supervisor fully informed about your clients and especially about those who seem that they might have a break with reality. Keeping in touch with your supervisor is one of the key ways to avoid a big surprise with regard to a client. Nonetheless, you should expect that sooner or later a client will have a break with reality (or will perhaps attempt or complete suicide) even though you did not anticipate it. When this happens, it is obviously quite important to process the event with your supervisor. This will be a good opportunity to learn something about the limits of psychotherapists to predict behavior as well as an opportunity to see what cues you may have missed, why you missed them, and how (or whether) you can avoid missing them in the future.

THE FEAR OF NOT LIKING THE CLIENT

Therapists, like the human beings they are, prefer some people to others. This fact is not a problem unless they deny it and insist they will enjoy all their clients or attempt to treat someone on an ongoing basis for whom they have a strong and active dislike. Sometimes it can be helpful to remember that disliking a client should be the beginning of a process in which you commit yourself to learning more about the client as well as more about yourself. If you try to deny that you are not all that fond of some clients, you make therapy much less likely to be effective. This is true for two reasons. First, if you pretend there is no problem, you are not motivated to solve it. Second, you are probably more likely to send mixed messages to the client if you feel one way but deny to yourself those feelings.

There are several different "surface" reasons why we may not like a client. These include value differences and disliking what clients are doing in therapy. We say surface reasons not to imply superficiality but rather to suggest that disliking a client often has dimensions beyond "value differences" or anger because a client has acted badly toward someone. As psychotherapists we are interested in the multiple reasons that help produce our dislike, and we rightly look primarily toward ourselves to understand the phenomenon. To understand your dislike of a client, there are several questions you may find helpful to ask yourself: (a) Does this person remind me of someone in my past I did not like? (b) Are the characteristics I dislike in the person a part of my personality or a part I defend against; that is, am I overidentifying with the client and trying to keep my own self-esteem by being angry about the traits I dislike in myself? (c) Have I stereotyped the person in some way so that I am responding to only one part of the client? (d) Am I keeping this person at a distance because I fear he or she will be too dependent on me? (e) Is this person I admire or like in some way but defend against my attraction by focusing on the behaviors I dislike? and (f) Has the client intentionally provoked me to be angry?

The assumption is made that an understanding of the basis of your dislike will lead to some diminution in your feelings. Additional changes in the way you feel may be effected as you struggle with possible alternative perspectives. For example, if you realize that you are keeping a client at a distance because you have stereotyped him or her, you might actively look for behaviors running counter to the stereotype. (You would also want to ask yourself why you were engaging in stereotyping in the first place. For example, perhaps you are unconsciously prone to make assumptions about individuals based on their ethnic, racial, gender, age, handicap, social class, or life style characteristics. Most psychotherapists pride themselves on being tolerant. It is typically very difficult for us to recognize in and admit to ourselves that we make judgments about people based on their membership in certain groups.)

In addition to trying to understand specifically why you dislike a particular client, a general suggestion is to refocus your efforts toward identifying the pain an individual is experiencing. It is very difficult to dislike a person when you are acutely aware of his or her suffering. Unfortunately, although understandably, many clients have, over the course of a lifetime, become very adept at hiding this suffering. What they show the therapist is the same toughness, the same obnoxiousness with which they have felt compelled to face the world. And so, over and over, and especially when the therapist finds him or herself disliking a client, the client's suffering must be held in focus in the mind of the therapist.

We would be remiss if we did not also point out that seeking supervision is a rather standard procedure in cases where you are discovering that you do not like a client. Often a supervisor (or peer) can help you identify key causal elements in your feelings about a client. Good supervisors do not condemn supervisees who seek help for problems like this one. If your supervisor seems unresponsive or judgmental, this might be a good time to discuss with him or her your expectations about supervision.

All these ideas assume that therapists are at least minimally motivated to "get beyond" their dislike of a client. We believe this is a reasonable assumption since we are convinced that the vast majority of therapists are highly motivated to deliver the best services possible. It is certainly true that a few psychotherapists are primarily motivated by a need for power or even an unconscious desire to punish. However, this book was not designed to be of much assistance in cases such as these.

Finally, we point out (as we do in more than one place in this book) that when you strongly dislike clients, perhaps the clients are telling you something about themselves through their behavior. This observation is not meant to let us off the hook for what we might learn about ourselves, nor is it a subtle way of blaming the client. We are just saying that perhaps a part of the picture is that your dislike of the client reflects a kind of response the client gets from others as a result of engaging in certain types of defensive maneuvers. Such information about, and understanding of, the client may prove extremely valuable in the therapeutic process.

CONCERN ABOUT THE CLIENT NOT LIKING THE THERAPIST

Generally, we as psychotherapists want our clients to like us. Some of this desire is reality based in that clients who do not like their therapists are more prone to be dissatisfied with therapy and to terminate therapy earlier. Furthermore, since there is a strong correlation between how clients feel about us and how they feel about their therapy, we often take clients' feelings toward us as some evidence about the effectiveness of therapy. This is also a reasonable assumption as long as we do not get too caught up in *equating* therapy effectiveness with the clients' feelings about us. If you see a client long enough, there are almost certain to be some negative feelings as you fail to live up to the impossibly wonderful qualities with which the client comes to imbue you (the issue of transference is discussed in a later chapter). Although many therapists do indeed dread having a client who is in the midst of negative transference, the concern we are addressing here is broader. We are speaking of the anxiety about whether any given client will, in a general sense, be favorably predisposed toward us. Although it is very unrealistic for us to expect that all clients will like us, we nonetheless hope secretly that a special kind of chemistry will be present in all our relationships with clients. Just as we should not expect that every client who walks through our door will be someone we are psychologically drawn toward, nor should we expect that all clients will find us to be a person they unambivalently enjoy. The client may initially and continually have a few reservations about you without making therapy either impossible or even difficult. On the other hand, as we have said, clients probably do need to believe that you have their basic interests at heart.

Aside from our realistic concern that clients who do not like us will profit less from therapy than they might otherwise, this concern reflects the basic issue of our wanting to be seen as a good person. The underlying false assumption is that to be loved by the client will adequately provide us with a strong and positive sense of self. In the worst case, we allow the client's love and admiration to become a substitute both for our own sense of self as well as for effective therapy. There is no point in denying that we want in some way to be liked by clients. Individuals who really do not give a damn about how others see them are not typically drawn to the profession. The question is not whether we need what have been called narcissistic supplies from clients but rather how we manage the need and how we try to be aware of it. As we implied earlier, it is very important to distinguish between how the client views you (feels about you), what kind of therapy you are doing with the person, and how you feel about yourself. Some of the issues involved will be unconscious ones, and that is in part why supervisors are so helpful.

CONCERN ABOUT LOSING CONTROL OF THE SESSION

As a beginning therapist, you likely have a number of fears about being unable to "control" what goes on in the session. As you probably know, there are many different philosophies among even experienced therapists about the advisability of trying to control what goes on in therapy. Furthermore, people mean various things when they talk about the therapist's responsibilities with regard to controlling the session. In our view, the chief responsibility of therapists in this area is to reasonably anticipate the consequences of various therapeutic approaches and to assist the client accordingly and in cooperation *with* the client. For example, if a client comes for the first time and seems to be having difficulty staying in touch with reality, one would certainly be advised not to ask the client to engage in some sort of fantasy. In this example, the therapist controls the content and process of therapy by not introducing a particular therapeutic technique.

On the other hand, one of the great lessons to be learned by all psychotherapists is that they cannot "control" any client. Certainly, we can often have input. But you will discover rather rapidly that clients often have a way of controlling their own lives that limits the role you will have. If you can give up your illusions of grandeur, you will be in a much better place to exercise the influence you *can* have.

All these issues aside, beginning therapists often fear that in certain kinds of ways they may lose control of what is going on. These fears of losing control are generally about prototype "emergency" situations, such as clients announcing that they are leaving the session early, clients actually storming out of the session early, clients "going strong" at the end of the session, clients expressing attraction toward the therapist, clients threatening the therapist, or clients crying uncontrollably. Of course, there are other situations you may worry about, but the above are several about which we often hear supervisees express concern or fear. There are three aspects of these various situations we would like to address. The first is the observation that each profession, as a result of the procedures it uses and the material it covers, lends itself to particular kinds of "difficulties." For example, as psychotherapists we rarely worry about whether the client is about to hemorrhage; on the other hand, surgeons must constantly worry about this issue. We make this point because it underscores what we hope will be some reassurance—namely, that there are actually a fairly limited number of high-probability difficulties that therapists tend to encounter. What this means is that there is an informal body of knowledge which is transmitted from therapist generation to therapist generation about what to do or not to do in these situations. For example, as we noted earlier, you do not need to spend a lot of time debating about whether you can date your clients. The answer is, "No, you can't." (Of course, you should not *criticize* your clients for wanting to date you.)

Second, there is unfortunately no real substitute for actually encountering and having to deal with some of these difficult situations. Certainly, reading books like this one and discussing issues in class and with your supervisor can help. But no matter how much information you have, it is not apt to eliminate all of your concerns about "losing control."

Third, it may seem paradoxical, but many of the situations involving therapist loss of control in the session are appropriately addressed in part by what we call common sense, that is, behavior suggested by common cultural knowledge. For example, if a client threatens to leave the therapist's office before the end of the session, few of us would be inclined to say, "You can't leave." There are several reasons why we would not say such a thing. We know it would likely make the person very angry and perhaps more likely to leave; and except under circumstances involving a legal situation, we would have no way of enforcing our injunction. Thus, one's lack of experience as a therapist does not mean that one lacks knowledge about the best course of action in a difficult situation.

With regard to the specific potential situations listed above, in the chapter "Questions Beginning Therapists Ask," we made suggestions regarding several of them. One on which we have not commented is uncontrollable crying. Unless the person has recently been or shows signs of being out of touch with reality, prolonged crying by the client is not something to worry about. You will find that crying does end. Certainly, one wrong thing to do is rush in to stop the person from crying because *you* are anxious. Do not be alarmed even if the person continues to cry for 10 minutes or longer. Remember, *crying will stop.* Of course, if you are very near the end of the session and the person is still crying uncontrollably, you will need to help the client compose him or herself at least a little. We are not talking about "cheering clients up" or denying their feelings; obviously, those sorts of interventions would be a mistake. On the other hand, we do not generally feel comfortable with the client leaving the session crying uncontrollably. Typically, under these circumstances, you would verbally recognize the importance of the issue with which you and the client were dealing, perhaps reassure the person that the two of you will be working on it together, and if you think it necessary, remind the client that he or she can call you for an additional appointment if one is needed. Generally, when clients are crying, we recommend that you not offer them tissues (unless they seem to be looking around for one), since symbolically you are saying, "It is time to stop crying." However, at the end of the session, it may be appropriate to do this just as a simple way of helping them compose themselves.

If there is some evidence of psychosis and the person's emotional state seems to be escalating, you may need to provide more cognitive structure (e.g., by saying, "Let's talk for a minute about your plans for after you leave here this afternoon"). In some cases, you may need to make specific suggestions. In part, such interventions may be needed to give the person a tie to reality. With some clients it may be important to implicitly remind them that a supportive person is in the room with them. It may sound a little strange to you for us to say that clients are reminded that "a supportive person is in the room with them;" however, individuals with tenuous ties to reality may withdraw far inside themselves when emotionally upset. With such clients, it is important that they be assisted in maintaining some connection to reality.

In summary, with regard to the therapist's concern about losing control of the session, we emphasize the following points: (1) It is a myth to believe that one can control another person; (2) Many difficult situations call as much for "common sense" as for intricate specialized knowledge; (3) Emergency situations calling for such specialized knowledge are not large in number and tend to be discussed in classes; (4) Concerns about losing control are perhaps best dealt with by having the good fortune, early on, of being forced to rely on your own skills by clients who don't bother to inform you in advance of the lively situation they end up creating for you. We should also add that if you are concerned about a particular "emergency" situation, we encourage you to ask your supervisor to demonstrate, in a role play, how the situation might be handled.

CONCERN ABOUT LOSING CONTROL OF EMOTIONS

In addition to fearing what the client might do in a session, psychotherapists also fear what *they* might do. They may fear that they may become angry or cry or in general that their emotions will be "stirred up." Our experience has been that therapists rarely "lose it" completely. Therapists don't tend to yell at their clients, sob uncontrollably, or jump up and pace back and forth as a result of emotional arousal. On the other hand, it is often the case that therapists find themselves irritated with a client, moved by a client's situation, or in some other way emotionally affected by what is going on in the therapy hour. Of course, one of the maxims accepted by many therapists is that there is often diagnostic information about the client contained in a therapist's emotional reaction. This issue will be discussed more in the chapter on transference and countertransference.

The concern about losing control of one's emotions carries with it an important dialectic. On the one hand, there is the knowledge that we will not be helpful if all we do is repeat with the client earlier unsatisfactory relationships. Furthermore, communication and therapy principles suggest that clients may have difficulty showing their problems if we continually evidence strong emotional reactions to them. On the other hand, therapists are human beings; they have emotional reactions. Furthermore, it may be helpful for clients to experience a relationship in which they know their impact is felt and can be processed.

In our view, this dialectic is resolved in part by therapists titrating their expressed emotional responses and also by their interposing cognitive processes between the experience and expression of affect. At first, these two processes may seem a bit cold, calculating, and academic. However, they are not meant to destroy spontaneity, and in fact they express what therapists actually do. We know of no therapist (or even *person* for that matter) who gives free expression to all affect or who does not routinely and frequently think about what she or he is feeling before expressing the feeling. When therapists say, as they sometimes do, "I just let the tears come to my eyes in the session because I was so moved," in part they may be suggesting that their cognitive activity did not produce a reason *not* to let tears "come to their eyes."

Another way of talking about this issue is to note that there must be some sort of balance between emotional involvement and distance. On the one hand, therapists who are completely wrapped up emotionally in their clients' problems are not likely to be of great assistance (although there must certainly be counterexamples, given the elusiveness of what heals in psychotherapy). On the other hand, as we have suggested before, therapists who have an iron grip on their emotional life, who are not at any risk for losing control of their emotions, may find it very difficult to understand the pain others suffer. In functioning as a therapist, there are much more serious problems than being moved by the suffering of others.

CONCERN ABOUT MAKING A DIFFERENCE

Over and over again we have supervisees raising, in one form or another, the concern of whether they are really doing their clients any good or not. The fear, of course, is that they are no actual help. We think it can be helpful for therapists to identify more specifically the kind of concern they are having. The fear that one is having little impact may represent any (or some combination) of several factors including the fears that (a) psychotherapy itself is of little value; (b) some particular clients cannot be helped; or (c) the therapist is simply ineffective at doing psychotherapy. Concerns about one's effectiveness can be exacerbated by infrequent supportive comments from one's supervisor. To the extent that this is a factor with several supervisors, the therapist may be receiving some valuable feedback about where talents do and do not lie. On the other hand, and especially at the beginning of training, therapists should work toward not taking critical feedback from the supervisor *too* seriously, both because the sample of people looking at their work is too small to ensure reliability and also because frequent mistakes as a beginning therapist do not suggest poor skills later on.

CONCERN ABOUT THE SUPERVISOR'S EVALUATION

As we note in other chapters, self-presentation is a powerful motive; this holds for clients, therapists, and supervisors alike. It is altogether natural that therapists have strong desire to please their supervisor. This desire, though it may in part be "external," is certainly not all bad in that it may reflect one's basic commitment to doing good psychotherapy. On the other hand, one of the more frequent mistakes we see made by beginning therapists is to wait too long to discuss with their supervisors feelings of inadequacy, fear of evaluation, and so forth. Supervisors certainly may be overly critical or unsupportive at times, but they are also often quite open and responsive to expressed therapist concerns. Discussing one's fear of evaluation may not eradicate the fear, but it will often increase the supervisor's sensitivity to therapist vulnerabilities. It doesn't hurt to remember that just as the therapist wants to do a good job, so does the supervisor. Our philosophy is, "Give your supervisor the *chance* to be helpful and responsive." If you don't get the help you need, at least you will know that you made the effort.

We might also add here that, despite supervisee fears to the contrary, there are very few situations in which a supervisor actually holds "life or death" power over the supervisee. In most training programs, if one supervisor sees only your weaknesses, that is not an insurmountable problem because you will be given other opportunities with different supervisors. Certainly, a poor evaluation is hard on anyone, but it may help to remember that training programs are not typically dictatorships in which one person holds ongoing life or death power over you. With regard to supervision, you are very rarely at the continuing whim of any one person.

Finally, we emphasize that in *good* supervision you are going to hear in one form or another that you made mistakes. Certainly, there is little reason for a supervisor to be nasty or hypercritical. But you should be very wary of supervisors who seem to be supportive of everything you do. In part, supervision is an opportunity for you to test your ideas and judgment against someone else. Whether you agree or disagree with that person's critique, it can be helpful to have it. Thus, as you worry about your supervisor being critical of you, consider what you would lose by *not* receiving criticism. Furthermore, as you worry about your supervisor's judgment of you, you might want to consider the ways you have rebounded from criticism before. Perhaps you can survive better than you first feared.

SUMMARY

Our fears as therapists are frequently healthy for a number of reasons. They serve to motivate us to understand the basis of our fear, which in turn provides us with a base on which to build additional skills. They also alert us to the fact that we suffer from shortcomings—a not inconsequential insight as we work toward helping others deal better with *their* suffering. Finally, our fears about not doing a good job as therapists are friendly evidence that we care deeply about the degree to which we are or are not helpful to our clients. This caring is a primary and indispensable part of being effective as a therapist.

4

CLIENT FEARS

He said this and smiled with a face as white as chalk. "Why is it he is smiling?" The thought flashed through my mind before I realized anything else. I too turned pale.

"What are you saying?" I cried.

"You see," he said, with a pale smile, "how much it has cost me to say the first word. . . ."

—*Brothers Karamazov*

In this chapter we want to review some of the concerns clients have about the process and outcome of psychotherapy. We believe that psychotherapists who are aware of the full range of concerns clients may have about therapy will be more adept at recognizing these concerns as they are indirectly expressed by the client. Additionally, to be aware of these concerns provides a stimulus for us to think about not merely what is at stake for clients but also how we can be responsive to the concern. One very obvious reason that we spend some time writing about client fears concerning therapy is that clients who are very dissatisfied about the process of therapy may terminate prematurely.

We have at least two goals in writing this particular chapter. Our first is simply to alert you to a number of fears clients may have as they enter therapy. Some of these fears are often conscious, others frequently unconscious. Some have rather clear implications for your initial behavior as a therapist with any client; others we describe chiefly so that you can think about what issues are involved and how you might handle a situation in which the client is clearly expressing the fear. Some of the fears may be overtly expressed by the client; others may only be inferred. A few of the fears may be expressed early on; others tend to emerge much more slowly.

A second and more indirect reason for writing about client fears is that psychotherapists need a good appreciation for the many internal obstacles clients often must overcome just to arrive at their first session. A keen appreciation for these difficulties gives one an empathic frame with which to "greet" clients and also strengthens our sense of respect for this person we call our client.

Another point we should perhaps underscore is that there may be an important relationship between concerns or fears clients have about therapy and the difficulty which brought them there. This is an example of Weinberg's (1984) point that as psychotherapists we need to ask "where else?" with regard to client behaviors. That is, when we observe a behavior which seems tied in some way to the client's concerns, we ask ourselves where else the client engages in similar behaviors; the more consistency we see across situations, the more likely are we to focus, with the client's help, on the relationship between the presenting problem and the consistent behavioral pattern. More broadly, we are saying that there is a link between the kinds of fears a person has about the process of therapy and the person's personality traits. For example, if a client says, "Can I be sure that what I say will be held in confidence?" we might hypothesize that the client may have difficulty placing trust in others. We say "may have difficulty" because the question is also a reasonable one by cultural standards. One might think of a continuum of client concerns about therapy. Variables of interest include the type of concern, presence or absence of situational variables likely to activate the concern, the relative sophistication of the client with regard to therapy, the emotional intensity of the client with regard to the fear, and evidence of the client having similar concerns in other situations. At one end we might see a client who has little knowledge about therapy, who has a pending legal case, who asks about confidentiality but doesn't seem obsessed by it, and who seems easily reassured by your answer. At the other end is a client who has been in therapy several times, who has no obvious objective reason (such as legal difficulties) to be strongly interested in confidentiality, and who repeatedly asks about confidentiality despite your reassurances. In the former case you have learned little about the person as a result of the issue of confidentiality being raised. In the latter case you have probably learned quite a bit and have certainly identified an area that deserves further exploration by the client and therapist.

A number of the fears we discuss will probably diminish rapidly if therapy progresses as we hope it will. Furthermore, we are not suggesting that all clients experience each of the fears we list. We are saying that these are typical and representative of the concerns clients may have about the process. For sake of discussion, we divide client fears into three broad categories: (a) how will I (the client) be treated; (b) how will I be viewed; and (c) will I like the effects of therapy. These are not conceptually distinct and mutually exclusive categories but serve as a way to organize the material. A number of these concerns are represented in an instrument developed by Pipes, Schwarz, and Crouch (1985).

HOW WILL I BE TREATED?

Clients have both hopes and fears about how they will be treated in psychotherapy. We believe that it is a rare client indeed who has no expectations or concerns about what the therapist will be like or what the therapist will do and say. Most clients have some sense that the relationship into which they are contemplating entering is somewhat of a one-sided affair. They understand, if only implicitly, that the therapist will not be very vulnerable, that they (the clients) will, and that the therapist will be in control of many aspects of the relationship. They also realize that they are coming to seek the help of the therapist (implying that the therapist offers something which cannot be, or has not been, found from other sources), while the therapist has not sought them out and apparently needs little from them. All of these facts (actually, *feelings*) are very much a part of clients' phenomenological world as they approach therapy. As if these things were not enough to strike fear and apprehension in the heart of the most self-confident client among us, clients are aware of two other things. First, therapists are unknown quantities—clients have little or no hard data about them. Can one be certain that this unknown person will prove to be benevolent? Second, and perhaps more importantly, most clients have had a number of relationships in which the other person has proved to be, at least in the eyes of the client, untrustworthy, punishing, controlling, unforgiving, or a major disappointment in some other important way. Like Antonio in the *Merchant of Venice,* clients have been led to believe that there is often a Shylock who will demand "a pound of flesh" for services rendered. Of course, this business of expecting (fearing) that one will be treated by the therapist as one has been treated by others is a part of what will need to be examined in therapy. The point here is that clients can be reasonably expected not to place their faith immediately in the therapist.

We will now discuss some of the specific concerns clients have about how they will be treated.

1. Will I be treated more like a case than a person? In part, this concern is about not being respected in a particular kind of way. Taking telephone calls during the therapy hour, being inflexible in response to reasonable requests, and not bothering to remember important events which the client has told you about are examples of treating clients as if their worth as individuals is not significant. As another example, there are some agencies in which clients in the waiting room may hear therapists discussing cases down a hall or in an adjacent conference room. Even when names cannot be discerned, imagine your own reaction if you are a client and you hear a therapist (maybe even your own) say, "Well, I'm just tired of listening to this client." Here the issue is not so much confidentiality as it is a question of basic sensitivity (or lack thereof) which communicates a sense of respect for all clients.

2. *Will the therapist be honest with me?* In part because clients believe that other individuals have not been honest with them, clients are at times concerned that the therapist will not be entirely forthcoming with them. This fear may also represent a projection of sorts in which clients have concerns about their own capacity to be straightforward in dealing with others. There is also a popular image of psychotherapists as never willing to give their own perspective, as always turning questions back on the client. But there is also another issue, as we see it, that has nothing to do with clients' experiences or the image of the therapist. We believe that the concern about the therapist being honest reflects a relatively sincere and healthy desire to be able to know how one is perceived by others. If not taken to the extreme, this desire reflects the recognition that knowing how you are affecting others gives you information which may help you make desired changes in interpersonal behavior. Yalom (1975) cited interpersonal learning (input) as the most helpful (as reported by clients) of 12 curative factors in group psychotherapy. Examples of this category include "learning how I come across to others" and "other members honestly telling me what they think of me."

3. *Will my problem be taken seriously?* Although clients generally come to therapy with an acute awareness of the troubles which they see as afflicting them, they are not so sure that these afflictions are important to anyone else. Perhaps they have come despite great indifference on the part of, or over the expressed objection by, friends, family, or spouse. Even if people close to them are supportive, clients may secretly harbor the fear that their problem will seem insignificant to the busy therapist. One trap which some therapists fall into is assuming that clients who present their problem as if the problem were not serious are not highly motivated about psychotherapy. In the chapter "Intake Interviewing," we note that clients at times present with a problem they feel is more socially acceptable than the one which is really bothering them. It is certainly important to keep this in mind. If the therapist can be trusted with a little problem, perhaps a larger one will be forthcoming. However, the point we underscore here is that in listening to the style in which the problem is presented, we must not be too eager to accept "presentation style" as reflective of the true inner experience of the client. Clients, having learned from the culture that expression of deep anguish is rarely rewarded, are apt to titrate the strong emotions they feel. They do this not just because they do not know the therapist but because they instinctively "dress up" their shortcomings and camouflage the "nasty" parts of themselves. Often, other people they have encountered have been willing to accept, and in fact have preferred to see, this false self. Indeed, clients themselves are often "satisfied" at one level to accept this false self. Here then is the fear—that the therapist will not take the client seriously, will be willing to accept the "dressed up" problem rather than caring enough to allow and encourage the client to be serious themselves about the difficulties with which they struggle.

4. Will the therapist share my values? Despite our occasional protestations to the contrary, psychotherapy is, in part, about values (Beutler, 1981; London, 1986). Bergin (1985) proposed a set of values to guide psychotherapy for which he felt there was general agreement among therapists. Jensen and Bergin (1988) concluded that there is consensus among mental health professionals about a number of values related to mental health.

Values are evident in our (at times hidden) goals for clients and in the methodologies we use to achieve those goals. Instinctively, many clients realize this fact and are concerned about whether there will be value differences and, if so, how these differences will affect both the interaction and outcome of therapy. That is, when clients are concerned about such differences, they are expressing a concern both about whether they will like, respect, and feel comfortable working with the therapist and also about whether the therapist will exercise an influence on them which they would view as unhelpful or destructive in some important way. These are not concerns to be taken lightly. If we view psychotherapy as a life-changing process (Bugental, 1987), the person with whom one enters into this process deserves serious scrutiny. We know from a long line of research that people tend to be attracted to those they perceive as similar (Byrne, 1971). Since we obviously want our clients to be attracted to us in a basic kind of way, this desire that we share basic values does not seem misplaced. This does not mean that all of our values should constantly be up for extended discussion; however, if clients initially want some information about something that is important to them, it is seldom a mistake to provide them with some information. If a client wants to know at the outset whether we are "pro-life" or "pro-choice," we should certainly not feel bound to answer the question as framed, but neither should we try to perform a verbal ballet that leaves the client wondering whether we are capable of making commitments to a reasoned position. Individuals who practice feminist psychotherapy have frequently expressed the idea that therapists should encourage clients to ask questions about the values of the therapist (e.g., Butler, 1985). As we noted in a previous chapter, questions clients pose to us often have multiple purposes, and we ignore this fact at the peril of good therapy. However, we must also try to strike a balance so that clients are given respect and credit for knowing about the things that are important to them.

We should also point out that although clients may have some concern about whether their therapists share their values, Epperson and Lewis (1987) found that clients strongly endorsed the statement, "Counselors should make every effort to keep their own values from influencing their clients." However, this finding in no way suggests that clients think counselors should have no values; rather the implication is that counselors should not *misuse* their influence. Since (as Epperson and Lewis pointed out) studies have shown no interaction between counselor values and client values, it appears that the concern clients have, rather than being, "Will the counselor share my values," might more appropriately be labeled, "Will the counselor use undue influence with regard to my values."

5. *Will the therapist understand my problem?* This concern is often related to the one about values. Clients may wonder whether the therapist will understand what it is like to be Jewish, Hispanic, male, female, gay, lesbian, etc. For example, at times a client may say, "Are you a Catholic?" or "Have you seen many people in therapy who are gay?" At other times the fear may be more indirectly expressed as in, "This culture does not know what to do about women," or "Nobody really cares about white males anymore." In most cases like these, clients are expressing feelings about their situation and trying to ascertain whether you have some sort of feel for what it's like to be in their shoes. Consider the following situation.

MALE CLIENT: Nobody cares about white males anymore.
FEMALE THERAPIST: Well, I agree that things can be rough. After all, reverse discrimination has become a reality.
CLIENT: Well, I'm sick of it.
THERAPIST: If I were a white male, I would be too.

Here the therapist has at least overtly suggested that she has an appreciation for the client's feelings. On the other hand (and even leaving aside the issue of whether "reverse discrimination" is a viable construct), she has perhaps been a little overly enthusiastic about trying to identify with the client. Furthermore, while we acknowledge that a discussion of cultural values and the culture's prejudice toward many subgroups can be of great effectiveness when timed well, we are generally of the opinion that psychotherapy works best when the focus is kept primarily (although not exclusively) on the individual rather than on cultural influences. (There are some differences of opinion among therapists about this issue. For example, individuals who identify themselves as feminist psychotherapists are explicit in emphasizing the role of society in contributing to client conflicts and difficulties [e.g., Butler, 1985; Gilbert, 1980]. From this perspective, some emphasis is placed on helping clients analyze how society may have contributed to their problems through processes such as racism or sexism.) Most therapists (perhaps excluding orthodox psychoanalysts) do agree that some relief from guilt and anxiety may be effected by helping the client identify some ways in which the culture and persons in the culture help make the client more vulnerable to those feelings. After all, for example, it is scarcely a myth that our culture has attempted to force ethnic and racial minorities into the proverbial melting pot and away from their ethnic identities. Most of us would likely agree that when people are forced away from their ethnic identities their self-esteem probably suffers, and this is not due to any characterological defect.

6. *Will the therapist be competent to help?* Naturally, this is not a fear which is generally expressed directly. Nonetheless, we assume that many clients do have this concern. One view of psychotherapy includes as a central tenet the degree to which the client perceives the therapist to be an expert (Heppner and Claiborn, 1989; Strong, 1968; Strong and Claiborn, 1982). Kokotovic and Tracey (1987) found that perception of therapist expertness was related to probability of clients

returning after an initial session, although only insofar as the variance overlapped with that of client satisfaction. McNeill, May, and Lee (1987) found that premature terminators viewed their therapists as less expert than did successful terminators.

Earlier we discussed the issue of clients inquiring about one's credentials. To reiterate, we do not force clients to discuss the "deep meaning" of asking about credentials. These are, in our view, legitimate and realistic concerns. In part, such questions express a concern about competency. However, as Paul Meehl once said, "The proof is in the pudding." We advocate answering questions like these straightforwardly and then demonstrating to the client by our skill and caring that we are indeed competent to help.

7. *Will I be pressured to do or say things?* Some clients bring to therapy a strange and varied assortment of conceptions and misconceptions about the therapeutic process. Both accurate and inaccurate ideas may come from friends, books, or television programs. Many clients are sophisticated enough to know that few therapists "force" their clients to do things clearly against clients' wills. On the other hand, this concern embodies and captures the spirit of a concern most clients do have—that of the extent to which they, rather than the therapist, will have control over the process. As therapists, we are sometimes prone to point our finger accusingly and say, "She has a great need for control," or "He is trying to take control of the sessions." We should not find it altogether surprising when people seem to want control over their lives! At its base, the desire to be in charge of one's life is viewed as a healthy desire. We say this knowing that it is certainly possible for this desire to be corrupted in the sense that it may become defensive obsession. Here we are merely emphasizing that clients who are mildly concerned about whether they or the therapist will be making the final decisions about what is best for them are implicitly expressing some basic drive toward good mental health.

It should be obvious that many clients come to therapy in part because they do not feel that they are in control of what seems, in their eyes, to be happening to them. Or more pointedly, they may have had many past experiences in which they were dependent upon someone and felt they had to comply over and over or risk losing love and/or support. These people have a very keenly developed fear that new relationships will prove confining, suffocating, or demeaning. They may expect therapists to be controlling from the beginning, but more often these sorts of people have a more subtle fear—the fear that they will be forced to strike a Faustian bargain to get the help they need. This fear takes the form of, "I will let you be in charge of me in order to get from you (the therapist) what I need." That is just one powerful example of why therapists must not place clients in the position of fulfilling *therapists'* needs. Inevitably, many clients will feel that they have no choice but to comply—no matter how much is demanded of them. Not merely does this convey to clients the message of the terrible price which must be paid for getting one's needs met, but it also conveys to clients the sense that love and support, rather than springing quite naturally from a relationship, are things which must be earned by certain kinds of behavior. The issue is not just that a heavy price is paid but that the person fears that there are always *conditions* with which he or she must contend.

    8.   Will I become dependent upon therapy (or the therapist) and then be abandoned? This is not a fear which is expressed early in therapy, and it is obviously not typically and overtly stated by the client the way we have phrased it. Nonetheless, it is assumed to be operative in the minds of many clients. For a number of reasons, we expect that clients will fear and resist being dependent upon the therapist. Broadly speaking, these concerns fall into two categories which may be reciprocally causal but which we separate for emphasis. The first revolves around the issue of how clients view themselves and how they feel about the various "selves" they might be or wish to avoid (Markus and Nurius, 1986). Thus, the idea of being dependent may conjure up associations of weakness or worthlessness. Examples would be clients who have been told by their parents all their lives things like, "Don't ever put yourself in the position of owing someone something," or "Don't ever love someone too much," or "Love them but make sure you leave them before they leave you," or "Only the strong remain free." These messages are not typically stated overtly by parents but rather are messages understood by children as they watch and listen to parents. In cases like these, clients have come to associate certain actions suggestive of dependency with a bad image of themselves. Thus, they make every effort to avoid placing themselves in situations which would suggest to them that they are in fact dependent on others. Having reached a point in their lives where psychotherapy seems like the only alternative to a bleak or painful life, they force themselves to "submit" to the dependency they fear by seeking therapy. This does not mean that they are comfortable about entering into the relationship, and it certainly does not mean that they easily allow their dependency to develop. For each time they are reminded of their dependency, they experience a kind of self-loathing—they fear that they are about to become what they have always viewed as bad.

      It is often quite difficult for therapists to understand this sort of attitude toward the self. After all, we are caring, competent people in whom others are to place their trust. But that is not the point. From the client's perspective, it may matter very little how caring or how competent we are. For to be dependent on anyone for any reason may activate self-hate. To get some idea of what this is like for clients, you might imagine that you feel sick for a period of time and then see a physician. Medication is prescribed which you are told will help make you well. But there is a catch. The medication has the disturbing side effect of making you feel very guilty every time someone does you the least little favor. And so you work very very hard to set up situations where you won't feel so badly about yourself. You probably also do a lot of thinking about whether you could just take half the dosage, or take the medicine less often, or in some other way reduce the side effects. Perhaps you try to pretend that the guilt you feel really isn't guilt. In short, you should struggle valiantly. But there is really no getting around the fact that you have become someone you do not particularly like— someone for whom you have little respect even though you don't feel you had much choice about the medication. This is exactly what clients do as they struggle not to be (or appear to themselves) dependent while simultaneously disliking the person they have become. This type of client may not fear the actual interpersonal consequences of dependency as much as they despise seeing themselves act in a manner for which they have always had little respect. With these clients, some attention will need to be given to their view of dependency and their view of themselves in therapy. If these views are not explored, the clients' negative view of themselves may undermine progress in other areas of their life.

Clients who view being dependent as a weakness often fear abandonment. There are a couple of reasons why this may be so. In the first place, a great many people seem to have learned the lesson that if they have been foolish there will be a price to pay. (This is perhaps especially true of males.) Second, some of this fear may be a kind of projection. That is, clients are unforgiving of their perceived weakness and perhaps imagine that under reversed conditions they would abandon the person.

Another reason people fear being dependent is that they fear the interpersonal consequences. For example, they may fear that they would be powerless to prevent psychological abuse, or they may fear that they would be powerless to prevent the loss of the person on whom they are dependent. This sort of fear of dependency is closely related to Freud's ideas of danger situations (one of which was "loss of the object" and another "loss of the love of the object" [Greenberg and Mitchell, 1983]). One certainly does not have to be a Freudian to believe that when individuals are dependent on another person it may remind them (whether consciously or unconsciously) of earlier experiences in which they were dependent and ended up losing, in one form or another, the relationship.

The client's fear of becoming (being) dependent upon the therapist and then being abandoned we assume in part reflects feelings about people in general. That is, there may be an expectation that anyone on whom the person comes to depend will in fact ultimately disappoint them in a major way. Their ideas (and feelings) are expressed by sentences such as, "I knew that sooner or later she would let me down," or "Nobody's perfect and that goes double for the people I've trusted," or even, "I don't intend to let him get close enough to hurt me." For people who fear becoming dependent and then being abandoned by the therapist because this has happened with other people, the relationship with the therapist assumes heightened importance. This is true for two reasons. First, as clients recapitulate their problem in the therapeutic relationship, they are presenting the therapist with a powerful opportunity to create an experience which disconfirms their fear about the consequences of trusting others. Since we view some trust in others as being a requisite for good mental health, it is very important for the client to experience that trust in others does not lead to abandonment. If the client can place no faith in the therapist, then there is no way for there to be a disconfirming experience. As we have noted, this is an assumption of the book—that an emotional experience with the therapist is more likely to lead to behavior change.

The second reason the relationship with the therapist is especially important if a person fears being abandoned is that in such instances the client, in order not to be vulnerable, tends to discount the ideas of the therapist and in general limit the impact and influence of the therapist. Thus, a poor relationship in such instances means that a key therapeutic ingredient, therapist influence, has unfortunately been at least partially neutralized.

At a more practical level, there are several implications of these facts for the practice of psychotherapy. For example, it is quite common even for clients who have done well in therapy to have the fear near the end of therapy that they have become somewhat dependent on therapy. We will discuss this issue in the chapter on termination. Furthermore, it is important to keep in mind that some clients are very prone to experience fear of abandonment if the therapist is about to go on vacation. When clients show the therapist a part of themselves which they do not like, they may feel especially vulnerable to abandonment. This is true because telling someone about the "bad them" both realistically and especially in fantasy makes them dependent upon that person in the sense that the therapist now knows how to exploit their weakness. Thus, they fear that the therapist will "damage" them and then leave. There is also a kind of potential symbolism here of the bad person (therapist) who might steal the client's secret. More specifically, once the client has confessed to the therapist, the client has lost control of what was once so well guarded. A milder form of this fear is when clients fear that they will be rejected (rather than completely abandoned) when they reveal the "bad" parts of themselves. We will discuss this issue a little later in this chapter.

It is unlikely that a client will initially and overtly express concerns about being abandoned. A possible exception to this rule is when inpatients (for example, in a VA hospital) see a series of therapists who are students on rotation. If you are to be a part of such a scenario, the two general rules to follow would be to offer the client an opportunity to talk about the issue and to avoid encouraging dependency. How should you go about offering the client an opportunity to discuss the issue? Consider the following example involving a female therapist and male client:

THERAPIST: I'm Sue Smith. Dr. Jones, the psychiatrist, said you wanted to see a therapist.

CLIENT: Are you another one of those students who is in training out here? How long will you be here?
[Note: The client's use of the term *another one of* is important. At best this sentence suggests a kind of benign curiosity about the therapist. More likely, the client has a well-developed set of expectations about what is possible with a student. The question "How long will you be here?" immediately alerts the therapist to the client's sensitivity about being left.]

THERAPIST: Yes, I'm a psychology intern. I'll be here for three months. I talked a little with Bill Johnson. I think you saw him for about three months, didn't you?

[Note: Obviously, the previous therapist did not introduce the client to his new therapist. At times this may not be possible, but it is generally best. Even though the client has implicitly raised the issue of being left, the therapist chooses not to process the fear immediately since she has just met the person. This is probably a wise decision.]

CLIENT: Yeah, he was around here for a while. He helped me quite a bit. Are you going to need those audiotapes like he did?

[Note: The first sentence suggests some hostility and again implicitly raises the issue of being abandoned. If we take at face value the client's comment about being helped, we see that clients can have positive feelings about their past therapy but simultaneously still be angry about being left. Notice that by asking about audiotaping, the client, for the second time, places the new therapist in the same category as his previous one. One might assume this sentence to carry with it elements of hostility. For example, there is the suggestion that the therapist will "need" something from the client, and there is also an implicit pointed reference to the therapist being a student. Some clients use this as leverage to reduce the therapist's power. Although these more negative purposes are certainly possible, it is also possible that the client is trying to offer the therapist what he can to be helpful. We are perhaps rightly suspicious of such a question, but we want to point out that the instinct to be helpful is not a cancer to be cut out. True, it may be overemphasized by some clients, but we need to be "on the lookout," so to speak, for behaviors which might in part represent positive, desirable aspects of the person's personality.]

THERAPIST: I'm glad you brought up the issue of taping. I will need to tape if that's okay with you. In fact, I have a form here I'd appreciate your signing if you don't mind.

[Note: Again the therapist chooses not to address the issue of the client's being abandoned. Since she is still in the first minutes of the first session, she is waiting for a more direct statement about the issue or a little more time to pass, whichever comes first.]

CLIENT: Well, I'll sign. [Pause] Could you tell me again how long you will be here?

[Note: The client is sending out such strong, frequent signals about the issue that the therapist should probably go ahead and try to process the issue even though it is fairly early in the first session. One reason the therapist would be reluctant to go ahead here is that it will be very difficult for the client to express anger about the person who helped him (assuming for a moment that this is his perception) to a relative stranger. Thus, the therapist will likely adopt a limited goal of making the issue as nonthreatening as possible while realizing that she will undoubtedly have to return to the issue later because any processing done now will almost certainly be incomplete.]

THERAPIST: I'll be here for three months. [Pause] I know that's a very short time.
[Note: The therapist does a nice job of placing the issue on the table without being overly threatening.]

CLIENT: Well, nothing lasts forever.
[Note: The client seems a little defensive, a little protective of himself and his previous therapist.]

THERAPIST: [Nods—Pause] Well, I was just thinking, you saw Bill for only three months, and now I'm here for only three months. That can be tough. I'm guessing that's not quite enough time for you to get to know someone the way you'd really like to.
[Note: Since the client sent out such strong signals, the therapist decides to push just a little. The issue is framed in positive terms rather than in negative terms (suggesting the possibility of anger could be an example of a more negative frame). The "positive" emphasis is appropriate here.]

In this example the therapist would likely continue both in the first session and in future sessions to afford the client the opportunity to express and explore his feelings of being abandoned. In fact, the therapist's continued alertness to this issue is one way of addressing the suggestion above that clients whom you know you will only see for a very limited number of times should not be encouraged to be dependent on you. It is also important, however, that such limited therapy not be turned into one extended processing of the previous therapy. So, while some time should be spent in "wrapping up" the previous therapy (assuming there has been some sort of problem), some common goals for the new therapy, however limited it is to be, must also be established.

9. *Will I be engulfed by the therapist?* The obverse of the concern about losing the therapist is the fear of being engulfed by the therapist. Thus, these two fears represent different aspects of one dimension, that being how the problem of closeness is to be addressed.

It is very important that the therapist not push for more intimacy than the client is capable of handling. So, for example, if the client says, "I'm not sure I can trust you," or "I'm not sure I want to tell you about it," the following sorts of comments would in our view be inappropriate:

"If you can't trust me, who can you trust?"

"You can't get better until you talk about it."

"You do realize that these sessions are confidential, don't you?"

"Maybe if you trusted me, you could trust others."

"Why can't you trust me?"

"Why don't you want to talk about it?"

"Nothing ventured, nothing gained."

Each of the above therapist responses has the effect of suggesting to clients that they ought to be open and trusting with the therapist. This is a demand by the therapist for intimacy which is inappropriate and which may heighten the client's fear that the therapist will overwhelm and engulf the client. When clients express anxiety about boundaries between themselves and the therapist, the therapist is advised to ensure respect for those boundaries in responding to the concern. In the above example, the therapist might consider one of the following:

"It seems reasonable not to trust someone when you barely know them" (assumes initial stages of therapy).

"It's tough struggling with the fear about what I might do if you show me your real self" (assumes client has been seen for a number of sessions).

"It sounds as if a part of you wants to go ahead and talk about it, but there's also another part; one that says, 'Be careful.' I'd like you to know that this is a place where *you* decide what's best for you."

Clients who had dominating parents may be especially prone to fear being engulfed by the therapist. These clients may also exhibit behaviors of the classic help-rejecting complainer. That is, clients who have never developed an easygoing acceptance of their autonomy may seek out advice and direction but then reject that direction or subtly sabotage the ideas which were solicited. In the first place, these clients can be very frustrating. The therapist needs to be alert to the possibility of being lured into a role which repeats the client's earlier pattern of seeking help and then rejecting it. On the other hand, the client who fears being engulfed may exhibit this fear by chronically remaining uncommitted to therapy. These clients stick their toe in the water, so to speak, but have a great fear of actually going for a swim. They are often quite attracted to therapy, especially initially, but then get stuck because they fear they might lose what little power and control they have carved out for themselves. Their self-image is quite fragile; there is a constant fear that someone bigger will swallow them up. For these people, being close is equated with loss of self. Typically, the therapist should move slowly, encouraging the development of some sort of self-identity and respecting client's needs to establish intimacy at their own pace.

10. Will the sessions be confidential? Some comments concerning this issue may be found in the chapters "Questions Beginning Therapists Ask" and "Ethical and Legal Issues." We make a few additional comments here because confidentiality is indeed a client concern. There is a very practical reason for the profession's insistence about confidentiality. Weinberg (1984) expresses this reason well:

> Confidentiality must become a speciality of ours. Our patients often trust us with information they would want no one else to have. Moreover, they trust us to explore the recesses of their souls, and along with them to uncover other facts

whose discovery is mortifying in its very prospect. They need confidence in our ability not to disclose information to anyone.

Not surprisingly, most patients are slow to arrive at this state of trust. They wait a long time before being willing to reveal themselves fully. They watch us narrowly, and if we seem aghast at anything they disclose, they may worry that we will have a need to discuss it with others, and they may retreat. There's a burden on us to be absolutely above reproach. (p. 64)

Weinberg (1984) makes a second interesting point related to confidentiality in psychotherapy. It is his belief that the client should also be asked to honor the principle of confidentiality since in his view this helps the client avoid diluting the impact of the session by talking to others and seeking their support. Although we do not practice asking the client to honor confidentiality, we believe that it is an interesting idea with sound reasoning behind it.

We emphasize that it is very important to avoid any actions which might give the impression that confidentiality is being compromised. This requirement goes beyond the strict rule of not revealing a person's identity. Thus, for example, suppose that you are at a party and are asked, "Have you ever seen a client who was bulimic?" You answer, "Yes, last semester at the VA hospital." The person says, "Did the client always act like the perfect child when he or she was growing up?" You say, "Yes, that did seem to be the case." You then go on to add, "It also seemed like the client wanted me to be perfect. There was a great deal of hostility. The client often criticized me at length." Although you revealed no names and very little identifying information, you have communicated to the person(s) with whom you are speaking at the party that you discuss clients at parties. Would we be surprised to learn that the listener, upon becoming a client, was concerned about confidentiality?

One of the authors once supervised a student who was seeing a client who was in prison for rape. The student told his wife one or two facts about the person, including why the client was in prison. The following week, the client, who knew that the therapist was married, asked, "Did you tell your wife why I am in prison?" The therapist had not anticipated that the client would ask such a question and was naturally very uncomfortable. The point is that it is very difficult to know how the subject of confidentiality will come up and what kind of impact your not being absolutely circumspect will have. There is, therefore, a very simple rule to follow: "Don't talk about your clients except to your supervisor."

HOW WILL I BE VIEWED AS A CLIENT IN PSYCHOTHERAPY?

Since psychotherapy always involves the client and at least one other person, we can say that therapy is a social process. One perspective on a social phenomena is that there are self-presentation motives operating in such processes. Baumeister (1982) has suggested that two such motives are to please the audience (i.e., to obtain rewards) and to construct one's public self congruent with the ideal self. The idea that there is a motive to please others or appear desirable has been described by Crowne and Marlowe (1960) and by Edwards (1957). The idea that there is a motive to have congruence between public self and ideal self is an extension of the ideas of Carl Rogers (e.g., Rogers, 1951; Rogers and Dymond, 1954). Baumeister (1982) described the desire to obtain consistency between the public self and the ideal self as "a means of, substitute for, or prop to self-fulfillment." He also noted that there may be an accompanying "motivation to convince them [others] that one is like one's ideal self." Citing Jones (1964), Baumeister suggested that if we can convince others that we are a certain way, we may be more prone to believe it ourselves. With regard to therapy then, the client is assumed to come with some sort of predisposition to appear reasonable, rational, and appropriate. More generally, we might say that clients come with a kind of agenda about the way they would like to be seen. Some of this agenda may reflect cultural predispositions in interpersonal environments. Perhaps most importantly, we are interested in the degree to which the client seems overly concerned about creating, maintaining, and controlling this image, whatever the image may be. Why are we so interested in this attempt by clients to control the image they create for us? There are two primary reasons, and they are related: (a) We want clients to realize, ultimately, that the relationship does not depend on their being a good person, and (b) we hope they will progressively spend less and less energy maintaining an image and more and more energy identifying their own preferences, expectations, etc.

First, as clients struggle (as they often do) to obtain our approval, we want them to understand that our approval is not contingent on their good behavior. Certainly, we have the hope that the client will behave (or at least learn to behave) in a more or less civilized fashion. But in fact, most clients who seek therapy already meet that criterion—most clients more than meet it. The great majority of clients have in some basic way come to expect that if they behave in some specified way, then they will be accepted. Rogers (e.g., 1951) called these expectations "conditions of worth." Psychotherapy attempts to turn this reasoning around. If clients are fully accepted, we assume that then clients' behaviors will be something that both they and others can enjoy, in part because behavior is not demanded but rather is expressive. There really are several different and powerfully positive processes at work here. The first is clients' discovery that not all the world places conditions on them. This realization is freeing in itself since clients can now dare to hope that they might be able to have good relationships. Thus, we hope that clients will come to expect helpful responses from others and that they will begin to seek out and create better interpersonal environments for themselves. Also, as they begin to see themselves as actually deserving of good treatment (not contingent on good behavior), they are less demoralized, more self-accepting, and less likely to subject themselves to rigid and punitive treatment. This is the process whereby therapists' accepting, tolerant attitudes are internalized by clients. In one form or another, and by whatever name it may be called, this process seems to be present in virtually all schools of psychotherapy. Furthermore, clients are greatly relieved to learn that neither good nor bad behavior can put the relationship at risk. It is who they are, not what they do, that forms the basis for the ongoing relationship. Finally, by showing that our approval is not for sale, we underscore within the *process* of therapy that despite clients' natural inclinations to seek our approval, this is not the goal to be sought. Rather, the goal is an identity for clients which is ultimately not dependent upon the therapist for validation. This does not mean that we should not be supportive. We are simply saying that as clients strive to create for us an image which they believe will bring rewards, we must help them work toward less and less dependence on this sort of approval. Simultaneously, we help them generalize this experience to their relationships with others.

The second primary reason we are interested in clients' efforts to control the image we have of them is that these sorts of efforts can take up enormous amounts of energy. We adopt an uncritical acceptance of our clients in part because we want them to be placed in an interpersonal environment where little energy is needed to maintain the acceptance of the therapist. If clients spend great effort to maintain an image with their therapist, we assume that similar efforts are made with others. Clients who work very hard at maintaining an image have very little time left over to explore, focus on, and carry out their own preferences. This leaves them frustrated because they are unable to express who they are and anxious because their sense of accomplishment and identity is based on an image subject to the interpretive whims of others. In fact, many clients enter therapy in part because they no longer are able to maintain a balance (which they often have spent so much energy doing and which they themselves may label as a "balancing act") between what they experience as their own needs and the needs of others. In part such "failures" in the balancing act create a crisis of self-image in which clients are left uncertain both about who they wish to be and who they think they are. When individuals are uncertain about the way they would like to be, they paradoxically engage in especially strong attempts to draw clear and coherent pictures for others of their self—hence the efforts to create and control the image the therapist has of them.

We know that clients may also have other motives which in part conflict with their need to be seen as possessing positive traits. For example, a part of their motivation for coming may be to confess or to shock. In any event, clients are invested in creating a certain image of themselves for the therapist and perhaps to some extent for others who may be aware of the fact that they are seeking therapy. We will now discuss some of those issues.

1.   Will the therapist think that I am a bad person? One of the more common (though not unimportant) fears clients have is that the therapist will see them as a bad person. Exactly what is meant by "bad" varies enormously from client to client. Some will think they have treated their spouses, parents, or children badly; others will think that they are morally bankrupt because they have squandered their potential or failed to speak out about injustice; and still others may be unable to specify (or may not even be conscious of) exactly why they feel like they are a bad person. But in each case clients may fear the same type of judgment from the therapist that they have pronounced upon themselves. If the therapist is uncritical and accepting, the fear is not realistic and thus becomes grist for the therapeutic mill. That is, the client's fear about rejection is something to be explored. As suggested earlier, when clients repeatedly experience *not* being thought of as a bad person, they come to be more forgiving of themselves. Although the various schools of therapy differ in their emphasis on the importance of the relationship between client and therapist, most either implicitly or explicitly suggest that the therapist must adopt a forgiving and tolerant attitude toward the failures of the client. There are at least three different processes whereby clients may not experience being accepted. Since the relationship between client and therapist is so important, it is critical that the therapist be alert to each of these possibilities.

First, as we have suggested above, the client may *expect* to be judged and therefore see evidence of such judgment when in fact there is little or none. This is an example of what Freud called *transference*. For example, if parents have been harshly critical, therapists will be expected to be that way also. More generally, we might say that people probably look for cues suggesting that what has happened in the past will happen again. One reason they do this is to order their world; a part of this ordering is a constructed continuity of experience about the self. Thus, even when evidence is scant, if it is of central importance to the self and if it is consistent with previous experience, it is likely to be information on which the client focuses. Furthermore, the client is likely to place trust in this information, even if it is at variance with other available data. This is a part of the process whereby clients actively (whether intentionally or unintentionally) maintain an ongoing fear that others think them to be bad persons. A related part of the process is that since people internalize (or emulate) individuals who have been important to them, they come to adopt the same attitude about themselves that others have had toward them. So it is not just that clients think they will be seen as bad since they have been treated that way in the past but additionally that they have come to believe that they *are* bad persons. What people already believe about themselves requires little confirmation. The expectation that one will be thought of as a bad person, coupled with the belief that one *is* a bad person, is something which the client may bring to therapy and which may be independent of any actual thoughts or feelings which the therapist has about the client. In our view, the therapist must be alert to this possible issue and where needed address it repeatedly, not merely in terms of the therapeutic relationship, but also in terms of the client's interpersonal relationships outside of therapy. Consider the following example:

CLIENT: My wife said it bothered her a lot when I came home late without calling.

THERAPIST: How did you feel about what she said?

CLIENT: Well, I know I shouldn't do it. I know she must think that I'm a clod.

THERAPIST: She said you were a clod?

CLIENT: No, but I could tell by the tone in her voice. She sounded just like my mother always did when she criticized me for staying late at the playground.

THERAPIST: Well, perhaps your wife was angry. On the other hand, perhaps she was mainly concerned about you or even wondering how you felt about her. It sounds like your first assumption was that she was being critical of you—it's almost like you expected that kind of response, that you're afraid that people are likely to think of you as a bad person.
            [Note: The therapist does not specifically comment on the client's statement about his mother but rather makes note of it as a potentially important issue.]

CLIENT: I know I'm basically a nice guy.
            [Note: The client overtly rejects what the therapist has said. At this point beginning therapists often stop, fearing they will offend the client if they continue to press.]

THERAPIST: You know this on one level, yet at another level continue to expect other people to pronounce judgments on your behavior—maybe the way your mother did when you were a child.
            [Note: The therapist does four good things with his/her comment: (1) acknowledges the client's reality ("you know this on one level"); (2) doesn't let an important issue drop but does that in a way that is not threatening ("yet at another level . . ."); (3) links the client's behavior to an emotionally charged part of the client's life (what he learned from his mother); and (4) broadens the issue slightly from one of being a bad person to the more inclusive one of assuming that others, rather than the client, are to be the judges of the client's behavior. Note also that the therapist is now tying the current problem to an issue (the client's mother) which was first introduced by the client.]

Clients like the one in the example above are likely to expect rejection from many people including the therapist. This expectation tends to make their behavior more rigid, more defensive, less adaptable, and less inherently enjoyable to themselves. Furthermore, as we said above, clients' expectations that they will be seen as bad persons heighten their awareness of, and sensitivity to, information consistent with their views, however limited the data are. Thus, one way in which clients may feel they are being judged as a bad person is if they have come to expect bad treatment from others. This expectation is seen as a combination of direct learning experience in which they are criticized by others and a subsequent internalized view of themselves as a bad person. Furthermore, we emphasize that parents and significant others may be critical covertly rather than overtly, and in such cases negative self-images can be especially difficult to overcome.

A second way in which clients may experience themselves as being a bad person is if the therapist is *repeatedly* intolerant, moralistic, or judgmental. Any of several factors may produce such a situation. These factors include (a) a long-standing personality deficit in the therapist; (b) a situation in the therapist's life which has temporarily affected his or her capacity to respond therapeutically; or (c) a client and therapeutic relationship which have raised issues which are not quite settled for the therapist and about which the therapist is somewhat defensive. These issues will be discussed more in the chapter "Transference/Counter-transference."

A third way in which clients may end up feeling like they are bad persons is when they from time to time provoke or elicit unsympathetic responses from the therapist. This may sound strange after we have emphasized how the therapist needs to have a "helpful" personality and after we have suggested that therapists' deficits may produce therapeutic failure. However, people vary widely in their capacity to elicit helpful and relationship-enhancing responses. Even therapists who are very supportive of clients and who do not suffer from emotional conflicts or personality deficits may occasionally criticize clients who are *good* at provoking others. These clients may then feel especially bad about themselves because they have been criticized but also because at some level they may realize that they have provoked this criticism.

We have just listed some ways in which clients may end up feeling bad about themselves. There are three primary reasons why clients' fears about being seen as a bad person must be addressed.

First, clients may be unwilling to discuss the things that are bothering them if they fear the fact would exacerbate their preexisting bad feelings about themselves. Second, the reduction of doubt about one's self-worth is frequently a therapeutic goal in and of itself. Third, fear about being seen as a bad person may set up a self-perpetuating cycle in which expectations are verified through various "cognitive errors" and then followed by defensive behavior which is self-constricting and which also elicits defensive and unhelpful responses from others.

2. Will my friends think there is something abnormal or bad about me if I come for psychotherapy? This fear (if it exists for a client) typically comes from some sort of interaction between cultural or environmental factors and personality of the client. For example, certain ethnic groups may be suspicious of "professional helpers" or have a view that emphasizes taking care of your problems by yourself or within your family or community. Some religious groups believe that psychotherapy is an instrument of "the devil" and threaten to expel any member seeking help. Another example would be the woman who is married to a man who might physically abuse her if he knew she was coming for therapy. The therapist must be especially sensitive to these cultural and environmental factors both because they are powerful maintainers of fear and also because they can have real and potentially damaging consequences for the client. Although you can offer support for the client coming to therapy, and even possibly additional help in the case of overt threats, it is very important to avoid pressuring the client toward continuing to seek help. It is only the client who can finally decide what is best, and it is the client, rather than the therapist, who will reap the potential consequences of ostracism, verbal or physical abuse, ridicule, or whatever if the client's interpersonal environment is not supportive of the client being in therapy.

Fortunately, the above examples are not "average" cases. More typically, the client's general concern about being evaluated by others is manifested. In many cases the assumption that others would be critical is untested. In fact, there may be some advantage to the client's gathering together enough courage to mention it to the person whose opinion is feared. For example, one Chinese student mentioned that his wife did not know he was coming for therapy. The student's therapist was of the opinion that cultural factors were an issue. Although the therapist did not actually encourage him to tell his wife, the client did so and was very relieved to learn that she was supportive.

Often clients want to deal with their fear and will introduce the topic by saying, "I haven't told my mother I'm coming for therapy," or, in the case of college students, they may want to know whether their parents will be informed about their visits. When clients volunteer the information that they have not told a given person about their therapy, there is almost always some sort of relationship issue involved. In the above example about the mother, there is a strong possibility that dependency issues rather than evaluation issues are more central.

One way a version of this fear may be expressed is when the client says something to the effect of, "Coming for psychotherapy means I have failed—I just don't want other people to know about my failure." The primary issue here again is not really the fear of being evaluated by others but rather the way in which the person looks at what he or she has decided to do (i.e., seek psychotherapy).

One area of social psychology which casts some light on this fear is the "false consensus" effect (Ross, Greene, and House, 1977). For example, Snyder and Ingram (1983) found that individuals who were anxious about test taking were more likely to express the intention to seek help after being told that their problem was a common one. Suls and Wan (1987) found no relationship between interest in psychological treatment and subjects' own estimates of the prevalence of their problems but concluded that information from experts concerning prevalence might help induce potential clients to seek help.

3.   Will the therapist think that I am more disturbed than I really am? There is something rather fundamental about the desire to be seen as we believe we really are. True, there is a fear on the part of some that they are frauds—impostors (Clance and Imes, 1979) who need to avoid being discovered. But many clients are seeking, as much as anything, to have the experience of being understood. In part they seek psychotherapy because others have failed to understand them, have failed to see the complexities and appreciate the nuances. The client is searching for a person who is willing to go into "the heart of darkness" with them—a person who is also willing to visit their secret shrines and stay long enough to meet the person's gods and devils. A part of the client wants to believe that if we can understand the exquisite balance, the peace treaty if you will, the client has worked out between these forces, perhaps we will appreciate the client. For example, there is evidence that people see themselves as having a rich, deep, and multifaceted personality (Sande, Goethals, and Radloff, 1988). This belief at times produces in clients a feeling of, for example, "If they only knew my mother, they would understand why I do what I do." But this desire to be known sets in motion a number of fears, including the fear that the therapist will "go too far" and see more pathology than the client believes is there. As is the case with many other fears, this one is influenced by both cultural factors and personality structure. Cultural factors of relevance include the popular image of the psychotherapist who "psychoanalyzes" the client and "makes a mountain out of a molehill." Certainly, in our culture there is a premium placed on what might be called one's understanding of reality and a capacity to adapt to it. Clients do not want an expert sitting in judgment of them who fails to notice adaptive strengths. After all, one possible outcome of being misjudged is being placed, nonvoluntarily, in a psychiatric unit.

Obviously, some clients are concerned about this issue not so much because they fear being seen as disturbed as because they fear they are disturbed and fear having this confirmed. Other clients are sensitive to evaluation, and their sensitivities may interact with an identity that is tied to a belief in one's hold on reality. In any event, the point we wish to stress is that clients are very sensitive to the issue of how disturbed they are viewed as being.

4. *Will the therapist find out some things about me that I don't want known?* A fear related to the one we just discussed is the idea that clients often have "secrets" which they, at one level, do not want revealed. We say "at one level" because we believe that most clients have a rather basic desire to tell the therapist about the things which are disturbing to them. This desire, however, may be counterbalanced by the fear of being known, of being vulnerable to another person. At times clients are quite aware of withholding their "secrets"; at other times they resist talking about these secrets but are unaware of their resistance. (Additional comments may be found in the chapter "Resistance.")

There are several reasons why clients may fear having some things revealed. These range from potential legal difficulties to issues about power and control that have little to do with specific content. Our general belief is that when clients try to prevent us from knowing certain things about them they have symbolically placed themselves in opposition to us. This may or may not represent a pathological process, and it is not necessarily easy to know the difference. Consider the following exchange from a fifth session involving a client who came for therapy because she was intensely jealous:

THERAPIST: So as I understand it, you don't, in your view, have any evidence that your husband has been unfaithful, but there's a kind of nagging fear that just won't go away.

CLIENT: That's right.
THERAPIST: Well, we've talked about this for five sessions now. I'm wondering if we might talk a little about how you viewed your parents' marriage. Does that sound reasonable?
CLIENT: I really don't want to talk a lot about the past. It's not that I mind, it's just that I've never thought one could solve problems by going back in time.

At this point of the interchange, it is difficult to know whether the therapist's suggestion has set off anxiety about her parents' marriage or whether the client's statement is a philosophy of life and behavior change consistent, for example, with that of someone like Albert Ellis (e.g., 1985). One clue suggesting that the person is expressing a philosophy of life rather than a specific conflict is that she frames the issue broadly rather than saying she doesn't want to talk about her parents' marriage. Certainly, we must understand that clients can appear quite reasonable in their defensiveness. However, we must also understand that we are foolish therapists indeed if we assume that every time the client "rejects" our suggestions or ideas a pathological conflict has been identified. What we do have to do when the client seems to disagree with our suggestion about how to proceed is to weigh as impartially as possible the evidence suggesting we might be off base and the evidence suggesting that the client is conflicted about the material. For example, if a client comes to therapy reporting difficulty in establishing new relationships but says that "the past is past" when describing his feelings about his wife who died six months earlier, there is certainly a strong possibility that the client doesn't want to discuss something he probably does need to discuss. The psychotherapy profession has gone to great effort, both in the legal area and in the professional attitudes fostered in training programs, to create an environment which allows clients not to hold things back. By doing this, we seek to calm naturally arising and reality-based client concerns.

5. *Will I appear foolish or weak?* Most clients come to therapy in part because they believe they have been unable to solve one or more problems confronting them. Whether the problem is highly specific, as in the case of an inability to board an aircraft, or rather diffuse, as in feelings of despair about the meaning of life, clients often see themselves as weak, inept, or worthless. Having this view of themselves, they suspect that others may also. We have all experienced the sharp pain of believing that someone thinks us foolish. We have also all had the experience of scrambling to portray ourselves as not foolish. We have worked to say just the right thing that lets others know that we are insightful, that we were being ironic if we at first seemed foolish, that we are not to be trifled with. There is not so much fear here of actually being damaged but the fear that we will seem as if we could be damaged.

As we have suggested elsewhere in this book, clients' desires to win our approval by being "good clients" serve to fuel the fear of appearing foolish. The client who believes that you can be bought off with good behavior has a very strong motivation not to appear foolish. But, of course, it is this image of the "nonfoolish" self that clients are ill-served in protecting because the image itself is a protective device preventing clients from disclosing and testing hypotheses about their worthlessness. With the successful image securely in place, clients are never able to deal with the deeper feelings of uncertainty about the acceptability of their "true self." As therapists, we must be careful to send messages which emphasize our interest in the deeper, at first unnoticed, aspects of the person. Such a message is ultimately reassuring to clients because they can then begin the process of giving up the image so carefully cultivated in previous relationships.

WILL I LIKE THE EFFECTS OF BEING IN THERAPY?

In addition to concerns about how they will be treated and how they will be viewed in psychotherapy, clients may also have fears about the effects or outcome of psychotherapy. We now briefly discuss four such fears.

1. Will I learn some things about me I don't want to know? Earlier we discussed the fear that some clients have of having the therapist discover things about them they feel uncomfortable having someone else know about. It is often the case that the deeper fear is of discovering something about oneself. More specifically, there is often a fear that a dreaded suspicion will be confirmed. Perhaps the client worries that he or she is an impostor, or uncaring, or mean, or has some other fatal flaw. In our view, the fact that clients have these types of fears makes psychotherapy both exciting and difficult. Initially, these fears may not be at all evident even though at some level the client had to fight against them to come to therapy. In short-term, highly focused therapy, these sorts of concerns may never be dealt with and in fact are in such cases inappropriate as a central focus. In longer-term therapy, this fear that one will have one's suspicions confirmed becomes extremely important, for an individual will struggle valiantly to prevent knowing fully what is feared. The parallels to phobic behaviors are obvious. Individuals who are phobic consistently avoid contact with the object or situation which they fear. The fear some clients have of discovering (or confirming) something about themselves is a fear of massive loss of self-esteem—something which clients work hard to avoid. Typically, the fatal flaw which clients fear they have has no more than a small base in reality. However, this base has often been extended and solidified by repeated destructive interactions with significant others. It is perhaps a strange paradox that people both look for evidence that they have some bad characteristics but also fear the "final proof" of this fact. Because of the nature of psychotherapy, clients may indeed see entering into it as having the potential to result in such a proof.

2. Will I lose control of my emotions? Some clients are concerned about whether they will lose control of their emotions either in the session or afterward. It would be fair to say that for many people this fear is rooted in reality since clients often do lose control of their emotions. Some of the concern about losing control is related to image concerns which we discussed previously. That is, clients may not want the therapist to see them while they are angry, or crying, or whatever. Many people have a view of themselves as stoic, as able to withstand and control emotional reactions. The idea that they might, for example, "break down and cry" is very frightening to them. They would not want this to happen while they are with someone, and they would not want it to happen while they are alone. In either case they experience themselves as weak, vulnerable, and lacking in dignity. This may be especially true of males.

Some people have so long overcontrolled their emotions that they fear they will either disintegrate or destroy others if they lose control. It is very important that the therapist help the client address this fear. The point is that the client is more likely to move toward better mental health if he or she (a) feels safe enough with the therapist to risk this vulnerable part of the self and (b) actively struggles with this issue so that there is better access to the spontaneous parts of the self. It is a serious mistake, in our view, for the therapist to adopt the limited goal of having clients feel comfortable experiencing their emotions in the therapy hour and leaving to chance whether the client is able to generalize this comfortableness. On the other hand, this is not to suggest that clients are encouraged to "let go" outside of therapy every time they feel like it. We are merely underscoring the idea that the client's fear of losing control emotionally is a concern about the self which includes but transcends what happens in the therapy hour.

3. *Will I find there is no hope?* Clients often see psychotherapy as a kind of "last resort." Short of suicide, they may view it as the most drastic action possible to resolve the problem. Obviously, if therapy were not to be of help, there would appear to be little hope of gaining relief. This is part of the reason clients may become so depressed in therapy if they do not feel they are making progress. It is not the lack of progress per se which brings discouragement but rather the belief that even though they have done "the most likely to be helpful thing," they see little improvement. In such a case, the ways they have tried to solve the problem in the past have not worked, and now the one last thing in which they placed their hope seems to have come up short. How can we as therapists fail to understand how discouraging this may be?

4. *Will therapy disrupt my relationships?* As psychotherapists, we know that the outcome of psychotherapy can involve the termination of, or radical change in, various relationships in which the client is involved before entering therapy. As Brody & Farber (1989) point out, "therapy initiates a process of change not only in the patient but in the significant other and their relationship as well" (p. 116). Some clients also realize this and may be apprehensive about it. For example, a client may say in the first or second interview, "You're probably going to tell me I should leave my husband since he beats up on me." Another client may say, "I'm not sure I want my wife to come with me to talk about this; we've had several friends who went to marital counseling and ended up getting a divorce." Generally speaking, clients' concerns about the way things are now outweigh their concerns about what might happen if they come for therapy—otherwise,

they wouldn't have come. Nonetheless, some clients need a kind of reassurance that you aren't out to tell them who they should sleep with, how they should treat their parents, etc. This sort of concern can generally be successfully dealt with by consistently refusing to give advice or be critical. In this way you signal that the client, rather than you, is in charge of any and all changes that will or might be made in relationships with others.

A slightly different situation involves sophisticated clients who worry that therapy will set in motion a set of changes in the self with accompanying interpersonal forces which they will be unable to control and which they fear will lead to a deterioration of some relationship. In our view, this is entirely possible; and if clients hint at this fear, we tend to state rather forthrightly that relationships do change, sometimes for the better and sometimes for the worse as a result of psychotherapy. It is important to remember that in these cases most clients are not raising some sort of unconflicted theoretical issue of how therapy changes people and their relationships. Most of the time there are issues about dependency ("I'm worried because I could never live without Bill"), or self-esteem ("I don't want to hurt Julie and would think badly of myself if I ended up divorcing her"), or both. There may also be unacknowledged secret wishes for a major change which people defensively cover up by talking about their fear of change.

When clients express a concern about how therapy may affect some of their relationships, we recommend you make it clear throughout therapy that they are in charge of their relationships, and we suggest that you acknowledge the possibility of major change if clients raise the concern. Most important, however, is the issue of being sensitive to the implied fears clients have about doing something that will affect their relationships. Consider the following example from a first session:

CLIENT: I've just been thinking so much about whether to come for therapy or not. My wife says we should be able to work these problems out by ourselves, and in some way I guess she's right. She's not willing to come to therapy.
[Note: The client is echoing some of the fears being expressed behaviorally by the spouse. By using the phrase "in some ways I guess she's right," the client "sits on the fence," so to speak, and has created a complex mixture which partially hides the client's deep anxieties about therapy.]

THERAPIST: Well, I gather that you also have some concerns about coming.
[Note: The therapist keeps the focus on the client and does this in a way that encourages the client to take responsibility for his own concerns. This response, while it may raise the client's anxiety level, may also partially relieve the client from the burden of creating a complex way to talk about his concerns. Of course, there is also the issue of the spouse's refusal (actually, *reported* refusal) of therapy. This must also be dealt with, but that, in our

view, should take a back seat to the fears the client has about being there himself.]

Clients' expressed fears about how psychotherapy might affect their relationships are a mixture of reality, myth, and projection. Almost always the expressed fear represents something quite basic such as wishes, **dependency**, self-esteem, or control.

SUMMARY

Clients may come to therapy with a wide assortment of fears. For discussion purposes we have divided these into three groups: (1) How will I (the client) be treated? (2) How will I be viewed? and (3) Will I like the outcome? In part, clients' fears are seen as part of the natural process whereby all individuals, including clients, ensure for themselves a safe and orderly world. Thus, fears are not something which should necessarily be eradicated as soon as possible but rather are to be used by both client and therapist as one of the ways to understand the client's personality organization. The process of dealing with the client's concerns about therapy is one of the many ways in which the client confronts her or his interpersonal vulnerabilities.

5

INTAKE INTERVIEWING

Be fond of the man who jests at his scars, if you like; but never believe he is being on the level with you.

—Pamela Hansford Johnson

In most mental health settings, clients who present themselves for treatment are first and routinely assigned to an individual for an intake interview. Who does the interview, how thorough it is, over what period of time it extends, the uses to which the information will be put, the question of whether the person doing the intake will also be the client's therapist, whether the intake will include tests, and the overall purpose of the intake interview are all issues which depend in large measure on the type of agency and the policies of that agency. Expressed another way, there is tremendous variation both between agency types (for example, a community mental health center versus a Veterans Administration medical center) and within any given type (for example, private practitioners vary widely among themselves in terms of what they do and don't cover in an intake session). Thus, it would be erroneous and misleading to speak of *the* intake interview. Roughly speaking, this chapter will describe intake interviewing as practiced at many community mental health centers and some university counseling centers. When we come to the part of the chapter which describes the topics to be covered in an intake interview, we will be describing an outline which is a composite of outlines used at agencies of various types. There are a number of chapters and books which you might find helpful in learning to do intake interviews (e.g., Hersen and Turner, 1985; Pascal, 1983; Pope, 1979; Rosenthal and Akiskal, 1985; Turner and Hersen, 1985; Wolberg, 1988).

We assume that before your practicum or internship placement you will have had some training in abnormal psychology. There are a number of helpful "overview of diagnostics" books including ones by Maxmen (1986) and Rowe (1984). A discussion of complex differential diagnoses is beyond the scope of this book.

Many clinics require that the intake therapist assign clients a diagnostic category from the *Diagnostic and Statistical Manual* (Third Edition [Revised] DSM III-R). The DSM III-R, which categorizes and describes mental disorders, is a publication of the American Psychiatric Association (1987). Because psychiatric diagnoses are used and discussed in so many settings and university courses, we recommend that students purchase a copy of this reference book. In addition to the complete reference, two "abbreviated" versions are available (at a reduced price), each of which contains all the classifications and diagnostic criteria. If you are unfamiliar with the DSM III-R, there are a number of training guides and casebooks which can help you connect "real" cases to diagnostic categories (e.g., Reid and Wise, 1989; Spitzer, Gibbon, Skodol, Williams, and First, 1989). (Note: As this book goes to press, the DSM-IV is under development but is not yet published. Most of the comments we make about the DSM III-R will likely also apply to the DSM-IV.)

OVERVIEW OF THE FIRST SESSION

Clinics which have a primary theoretical orientation to the exclusion of other orientations will typically encourage or mandate a specific type of intake. The most obvious of these would be a clinic specializing in behavior therapy. (There are many good books describing behavioral assessment. Two of these are *Behavioral Assessment: A Practical Handbook* [Bellack and Hersen, 1988] and *Behavioral Assessment of Adult Disorders* [Barlow, 1981].) If your placement is in a specialty clinic (other examples might include alcoholism treatment facilities and family therapy clinics), you will presumably have had some previous training/course work readying you for such a placement. This chapter will not attempt to cover specialty intakes.

During the intake there are at least a few things to be determined and accomplished which do not generally depend on clinic orientation or even policy guidelines since all organizations/centers offering therapy do share some commonalities. For example, no matter where you work, one of the things you naturally are trying to ascertain during the first session is the nature of the presenting complaint. We will discuss this particular aspect of the intake interview when we give a comprehensive outline. At this point we will mention two things all intake sessions typically should include.

Is Psychotherapy (at This Agency) What the Client Needs/Wants?

One important outcome of an intake session is that you as the therapist should have some idea about whether the individual is in the right place for the help she or he is seeking. If a client wants her husband to stop beating her, she may need a therapist, or she may need only an attorney. If a client is seeking biofeedback, there is the question of whether the agency provides such a service. If a client wants to be in a group because he is lonely, the clinic may or may not be the place for him. If the client abuses drugs and alcohol, the alcoholism treatment program may or may not be appropriate.

It is also important to note that clients, even in cases which seem fairly straightforward to us, do not always know how to ask for what they want or may be initially reluctant to be specific. In such cases clients may go on and on about a problem, for example, how upset they are about their job, when all they really want is information about career options. As therapists, we are rightly skeptical when an individual makes what at first seems to be a simple request for help related to problems we see as complex. We should also be careful, however, to do our best to find out what the client is asking for before we plunge in deeply to assess the problem. Thus, there are at least three reasons why we should not be too quick to come to a decision about what the problem is: (a) Clients may have little insight about what is really bothering them and may be trying to solve the wrong problem; (b) Clients may consciously or unconsciously be holding back on telling you the real problem as they see it because they are fearful; (c) Clients may not even be asking for what we think they are asking for—at times we simply misjudge people because we are too eager to "get started."

Of course, there are also cases in which the client attempts to intentionally deceive the therapist or in which the client is malingering (Rogers, 1988). A discussion of these issues is beyond the scope of this book; however, common sense would suggest that one might expect these problems more frequently within a nonvoluntary client population (e.g., prison inmates).

We also emphasize that clients' expectations (anticipations and preferences) about their role and the therapist's role in psychotherapy are seen as key ingredients in the process and outcome of therapy (Tracey, 1986; Tracey and Dundon, 1988; Tracey, Heck, and Lichtenberg, 1981). (We should also note, however, that some data suggest that expectancies are not related to process and outcome in simple ways [Hardin, Subich, and Tichenor, 1988; Tinsley, Bowman, and Ray, 1988].) The intake session represents the initial point at which we begin to discuss with clients these important expectations.

Case Disposition and Assessment of Seriousness

A second important outcome of the intake session is related to the issue just discussed. This second issue is that at the end of the intake session you must be able to decide, at least preliminarily, what action is to be taken. There are several "subcategories" which fall under this heading. First, we should note that before you can take action on a case you will have to know both the general guidelines used by the agency following intake and also what special supports/services are offered. One model which is widely followed involves having, a day or two after the intake session, a group discussion concerning the case by the professional staff working at the center. This procedure, called "staffing the case," may involve psychologists, psychiatrists, social workers, and trainees. The outcome of the staffing is to decide on a general course of treatment and the assignment of an individual therapist when appropriate.

Another part of deciding what action is to be taken involves an assessment of the seriousness of the situation. Circumstances involving suicidal or homicidal threats or ideation require that you bring the case to the attention of your supervisor as soon as possible. If, for example, you do an intake session on Monday with a client who is suicidal or homicidal, you should not wait until Friday staffing to discuss it with your supervisor. Assessing suicidal potential will be discussed later in this chapter. Assessment and treatment of the violent (or potentially violent) individual (e.g., Roth, 1987) is beyond the scope of this book, as is crisis intervention in general (e.g., Gilliland and James, 1988; Slaikeu, 1984).

In addition to the special circumstance of homicide and suicide, another important issue in assessing seriousness is the question of whether the individual is psychotic. Most clinics require or at least strongly encourage the intake therapist to make a referral to the clinic psychiatrist if the individual is suspected of being psychotic. Cases requiring the utmost care are those in which homicidal or suicidal states are mixed with a picture of psychosis. For example, clients may report hearing voices that tell them to hurt themselves or someone else. (These are called "command" hallucinations.) Later in the chapter, we will outline the mental status exam, which helps determine if a person is psychotic. At this point, however, we will make a few general comments about psychosis which may serve as a review for the reader.

Despite widespread use of the DSM III-R, staffing and supervision frequently focus on more broad categories such as "psychosis." Thus, the question is often asked, "Is the client psychotic?" or "Do you see any signs of psychosis?" The exact meaning and intention of such questions vary from professional to professional and from clinic to clinic. In its broadest sense, the term is meant to include any behavior, thought content/process, or emotion observed by the therapist or reported by the client suggesting a gross distortion of reality, particularly if the break with reality appears to be uncomprehended by the client. Other definitions, though related, draw a distinction between a thought disorder (as in the schizophrenic disorders) and affective (or mood) disorders (as in manic illness or major depression). The DSM III-R does not explicitly define psychosis but implies in several sections that one or more of the following should be present before the word *psychosis* is appropriate: (a) delusions; (b) hallucinations; (c) illogical thought; (d) incoherence of speech (including more severe as in the case of nonsensical statements and less severe as in the case of tangential statements, inability to follow a line of reasoning, etc.); or (e) behavior that is grossly disorganized or catatonic. Presence of any of the above five symptoms, particularly if severe in form and uncomprehended by the client, generally justifies a broad diagnosis of psychotic.

We also mention here a few other terms related to the area of psychosis that are sometimes used by professionals and which you should know since they are used from time to time in duscussing an intake interview.

Organic psychosis refers, in the strictest sense, to any psychotic condition in which there is known to be, or there is strong presumptive evidence for, actual tissue damage to the brain or central nervous system and for which there is believed to be a causal connection between the psychosis and the tissue damage. Considered more broadly, the term is also applied to psychotic conditions (whether temporary or permanent) presumed to be directly related to a physiological process (including, for example, hormonal dysfunctions, ingestion of certain types of drugs, etc.). *Functional psychosis* refers to those psychotic conditions for which we have no strong evidence that there is tissue damage or tissue change. The word *functional* was originally used to imply that the psychosis served a "function" for the ego—for example, retreat from reality to prevent being overwhelmed. The functional psychoses have traditionally included the schizophrenias, the paranoid disorders, and the affective disorders. *Reactive psychosis* generally refers to any psychotic condition which follows a situational stressor or other identifiable cause. The term is also an actual DSM III-R category, and when used in that way, the symptoms must be attributable to a stressor and must not last more than two weeks. More broadly, the term implies a distinct beginning of symptoms which have not persisted over a long period of time. In contrast, the term *process psychosis,* which is *not* a DSM III-R category, refers to a psychotic condition in which there is no identifiable onset of symptoms or in which there is a chronic condition showing little improvement over time. *Psychosis in remission* refers to an individual with a previous history of psychosis but whose symptoms are not now severe. An example would be an individual who had been psychotic but who now showed only blunted affect, with perhaps some evidence of mild delusions.

Another component to considering what action should be taken after the intake session is deciding which staff therapist might be appropriate for this particular client. As we mentioned, some agencies do a staffing on each new client, and the decision about who will be the therapist is made at the staffing. Other agencies allow the intake therapist to make an assignment based in part on the type of problem, client dynamics, client preference if expressed, and in part on the caseload currently assigned to each staff therapist.

One of the long-debated questions concerning assignment of a therapist is the extent to which expressed client preference should be taken into consideration. Some therapists view "preference" as an early testing of boundaries, a bid for control, or as an expression of fear or anger. Our perspective is that if the client expresses a preference in terms of gender, ethnicity, age, religious belief, or similar variable, the intake therapist should discuss with the client the basis for the request. Such a discussion may illuminate important therapeutic considerations. If the request seems reasonable and can be honored, we believe that it generally should be. On the other hand, when clients are not overly suspicious or hostile, the intake therapist may suggest that they reconsider their preference. Consider the following example of a client initially seeking services for anxiety on the job:

CLIENT (MALE):   I would like to see a male therapist.

THERAPIST: Any particular reason for your request?

CLIENT: Yes. My mother was an alcoholic, and I can't trust women very easily.

THERAPIST: It's possible you might be able to see a male therapist. I'm not sure who is available right now. It sounds like you wonder if you could make yourself vulnerable to a woman after growing up with an unpredictable mother.

CLIENT: Well, I think you might feel the same way if you had been through what I've been through.

THERAPIST: Yes, I think I very well might. [Pause] Let me throw out an idea. Could it be important for you to work with a woman as therapist for that very reason? I'm guessing, and it's just a guess at this point, that a part of you would like to learn to trust women with some of the vulnerable things about yourself. So one way to work on that would be to face the challenge right from the beginning. What do you think?

Two considerations in assigning a therapist to a client are the anticipated length of therapy and the presenting problem. In the above example, a client seeking vocational information or brief vocational counseling should perhaps see a male therapist since it might take quite some time for the client to trust a female therapist, even with regard to discussing career options. Or if for whatever reason it is known or believed that the number of sessions is to be limited, a male therapist should be seriously considered since, as we noted, working through the mistrust might take a long time, leaving unattended the client's presenting problem.

Another consideration about action to be taken after an intake interview is whether the individual should be referred to individual or group psychotherapy. Assuming each of these modalities is available, there are a few general guidelines which tend to be followed by many therapists faced with this decision (e.g., see Yalom, 1975). Clients who are extremely hostile should generally not be referred to groups because such clients frequently disrupt the group process over a considerable number of sessions. Also, clients who are expressing severe stress likely to result in suicide, homicide, or reactive psychosis should be initially referred for individual psychotherapy. A third group of individuals who should initially receive individual therapy is comprised of persons who are painfully socially anxious. These individuals need to make at least a little progress toward feeling better about themselves before being in group therapy, since otherwise they are likely to retreat so far that they profit minimally from the group. Obviously, individuals who are in the midst of a psychotic reaction should not be put in groups. Individuals suffering from a personality disorder should be evaluated with special care before referral to groups because some of them tend to be very disruptive of group process while simultaneously profiting little from the experience.

Referral following intake will be affected by whether your agency has a waiting list and, if so, the criteria for being placed on a waiting list as opposed to being seen more or less immediately. If it appears that clients must be placed on the waiting list, it is very important that they understand what alternatives are available and what they should do in the event of a crisis while they are still waiting for an available therapist.

Finally, in terms of disposition, a decision must be made about whether to refer the client for an evaluation regarding the appropriateness of medication. This evaluation, like ones involving psychoses, will usually involve referral to a consulting psychiatrist. The general rule here is, "When in doubt, refer." Clients to be evaluated for medication include individuals who are incapacitated with anxiety, individuals who are very depressed or manic, and individuals who appear to have a thought disorder or are otherwise out of touch with reality.

PHILOSOPHY OF THE INTAKE SESSION

The Client's Vulnerability

Perhaps the first and most important consideration in the first session is to remember that the client is usually in a state of vulnerability; hence, sensitivity on the part of the therapist is an obvious necessity. It is unfortunately the case that students are sometimes thrown into initial practicum settings with little or no training in how to talk to individuals in a crisis. Even if you have had considerable training, there may be a great fear on your part that you will not get through the "intake form" in the time allotted or that you will fail to ask a key question if you do not race "full steam" ahead. It is imperative that you remember in this first session the simple fact that a human being sits across from you, a person with hopes and dreams which have often been dashed. There may also be great fears, gnawing suspicions (not infrequently of the therapy process in general, and you in particular), and towering rage which has perhaps been camouflaged beneath a tranquil exterior. Often the people have come to therapy only under great pressure (whether internal or external) and in spite of the deepest of misgivings. Perhaps they have put aside, for the moment, their abiding fear that no one can help them; or perhaps they have promised themselves that they will make one more effort to carve out for themselves the kind of life for which they long. It is into this emotional whirlwind the therapist steps.

In many cases, clients have pondered for a very long time (maybe years) whether they will seek therapy. In the intake session, that magic moment which they have so feared yet in which they have placed so much hope has arrived. At such a time, your behavior—the way in which you respond to them—may have a tremendous impact. In such circumstances it is imperative that you remember that the intake questions exist for the purpose of helping the client, not vice versa. We are not suggesting that the questions are unimportant—far from it. Rather, we point to the importance of responding with sensitivity as individuals begin the process of trying to explain what has gone wrong in their life. No therapist wants to be guilty of overidentifying with clients; however, it is imperative that what the client is saying is registering with you as important, that it makes some difference to you whether this person goes on in pain or is able to change. One of the therapist's greatest tools is that he or she is able, with each new client, to resonate to the expressed pain. Kopp (1972) has described his philosophy about being able to resonate to the feelings of others:

> As a psychotherapist, I am no longer willing to accept anyone as my patient to whose pain I do not feel vulnerable. If someone comes to me for help whom I do not experience as the sort of person who is likely to become personally important to me, I send him away. (p. 23)

Kopp goes on to say that the reason he does this has little if anything to do with the desire to be helpful to any given person but rather has a great deal to do with taking care of himself. We are not suggesting on what grounds clients should be selected; however, we are suggesting that doing therapy involves a process in the therapist which is far more personal than setting out to repair a broken clock. If you can (and do) sit in intake after intake and feel nothing, you probably need either to (a) get in therapy yourself; (b) get a new clientele with whom you can identify at least a little; or (c) find another vocation. Conversely, if you are consistently overwhelmed by the problems people bring to the intake session, you will, of course, need to work on yourself.

Respect for the Client

A word which often comes up in discussing how we treat (or don't treat) clients is *respect* (e.g., Hymer, 1987). As you approach conducting intake interviews, a good foot to start off on is to consider what kind of respect you would like shown to you if you were the client. It is a well-established fact that a significant percentage of clients come for an intake session and then never return. Naturally, there are many reasons for this fact. But one reason most certainly is that clients come expecting to be treated with respect, and for some reason, some are not.

A part of showing respect for clients is to ensure that from the beginning clients be given credit for the strengths they have, including their willingness to come for therapy. There should be an implied promise that they will also get credit for progress in therapy. Naturally, some clients will take every opportunity to degrade their own accomplishments. A few will accept recognition appreciatively of their achievements and strengths. The majority will have some ambivalence about recognition offered by the therapist. To the extent that ambivalence or rejection of accomplishments (as remarked upon by the therapist) are prevalent, a potent therapeutic area has been opened and is thus easily identified by the intake therapist. This is one of the positive outcomes of recognizing the client's strengths. A second is that even when ambivalence is present, a part of the client which is healthy can begin to use this feedback, and to that extent the client will feel respected. Naturally, we are not suggesting that during the intake session the therapist counterpose an appreciation for the client's strengths to the concerns, self-doubts, and personal limitations expressed by the client. To say to a client who has just expressed doubts about his or her appearance, "Well, you look nice today," is an example of an attempt gone wrong to recognize client strengths. A general rule in the intake session is, "Don't contradict the client."

We might hazard a guess that therapists are now more likely to recognize *and use in therapy* the idea of client strengths. For example, a complete DSM III-R diagnosis includes a statement about the client's highest level of functioning in the past year in each of three areas.

Tarachow (1963) has commented on the importance of giving clients credit:

> He thus also gets part of the credit in case he gets well. Never rob a patient of that. If you rob a patient of that credit, you will not permit him to be cured. A patient must be able to take as much credit for the improvement as you do. If the cure becomes something you do to the patient or for the patient, you rob him of something that is quite important and he will certainly resent it.
>
> If you take the tack, I will help you, I will do this for you, the patient will come session after session, week after week, waiting for you to cure him. He will bring his body. You are supposed to give him the cure. Patients can become spectators of their own treatment. So, divide the burden, divide the responsibility, divide the credit, divide the blame. (p. 168)

One example of not showing respect is to communicate that you know more about clients' dynamics than they do. When doing an intake session, you must realize that *you* are the untutored one—it is *you* who is here to learn and to listen. And if you do that well, if within an informed framework you have a respectful and patient eagerness to know clients, clients will let you know their secrets—they will teach you what you need to know of them, and they will also forgive some of your inevitable stumbling, fumbling efforts to be effective. Kegan (1982) has described in cogent fashion how one must first listen well before being a psychotherapist:

> In part, it is a professional helper's persistent recognition that her own meaning for a set of circumstances might not be the same as her client's that leads us to call her a sensitive listener; her understanding of what goes into the way her client makes meaning and what is at stake for him in defending it that leads us to call her a psychologist; and her understanding of what to do with her understanding that leads us to call her a therapist. It is advisable that before people become therapists they pursue the first two callings. (p. 3)

Thus, being a good therapist is much more than listening well. However, in the intake session it is seldom necessary for you to perform heart-stopping displays of clinical acumen; what you first want to have happen is for clients to go away believing that they have been listened to—that their problem has been *heard*. In his short story "Misery," Anton Chekhov (1918/1959) gives a powerful example of one's desire to be heard. A sledge driver, Iona Potapov, tries repeatedly, and unsuccessfully, to tell other people about the recent death of his son. Chekhov writes:

> The misery which has been for a brief space eased comes back again and tears his heart more cruelly than ever. With a look of anxiety and suffering Iona's eyes stray restlessly among the crowds moving to and fro on both sides of the street: can he not find among those thousands someone who will listen to him?
> . . . His son will soon have been dead a week, and he has not really talked to anybody yet. . . . He wants to talk of it properly, with deliberation. . . . He wants to tell how his son was taken ill, how he suffered, what he said before he died, how he died. . . . He wants to describe the funeral, and how he went to the hospital to get his son's clothes. He still has his daughter Anisys in the country. . . . And he wants to talk about her too. . . . Yes, he has plenty to talk about now.

Chekhov ends his story with a poignant scene of a man who cannot find another human being to respond to him:

> He puts on his coat and goes into the stables where his mare is standing. He thinks about oats, about hay, about the weather. . . . He cannot think about his son when he is alone. . . . To talk about him with someone is possible, but to think of him and picture him is insufferable anguish. . . .
> "Are you munching?" Iona asks his mare, seeing her shining eyes. "There, munch away, munch away. . . . Since we have not earned enough for oats, we will eat hay. . . . Yes, . . . I have grown too old to drive. . . . My son ought to be driving, not I. . . . He was a real cabman. . . . He ought to have lived. . . ."
> Iona is silent for a while, and then he goes on:
> "That's how it is, old girl. . . . Kuzma Ionitch is gone. . . . He said good-by to me. . . . He went and died for no reason. . . . Now, suppose you had a little colt. . . . And you were own mother to that little colt. . . . And all at once that same little colt went and died. . . . You'd be sorry, wouldn't you? . . ."

The little mare munches, listens, and breathes on her master's hands. Iona is carried away and tells her all about it. (pp. 14–16)

Thus does Chekhov illustrate dramatically the very basic human need to be able to tell one's story.

Communicating Hope and Involvement

If the first thing to remember about the intake session concerns the client's vulnerability and our concomitant responsibility to respond with sensitivity and respect, a second process we must nurture is the one of communicating a certain degree of hopefulness concerning the client's problems. In absolutely no way do we want to imply that the therapist should downplay the seriousness of the presented problem (such an act would represent a lack of respect as a minimum), nor do we mean to suggest that the client should be misled into thinking there is hope where there, in fact, seems to us to be none. However, as Frank (1973) noted, ". . . Unless the patient hopes that the therapist can help him, he will not come to therapy in the first place, or if he does, will not stay long; and his faith in the therapist may be healing in itself" (p. 137).

You will find that clients often ask very directly about this issue of hope. For example, they may ask in a seemingly joking fashion, "Well, Doc, is there any hope for me?" or they may be more oblique by saying something like, "I'm not sure I can get better," or "I've just about given up hope," or "I can't see any reason to get my hopes up," or even "I'm tired of trying." In each of these statements, the client is in all likelihood, among other things, pleading with the therapist to provide some glimmer that things might be better. This plea is a treacherous pitfall into which many an unsuspecting therapist has fallen. Although experienced therapists differ widely in how they respond to such pleas, the majority probably tread a middle ground so that they do hold out some hope yet avoid being unrealistic. (Frank [1973] noted that success in therapy seems to be related in part to the congruence between patient expectation of therapy and their actual experience in therapy.) Furthermore, therapists try in the intake session to resist starting a pattern in which the therapist is expected to assume responsibility for the "cure."

Just as there are dangers in offering no hope, there are also risks involved in offering too much hope or the wrong kind of hope. Tarachow (1963) has described more than one of the problems which can arise if you give the client a "good prognosis" in the first session. In the following discussion with psychiatric residents, Tarachow reveals a subtle reason for not promising a cure:

DR. TARACHOW: What are the dangers of giving a good prognosis without any reservations or even with qualifications? What are the dangers of giving a prognosis to a patient at the end of the first interview?

RESIDENT: Well, the patient has the need to counteract you, as the person or the therapist; this person may rebel against being helped because it now presents a challenge to him not to be helped, to show you up.

DR. TARACHOW: Yes that may well be true. A patient who is stubborn and perverse will want to upset your apple cart. On the other hand, a patient may have been afraid to do something. A patient presented himself for treatment; he was afraid to play the saxophone. That was his phobic symptom. In my youthful and enthusiastic fervor I told him, "Why of course, I'll help you play the saxophone." He never returned because I had simply burdened him with more anxiety. He had had enough anxiety while not even touching the saxophone, before he came to see me. My ready promise of a cure was a threat that he would have to play it; he did not return. But these are still not the issues I am after.

RESIDENT: I was going to mention the second point, but you apparently are not after that, that you might frighten the patient. He had mixed feelings about coming to treatment in the first place, as you brought up, and if you promise him a cure this may frighten him.

DR. TARACHOW: Well, all of these things are true and you should be aware of them. Premature mention of cure may be disastrous. But something else is more central and you should be aware of it. It is the following: By the end of the first interview the patient has not told you very much. He has perhaps avoided telling you his worst problem. He has avoided telling you why he thinks he is incurable. You know, patients have various levels of thinking. While talking to you they are thinking of something else at the same time. With all the completeness that I say we can attain in the first interview, there is still the other factor. The patient cannot tell you all, either consciously cannot tell you or because he has forgotten or because he is ashamed. But for the moment we shall deal with things he consciously cannot tell you. He cannot tell you the things which he regards as his most shameful problems. So, at the end of this interview at which he has not even told you what bothers him most, you tell him that you can cure him. He regards you as a fool, and correctly so, and he need not return to you. The best attitude is to indicate that you think you can help the patient to help himself. (pp. 166–167.)

Thus, Tarachow's discussion highlights three reasons for not offering too much: it may raise resistance, it may frighten the client, and more subtly, the client may lose confidence in you. The chapter "The Therapeutic Stance" contains additional discussion and suggestions concerning offering appropriate hope.

We shall also note that some clients are asking not just is there hope but also how much will it cost in terms of anxiety, psychic pain, etc. In these cases, for both ethical and legal reasons, as well as for psychotherapeutic ones, it is best to tell the client that some degree of cost will be involved. These costs need not be described in rigorous detail (in fact, they cannot be reliably predicted), but neither should they be underplayed. Strong commitment to ongoing therapy may actually be made more difficult for the client if we describe the process as easy. It is also important for a number of reasons to give the client the best estimate we have of how long therapy may take. In clinics where there is a limit imposed on how long therapy may continue, this information should also be communicated in the initial session, and of course, that factor would also have to be considered along with others in deciding with the client whether this is the place for him or her.

Interviewer Bias

It would perhaps be impossible to construct a complete list of the many ways in which intake interviewers might be biased or in which they might make errors of judgment based on stereotypic thinking. Furthermore, "political" influences on our current diagnostic system seem to be present, even though the nature and meaning of these influences is in debate (Schacht, 1985; Spitzer, 1985). Thus, perhaps one should speak of the possibility of both diagnostic classification bias as well as interviewer bias. Although a comprehensive discussion of bias is beyond the scope of this book, we do want to at least introduce for further consideration and reading two areas which have received attention in the literature and about which the intake interviewer must be concerned. These include gender issues and cultural/ethnicity issues.

Gender issues.   Gilbert (1987) expresses directly the idea that gender is an important interpersonal variable:

> Gender effects are powerful and pervasive. Knowing whether a person is male or female not only is essential to comfortable interpersonal interactions but also often makes a significant difference in how we relate to that person, both within and outside of the therapeutic setting. (p. 555)

One of the first empirical studies to draw linkages between gender and mental health issues in assessment was that by Broverman, Broverman, Clarkson, Rosenkrantz, and Vogel (1972). In what has now become a classic study, this group concluded that the judgments of clinicians about the mental health of clients followed the traditional sex-role stereotypes of the culture. More recently, Kaplan (1983a) hypothesized that the diagnostic system currently in use in the United States suffered from certain flaws which could be related to gender stereotyping. (See also, Kass, Spitzer, and Williams [1983] and Kaplan [1983b].) Caplan (1984) and Russ (1985) have commented, for example, on the way in which the construct of masochism has been inappropriately applied to women. Werrbach and Gilbert (1987) have discussed gender stereotyping as it is related to male clients. The key point we stress here is that interviewers must be aware of the ways in which their gender stereotypes may influence their diagnostic judgments about clients, as well as treatment recommendations. For example, it may be very unhelpful to label a woman as masochistic when her husband has threatened her life if she attempts to leave the battering situation.

Cultural/ethnicity issues.   As Smith and Vasquez (1985) point out, "Increasingly, counselors and therapists are being confronted with the very real possibility of counseling persons who are different from themselves" (p. 531). Assessment of individuals from diverse ethnic and cultural groups (e.g., Comaz-Diaz and Griffith, 1988; Lonner, 1985; Pedersen, Sartorius, and Marsella, 1984; Zuniga, 1988) may be made more difficult both by uncertainty regarding clients' acculturation status, as well as the assessor's ignorance concerning the culture of the client. Potential difficulties range from the question of whether test norms should be different for different groups (e.g., Gynther, Lachar, and Dahlstrom, 1978) to the meaning of various nonverbal communications (Jensen, 1982). Although specific recommendations concerning interviewing clients who are culturally different are beyond the scope of this book, we want to emphasize that assumptions made about one cultural group do not generalize to other groups. We also wish to emphasize that there are wide differences *within* all cultural groups and that social class and other social variables often interact with ethnic and cultural variables. The fine line which must be tread by the interviewer lies between general knowledge of the cultural or ethnic group on the one side and sensitivity to individual differences on the other.

CONDUCTING THE INTAKE INTERVIEW

Client Forms

In most agencies, the client will be asked to complete a form before seeing an intake therapist. These forms may range in complexity from a "name-address" card to a form several pages in length asking for a report on symptoms, family history, previous psychotherapy, and so forth. If the client fills out any form more involved than "name-address," we encourage you to look it over (assuming it is available to you and it usually is) for any clues about the client's personality. The carefulness (or lack thereof) with which clients approach this task, items they leave out, the detail with which they describe their problem, and so forth all convey information to you about them. Clients not infrequently use such forms to underscore how they are feeling. For example, if a question on the form asks about age of parents and the client writes, "My mother died 5½ months ago," you can see in the response the energy which is going into struggling about that event. As you look over the intake form, you should be formulating very tentative hypotheses and raising questions in your mind about the client. The point is not to place the client in a fixed category but rather to begin the process of collecting data which will assist you in being sensitive to clients and their difficulties.

Rationale for Questions

In the intake session, a large number of questions are being asked. The need for some of these will be obvious to the client. For example, most people coming to a clinic expect to be asked something like, "What brings you here today?" or "How long have you had this problem?" On the other hand, the client may not have any idea why certain other questions are asked. For example, in a mental status exam (to be discussed later in the chapter), we may ask them to count backwards from 100 by 7s. Or we may ask them the meaning of certain proverbs. Later, after the mental status exam and during another part of the intake, we may ask questions like, "Do you take drugs and if so, what are they?" or "Have you ever been in trouble with the law?" or "When did you have your first significant sexual experience?" In the mind of the client, these questions may range from the unnecessary to the intrusive. Particularly if they have never previously received psychological help and are not psychologically sophisticated, they will probably not understand why they should be asked these questions if their presenting problem concerned something like anxiety on the job.

Thus, before proceeding deeply into the intake you will need to describe briefly for the client the kinds of questions you will be asking. Our experience has been that this explanation need not (and indeed, should not) take long. One mistake you may be tempted to make is to overexplain the need and basis for the questions. This tendency to go into too much detail comes in part from the training one receives in graduate school where elaboration is reinforced and also from a defensive fear that the clients may demand to know something more about the questions than we will be able to answer. Or perhaps one more step removed, we may become obsessive about our tools when we are least confident of our ability to use these tools.

One thing you may wonder about is timing. That is, at what point in the hour should you move into asking the questions you are expected by your agency to have answered by the clients yet which the client does not seem to be addressing as he or she talks about the presenting problem. The timing will vary from client to client. If the client is in great crisis, you may delay some of the more standard questions which don't seem to have direct bearing on the case until a second session. In some clinics the assigned therapist is expected to complete intakes which for whatever reason were not completed by the intake therapist. We have found comments similar to the following to be effective: "I need to ask you a few more questions which we ask all clients to answer. Some of these may even sound a little strange to you. But we do need to ask them." As you ask questions which your agency requires but which may seem unrelated to a presented symptom, you should look for links which might not have occurred to the client. For example, one intake question we may ask the client concerns interests and hobbies. If a socially anxious client says, "Stamp collecting, reading, and crossword puzzles," we might say something like, "Does your anxiety interfere with any of your other interests?" It may or may not have occurred to clients that their hobbies may in some sense reflect their presenting problem. By linking what at first seemed to be irrelevant questions to the client's problem, we make the intake process smoother, enhance the credibility of the therapeutic process, and begin that process by fostering insight.

Description of Format

It cannot be emphasized enough that clients often come to therapy in a state of anxiety about their life, fear and distrust about the therapeutic process, and ignorance concerning what will be expected of them and what will happen to them. Some research (e.g., Parrino, 1971) has shown that role induction procedures may be helpful to prospective clients. Wollersheim, McFall, Hamilton, Hickey, and Bordewick (1980) have described how providing a treatment rationale may assist the psychotherapeutic process. Heitler (1976) reviewed various techniques that can be used in preparing unsophisticated patients for therapy. We believe that people who are given some knowledge about what to expect, and who have a grasp of the format to be followed, are more receptive to therapy for two reasons. First, knowledge in the face of uncertainty can have a direct ameliorative effect on the concomitant anxiety. Second, by describing for clients what is to be expected, we communicate our respect for their right to know what should and will happen. As in the case of describing the questions for the intake sessions, the description of the overall format for receiving help from the agency should be brief. Normally, the description will include the following: (a) whether the intake lasts more than one session; (b) how contact is to be made after the intake; (c) when the client will know who his or her therapist will be; (d) what procedures are to be followed regarding testing and in general what testing will cover and how long it will take; (e) a description of any psychiatric consult which seems needed; (f) an opportunity for the client to ask any questions he or she may have about therapy; and (g) a short role induction procedure describing in very general terms what is expected of the person in therapy (some clients will obviously not need this part of the description, and many therapists prefer not to comment on it except under unusual circumstances).

Some of the clients who will not need to be seen/evaluated by a psychiatrist will be disappointed upon being told they will not see a psychiatrist; some clients who will need to be evaluated by a psychiatrist will be upset by this development. The issue of the working relationship between the individuals who deliver psychological services and the psychiatrist is an important one. If you are uncomfortable with this issue, the client's anxieties about the power and status of various help-givers is sure to be magnified by your own anxiety. Thus, when you are getting started, you might want to practice with a fellow student answering questions such as, "Why can't I see a real doctor?" or "Is it really necessary for me to see a psychiatrist?"

In inpatient settings such as VA hospitals, a psychiatrist will generally see all patients who are admitted. If you have been assigned to do intakes in such a facility, the topics you cover, as well as the description of the overall format which you will provide the client, will vary depending on when the psychiatrist (as well as other treatment team members such as social workers) sees the client and what topics are covered. It is imperative that you understand how your help fits into the overall scheme of service delivery by the agency.

MENTAL STATUS EXAM

Depending on the agency, the intake therapist may be asked to administer a mental status exam. In other agencies, this part of the interview may be handled by a psychiatrist. In either case you should be familiar with the components of the mental status exam and have some understanding of how the exam is administered. As we have noted previously, the thoroughness of this part of the interview varies widely by agency. In hospital settings the examination is usually rather thorough; in private practice it is usually brief if used at all; its use at community mental health centers probably falls somewhere between these two types of agencies.

We divide the examination into five major parts. Each part, in turn, consists of one or more components. Various components may be left out of the examination in cases where the probability of obtaining useful information is very low. For example, a client seeking service from a private therapist and presenting with moderate anxiety about a job change might not be asked about hallucinations without some evidence to suggest a more serious problem. The five major parts are Behavior, Thinking, Feeling, Data Gathering Apparatuses, and Symptomatology and are described below (see appendix A to this chapter for a summary of the intake interview).

Behavior

Appearance.   As an examiner there are two key issues to focus on. The first is merely to describe what clients are wearing (dress, high heels, etc.) and how they look (neat, disheveled, etc.). The second is to consider whether clients' dress and appearance are consistent with their age, occupation, and socioeconomic status. A student presenting in denim "cutoffs" is not viewed the same as a business executive presenting in the same attire.

Interview behavior.   Here we are interested in what clients actually do during the interview. For example, are they constantly tapping their foot? Do they sit rigidly erect? Do they smile through most of the interview? Do they speak softly or loudly? Are any speech impediments noted? The concept of behavior also includes the clients' characteristic way of interacting with the examiner. For example, we note whether clients are generally cooperative, suspicious, coy, and so forth.

Thinking

Judgment.   When we say "judgment," we are speaking of the client's ability to make effective decisions in both the social and personal realm. This aspect of thinking may be assessed in one of three ways. First, questions from tests like the Wechsler Adult Intelligence Scale may be used. Examples include, "What would you do if you were in a theater and saw a fire?" and "What would you do if you found a letter that someone had dropped that had a stamp on it?"

A second way to make this assessment is to ask one or two questions of your own making such as, "If you wanted to change jobs, how would you go about it?" or "If you met a stranger who wanted to borrow $1,000, what would you do?" A third way to make this assessment is to try to draw inferences based on the person's responses to other parts of the interview. For example, in the complete intake interview, we ask the question, "How have you tried to solve your problem?" In addition to having therapeutic implications, the answer to the question gives us some information about the person's judgment.

Thought content.   Quite literally, we mean by this category what sorts of things does the person seem to be thinking about. There are several specific types of phenomenon for which we are interested in checking: (a) delusions, (b) obsessions, (c) homicidal ideation, (d) suicidal ideation, (e) ideas of reference, and (f) ideas of influence. If any client reports homicidal ideation, you should as a minimum discuss this issue with your supervisor immediately following the session. In the session itself, you should ascertain whether clients have previously acted on their aggressive feelings, what weapons they own, whether there is an identifiable person who is being threatened, to what extent clients seem to be rational, and the extent to which the conflict seems to be escalating. Courts have frequently ruled that you have a duty to protect third parties if you become aware that their lives are in danger (Fulero, 1988; Mills, Sullivan, and Eth, 1987). Because of the potentially conflicting ethical, legal, and clinical issues, as well as the difficulty in predicting violence, homicidal ideation is among the most difficult situations faced by therapists. If you are a beginning therapist, consultation and supervision are a must. If for none other than legal reasons, you are required to take seriously statements such as, "I could have killed her," even though your initial impression may be that the statement is nothing more than a metaphor.

We will discuss the issues of the suicidal client in greater detail later in the chapter.

Thought processes.   We are interested in at least two aspects of thought process: form and rate. By form we mean both the degree of logic inherent in the apparent stream of thought and, more broadly, the degree to which associations of words, phrases, and concepts are organized and "tight." Loosely organized thoughts may include, for example, circumstantial or tangential thinking. At the extreme end of the continuum would be phenomena like "word salad" in which one sentence, phrase, or word follows another but appears to the objective observer to be unconnected. The rate of thought is reflected, in part, by rate of speech but is also inferred when clients say things like, "My thoughts are coming too fast—I can't say them."

Intellectual functioning.   There are several aspects of intellectual functioning which are typically checked in a complete mental status exam. These include (a) abstract versus concrete thinking (often checked by asking the client the meaning of proverbs such as, "People who live in glass houses should not throw stones," or "A rolling stone gathers no moss"); (b) ability to concentrate (often checked either by memory for digit span or by serial sevens or both); (c) fund of information (checked by asking questions such as, "How far is it from New York to Paris?" or "Name three presidents of the United States after 1900").

Memory.   Three types of memory (immediate, recent, and remote) are checked. Some variations in definition exist, but *immediate* normally refers to a few seconds and may be checked by digit span or by asking the person to repeat the last question you asked. *Recent* normally includes the last six months, and *remote* is anything longer than six months. Individuals suffering from an organic impairment may do poorly on this aspect of the exam. Individuals who are anxious may also do poorly on the immediate recall task due to their inability to concentrate.

Orientation.   Here we wish to know whether the individual is "oriented" to person, place, and time. Thus, we ask clients if they can tell us where they are, what the approximate date and time of day are, and who they are. Disturbances as to time are seen most frequently, followed by place and person. We expect individuals to be within one or two days of the actual date and within two or three hours of the actual time. Special circumstances may change these expectations, but the great majority of clients will fall within the boundaries indicated, and those who do not should be carefully evaluated.

Insight.   In this category we are interested in whether persons realize that they have a problem and to what extent they have an appreciation for how it came about.

Feeling

Some authors make a distinction between affect (by which they mean level of intensity or degree of lability) and mood (by which they mean the general type of feelings evidenced by the client during the session). In any event, the mental status exam includes (by whatever name) observing to what degree the client's affect changes quickly (labile affect) and to what degree intensity of affect is or is not manifested.

Data Gathering Apparatuses

Sensorium.   This category represents our desire to know whether the person's five senses are functioning adequately. Hearing impairments and blindness are examples of phenomena reported.

Perceptual processes.   The presence or absence of hallucinations are noted. If not brought up by the client, the subject may be introduced by asking something like the following: "People often have unusual experiences when they are under stress as you have been; has anything unusual happened to you lately?" If the patient says no, but there is reason to believe hallucinations might be present, a follow-up may be added: "For example, some people in crisis see or hear things that other people don't; has anything like that happened to you?"

Symptomatology

We are interested in any psychological symptoms or any physical symptoms which might have their basis in psychological functioning. Because of their severity and/or frequency, one especially notes depersonalization, derealization, phobias, other anxiety states, depression, eating disorders (e.g., Foreyt and Kondo, 1985), and alcohol (e.g., Caddy, 1985) or drug abuse. One should also be alert to the possibility of the client's having been a victim or perpetrator of child abuse, incest (Coutois, 1988), rape, or battering. Recent activities which appear to have the potential to harm self or others are noted here irrespective of whether the client has denied suicidal or homicidal ideation.

FORMAL INTAKE INTERVIEW

We have already noted that the areas covered during an intake session vary from setting to setting. What follows is an outline of a rather complete intake interview divided into five major sections. Although all items in the categories may not be completed in all agencies, most agencies do in one form or another, or under one name or another, cover the five major areas.

Presenting Complaint

One of the most important aspects of an intake session is to begin the process of discovering what brought the client to therapy. We say "begin" because a significant percentage of clients cannot or will not tell you straight away what is truly bothering them. This does not mean that you should be intensely suspicious of the client's motives; rather, it means that you maintain a readiness to discover deeper levels of what the client wants or needs. Whether you do or do not have reason to believe that the client is "holding back" his or her real reason for coming, there are several aspects of the presenting complaint which will need to be explored. First, we are interested in the *duration* of the symptom (complaint). For example, did the headaches start last week, a year ago, or in the first grade? How long has the person been depressed? When was social anxiety first noticed? Second, when possible, we would like to know the *circumstances surrounding onset.* For example, was there a stressful event? Did the symptom begin suddenly or gradually? Third, we wonder about the *degree to which the symptom(s) disrupts the person's life.* As we noted earlier, a complete DSM III-R classification includes an analysis of the individual's highest level of adaptive functioning in the past year. Fourth, we look for obvious *consequences* of the symptom. Although behaviorists, among the many theorists of psychotherapy, are perhaps the best known for studying consequences, in reality all schools of therapy are interested in the consequences (outcome, end product, result, etc.) of symptoms. For example, family therapists are often interested in what the symptom does for the family. Psychoanalysts are interested in the motivational state of individuals who have symptoms and thus by inference are interested in how the symptom affects the individual. Gestalt therapists are concerned with the process whereby individuals create certain outcomes. The "complete" set of consequences of the symptom will, of course, not be known at the end of an intake session (if ever). Nevertheless, this is the time for both therapist and client to begin understanding, for example, how the individual's problem fits into the larger picture of his or her life style, how the client accomplishes goals, what the client gets out of these goals, and so forth.

Fifth, we want to know *how the person has tried to solve her or his problem.* This information tells us something of the person's resources and coping mechanisms and also helps us identify interventions which might be unsuccessful. For example, clients who report dissatisfaction with their job and who have never brought the issue to the attention of their boss represent a situation requiring a different intervention than persons who have had several nasty fights with their superior. Gaining a grasp on how the person has tried to solve his or her problem also enhances the client's belief that the therapist understands the subtleties and nuances of the problem, the difficulties inherent in trying to solve it, and the credit due the client for struggling valiantly. Of course, such a belief on the part of the client is easily destroyed if the therapist suggests (particularly if covertly) the stupidity of trying to solve it that way. Rather than passing judgment on the effort, the therapist is encouraged to acknowledge the efforts made by the client. Later, you may be able to suggest an alternative perspective on the problem. In the initial session, however, you have not yet earned the right to help the client. You are therefore encouraged initially to do some struggling yourself to understand how the other person is struggling before offering bits of wisdom or interpretation.

Sixth, we would like to know how the individual came to this particular mental health clinic. For example, was it a referral; if so, from whom and under what circumstances? Was the person pressured into coming? Has something happened recently to make coming seem more necessary or desirable? For example, has the symptom become more pervasive or intense or in some way begun to make the person's life more difficult? Perhaps the most typical pattern is for an individual to be suffering from a problem over a period of time and then to have an experience which seems to galvanize him or her into action.

Finally, in terms of presenting complaint, we need to get some idea of what the person expects in terms of symptom relief or other help. Naturally, we understand that an individual's expectations and goals may change over the course of therapy (Sorenson, Gorsuch, and Mintz, 1985). Nevertheless, the initial expectations, particularly concerning symptom relief, are something we ignore at the risk of premature termination.

Current Functioning and Living Situation

Some of the information of interest in this category should be obvious. For example, we want to know if clients are living with anyone else. Are there children, parents, siblings, housemates? How do they use their leisure time? Where is the person currently employed?

The ability to locate and keep a job has long been one of the important practical measures of an individual's level of functioning. Furthermore, we note whether the individual's current employment situation appears to be commensurate with education level, tested intelligence (if known), level of aspiration, and other known strengths and weaknesses. Answers to these questions provide a piece of the diagnostic puzzle. For example, dependent personality disorders frequently report stress in their jobs.

Is the person currently suffering from a significant disease? What drugs, whether legal or illegal, are being taken, how often, and in what amounts (for example, how much liquor is being consumed and in what pattern)? In particular, questions about current alcohol abuse should be asked in fairly specific terms. Drug abusers are notorious for denying and minimizing their habit. Therefore, answers to questions like, "Are you a heavy drinker?" or "Do you have any problems with alcohol?" or even "How often do you become intoxicated?" are rarely illuminating. If you have any suspicions that alcohol abuse is likely, you should ask specifically about the number of beers consumed each day, the number of ounces of hard liquor, etc. You will need to ask about all categories of liquor (hard, beer, wine) since a significant percentage of individuals, in an effort to deny their problem, may think of drinking problems as referring only to individuals who consume hard liquor.

As judged by the number of books being published and the number of articles concerning the subject now appearing in professional journals, medical psychology is an increasingly visible subspecialty. One aspect of this specialty is a recognition of the interplay between physical disease and psychological state. Thus, when we ask about current illnesses and medications, we do so not out of idle curiosity but rather because we now know some very important links between the physical and the emotional. For example, diabetics are often subject to fluctuations in blood sugar levels which in turn may produce irritability and loss of concentration. Long-term use of steroids may produce a type of psychosis. Hyperthyroidism may produce anxiety and panic attacks. We do not want to treat an individual for neurosis when in fact the problem lies in the thyroid gland.

Finally, in this category we include questions about recent significant events—job loss, new baby, moving, divorce, death, promotions, etc. We ask about this issue, not merely because significant events can help produce symptoms, but also because it is often easier for clients to feel understood when they know you have some grasp on the important happenings in their life.

Family History

Systems of psychotherapy vary widely in their emphasis, or lack thereof, on the importance of the family in the development of psychopathology. Perhaps even more diverse are perspectives on the role of the family in *ameliorating* psychological problems. In most settings, however, it is customary to get at least a few basic facts about the family of origin. We usually ask (if this information is not asked on the forms completed by the client) for the parents' ages, whether married, divorced, or/and remarried, date of death if deceased, and parental occupations. A question is also usually asked about siblings, how old they are, and their occupations. Also of primary interest is a short description by the client of the family environment during formative years, a brief description of father and mother, and any psychological problems in the family which were noted by the client.

As suggested earlier, if your theoretical orientation is, for example, family systems theory, you will ask many more questions under this category.

Personal History

There are a number of questions which are typically asked under this category. We need to know whether there was any trauma during birth (especially important are events which might suggest the possibility of organic problems), presence of scars (which may suggest a history of aggression [fights] or accident proneness and hostility turned against the self), and history of operations and severe illness (which may suggest a propensity to somatize conflicts).

Personal history also includes marriages, divorces, birth of children, legal difficulties, and past drug usage (important in understanding possible organic problems, acting out, and tendencies to retreat/escape from problems). We want to know something of the person's development of interpersonal relationships, sexual development, and work/school history. Finally, we are interested in the individual's perceptions of his or her strengths and weaknesses, how those developed, and what specific events the client sees as having contributed significantly to the kind of person she or he is today.

Previous Treatment

It is very important to ask about previous psychological treatment. There are several things you need to know about such treatment. First, obviously, you want to know when it took place. Second, we ask about the general circumstances surrounding the treatment; this is, what the treatment was for, living circumstances at the time, etc. Third, the therapist should ascertain what specific type of treatment was received (drugs? desensitization? electroshock?) and how long it lasted. Fourth, the client should be asked about his or her perceptions as to the success or failure of the treatment. And finally, you should at least briefly inquire about the client's expectations as a result of having received the treatment. If at all possible, you should obtain a release of information allowing you to contact the previous therapist for information about the client's treatment.

In fact, the therapist may spend many sessions slowly discovering the impact of previous treatment; the above brief questions are not meant to deny the subtleties involved in this process.

THE SUICIDAL CLIENT

The comments we make here are applicable to therapy sessions other than the intake session. We include them here because any good intake includes a sensitivity to the possibility of suicide.

Client Cues and Suicide

There are a number of risk factors we use in the evaluation of potential for suicide. One set of risk factors we will not discuss are those arising from demographics: age, gender, ethnicity. If these are of interest to you, almost any book on suicide discusses them at least to some extent. We will not discuss them because we believe, for example, that to say that a person of one gender is less likely to commit suicide than a person of another gender may invite a reliance on statistics rather than clinical cues.

As we mentioned at the beginning of the chapter, one goal of the intake session is to make an assessment of how serious the problem is which the client and therapist are confronting. Certainly, if there is a strong possibility for suicide, a serious problem is at hand. How do we approach the issue?

The first thing you need to know about suicide is that if you have any reason to believe that it is an open option for the person, you should do a complete assessment of the potential. An even safer route is simply to ask the client directly about the issue during the intake (earlier in the chapter we listed homicidal and suicidal ideation as a component of thought content). Therapists doing intakes vary as to whether they ask directly about the issue in the absence of cues. As a minimum, we can certainly say that if cues are evident in the interview, ask! Whether cues are or are not present, asking about suicide is never wrong. There are a number of myths about suicide. Perhaps the worst one is, "If you ask about suicide and the person had not considered it, you are putting the idea into his or her head, and the person may go and do it." Without getting into a debate about whether this is or is not theoretically possible, let us say most emphatically that we have never known a good, experienced therapist who was timid about asking clients about suicide. On the other hand, beginning therapists almost always are fearful of asking direct questions unless the client brings it up. It is very important that you work on your anxiety about the issue, for example, by discussing it with your supervisor. As we are suggesting, this myth about suicide is widespread among beginning therapists. Therefore, there is nothing unusual about your fear. You can take solace in the fact that there is, as far as we know, consensus among experienced therapists that asking about suicide does not *cause* suicide. It is entirely possible that by not asking a client about suicidal thoughts you will lose an opportunity to help prevent suicide.

If you do not ask all your clients about suicide, there are some cues which should prompt you to ask. First, we believe that any person who reports moderate or severe depression should be asked about suicide. (In three samples of college students, Westefeld and Furr [1987] found that *all* students who reported attempting suicide also reported depression.) Second, persons who have recently engaged in an activity potentially dangerous to their life should be considered a suicidal threat (for example, driving their car at a high rate of speed on narrow roads). Third, if the client makes philosophical or abstract statements about life and/or death, this should be considered a cue (for example, "Most people are cowards, they can't face the idea of dying," or "Why should I get upset, life is so transient anyway"). Fourth, you should be sensitive to any behavioral cues which might suggest suicide. For example, get more information if the client "lets slip" something like, "I'm making a will." Finally, the client may make vague or not so vague reference to suicide (for example, "I'm not sure I can go on," or "Is it really worth living like this?" or "People would be better off if I were not around," or even "I guess the only way I could get even with them is to kill myself"). If any of the above cues are present, you are a foolish therapist indeed if you do not ask about suicide.

Let us suppose that one or more of the cues are available, and you ask rather directly, "Have you considered killing yourself?" Let us further assume that the client answers something like this: "Well, once or twice I have thought about it; it scares me now to think about the possibility." This sort of situation, and the many variations of it, calls for a further assessment of suicidal potential.

Assessment of Risk

In this discussion we will mention a number of questions, the answers for which help provide a clearer picture of the degree of risk. We cannot emphasize strongly enough the fact that even when risk for suicide does not seem to be high, the presence of any risk is to be taken seriously. An outline of risk assessment can be found in appendix B to this chapter.

1.   What is the history of previous suicidal attempts? The more attempts which have been made and the greater the lethality, the greater the risk when suicide has been threatened.

2.   What is the frequency of the suicidal ideation? Generally, a person who thinks about suicide once a month is at less risk, all other factors being equal, than a person who thinks of it each day.

3.   What is the nature of the suicidal ideation? Highly specific thoughts about suicide are considered more dangerous than vague ones. We refer here not to the nature of the plan (discussed below) but rather to specific thoughts ("If I were dead, I wouldn't have to suffer anymore; what would be the easiest way to die?") compared to general ones ("Life is the pits.")

4.   What is the typical duration of the ideation? For most people, thinking about suicide is difficult; when the thought comes into our minds, we tend to block it out or stop it in some way. The person who is no longer able, or no longer has the inclination, to stop thinking about it is at greater risk than the person still able to block out thoughts after a few minutes. So if every time a person thinks about suicide (whatever the frequency) he or she dwells on it for three or four hours, that is generally more serious than the person who only thinks about it for five minutes.

5. *How strong is the person's ego?* By this we mean such things as how capable do individuals seem to be in terms of resisting dangerous impulsivity, does their rational self-interest appear to be intact, to what degree do they exhibit confidence in their judgments, and to what extent do they appear to be confused?

6. *Is there a social network which the person perceives as caring?* The assumption is made that individuals who commit suicide are not well connected to friends or relatives. Of course, the number of casual friends has little to do with suicide.

7. *What is the individual's assessment of his/her likelihood of committing suicide?* For example, we often say something like this: "We have been talking for a while today about your fears that you might try to kill yourself; is this something you think you might actually do or is it more that you are trying to say how bad you feel?" You will find that people give very different answers to this question, ranging from, "Yes, I might do it," to "No, I was just thinking about it; I don't think I would really do it."

8. *Is there a plan?* This question is a must when making an assessment of risk. Any case in which there is a plan is generally considered by therapists to be much more dangerous than a situation involving no plan. On the other hand, just because there is no plan does not eliminate risk, especially for individuals prone to impulsiveness.

9. *Is the plan specific?* For example, "I'd get my father's gun; he keeps it loaded, and I know where it is" would represent higher risk than, "I guess I could get a gun—I don't know where."

10. *Are the means readily available?* For example, individuals who have collected enough pills to kill themselves are at greater risk than clients who propose to start saving their prescriptions.

11. *How lethal is the plan?* We emphasize that any plan to end one's life is in one sense lethal. Nonetheless, the situation is *very* serious with a threat such as firearms because the outcome of their use for suicidal purposes is so often fatal.

12. *How likely is rescue?* Assuming the same means (let us say "taking pills when I get home from work" as an example), individuals who live alone and whom no one visits are at greater risk than individuals who frequently have people stopping by to visit.

13. *What has been the person's coping style in similar situations?* Individuals who have had a serviceable coping style in the past but who can no longer use that style are generally considered at greater risk than individuals who still have that option open but aren't exercising it for some reason.

14. *What is the person's perception of the effects of suicide on others?* Individuals who say something to the effect of, "Nobody would care; nobody would miss me; the people who know me (or my family) would clearly be better off if I were gone," are considered a greater risk than individuals who say, "Well, I think it

would hurt my father, and I wouldn't want to do that." When we say that individuals in the former category are a greater risk, we are of course not referring to instances in which people say they don't want to hurt others but unconsciously do want to hurt them.

15.   *What diagnostic category comes closest to describing the person?* We ask this because there are some diagnoses which make suicide more likely. These include agitated depression, psychotic depression, bipolar depression, involutional melancholia, and command hallucinations of a self-injurious nature, particularly when combined with delusions. Chronic alcoholism raises the probability for any individual.

16.   *Is the person psychotic?* Psychosis, in and of itself, does not automatically imply great suicidal risk. However, psychoses in general make prediction more difficult.

17.   *Are there behavioral suggestions of suicide?* We listed this earlier under "cues." Behavioral cues should also be considered risk factors. These include making a will, giving away prized possessions, checking on insurance policies, and organizing business affairs.

18.   *To what degree are helplessness, hopelessness, and exhaustion present?* The feeling of helplessness suggests that individuals perceive that they have no control over what is happening to them. Hopelessness suggests that the situation, as far as clients can judge for themselves, will not get any better. The presence of exhaustion suggests that clients have already struggled to the point that they believe they have few or no resources left.

19.   *Can the client identify any reasons why she or he wants to live?* Individuals who still have something positive to "hang on to" are generally a little lower in risk than individuals who can think of no reason to go on living.

Each of the above items is relevant to the degree of risk in a given situation. In more general terms, and as a way of summarizing this section, be sure to check the suicidal history, the nature of any plan, the general ego strength, level of involvement with others, and whether there are behavioral indicators present.

Working with Suicidal Clients

As with the issue of making an assessment of suicidal risk, space permits only a brief discussion of principles for working with suicidal clients. We list a few principles as a way to help you begin thinking about what to do when you are confronted with a suicidal person.

1.   *Make an assessment of the risk* (see comments above).

2.   *A contract is used by some therapists.* In other words, you essentially ask clients to agree not to kill themselves while they are in treatment with you. If they won't agree to this, you might try for a contract that lasts until the next therapy session. Thus, some therapists essentially say, "I'm going to make an investment in you. I'll stick with you when the going is tough. Would you be willing to promise to stick with me?" You will find some clients willing to do this, some not.

3. *Avoid power struggles.* The client already feels like she or he has lost control. Threatening suicide is thus an attempt to get control back (death being the ultimate control in one sense). The last thing the client needs is another power struggle.

4. *Offer involvement.* This is the greatest power you have. Don't promise more than you feel or can give.

5. *Take all threats seriously and communicate the fact that you intend to do so to the client.* Unfortunately, you may on occasion hear a person (maybe even a therapist) say, "The client hinted at suicide, but I didn't say anything because I didn't want to reinforce that kind of behavior," or "The client threatened suicide, but it was obviously just an attempt to manipulate me." We do not believe that such formulations are particularly helpful. Rather, they are often dangerous. It is very important to distinguish between recognizing some of the dynamics of suicidal threats (yes, such threats can be used to bring about desired ends, including "getting attention") on the one hand and how you will react on the other. Just because we may view a behavior (in this case a suicidal threat) as instrumental in attaining a variety of goals does not mean that we should not respond to it. In any event, we generally do try to help clients discuss all aspects of their feelings.

6. *Make suicide seem real and don't glorify it.* We generally call suicide "killing yourself" so as to make it seem real.

7. *Find out what they hope to accomplish by committing suicide.* This will tell you something of the problem and may point toward a solution.

8. *Offer hospitalization if actualization of the threat seems likely. Make sure such action is their choice, if at all possible.* Individuals who are very frightened by their ideation may find relief in just knowing that this option is available.

9. *Share responsibility—consult with supervisor and peers.* This can help relieve the pressure even if you don't get any new ideas, which you usually do.

10. *Watch for countertransference; be aware of your own feelings and attitudes about death and suicide.* To the extent we are uncomfortable about death, it will be hard for us to listen well to someone considering death.

11. *Help the client be aware of and focus on the ambivalence.* If the client is discussing suicide with you, she or he has not yet decided to die. As a therapist you must "take advantage" of the ambivalence.

12. *Attempt with the client's assistance to remove means to carry out any expressed plan (e.g., guns, pills, etc.).* This is a simple principle but one which helps save lives, especially with impulsive people. Obviously, not all clients will permit this action.

The above are meant to raise a number of the issues important in working with suicidal individuals. As we said earlier, we encourage you to read more on the important topic of suicide.

OPTIONAL QUESTIONS

Like psychotherapy, intake interviewing is in part a creative process. Thus, while there are indeed a number of areas which should be "checked" during an intake interview, the way in which these questions are asked is not bound by any rigid rule. You will discover, if you have not already, that most experienced therapists have developed particular questions they like to ask in an intake interview which they believe are especially helpful in assisting them to understand the client.

You will find it very difficult to learn about these nonstandardized questions by reading books. Seeking out opportunities to observe experienced therapists and asking supervisors to talk informally about how they conduct intakes are two ways of learning about this type of question. To give you some idea of what we mean when we talk about questions that are not part of a standard intake session, we have given two examples below. These are for illustration only—you are encouraged to develop your own creative questions.

"Is there anything else about you that we have not discussed that you think I should know?"   Actually, some version of this question is often asked at the end of the intake. Notice, however, the particular way in which this question is asked. The phrase, "that you think I should know about," not merely asks, "Is there anything else?" but structures that issue in such a way that the client is made to feel an active part of the therapy. In particular, the client is faced with the dilemma of asking him or herself what the key ingredients will be in the interchange which is to follow. Implicitly, the issue of trust is also raised. Furthermore, the client, not the therapist, is responsible for deciding what is important. Such a question, particularly following many questions whose importance are set by the therapist, springs the client-therapist encounter into an entirely different phase. The answer to this question is important and often very illuminating since we cannot hope to ask about all important things in the client's life. Just as important, however, is the set of processes set in motion by asking the question.

"Is there anything about you that most people tend to misunderstand that you would like me to understand?"   This question is a variation of the first one but emphasizes more heavily the special relationship between client and therapist. It also raises more straightforwardly (and therefore more threateningly) the issue of vulnerability. Like the first question, it allows the client to teach the therapist about him or herself.

We emphasize strongly that the above questions are not necessarily good ones to ask all clients. We encourage you to think of the intake session as a time to "get a few facts" but, more importantly, also as a time to begin the creative process of understanding deeper aspects of the client.

DIMENSIONS OF INTEREST TO THERAPISTS

As we have said more than once, the kinds of "intake" questions one asks and even the number of questions asked certainly depend in part on one's theoretical persuasion. Nonetheless, we recognize that legal and ethical constraints meld with what we will call "common clinical procedures" to produce a set of intake procedures common to many settings. Similarly, we can say that there are some dimensions which psychologists, as a group, tend to be interested in when thinking about clients. These dimensions are often implied in academic course work, but they are often brought into clear relief only when one reaches practicum. Listed below are a few questions which address dimensions of interest to psychologists. Again, the implicit model is somewhat eclectic, but you will find that if you are prepared to address these questions, questions asked in staffings about the client you saw for intake should not catch you completely off guard. Put another way, the questions listed below are examples of ones often asked by psychologists when an intake session is described in a staff meeting.

   1.   How does the client's relationship with one type of person differ from his or her relationship with other types of people? For example, does the person interact differently with men and women? Does the client have special difficulty with authority figures?

   2.   How does the client present him/herself? For example, does she appear confident? Does she emphasize her intelligence? Does he present himself as a victim? Does he suggest that he usually handles things by himself?

   3.   How does the client handle anxiety? There are very few if any systems of psychotherapy which do not acknowledge the centrality of the role of anxiety in pathology. Therefore, how the person goes about attempting to control significant anxiety is always important. Of interest are both the intrapsychic processes used by the client (denial, projection, etc.) and the interpersonal ones (retreating, attacking, seeking support, etc.).

   4.   Does the client differentiate reality from fantasy? As discussed earlier, when you are seeing a client, a part of the assessment you are making is an attempt to understand the degree to which the person is "in touch with reality." A slightly different but related question which is often asked by colleagues when you present a case is something like, *"What is the level of insight for this person?"* Some theorists, for example Ellis and Beck, make the client's ability to think logically about reality, the self, and the future a hallmark of good mental health.

   5.   For what is the client asking? We commented earlier about this component of the intake interview. We repeat it here to remind you that professionals often ask this question in staffing.

   6.   What are the themes in the client's comments? Of course, this question is one which should be asked about all client sessions, not just intake sessions. It is especially important to ponder this question in the case of the individual who presents with several concerns. That is, is there an underlying theme which connects the several complaints? For example, do the client's temper outbursts seem to happen when she or he feels humiliated, or does the client seem to return throughout the session to the issue of feeling inadequate?

   7.   What feelings does the client evoke in the therapist? This sort of question is frequently asked for two reasons. First, it may alert the individual who will see the person in therapy as to potential difficulties in terms of countertransference.

Second, and more broadly, an awareness of what types of feelings are being kicked off in the intake interview gives us some clue as to how the client interacts with others and the feelings that person produces in others.

8. *What has changed to bring the client in now?* We have discussed this issue earlier and mention it again to emphasize that it is a question frequently asked at staffings.

The above questions are listed as examples only and are meant to give you a brief idea of some of the kinds of dimensions in which psychologists as a group tend to be interested.

TESTS

Agency Policies

The tests which are routinely assigned for clients to take vary widely (see Lubin, 1984, 1985 for a description of the frequency with which various tests are assigned as a function of type of setting). Most agencies have a battery of tests which they administer to all clients and then a wide range of other assessment instruments which may be administered depending upon the judgment of the intake therapist or a consulting psychiatrist or psychologist. A discussion of what instruments you should use under what conditions is beyond the scope of this book. However, as discussed below, it is critical that you know something about the instruments which will be assigned. Even if you will not be utilizing the results, another professional presumably will. As an intake therapist, you need to be able to describe (in general and layperson's terms) for the client the reasons why the selected testing procedure is being followed. Before doing any type of assessment, including assigning objective tests, you should take appropriate course work preparing you for this endeavor. The few comments we make here about testing are designed to highlight critical areas; in no sense should reading this brief section be seen as a substitute for appropriate training in assessment.

Testing Pitfalls

As an intake therapist who may describe testing procedures to clients, you must keep in mind that testing is a sensitive area for some clients. For almost all clients it may become a problem area if not handled well. For example, it is not uncommon for clients to respond to a request that they be tested with the feeling that they are being treated more like a case than a person. Or they may be offended by what they perceive to be the intrusiveness or irrelevancy of some or many assessment questions (e.g., on the Minnesota Multiphasic Personality Inventory [MMPI]). If prone to paranoia, clients may fear that the testing will "trick" them into revealing things they prefer to leave unsaid. At an unconscious level, some clients may welcome the opportunity to "expose" themselves yet be frightened by this very same opportunity (Schafer, 1954).

On the other hand, if clients are dependent or naive, they may welcome the opportunity to jump headlong into "finding out" things about themselves via testing instruments. Often clients will say something like, "I'd like to take that test that tells you what kind of people you work best with," or "Can I take some personality tests to find out about myself?" or "I want to take the test that would tell what I should major in." In such cases we try to steer a middle course in which the tests are acknowledged as potential contributions to self-knowledge while they are also described as adjuncts to therapy. An obvious general rule is that any client requesting a test must be evaluated closely in terms of whether the test requested is the assessment instrument of choice. Of far greater importance than whether a test is or is not given is the client's motivation for *requesting* it and the client's personality functioning as revealed by the ensuing discussion.

Test Selection/Description

Although this part of the chapter is about testing more than therapy, we include it as a brief reminder since, as we noted, the intake therapist at times recommends tests to be administered.

In terms of selecting tests, there are a few principles which should be followed. First, one never selects a test based on some vague desire to "understand" the client. Testing is a form of referral (in the consultation sense). The basic rule in referral is that there must be a referral question—a reason for the testing/assessment. Thus, all tests are assigned on the basis that a question which we do not know the answer to needs to be answered.

Second, no test is assigned which has not been taken by the person assigning it. If the agency for which you work routinely assigns a personality test with which you are unfamiliar, you must make a point to take the test yourself. Obviously, you must also read the manual. Reading reviews in the Mental Measurement Yearbooks is also highly desirable. If you are not involved in interpreting or directly using the results, you may be tempted to shortcut some of the above recommendations. If your ethical responsibility to know what you are assigning is not sufficient inducement to carry out the above recommendations, let us suggest that as a practical matter other treatment team members, as well as the clients themselves, will expect you to have done the above, and you may save yourself a great future embarrassment by taking time to at least do the minimum.

Once the test has been selected, there is the question of how to describe it to clients. In most settings, there should be a brief discussion of each of the following with the client: (a) a general description of the instrument; (b) why it was selected for the client; (c) how long it will take to complete the instrument; and (d) any necessary description of the administrative procedure to be followed (when the test is to be taken, whether it will be oral or written, etc.). Again, a middle course is to be followed in which one adequately covers the points without trying to provide too much technical information.

Occasionally, clients may question you about a test, even going so far as to ask, "Is this test valid?" Under such circumstances, the vast majority of clients are *not* asking a technical question about validity coefficients but rather are saying something like, "Will it really help me to take the test?" For example, one student described the MMPI to a client by telling the client that it had been normed on persons who were mentally ill but was now used more widely. This description is a poor one for a number of reasons; we cite it here as an example of over-responding, which in turn makes the client more, not less, anxious.

Finally, we would like to emphasize that to many clients there is a certain amount of magic in tests; however, your specialty is psychology, not magic. Therefore, avoid describing tests in mysterious terms. Schafer (1954) vividly describes what he calls the "oracular aspect" of the tester's role:

> Still another contribution to the tester's oracular conception of his role may be made by the patient; patients commonly ascribe magically insightful and influential powers to doctors, therapists, and their agents.
> The tester, when he chose clinical psychology as his life work, may have been seeking just such an oracular role. Testing—or therapy—may be to him a royal road to omniscience—short, broad, smooth, and well-marked. One sees this conception in blatant form in many young graduate students of clinical psychology for whom there is no response they cannot interpret, no contradiction they cannot resolve, no obscurity they cannot penetrate, no integration they cannot achieve. (p. 23)

We encourage you to resist the temptation to assign tests, particularly multiple tests, if you cannot clearly outline how each will be used to benefit the client in therapy. Reasons such as, "So I can get a handle on what is going on" are not an adequate basis for assigning tests.

SUMMARY

The intake session is a critical contact between a client who (presumably) is asking for help and a person who proposes to be of assistance. Although agencies may vary in the degree to which they require information about clients, psychologists generally agree that the first contact must include the following: (a) finding out in at least a general way why the person is seeking help; (b) helping the client ascertain whether psychotherapy is the best form of assistance for the problem; (c) assessing the seriousness of the situation; (d) ensuring as best one can that the client experiences being respected (is taken seriously, is listened to, etc.). Within this framework, much latitude exists in terms of specific questions asked by the therapist, amount of detail sought, and degree to which potentially relevant areas are explored at the initiative of the therapist. Clients in crises should not be pelted with questions from an agency outline. Therapists best proceed with (a) Some faith in their capacity, over the long haul, to make sense of confusing problems; (b) Tolerance for clients who cannot or will not "lay the facts on the table;" and (c) A commitment to respond with respect and caring for the individual seeking help.

APPENDIX A:
OUTLINE OF AN INTAKE INTERVIEW

General Considerations
* Assessment of whether therapy is appropriate
* Assessment of seriousness

Mental Status Exam
* Behavior (Appearance; Interview Behavior)
* Thinking (Judgment; Thought Content; Thought Processes; Intellectual Functioning; Memory; Orientation; Insight)
* Feeling
* Data Gathering Apparatuses (Sensorium; Perceptual Processes)
* Symptomatology (e.g. Depersonalization, Derealization, Anxiety disorders, Depression, Eating Disorders, Drug Abuse, Child Abuse, Domestic Violence, etc.)

Formal Intake
* Presenting complaint
* Current Functioning and Living Situation
* Family History
* Personal History
* Previous Treatment

Dimensions Often of Interest to Therapists
* Relationships client has with various types of people
* Client self-presentation
* How client handles anxiety
* Capacity of client to differentiate reality from fantasy
* What the client is asking for
* Themes in the client's comments
* Therapist feelings evoked by the client
* Recent changes that have brought the client in at this time

APPENDIX B:
ASSESSING SUICIDAL POTENTIAL

* History of previous suicidal attempts
* Frequency of suicidal ideation
* Nature of suicidal ideation
* Strength of the person's ego
* Social network which the person perceives as caring
* Individual's assessment of his/her likelihood of committing suicide
* Existence of plan
* Specificity of plan
* Readily available means to carry out plan
* Lethality of plan
* Likelihood of rescue
* Person's coping style in similar situations
* Person's perception of suicide on others
* Diagnostic category closest to describing the person
* Presence of psychosis
* Behavioral suggestions of suicide (e.g., self-injurious behavior)
* Presence of helplessness, hopelessness, and exhaustion
* Client's identification of reasons he or she wants to live

6

THE THERAPEUTIC STANCE

The patient needs an experience, not an explanation.
—Frieda Fromm-Reichman

The atmosphere and the norms that indicate to your clients what therapy with *you* will be like are conveyed from the very beginning of your first session with them. Whether you feel prepared for the first session or not, your clients will be responding to the conscious and unconscious cues you reveal, and their behavior will adjust accordingly. If you are timid and self-conscious, they will likely understand that they must take charge of the session if anything is to happen. If you are calculated and impersonal, they will sense your lack of empathy and may well feel that this is a dangerous place for them to disclose. If you are uncomfortable with your therapeutic power and compensate by adopting an unprofessional chatty or flirtatious manner, they will tend to respond by treating you like a cohort. What we are suggesting is that it is primarily up to you, the *therapist*, to set the climate for the client (Yalom, 1980; Bugental, 1987). Further, we believe this communication will in fact take place in subtle ways, regardless of your awareness or wishes. It is thus very important to give considerable thought to what your function as a therapist is and to what your expectations for yourself and your clients must necessarily be if client growth is to be facilitated.

THE THERAPEUTIC RELATIONSHIP

For therapy to take place, an alliance must be forged between the client and the therapist (e.g., Gelso & Carter, 1985). This means much more than that the client feel liked by his or her therapist, although that is usually part of the client's experience. Clients may feel liked, but unhelped. An alliance also suggests more than rapport, or comfort, or reassurance. The term *alliance* suggests, to us at least, that two parties share a common goal, a mutually defined direction or destination. Therapists and clients do not get together simply because they enjoy each other's company; they meet because they share a joint commitment to the client's growth. If either of them wavers in this overall commitment, the alliance is jeopardized.

We are obviously referring to more than routine, first-session goal setting. In our experience, in fact, hasty and inauspicious agreement by the therapist to the client's presenting goal(s) can be a serious mistake. A male college student may come to you, for example, with the goal of becoming more comfortable with the opposite sex and may desire from you advice and foolproof methods to enhance his attractiveness. For you to collude in such an agenda is to suggest to the client that relationships can be unilaterally engineered, that intimacy can be demanded rather than created, and that, at bottom, he can force others to love him. Rather than accept such an agenda without question, you may instead choose to begin the process of forming an alliance with him by, in this case, disagreeing with his self-diagnosis and prescription. Your passivity or indulgence not only would not foster a therapeutic alliance but would probably preclude it. If a therapist cannot offer his or her expertise to the process, therapy is doomed. Something else may be taking place, but it will not be therapy.

Students often see their choices as bipolar: Either they can submit to their clients, or they can dominate and impose their own agenda. Such a conceptualization misses the crucial understanding that therapy, like other relationships, is an interactive process. One can and must offer one's self—judiciously and professionally, but still unmistakably—to the relationship. The key word here is *offer*, as opposed to *impose*. The therapist's own maturity and interpersonal skills are, of course, requisite; otherwise, the client will be invited to participate in yet another immature, dysfunctional relationship—hardly an appealing prospect.

If you can view one of your primary therapeutic responsibilities as the consistent offering to your clients of what might well be the first caring, nonexploitative relationship in their lives, you will have taken a major step toward clarifying your therapeutic role. This approach to therapeutic responsibility will demand that you fully internalize your professional training—not hide behind it in some plastic two-dimensional role—so that *what you know* is blended with *who you are*.

Bowlby (1988) describes the therapeutic role in terms of his attachment theory. He suggests that the therapist's major task is to assume the role of an attachment figure, who provides a secure, trustworthy base from which clients can explore and reassess their working models of attachment figures and of themselves. Similarly, Yalom (1980) argues eloquently for the therapeutic relationship to be a model which teaches clients what they can get from others. We believe that for clients with deprived, abused, or very protected backgrounds, such learning may be especially important.

Oliver Bown, as quoted by Rogers (1951, pp. 160–171), makes the point even more strongly that therapists must find a way to offer themselves fully to the therapeutic relationship. He suggests that the therapist must be willing to *need* the client—not in specific, pointed ways, but in the experiencing of a deep, profound desire for human connection with him or her. To hold back, according to Bown (Rogers, 1951, p. 162), to hide behind a professional façade, teaches the client at an unconscious level, "'Do not be free in this relationship. Do not let yourself go. Do not express your deepest feelings or needs, for in this relationship that is dangerous.'" Bown goes on to suggest that when he is free to act on his motivation for relational connectedness he is left with the sense of giving everything he can to the therapeutic relationship—which in turn leaves him with no sense of withholding or guilt. And *that* certainty within himself frees him to say no to specific client demands or requests, without a feeling of rejecting or letting down the client.

This understanding of limit setting—that it grows out of the reality of who the therapist is and what she or he can offer—is subtle and fine but an extraordinarily important concept for therapists to grasp. For many of us, setting limits is associated with punitiveness, which we see, accurately, as antithetical to a therapeutic experience. To understand that having limits in the therapeutic relationship is instead not only allowable but indeed something we offer, to fully internalize that learning, can be immensely freeing.

Irvin Yalom (1980) writes about the myth of the "ultimate rescuer." Many clients, be believes, will come with the unconscious hope not of learning to be more completely self-responsible but of having you rescue them from their pain and isolation and humanness. They will seek in you the ultimate rescuer that their parents and spouses and friends have failed at being. One of the ways you will help them take responsibility for themselves is for you to fail in this role, and the most important way for you to achieve this therapeutic failure is to acknowledge your limits regarding who you can be and what you can do. As Yalom says, "Earlier I stressed that one priceless thing the patient learns in therapy is the limits of relationships. One learns what one can get from others but, perhaps even more important, one learns what one *cannot* get from others. . . . The ultimate rescuer is seen in the full light of day as only another person after all. It is an isolating moment but . . . an illuminating one" (pp. 406–407).

The ideal therapeutic relationship, then, in our view, is one in which the therapist is committed to being fully present, to offering the best of who she or he is, and also to unashamedly offering realistic limits. While it is similar to other healthy forms of love and caring in several key aspects, it is different in one very important way: The therapeutic relationship is not reciprocal.

This lack of reciprocity will be experienced by the client as both blessing and curse. On the one hand, having your undivided attention frequently feels wonderful. (As a client said, "Therapy means never having to ask how *your* week was!") It is exactly your commitment to providing an environment where the client's potential can be actualized that makes therapy work. On the other hand, clients will at times rail against the lack of reciprocity and perhaps feel enormous vulnerability because you don't need them as much as they need you. They will worry, and rightly so, that in ten years you will have forgotten much of what they spoke of, while they may remember whole sessions with considerable clarity. The lopsidedness of that arrangement can be quite disturbing to them. Arguing with them that the benefits of therapeutic nonreciprocity outweigh the costs is probably less helpful than your understanding their vulnerability. They are right. Nourishing as the therapeutic relationship may be for them, one of its realities is that you will be more important in their life than they are in yours. The sadness they (and you) may feel because of that inequity is partly what will motivate them to leave, to outgrow their attachment to you in favor of potentially more reciprocal relationships. If you have done your job right, they will leave because, in this important aspect, they want more than you can offer.

Let us move from a general overview of the therapeutic relationship to something more specific. An assignment we sometimes find helpful for our graduate students is to write down their tentative definitions of psychotherapy. Take a sheet of paper, if you will, and try it. What is therapy, really? What makes it different from friendship or mentoring? Why does it work? What are the essential healing ingredients? After you have a working definition at the top of the page, draw a line vertically down the middle. On the left side of the page, *referring back to your definition,* list the specific responsibilities the therapist must assume for this kind of therapy to work. You might want to consider such things as relationship skills, knowledge base, ethical considerations, self-awareness, etc. Now on the right side of the page, write down your formulation of responsibilities clients must assume to benefit from therapy. Some of these responsibilities will parallel the therapist's, and others may occur to you that have no apparent therapist parallel. These tentative lists should be important in helping you clarify your expectations for your self and your clients and thus in creating the kind of climate you believe is important in therapy.

THERAPIST RESPONSIBILITIES

Many of what we consider specific therapist responsibilities are spelled out at greater length in other chapters. At this point we will provide only a quick and somewhat arbitrary review. We will not cover at all in this summary your specific legal and ethical responsibilities, although we assume you give them careful consideration.

Clear therapeutic priorities. Your primary responsibility can be stated very simply: *You are responsible for helping the client.* That is your function. If you keep that firmly in mind at all times, it will simplify many ongoing therapeutic decisions you will need to make. Your function is not to be entertained, or to make the client like you, or to enjoy hearing yourself say wise things. When you wonder how or if to express anger, or whether to comfort or confront, or whether or not to self-disclose or tell a joke or use hypnosis, the question to always ask yourself is, "Will it help this client at this time?" You may not always know the answer, but at least you will be asking yourself the right question. As we have underscored many times, the client's needs come first in the therapeutic hour, and your preferences must be secondary.

Emotional availability. As discussed both earlier in this chapter and in the Introduction, we believe that one of your primary responsibilities as therapist is to be emotionally available to your clients. They need to be able to sense your understanding and support to feel safe enough to risk being vulnerable with you. Put another way, to trust you, they must experience you as trustworthy. As Bachelor (1988) suggests, clients may "receive" your empathy in several modes, but the importance of your experiencing and then communicating to them your understanding of their inner world is clear. If your biases interfere with your ability to empathize with certain client situations or feelings, it is up to you, perhaps with the help of your supervisor, to work through those biases.

Objective assessment. Another responsibility of yours is to offer, in addition to your emotional availability, objectivity. You need to be able to assess your client's behavior and mood and thought processes well enough to diagnose, plan effective treatment, and evaluate progress. Further, you must not identify so closely with them that you lose the ability to understand their contributions to their dilemmas and concerns. There is a difference between empathy and gullibility. If you totally buy into your clients' version of life, accepting their renditions of blame and hopelessness and impotency as the absolute truth, then you have little to offer them beyond a fused relationship. In Reik's (1948/1972) term, you need to learn to listen with a "third ear" if your goal is to encourage their growth rather than just to support their world view.

Therapeutic knowledge and skills. Another of your responsibilities as a professional is to gain a thorough grounding in theory and skills helpful in therapeutic sessions and to keep that base up-to-date. Actually, this flows directly from your primary goal of being helpful to another. Ongoing professional development feels like an obligation only to those who have become more invested in making money or meeting credentialing requirements or making superficial attempts to stay out of ethical hot water than in offering a quality helping relationship. To the professional whose top priority is being of help to her or his clients, staying up-to-date through reading, workshops, consultations, and conferences is second nature. Appropriate guilt for therapists comes from realizing they have wasted a client's time and money by not staying abreast of current advances in theory and treatment. There is no way to know everything about therapy, of course, but the conscientious, thoughtful accumulation of knowledge is as expected of therapists as it is of other professionals. The damage to clients caused by negligence can be just as harmful, whether the cause was fraud or being "too busy to read."

We would like to mention that professional development should not be limited merely to learning approaches that reinforce one's own biases. If, for example, there is considerable evidence that eating disorders respond to a particular type of intervention, but the therapist prefers a different approach, it would be unprofessional for the therapist to deal with his or her cognitive dissonance by ignoring the new literature. Somehow, we must come to terms with newly emerging information, even when we don't like it, and must attempt to assimilate it into our own theoretical base.

Self-understanding.   The kind of self-knowledge just alluded to—awareness of one's biases—is another important responsibility therapists assume in order to provide clients with professional help. Hopefully, students will not only have a personal commitment to self-awareness and continued growth but will also have supervisors who can help them pinpoint areas they may need to address. We are strong advocates of students entering therapy to work on relevant issues. Whether or not you elect that route, however, it will be important for you to identify and explore issues and biases that interfere with your providing effective therapy. Such prejudices as sexism, racism, and ageism should be obvious, of course, but it is also important to continue to evaluate other assumptions one makes about certain behaviors and groups of people as new relevant information comes to light. For more on this issue of self-awareness, refer to the chapters "Intake Interviewing" and "Ethical and Legal Issues."

The area that, in our experience, students evidence the most general need to explore is the general propensity to assume a rescuer role (which, of course, complements the client's hope for an ultimate rescuer). It is very helpful for student therapists to identify when and how they tend to assume responsibility for rescuing certain kinds of clients and to recognize that their urgency to make sweeping changes for clients may well represent a lack of respect for the clients' actual and potential strengths. Some students have found it worthwhile to look closely at their role in their own family of origin. They sometimes discover that their inclination to assume responsibility for others is rooted in the identity they formed as a result of early family patterns or in unresolved childhood grief (Bowlby, 1981).

CLIENT RESPONSIBILITIES

In the early stages of learning to provide effective therapy, it may be just as important to reach a beginning understanding of your *client's* responsibilities as your own. Most beginning therapists, if they err in one direction or the other, expect too little—or perhaps the wrong things—of their clients, often for many sessions, before they start to grow impatient and then suddenly feel annoyed because their clients aren't "trying" hard enough. Giving thought ahead of time to what your clients will need to offer to the process to benefit from therapy should help you in conveying such expectations from the beginning. You cannot force your clients to meet your expectations, of course, but you can indicate matter-of-factly and consistently that therapy will have more impact if they carry their part of the load. With experience, you will gain new ways that fit your style to encourage clients to approach therapy responsibly. Ultimately, of course, you may need to terminate clients who are not committed enough to therapy to fulfill their responsibilities.

The guidelines we offer here regarding client responsibilities are clearly not "cookbook" rules. We expect that you will give careful thought to how they apply to each of your clients and check out with your supervisor such issues as timing, confrontation strategies, etc.

Openness to help.   As mentioned earlier, we assume that the clients you will be seeing in therapy are "voluntary." By this we do not mean that they must be totally free from ambivalence, that they will show no resistance, or that they will necessarily be compliant. We do suggest, however, that they must be at least somewhat open to being helped. If their investment in defending against your input is very high—for whatever their reasons—you need to be aware of that process, and at some point you will probably need to address that issue with the client. Sometimes informal humor, or empathy, or strategic interventions will serve to defuse some of their defensiveness, but it must be acknowledged that ultimately such clients have veto power. You cannot "do therapy" without minimal client cooperation.

It may help you understand the therapist's basic helplessness when faced with unyielding client defensiveness if you identify with the client for just a moment. Imagine that someone you were locked into a power struggle with forced you somehow to see a professional whom you distrusted and/or feared. If you were completely convinced that making yourself vulnerable to this person would result in a major loss of power or sense of failure for you, there would probably be little the stranger could do to "seduce" you into trusting him or her. There are some things a therapist could perhaps say or do that might make trust *easier* for you, but you could not be controlled. Trust cannot be forced, only encouraged.

Exploration of affective issues.   Another factor that influences the success of therapy is the client's willingness to explore affective issues. Even if your approach is largely cognitive/behavioral, you will need for your clients to introduce those problem areas to which they experience negative emotional reactions. While this seems too obvious to deserve mention, it is surprising how many clients are reluctant to do it. One of the common reasons for this hesitancy may be that they may want you to like them, to be proud of the progress they have made, and they may fear that they have used up their quota of your acceptance. You may need to remind them (and perhaps yourself as well) that hiding problem areas rarely results in their disappearance, fervently as one may wish it. Further, the more deeply the personality restructuring hoped for in therapy, the more crucial it is for clients not just to introduce affectively ladened material but to explore it as openly as possible. Not much happens therapeutically if the client and/or the therapist retreats from emotional explorations into mere intellectual discussion of important issues. Clients benefit most from therapy when they are willing to give up the control involved in "rehearsing" material and can instead let themselves respond spontaneously in the therapeutic moment.

Willingness to make behavioral changes.   A final responsibility of clients we would like to mention is to be willing to make different choices in behavior when they leave the therapist's office. Again, this seems obvious. Nonetheless, many people continue to come to therapy less because they want to change than because they want others to change. Or perhaps they want the therapist to make the changes feel risk free, and so they wait for an injection of courage. Or sometimes they come because they like the intimacy of therapy and wish to continue it indefinitely. When it begins to occur to a therapist that some of her or his "best" clients—those who are open and trusting and transparent and willing to explore virtually any topic—do not seem to be making much progress, it often helps to ask them what all of this exploration has led them to do differently outside of their therapy sessions. Significant changes for clients will not occur until they experience life in new ways, and an indigenous part of that process is almost always their *first* attempt at making risk-taking changes. Increased psychological freedom tends to accompany change, not necessarily precede it (Fried, 1980; May, 1981).

GUIDELINES FOR EARLY SESSIONS

We assume you are somewhat familiar from previous courses with the usual three-stage model that Egan (1986), Carkhuff and Anthony (1979), and others use to portray the counseling process. Our comments at this point are intended to build on the relationship-building skills you have already practiced in a pre-practicum environment.

    1.   When in doubt, *listen.* As discussed in the chapter "Listening," there is

so much to understand about any given client, it is critical that the therapist listen intently to what is being said. Your focused, concentrated listening should be available to the client from the very beginning, as you both try to identify and sort through his or her main concerns. Since clients often feel defensive when cross-examined, we suggest saving your questions for the crucial issues, rather than wasting them on minor details.

2.   Interact unapologetically. Your best qualities, whatever they are—humor, warmth, playfulness, sensitivity, artistry, analytical skills, etc., need to be available for you to use therapeutically. Tentativeness and tiptoeing around clients not only provides them with a poor model of how to relate but costs you credibility. Obviously, we are not suggesting that you are licensed to behave totally impulsively. What we are underscoring here is that you should work to include in your professional style the best part of your typical interpersonal behaviors.

3.   Offer appropriate hope. Many of your clients will come to their first session feeling anxious and demoralized. As Tracey and Dundon (1988) indicated, clients' expectations will vary widely. Some of them will have reasonable expectations for the help therapy can provide, some will have an investment in proving to you that nothing will help, and some may want to be rescued from their responsibilities for making changes. All of them deserve your support and willingness to offer appropriate hope. (Can you imagine your own dismay if you were in pain, went to a physician, and spent an hour explaining your concerns, only to have him or her look at you blankly at the end and say, "Well, we'll see. Who knows if you can be helped or not?") As Jerome Frank (1973) noted, clients without hope do not stay in therapy.

In addition to the comments we made about instilling hope in the chapter "Intake Interviewing," we will offer here a few more relevant points that may help you in your beginning sessions with clients.

One source of hope that you can almost always offer, whether you state it this directly or not, is your belief in clients' potential to change. People *do* change; we are in the process of changing all the time as we respond to external stimuli and deal with our own changing motivations. Certainly, deep, lasting personality changes are more difficult to achieve and take more time than simple behavior adjustment, but both are possible and in fact often interact.

Another source of hope you can offer new clients results from your listening analytically. The accurate and empathic labeling of client concerns is potentially relieving to many clients. When a large part of one's life feels out of control and overwhelming, it can feel very helpful to recognize that the concerns have some parameters. The challenge for the therapist is to summarize the issues with enough empathy that the client does not feel discounted. For example, a therapist, after listening for 30 minutes to a new client, may well say something like, "Let me play back to you what it sounds like, and tell me if I'm on target. One area of your life that's driving you crazy is your relationship with your mother-in-law. You seem to get along fine with the rest of your family and your husband's, but you feel like throwing in the towel with her. And a second area you've indicated you may want to focus on is the stress you're experiencing at work with your boss, who, even though you've tried pretty hard for months, seems to be very critical. Are those the two areas you see as most important for us to work on?" That approach hopefully serves to begin the process of negotiating target issues with the client but does not convey the same condescending distance as a summary like, "So, you need to improve your relationship skills with your husband's mother and work on your authority problems with your boss. Right?" Helping clients see some sort of order to the chaos of their lives is a way to renew their hope that progress is possible, but that order needs to be suggested respectfully and empathically.

A third avenue for instilling hope is to offer therapeutic direction, especially if that direction includes references to your client's perceived strengths. Often this involves offering a new perspective. For example, to follow up on the mythical client we just alluded to, the therapist might say, "One thing that strikes me about you, Mrs. Smith, is your willingness to be very honest with yourself and me about your feelings regarding your mother-in-law. I think that if we can get to the root of some of those reactions—and perhaps also take a look at your feelings about your husband's role in this—you may discover that there are some new ways to deal with her that don't leave you so frustrated." Even if, in your initial assessment, there is no immediate relief possible as, for example, in dealing with a client's anticipatory grief regarding a dying wife, you may be able to ease his confusion by saying something such as, "I know what you're going through now is very painful for you. At this point in your life, there just don't seem to be a lot of options. Coming to therapy, though, may help in a couple of ways. You'll have some support so you won't have to make sense of it all alone, and as things shift a bit in your wife's condition, we may be able to discover some alternative ways for you to be there for her and still take care of yourself."

4. Negotiate when possible. The give-and-take in the therapeutic relationship is a reflection of mutual respect and should be present from the first session. Negotiating, in this context, means your finding a middle ground between dogmatism and tentativeness. To be clear in your perceptions and your statements of them is certainly desirable, but it is equally important to be flexible. The client, ultimately, must be the expert on himself or herself. Hence, you will probably find it helpful to blend most of your empathic, clarifying, or challenging interventions with the attitude, if not the actual words, of, "This is what it sounds like to me. Does that fit with *your* understanding? Do you agree? Does what I've said make sense/ring true for you? If not, how would you change it?" The alliance you are trying to forge between the two of you can only be created when you and the client both work, and you work *together* (Hammond, Hepworth, and Smith, 1978). You will likely convey this respectful willingness to "negotiate" with the client by saying things like, "You've mentioned three main issues. Which would you like to begin with?" "Which would be a better time for you for our regular session, Tuesday at 2:00, or Wednesday at 4:00?" "I'm not

sure what you mean by 'feeling down.' Does that mean you feel mainly bored, or depressed, or angry, or what?"

5.   Mix empathy and challenge. In our experience, it is not uncommon for student therapists to begin by being warm and empathic and then, when they have decided the listening/exploring stage should be over, to become quite task oriented and dry. Their attitude seems to convey an OK-the-fun-is-over-now-down-to-business message, and the sudden switch can leave clients feeling bewildered and vaguely betrayed. We think it works better to blend empathy and challenge, hopefully from the beginning of the first session. The empathy should emerge automatically from the therapist's understanding of the client's subjective world, and there is no reason for that understanding or the verbalized communication of it to decrease over time. Challenging the client to do *more*—to change an unproductive behavior, to be more honest about her or his conflicted feelings, to take more interpersonal risks, etc.—is not in contrast to empathic understanding but is an adjunct to it. The inexperienced therapist, for example, who has been suppressing her or his impatience with a depressed client's reluctance to make behavioral changes, is likely after about three sessions of forced "empathy" to have a dialogue something like:

THERAPIST:	So, how was last week?
CLIENT (SIGHING HEAVILY):	Oh, about the same.
THERAPIST (EXASPERATED):	How are you going to feel better, Mr. Jones, if you won't make any changes! I can't do it for you, you know! Now, are you going to follow through on your agreement or not?

Such an exchange is likely to be in marked contrast to the fourth session with a therapist who, from the beginning, has communicated both an empathic awareness of the client's depressed affective state *and* the conviction that that depression will probably lift somewhat when the client takes a more active stance in life.

6.   Set concrete limits as appropriate. The clearer you can be about your responsibilities as therapist and what you see as the client's responsibilities, the easier it will be to set specific appropriate limits that reinforce those responsibilities. If, for example, you are to work with a client who has a history of irresponsible behavior and the client appears for the first appointment 15 minutes late, it is probably inappropriate to "take up the slack" for that client by continuing an extra 15 minutes at the end of the allotted hour. Other limits you may need to clarify and enforce might have to do with prompt payment, early cancellations of appointments, completion of homework assignments, and such treatment contingencies as attendance at AA meetings. As you state and enforce appropriate limits, it is important to be able to do that nonpunitively and matter-of-factly. If, in fact, you find yourself angry with your client for "making" you

enforce limits (such as ending sessions on time), it is time for you to take a look, with your supervisor, at your own countertransference issues.

7.   Ally yourself with client strengths. Your clients, like the rest of us, have the potential to demonstrate courage and resilience and strength, as well as the capacity for self-destructive passivity and manipulativeness. If, in the first session, you can identify and align yourself with the healthy part of the client's personality and refuse to collude with his or her pathology, you will have begun to establish the kind of "therapeutic alliance" we have previously referred to. In effect, you will be saying yes to certain forms of relating (e.g., mutual respect, caring, honesty, commitment to focusing on important issues, etc.) and no to others (e.g., game playing, flirting, tangential story telling, irresponsible collusion, etc.). In our experience, this expectation conveyed by therapists that good therapeutic work will come from their clients comes from the therapist's genuine respect for clients. Such expectations tend to permeate their interactions from very early in the first session (Bown, January 1976, personal communication).

8.   Indicate willingness to learn. Particularly if you have a suspicious or hostile client, it is important to demonstrate appropriate humility. Paradoxically, therapists often *gain* credibility by acknowledging outright and unapologetically that the client will need to teach them specifics about the client's life. Such client contributions certainly include, but are not limited to, information about that client's background, feelings, and motivations; education regarding the client's culture and life context; and ongoing feedback to the therapist about his or her therapeutic impact. The distinction that we are suggesting here is that you are the expert on therapy but that clients need to be the experts on themselves (Koile, 1988).

SUMMARY

The therapeutic relationship is one that is created anew with each therapist/ client combination. It is incumbent upon therapists to clarify for themselves what the substance and the parameters of the relationship need to be to promote client growth and then to actively work to promote such a climate. What the client experiences with you may have far more impact than any specific interventions you might make. Defining for yourself what your therapeutic stance needs to be—and what clients also need to offer to the process—can help you create these norms from the beginning of therapy.

7

LISTENING

Whom shall I tell my sorrow to?

—Russian folk song

Empathic listening is a therapeutic skill especially discussed by Rogers (1951, 1961) and his followers (Carkhuff and Anthony, 1979; Boy and Pine, 1982; Egan, 1986) and by Kohut (1977). While the person-centered and object relations writers vary somewhat in how they define *empathy,* the core ingredient is listening deeply enough to the client's world to be able to resonate to it and express it in one's own words. Writers from other orientations (Reik, 1964; Langs, 1978; Koile, 1977; Lazarus, 1976; Berger, 1987; Roth, 1987) also stress the importance of listening carefully to what clients say—and do *not* say—in order to be able to understand the depth and nuances of their meanings.

Most beginning therapists consider themselves "good listeners." Perhaps someone has told them so. Perhaps they only wish it were so. Even if, however, they have acquired some social listening skills, it is unlikely that they have much understanding of what therapeutic listening involves unless they have been in therapy as clients. The focused, professional attention to another's communication that is the essential hallmark of psychotherapy is an intricate, demanding skill that no therapist fully perfects. For who can fully understand another?

Nonetheless, we can continue to hone our listening skills, learning to use ourselves as we resonate to our clients' words and nonverbal expressions.

There is a difference between social listening and therapeutic listening. Social listening is largely a matter of not interrupting, of nodding from time to time and smiling when appropriate. Mainly it involves encouraging someone to continue talking, but at the same level. To be able to listen therapeutically requires much more. One must remain in much closer emotional contact with the client than with a social acquaintance, but also more clearly separate. Losing oneself and fusing with the client reduces one's therapeutic potential to zero. Similarly, distancing oneself is equally destructive. Distancing feels safer for therapists and helps ensure their objectivity, but it can leave the client—especially the client exploring painful or shameful material—feeling alone and incredibly vulnerable. Few therapists, even the most behaviorally trained, deny the importance of the therapeutic alliance that is forged by emotional bonding. Allowing oneself to resonate to the client's feelings, without fusing, however, requires much practice.

Let us imagine a hypothetical client, Helen, who comes to an agency for counseling. She is trying to deal with the death of her ten-year-old son Jeff. Imagine that only two therapists are available to see her—one, a female, too prone to be distant with clients, and the other, a male, too prone to overidentify (fuse) with clients. The dialogue with the female therapist might go something like this:

CLIENT (IN TEARS):	I just don't know how to keep going. I miss him so much, and I feel so guilty!
THERAPIST:	Helplessness is a common enough reaction, and your guilt is probably irrational. Both will diminish in time.
CLIENT (SOBBING):	But how do I make it through *today?* And tomorrow? My other children need me, but I can't seem to do more than go through the motions of taking care of them!
THERAPIST:	Sounds like the grief has been a springboard into questioning your adequacy as a mother.
CLIENT:	Oh, I don't know. I just know I hurt so much! Can't you help me?
THERAPIST:	The grieving process takes time, you know. First one goes through denial, then anger, then . . . .

This therapist has insulated herself from the mother's pain. Rather than trying to understand and stay in emotional contact with Helen as she expresses her reactions to her son's death, the therapist backs across the room emotionally and responds with intellectual interpretations and explanations. Helen is likely to leave feeling angry and exposed. Probably she will not return.

The dialogue with the male therapist might go something like this:

CLIENT (IN TEARS):	I just don't know how to keep going. I miss him so much, and I feel so guilty!
THERAPIST (ALSO IN TEARS):	My God, it must be *terrible* for you! I don't know how you're doing as well as you are. To lose a child . . . ! (sobbing)
CLIENT (NO LONGER CRYING):	It's the guilt that's the worse part. I keep feeling that I should have been able to help him more.
THERAPIST (STILL CRYING):	Oh, I *know.* The worst feeling in the world must be to watch a child die and not be able to help. You *poor thing!*
CLIENT:	Can you help me?
THERAPIST (REACHING FOR TISSUE):	Well, I'll try, but this is so *painful.* How awful you must be feeling! (begins to cry again)

This therapist has so completely identified with what he *assumes* Helen is going through, no therapy can take place. By abdicating his separateness, he has rendered himself impotent to offer more than emotionalism. At best, Helen is likely to feel overwhelmed by such "empathy." Perhaps she will realize that her assigned role requires a switch from client to comforter. More likely, she will feel angry and uncomfortable with the therapist's presumptuousness and self-indulgence and will not return for a second session.

What does Helen need, then, rather than distance or emotional engulfment? She needs a therapist who has the ability to tolerate and resonate to her pain without needing either to dilute or to identify with it out of her or his own needs. To be such a therapist requires a great deal of emotional strength. It is a bit like swimming very close to a deep, powerful whirlpool; the challenge is to be close enough to the emotional energy to understand what the client must be experiencing without getting swept down into the suction oneself. We are of no help as therapists if we are either drowning with the client or miles away on dry land.

Roth (1987) discusses several personality qualities of a good therapist. Among other traits, he mentions that the therapist must have an insatiable curiosity, blended with empathic appreciation of others' experiences. Such a therapist is familiar with the shadings of human pain but does not feel pressure to understand *this* client prematurely. Stated differently, the therapist's mind and heart must be engaged simultaneously. The mind must stay open, not jumping to conclusions, willing to tolerate ambiguity and contradictions while waiting for the client's major themes to emerge. Meanwhile, the therapist's heart, or humanity if you prefer, must be able to resonate to the client's affective world. The outcome is a simultaneous processing of information by the therapist's cognitive and empathic capabilities. It is this interchange between two parallel internal processes that in part distinguishes the professional therapist from the "good listener."

We would like to stress that this kind of therapeutic listening is a professional stance that can be *learned,* although much practice is necessary before the balanced awareness becomes relatively automatic. Our experience in working with many student therapists has led us to conclude that far too large a percentage of them underestimate the amount of practice a new skill requires before it becomes a ready part of their repertoire. Most quality professionals—from concert pianists to tennis pros—practice hours a day for several years before they expect excellence of themselves. Whether you consider therapy an art or an accumulation of skills, it is important to work regularly and patiently at improving your abilities. Difficult as it may be to learn, this therapeutic listening process will be of immense benefit both to you and to those with whom you work.

For you, it is a process that allows (indeed, requires) you to use all of yourself. Your feelings, your associations, your humor, your theoretical understandings, your insight—all of these will become increasingly available as you sit with a client, listening and trying to understand him or her as deeply as possible. If you find yourself leaning too far in the intellectual and distant direction, your emotional resonance to the client should pull you back upright, and if you begin to fuse and identify, your cognitive components should serve to rebalance you. There will surely be times when you will feel yourself off balance, but your recovery will become quicker as you practice.

For the clients on the receiving end of such therapeutic listening, there is often a dawning sense of incredible relief. *Finally* they are in an environment that offers the emotional closeness they need to feel safe (or at least safer) and the clarity and objectivity that helps them separate truth from illusion. This combination of safety and clarity offers clients hope. In time, many clients consciously or unconsciously incorporate their therapists' listening stance into their own relationship with themselves and begin to offer themselves what has been so helpful in therapy. They begin to experience, within themselves, the combination of patient compassion and encouragement to see the truth that they have received in therapy. In a sense, the therapist thus provides a model for the client of how to listen to himself or herself.

SIGNALS OF POOR LISTENING

Once you have something of an idea of what therapeutic listening feels like within yourself when you offer it, it is often helpful to pinpoint those states which are clearly *not* listening. (We will not address the obvious here—the times your mind wanders to tonight's dinner menu, etc.) During the therapeutic hour then, when you find yourself drifting into one of these other stances, hopefully your alarm bells will go off so that you can bring yourself back on center. *Alarm* is an appropriate brief reaction, for in a profound sense, you will have begun to approach unethical behavior. Listening to the client means that you are putting her or his needs *first,* which of course is your primary ethical obligation; not listening almost always is an indication that your own needs have superseded the client's. Therapy has given way to exploitation, however subtly.

Performance anxiety. Most beginning therapists have urgent needs to be helpful, especially if the client is paying for therapeutic services. There is a point, though, when the desire to help the client becomes a desire to do it "right," and instead of listening to the client, students begin listening to themselves, as they feverishly attempt to retrieve from their data banks what they are *supposed* to say in the current situation so that their supervisor, fellow students, mother, or whoever will be proud of them. The client's needs get left in the dust as the student becomes preoccupied with looking good. It is absolutely crucial to remember that clients have come to you, and you have agreed to see them, because they need something a professional can offer. That is the contract. That is what you promise implicitly each time you close the door and ask them to sit down. Any time you put your own needs ahead of the client's—including your perfectionist needs to look good—you have violated that contract. If you must worry about your image or your grade, we encourage you to do it on your own time, *not the client's.*

Disapproval of client affect. It is easy to be a supportive therapist when you like your clients, sympathize with their values, and are proud of the changes they are making. It is trickier to establish an alliance when you disapprove of their behavior (e.g., child abuse, excessive dependency, dangerous irresponsibility, etc.). Many therapists manage it by distinguishing between the client's needs or feelings (which can often be supported or at least validated) and client behavior (which might require therapeutic confrontation). But what do you do when you don't like their feelings? What most beginning therapists do—inappropriately— is quit listening.

Let's go back to Helen. Suppose she left the first agency, where she had had access to only those two inadequate therapists, and has somehow located you. You get off to a good start. You avoid the errors of the other two and successfully establish a good therapeutic relationship. During the fifth session, she begins to talk of her earlier desire as a teen-ager to have a baby "to play with" and reports that this child, Jeff, was born when she was 18 years old. During her sixth and seventh sessions, she discusses her deteriorating marriage, and you begin to suspect that she had turned to Jeff to meet her emotional needs for intimacy. Perhaps you have some trouble accepting that. By the tenth session, her neglect of the other two children has become a clear pattern, one which began before Jeff's terminal illness. You find yourself feeling increasingly judgmental of her narcissism and immaturity. The more you listen, the clearer it becomes that the family system was dysfunctional from the beginning and that Helen and Jeff's relationship had been particularly enmeshed. Now, as you try to help her explore her grief, you discover yourself thinking that she has no right to feel what she does, that she *shouldn't* have been so symbiotically attached to him in the first place. Each time she mentions her sense of loss, you notice your inclination to minimize her feelings so that they will be more in line with typical parental grief. In short, you disapprove of what seems to you to be grief over an exploitative and potentially incestuous relationship.

To be able to help Helen, however, you will need to find some way to follow the advice of one of the authors' supervisors: "No, no! You have to start where they're *at*!" You could pretend, if you wanted, that by ignoring certain client feelings they would go away, but doing that would waste the client's time and money, damage the therapeutic relationship, and increase your own frustration. Better to remind yourself that your client needs very much to be heard and that your job is to help her express and understand the various textures and shades of what she feels. If, in fact, Helen's family relationships are dysfunctional, they will much more likely improve by acknowledging and exploring what *is*, rather than by denying feelings and motivations because of your disapproval.

As you gain more experience, it is worth paying attention to the patterns that evolve regarding which client feelings you have trouble accepting. Granted that many motivations lead to dysfunctional client behavior, why do only certain of these feelings and motivations hook you? What you may discover is a form of countertransference seldom discussed—that is, when the client elicits reactions from you, not which you previously felt toward someone else, but perhaps which you felt toward yourself in a similar situation. For example, a therapist who judged herself harshly for feeling ambivalent in an earlier relationship may well find that she has little patience with a client struggling with ongoing ambivalent feelings about his wife. Another therapist, who spent many years struggling to overcome his dependency on an autocratic father, may find himself dealing with very judgmental reactions toward a passive, dependent wife of an alcoholic. Taboos that we have imposed on ourselves we are likely to impose on others, regardless of their intrinsic wisdom or applicability.

Therapist overcontrol.   Another signal of obstructed listening is therapist attempts to change the client's behavior. Often this takes the form of advice giving, lecturing, rescuing, and other variations of controlling. It is not that offering a client information or advice is always inappropriate; sometimes, in fact, clients truly do not understand a psychological concept that might aid them in making responsible decisions. Generally, most experienced therapists offer advice rarely, but doing so is not always untherapeutic. What we are suggesting that you monitor is your motivation for wanting to do these things. Again, the issue is whose needs are you meeting, yours or the client's? If you feel disappointed, hurt, or annoyed when your wisdom is ignored, that is a very strong indication that your motivation was self-serving.

Therapists attempt to change or control clients as a result of crossing boundaries and trying to take responsibility for improving the client's life. Berger (1987) talks about "dispassionate compassion" as the proper stance to take in therapy. When we start feeling passionate regarding our clients, when we feel a strong need to help them or change their minds or teach them a lesson, then we have once again lost the separateness that is the hallmark of therapeutic intimacy. It is not enough to care for our clients. We must learn to care *well,* and that means, among other things, letting them be responsible for making their own choices. As Rosenthal (1971) explained:

> This is part of the paradox of therapy. I am dependent upon the patient for my very existence as a therapist, and therefore for that measure of my self-esteem which derives from my being a therapist; yet to be effective and uncorrupted by the demands of the patient, my self-esteem must be independent of him. If I don't care, I can't help him; if I care too much, that is, if I want too much for myself, I can't help him. Only by letting him alone can I really be with him and help him, yet letting him alone feels like I'm not doing what I'm supposed to be doing. It's like learning not to slam down on your brakes on icy pavement. (p. 6)

Sometimes that can be very hard. When a client you like continues to behave in ways that sabotage her or his deepest goals or does things that are clearly self-destructive, it is not easy to remain dispassionate. If, for example, the gradually improving bulimic you have been working with suddenly feels under stress, resumes purging, and loses five pounds, you are likely to be frustrated and very concerned, and it will be difficult not to overreact.

There are two points we would like to make that may be helpful to remember when you are tempted to overcontrol. First, if lectures or simple advice were going to work in these situations, they probably would have worked before now. Very likely, either the client's friends or family have been delivering lectures or advice for years, or the client himself or herself has been trying to control the behavior with self-threats and judgments. That approach rarely works, so there is no need to try it again. Second, and more to the point, as Rogers (1951) discussed at length, a major paradox takes place: Deep changes are much more likely to occur when the client feels accepted *as is,* when there is an absence of therapeutic pressure to be or feel differently. Strangely, when you can offer acceptance and permission not to change, many clients feel freer to change more. And even in those situations when no immediate change is forthcoming, at least the client will not feel it necessary to lie to you about nonexistent changes in order to maintain your good will.

Certainly, there will be many times when you will point out to clients that their behavior seems to be in discord with their goals. There may be times when you will choose to do that forcefully. But before you do it, check your emotional urgency by asking yourself: If I offer this intervention and it is ignored or resisted by the client, can I accept that and maintain therapeutic contact? When your answer is no, we encourage you to consider that your real work may need to be with yourself rather than with the client and to explore with your supervisor the sources of your urgency.

LEVELS OF LISTENING

One difficulty that many beginning therapists have is in deciding how and what kind of direction to give to a client's revelations. The guidelines seem contradictory: On the one hand, supervisors encourage acceptance and respect so the client can feel free to explore important issues, but on the other hand, they insist that the client should not be allowed to wander indefinitely or to manipulate the therapist. While the issue of how and when to provide direction to a session is too complex to address comprehensively here, we can say that the level at which the therapist listens greatly influences the direction of a session.

Listening for content.   Students typically fear that if they have several clients, they will somehow get them mixed up and end up saying, "So, how's the snake phobia?" to the career client. While seasoned therapists do occasionally forget important client material, such lapses are unusual if the client was given full attention during each session. Particularly if the therapist was in tune emotionally, he or she likely constructed images or other impressions as the client's "story" unfolded, and these visualizations can be the avenue to remembering considerable material.

It is impossible, of course, to remember every single thing every client says. Nor would it be particularly wise to try. If you are using all of your energy trying to memorize each piece of data the client offers, you will surely miss the essence of the communication. Clients thankfully tend to be quite forgiving of small lapses; they do, however, feel hopeless and betrayed if the essence is discounted or forgotten. The question to ask yourself then, as you listen, is, "What does the client *mainly* need me to understand?"

Keeping this clear guideline in the forefront of your mind, especially in the initial sessions, will do two things for the therapeutic process: (1) It will mean that the questions you ask will not be wasted on trivia. No client appreciates being interrupted during an emotional outburst to be asked, "Wait. What time did you say that happened?" He or she will, conversely, be more tolerant of questions like, "Help me understand why this is so infuriating for you. Was this episode the final one in a long string of similar incidents?" (2) It will focus your listening and subsequent responses in such a way as to discourage client rambling or unnecessary storytelling. In effect, you will convey the message, "I want to get to the heart of your concern so I can help you as fully and quickly as possible."

On those rare occasions when you do forget important information, our suggestion is that you be honest. A simple statement like, "I'm sorry. Tell me again about . . ." is generally easily accepted by most clients.

There is one thing you can be sure of if you are listening for content as well as you should be: Some of your favorite stereotypes and biases will be shattered. You will find mothers who are homicidal, ministers with sexual fetishes, school board members having affairs with high school students, homosexuals who are deeply religious, skid row alcoholics who write beautiful poetry. You will discover that we humans are capable of dazzling courage and selflessness, as well as dangerous sociopathy and closed-mindedness. In short, you will discover that your clients are as complex as you.

Listening for feelings.　　If you have been progressing through a typical counseling training sequence, you have probably practiced "reflecting feelings." Perhaps you have learned how to paraphrase and pinpoint affect in a variety of ways, from the brittle "you-are-feeling-(blank)-because-" formula to more elegant neurolinguistic programming techniques. *How* you let your clients know that you understand what they are experiencing emotionally is much less important than *that* you do it. Our impression is that many of the "yes, but" responses that therapists complain of from their clients are less "resistance" than they are a manifestation of the client's feeling misunderstood. Unless you have a clear reason to believe otherwise, we suggest you take each "yes, but" as a signal from the client that you are inappropriately moving into your own agenda and need to slow down instead and listen again to what the client is trying to tell you.

There are differences between sadness, melancholy, nostalgia, depression, and grief. As you listen to the nuances of feelings that your client expresses, both verbally and nonverbally, it is worth the time it takes to pinpoint as accurately as possible what emotions he or she seems to be experiencing. The look of surprised relief, often accompanied by tears, that comes across the face of the client who hears you accept, clarify, and express accurately the depth and breadth of her or his feelings, that look is worth the effort. For some beginning therapists, this will require enhancing their affective vocabularies. Other therapists will learn to capture the client's emotional state with a metaphor, an image, a line from a song.

What that look of relief represents, besides a more relaxed client, is that you have begun to earn the right to intervene. As Earl Koile (1978) points out, being heard is a prelude to the client's ability to hear you. And if he or she cannot hear you, then all of the therapeutic wisdom and insight you offer is wasted. Influence is not automatically accorded to you because of your training. You must earn influence anew with each client, and your ability to make the client feel heard is your primary avenue toward earning it.

If you are distrustful of your own feelings, you will have a very difficult time aiding clients in exploring theirs. An exercise that you may find helpful is to find a list of affective words and go through them one by one, briefly capturing the sense of each one before you go on to the next. Try to resonate to each one. Which feelings or groups of feelings did you find yourself either actively defending against or perhaps cavalierly breezing through? Are there predictable patterns to your discomforts? Can you tolerate the feelings of intense grief, shame, fear, and rage? Surprisingly, and this may fit for you, some therapists tolerate their own and others' "negative" emotions well but block on "positive" ones such as joy, delight, and love. Discovering which emotions make you feel especially vulnerable and out of control is essential, since until you can gain greater acceptance of them within yourself, you cannot hope to be of much help to your clients as they explore similar ones. Never assume you will be able to "fake it"; clients can pick up on very subtle cues regarding what you are uncomfortable with, and you may inadvertently teach them that they cannot trust you to help in exactly the areas they most need assistance. There is no alternative—you must work on yourself to gain greater familiarity and competence with the whole range of human emotions.

One therapist we know learned this at the probable expense of a vulnerable client. She was completing her internship and had begun to earn a reputation as a therapist familiar and helpful with grief and loss issues. Accordingly, when she was assigned a 19-year-old woman concerned about losing her remission from leukemia, she assumed she could be helpful. She was, after all, relatively comfortable with sadness, fear, anger, hope, and longing. During the fourth session, her client began shaking. The client whispered that she was remembering her fear, not of the disease itself, but of the depersonalization she experienced in the large cancer hospital she'd been in for months of treatment. Within minutes, she was in a state of panic at the thought of having to possibly reexperience that, if in fact she lost her remission. Sensing her panic, the therapist moved immediately into empty reassurances and immediate problem solving. It would not be that bad, the client was older now with more resources, they would figure out how to be more assertive with the hospital staff, etc. Her words seemed to have no impact on her client's fear, and the client did not return for another session. In retrospect, the therapist realized that she had taught her client that she could talk about many things with the therapist but not her terror. The therapist could not handle that; the client would have to deal with it by herself. The therapist slowly realized that she had treated her client's panic as she treated her own—by running from it. That experience, and the learning which followed, prompted her to tolerate her own panic more willingly and to explore it in more depth with her own therapist.

Listening for themes. Transactional Analysis (Steiner, 1974) discusses "life scripts." Adler (1931) talked about "guiding fictions." Michael Novak (1970) called them "myths." Regardless of the terminology used, the gist of these constructs is the idea that all of us grow up, and usually live out, certain unquestioned assumptions about ourselves in relation to the rest of the world. For those of us who are lucky, these scripts are relatively functional and allow us some degree of flexibility and happiness. For those less lucky, the scripts are more likely pessimistic, cynical, and hopeless. Life has somehow taught these people, or perhaps they have taught themselves as they tried to make sense of life, that there were few options available to them and most of those wouldn't work. Many of your clients will come in with these unconscious negative or unrealistic assumptions; part of your role may be to help them identify and change the ones that sabotage their greater fulfillment of potential.

As you listen then for these deeper themes, it may help to focus on three overlapping areas: themes regarding self, themes regarding others, and themes regarding life.

1. Themes regarding self. Thomas Harris (1967) made the gross distinction between people who feel generally "OK" about themselves or "not OK" Simplistic as that sounds, it is not a bad place to start. Listening to a client, do you hear a pervasive sense of inadequacy? Does it seem as if he or she has trouble claiming the right to set limits or to disagree with authority or to make mistakes? Are the client's self-doubts so overwhelming that much energy is spent second-guessing others so as not to offend them? Or, conversely, is his or her self-assessment so grandiose that negative feedback is routinely discounted or distorted? What is the client's capacity for self-affirmation in stressful or rejecting environments? Obtaining this overall sense of the client's resiliency and self-esteem can be very helpful as you form your diagnostic impressions and treatment goals. Among other things, this gross barometer can give you a sense of how quickly to look for client progress, since, everything else being equal, the lower the client's overall self-esteem, the slower change is likely to occur.

We suggest you also look for exceptions to the pattern you have found. The client who appears to be quite confident and self-assured when dealing with her family and professional colleagues may nonetheless feel unattractive and insecure in intimate relationships. Similarly, the male veterinarian student who feels inadequate in apparently all interpersonal relationships may blossom into a decisive, compassionate caretaker when treating a sick animal. These fluctuations in self-esteem and behavior sometimes appear as almost untouched compartments within the client, and exploring them can dramatically enrich your understanding of his or her dynamics.

Much of what you will probably be attempting with your clients—a meta-goal, of sorts—is aiding them in achieving a healthier relationship with themselves. As a client of one of the authors said, "I am beginning to treat myself the way I try to treat others, and it feels damn good." As clients learn to treat their human frailties with more acceptance and matter-of-factness and as they learn to treat themselves with a balance of nurturance and realistic demands, a side benefit is that their relationship with others will likely improve also.

2. Themes regarding others. We will examine in greater depth some of the typical patterns that emerge in relationships in a later chapter. At this point, we want to highlight only the most obvious themes you are likely to hear with clients. You will quickly discover that much of how they treat others is related to how they treat themselves. The client, for example, who feels one-down and apologetic is likely to defer to those seen as more powerful (although with some frequency this difference may be cloaked in counter–dependency).

The relative power that a client accords to himself or herself and to others is probably the first pattern you will notice. As you help clients deal with their relationships with significant others, you will probably be helping many of them assume more power and use it effectively. It will behoove you to have a good understanding of power and influence and the effects of using them in different ways. You may also have some clients whose style is more powerful than their self-image, leaving them bewildered as to why they elicit some of the negative responses they do; these clients may need your help learning to orchestrate themselves to be "softer" when others feel threatened. Again, as with other patterns, it is helpful to look for exceptions to the rule as you sense the client's behavior changing in different roles. Some shy, "powerless" people, for instance, dramatically rise to the occasion when they take a role that requires decisiveness and assurance (e.g., teacher, doctor, etc.).

Another similar theme to listen for is trust. Whom do your clients trust? Do they typically trust one gender more than the other? Do they tend to trust people who deserve their trust? Is their trust all or nothing, or are they able to trust tentatively and continue to evaluate the other person? How do they respond when their trust is violated? Have they attempted to cover their vulnerability with an overlay of distrust and cynicism? It should go without saying at this point that many of these patterns will be hinted at in their relationship with you, since the intimacy of therapy provokes such strong reactions.

You may want to look also at the distance clients prefer to keep in relationships—which may or may not be a reflection of trust—and whether their needs and those of their associates are being met by their chosen stance. Many, but not all, clients desire more intimacy than they have in their lives and need to learn to approach others and to invite them closer. Some, however, may be quite comfortable having a relatively formal style with only a few close associates, but their formality and distance may be troublesome to others. It may be important for you to monitor yourself at this point, lest you automatically try to impose your style on someone who is managing fairly well with his or her own.

Finally, we would like to suggest attending to a set of themes that cuts across some of those previously mentioned. To get a measure of the client's overall relationship skills, ask yourself, "What is his or her capacity to say yes to others and to say no?" For healthy relationships, both sets of skills are necessary. To be able to affirm others and to accept affirmation is crucial if bonding is to occur. But it is certainly as important to be able to protest, to resist undue influence, if necessary to reject—and to be able to respond to these nos from others. Saying and hearing the word *no* is frightening for most clients, since associations with parental rejections are so strong, but the skill is vital if clients are to learn to be both in relationship but separate. Again, we would note that *your* comfort in saying yes and no to the clients, in affirming and setting appropriate limits, is what he or she will take away more clearly than the specific lessons you try to impart.

3. *Themes regarding life.* Although listening to your clients' themes in relation to themselves and in relation to others will teach you a great deal about their general approach to life, we believe you will find that the whole is indeed more than the sum of the parts. There are overarching values, dreams, and fears that seem to determine the stance a client takes toward his or her life (or destiny, if you prefer) that are often subtle and unconscious but extremely powerful forces. To get an intuitive sense of your client's stance (or combination of stances), you will need to give up your intensely focused listening and instead rely on listening "around the edges."

One way to look at your clients' approach to life is to see their possible choices as lying on a continuum. To modify a bit of some of Rollo May's (1981) thinking, we suggest one end of this continuum be categorized as surrender; at the other end is rebellion. Two less extreme points might be called cooperation and challenge.

+_____+_____+_____+
Surrender   Cooperation   Challenge   Rebellion

Most people have one preferred stance, although many of us shift somewhat when circumstances change. As you consider your clients and their adopted postures, consider also your own and try to obtain some objective assessment of the costs and benefits of each approach in different life conditions.

Surrender, or resignation, is typically associated with a victim stance. The person in effect relinquishes his or her own will and bows to forces perceived as greater. It may help to distinguish between "giving up," which often signals passivity and premature abdication of responsibility, and "giving in," which is seen by many as the appropriate religious or psychological response to life and death. Both are subcategories of surrender, but the latter certainly involves more conscious choice and is usually considered more clearly psychologically defensible.

Cooperation is often an optimistic, sometimes playful approach to life. People who cooperate often see themselves as "lucky," so fate is perceived as ultimately on their side. Some cooperators are surely just naive to the deeper injustices and sorrows of life, but not all fit this stereotype. Others are strong, positive, inviting people who have a knack for approaching people and situations in such a way as to elicit positive results.

The third group, challengers, are recognized by their ability to focus easily on perceived inconsistencies. Often they refuse to accept usual ways of behaving and thinking and offer instead new, innovative suggestions. For these questioners, their integrity feels subtly undermined by automatically accepting traditional guidelines, and they feel more alive and engaged when adopting a somewhat combative approach to life. Such people often register dissatisfaction with established norms and can be difficult to work or live with, but they demonstrate considerable energy and adventurousness as they forge new, creative pathways.

Rebels are at the extreme end of the continuum. Certainly, social revolutionaries fall in this category, but so also do cancer patients who defy medical "wisdom" and live longer, Mother Teresas who take on impossible projects and accomplish miracles, and parents who circulate petitions demanding changes in unfair school policies. Those who defy what others see as inevitable are often troublemakers and are always discomforting, but their courage and vision is sometimes both inspiring and enlightening to those in the other three categories.

Part of your job as a therapist may be to listen to your clients well enough to help identify their chosen stance, aid them in assessing how such a stance both costs and benefits them, and encourage them to make their choices in relation to life more fully conscious and intentional.

SUMMARY

Therapeutic listening requires that therapists be able to offer not only an objective analysis of the client's psychological problems and personality style, but also consistent emotional availability. This balance of intellectual analysis and empathic understanding is a skill that generally can be learned by students although it does require much practice. Part of such learning often involves becoming aware of why one is not listening and then making appropriate corrections.

Therapists from different theoretical orientations tend to listen for different kinds of material, at different levels. Whether one listens at strictly a content level, or listens more deeply for feelings, or more deeply still for client themes, the depth of the listening often determines the direction in which the client will move. As a general guideline, the more fully the client feels understood, the more influence he or she accords the therapist.

8

TRANSFERENCE/ COUNTERTRANSFERENCE

When all is said and done it is impossible to destroy anyone in absentia or in effigy.

—S. Freud

The idea of mother means, first of all, unqualified, unwavering love, no matter how obnoxious and unadorable the years have rendered us. And, second, it signifies that once there existed another living soul who knew about and had been in intimate contact with our purest and most unblemished childhood self, the self we still believe we are, the self with whom we still commune in our interior conversation, the self that, despite all the evidence to the contrary, still insists, still knows, that we are good.

—Tova Reich

TRANSFERENCE

Definitions

The word *transference* has been defined in a number of ways. Frequently, the central tenet is that feelings and attitudes toward a person early in life are transferred (or displaced) onto the therapist. A key assumption is that the therapist has done nothing (or very little) to evoke these feelings. As Weiner (1975) pointed out, if the client says, "I must be a boring person," after the therapist repeatedly yawns, we perhaps have learned little about the client. If, however, the client makes this statement and there have been no yawns (or similar behaviors) by the therapist, an important therapeutic issue has perhaps come into focus. Freud first viewed transference as an obstacle to treatment but later came to believe that transference was the key to a successful outcome in psychotherapy (Storr, 1979).

It was a part of Freud's genius to discover that under certain conditions (and especially under those practiced by Freud) clients often behave toward their therapists as if their therapists were their parents. It is now generally accepted that his sort of transference is greatly influenced by the therapist's behavior and that its "recognition" by the therapist is highly (though perhaps not completely) dependent upon the therapist's theoretical orientation. In short, therapists who are not predisposed to psychoanalysis may not see a great deal of transference.

Another way that the word *transference* is sometimes used is to describe any overly emotional reaction to something the therapist does or says. In this view transference *may* be the result of displaced attitudes but may also more generally represent "exaggerated" reactions to internal conflicts or a stressful environment without reference to any specific person. In classic psychoanalytic theory, this second definition is subsumed by the first.

A metaphorical example of transference from this second perspective can be found in *Moby Dick* (Melville, 1851/1930). Even though there is a partially rational reason for him to be angry with the white whale, Ahab reacts to the whale with emotions that go far beyond what reason alone might suggest:

> . . . ever since that almost fatal encounter, Ahab had cherished a wild vindictiveness against the whale, all the more fell for that in his frantic morbidness he at last came to identify with him, not only all his bodily woes, but all his intellectual and spiritual exasperations. The White Whale swam before him as the monomaniac incarnation of all those malicious agencies which some deep men feel eating in them. . . . deliriously transferring its idea to the abhorred White Whale, he pitted himself, all mutilated, against it. All that most maddens and torments; all that stirs up the lees of things; all truth with malice in it; all that cracks the sinews and cakes the brain; all the subtle demonisms of life and thought; all evil, to crazy Ahab, were visibly personified, and made practically assailable in Moby Dick. He piled upon the whale's white hump the sum of all the general rage and hate felt by his whole race from Adam down; and then, as if his chest had been a mortar, he burst his hot heart's shell upon it. (p. 267)

Like the white whale, the therapist may become the focus of the pent-up frustrations, the difficulty of changing, and the dashed hopes of the client. It is a part of the therapist's job to be the object of this anger and disappointment without retaliation and, in fact, to do so in a continuing environment of care and respect for the struggles of the client.

The definitions of transference as displaced attitudes and transference as exaggerated reactions are actually compatible from a theoretical perspective. We are drawing a distinction here only because you may hear people use the term in either way.

Carl Rogers (1951) takes a position on transference which overlaps but also contrasts somewhat with the traditional psychoanalytic position. Rogers distinguishes between what he calls the "transference attitude" and the "transference relationship." Rogers says:

> If transference attitudes are defined as emotionalized attitudes which existed in some other relationships, and which are inappropriately directed to the therapist, then transference attitudes are evident in a considerable proportion of cases handled by client-centered therapists. (p. 218)

Although Rogers goes on to say that in contrast to psychoanalysts, client-centered therapists do not foster the development of a transference *relationship*, it is clear from the above quote that he does give credence to the idea that many clients have feelings about their therapists which are based less on the reality of the current situation than on feelings about prior relationships. Thus, theorists as diverse as Freud and Rogers agree that feelings are often "transferred" to the therapist. This agreement is a good example of what we call common clinical wisdom.

Transtheoretical Perspectives

Orthodox psychoanalysis aside, the concept of transference is now generally seen in a rather broad context. That is, technical transference (displacement of specific feelings) is only part of a much larger issue involving prior learning experiences. In this view, clients' behaviors may demonstrate parallels to behavior toward earlier figures, but this process of behavior transfer is one all people do to one degree or another. Each person brings to an interpersonal encounter a set of prior learning experiences which in turn shapes expectations, behaviors, and attitudes toward the person encountered. These expectations and attitudes are in operation before the other person says or does anything. The learning experiences which help shape client expectations involve childhood experiences with parents, siblings, and peers; emotional involvement in sexual relationships; the experience of working with, supervising, and being supervised by others; books and articles which have been read (for example, about human nature or psychotherapy); and information obtained from friends and acquaintances about a variety of issues, including psychotherapy. Thus, when clients come for therapy, they have already formed some impressions about what a psychotherapist does or does not do. These impressions in turn affect the behavior emitted by the client toward the therapist.

We assume that most therapists agree that previous experiences shape how clients will respond to their therapists. Therapists, however, depending on their theoretical orientation, vary widely in terms of how much *emphasis* is placed on this idea that one's previous experience shapes one's feelings and attitudes toward the therapist. In particular, therapists are at odds about how strong the relationship is between therapeutic effectiveness and degree to which transference is discussed and processed. Therapists who are more cognitive-behavioral in their orientation, while acknowledging the role of prior experience on attitudes toward the therapist, do not emphasize this construct. Psychodynamic therapists, as well as interpersonal therapists, are typically more interested in the construct and see it playing a more pivotal role in treatment. However, we emphasize that whatever your orientation, you should be alert to how the client may handicap his or her progress by acting as if you are like hurtful and unhelpful people in the past. Progress may also be hindered if clients continually view you as able to solve all their problems.

Types of Transference

Generally, we speak of two types of transference: positive and negative. The way in which these are "handled" depends on the goals and type of therapy (e.g., Wolberg, 1988). One may also speak of specific transference (when a client treats the therapist as if the therapist were a specific person in the client's past) as contrasted with general transference (when the client treats the therapist the way most people in the culture treat authority figures) (Weiner, 1975). The literature on transference contains other constructs as well, such as transference neurosis. A discussion of all these issues is beyond the scope of this book. Here we merely highlight what is meant by positive and negative transference.

It is generally assumed that the majority of clients rather quickly grow to like or at least respect their therapist. The initial *liking* is sometimes called positive transference. It is transference in the sense that the client does not really know much about the therapist but is presumed to be responding to the non-critical, accepting demeanor of an authority figure on whom the client is counting for help. Most clients who do not develop some minimal liking for the therapist are assumed to drop out of treatment. Positive transference is even better illustrated by the period (if it occurs) when the therapist, in the eyes of the client, "can do no wrong, has no faults, and always understands exactly what the client is thinking and feeling."

Negative transference (or whatever you would prefer to call it), if present early in therapy and left unaddressed, may at best greatly impede treatment and at worst contribute to client dropout. There are primarily two types of negative transference. The first may happen quite early in therapy (perhaps even in the first session). These situations involve clients who are mistrustful and/or hostile toward the therapist because the therapeutic relationship reminds them of an earlier important relationship which was difficult for them and about which they have ambivalent or negative feelings. (These situations often contribute to the client's "resistance," discussed in the next chapter.) The second type of situation, when it occurs, happens later in therapy. These situations arise when clients realize that the therapist cannot and will not fulfill all their needs and is not perfect. The second type of negative transference is not likely to emerge in short-term therapy.

A general rule (and it is *very* general because of the complexity of this issue and wide differences among therapists) is that positive transference is not something you should comment on at the beginning of therapy. Furthermore, negative transference should be controlled, particularly at the beginning of therapy. This is typically done by the therapist's avoiding confrontations, being supportive, and avoiding falling into roles representing people which the client has had difficulty getting along with in the past. For example, if the client says, "My father always gave me too much advice," the therapist is ill-advised to give advice initially. Later the therapist may wish to help the client work through the dependency issues involved in resenting the father's advice. This process might indeed entail some degree of negative transference. As we said, however, this would (should) not happen near the beginning of therapy. The risks of the client's dropping out are far too great.

One important point to remember is that negative and positive transference often accompany each other. In particular, negative feelings may follow strongly positive ones. For example, when clients can initially find no fault in the therapist, they have thus set up a situation in which they are easily disillusioned when the therapist does not perform in a consistently perfect fashion. Certainly, some clients will evidence primarily positive or primarily negative transference. Perhaps just as often, and especially in settings where one sees numerous clients with serious disorders, one will see a pattern of overvaluation and idealization of the therapist, alternating with a pattern of irritated discontent as the client discovers that the therapist does not measure up to the ideal person the client imagined the therapist to be.

Components of the Client/Therapist Relationship

Traditionally, in order to discuss transference, writers have referred to three components of the therapeutic relationship: the real relationship, the working alliance, and the transference relationship (Weiner, 1975). The term *real relationship* refers to the part of the therapeutic relationship that is based solely in the reality of two people meeting and talking. For example, it is customary in our culture to say hello (or some variant thereof) when seeing a person after an absence. When the therapist and client say hello to each other, they are seen as acting in the real relationship. Or, suppose that the therapist is 30 minutes late and offers no apology or explanation. If the client becomes angry and expresses the idea that the therapist is insensitive, this action would be a part of the real relationship since in American culture it is considered rude to keep a person waiting for 30 minutes with no explanation. (This example also highlights how cultural factors may help define what is or is not considered transference.)

The *working alliance* refers to the special rules which surround the therapeutic encounter. For example, the ideas that clients will talk about their problem, that the therapist is entitled to ask questions, and that the therapist will not, except under very unusual circumstances, divulge the content of the conversation all refer to the working alliance. (In other chapters of this book, we make reference to the *therapeutic alliance*. It is a less technical term than *working alliance*, but both terms imply a shared effort under the conditions of psychotherapy.)

Finally, the term *transference* is reserved for all the remainder of the behaviors and attitudes of the client toward the therapist. Another way of saying this is that transference is represented by actions and feelings by the client which are based neither in the reality of two people having a conversation nor in the reality of the psychotherapy treatment arrangement (or contract) but rather are based primarily on the false assumption that the therapist is very much like someone in the client's past. It is important to emphasize that this "person in the client's past" may be an actual person or a person constructed in the imagination of the client. For example, clients may have been mistreated by their parents and other adults but longed for a protector and savior to come to the rescue. In turn, the therapist may be treated as if he or she were in fact that savior. This too would be considered transference.

Why are these distinctions between the real relationship, the working alliance, and the transference relationship drawn? Again, the answer depends on one's theoretical orientation. However, there does seem to be some common ground. Most orientations, whether implicitly or explicitly, give some emphasis to rationality—that is, to the client's capacity to distinguish between what is "real" or "reality based" from what is not. Even the person-centered perspective (which is much more focused on the phenomenology of experience rather than on "reality") talks about treatment progress as involving progressively less and less distortion of experience and as involving a movement toward a more accurate understanding of one's experience. Rogers (1951), in describing an example of successful therapy, says, "As this process goes on, the overall generalization, Mother is a bitch and I can't possibly get on with her, is seen to be inadequate to fit the complex facts of primary experience" (p. 143). Thus, although various theories may place different emphases on the importance of transference and may suggest different ways of using it, we are underscoring that most therapies have as one of their goals the capacity of the client to differentiate between the figures in one's past life and the figures (including the therapist) in one's current life. There is also the related capacity to respond to current figures, including the therapist, based on objective experiences in the present. Some therapists believe that the process whereby one comes to be able to make this distinction, both emotionally and intellectually, is the essence of therapy. Other therapists would see this distinction as part of a larger issue of the need to think rationally.

Many therapists would agree, however, that discussions concerning the "real" or rational part of the relationship should receive less focus than the transference or irrational part of the relationship since clients seek help for those parts of their lives in which they are not functioning well. Another way of saying this is that the therapist gains little by commenting on culturally typical (real relationship) behavior. Thus, in the example above of the hypothetical therapist who was 30 minutes late, there would be little point in saying to the client, "Do you always get upset when people make you wait?" If the client were to repeatedly bring up the issue for several sessions even though the therapist had apologized, the therapist would certainly be remiss if he or she did not help the client look at this process, since the issue would have moved from being a part of the real relationship to being a transference issue.

Even though we are emphasizing that attention to the "transference relationship" may often be helpful, this focus also has limits. While being alert for the many ways in which clients may repeat with us previous unsatisfactory relationships, we must also be keenly aware of the here-and-now, actual relationship that exists between us and the client. Yalom (1980) has expressed well the idea that it is a mistake to be overly infatuated with transference:

> To summarize, a singular focus on transference impedes therapy because it precludes an authentic therapist-patient relationship. First, it negates the reality of the relationship by considering the relationship solely as a key to understanding other more important relationships. Secondly, it provides therapists with a rationale for personal concealment—a concealment that interferes with the ability to relate in a genuine fashion with patients. Does this mean that therapists who faithfully maintain a detached, objectifying, "interpretation-only" posture toward patients are ineffective or even destructive? I believe that, fortunately, such therapists and such courses of therapy are exceedingly rare. Here lies the importance of the "throw-ins" in therapy: therapists despite themselves and often unbeknownst to themselves reach out in a human manner in off-the-record moments. (pp. 413–414)

Development of Transference

There are several reasons why transference develops. An understanding of these factors contributes to a wider perspective on the psychotherapeutic process and to an enhanced ability to deal with transference issues.

Anonymity of the therapist.   We mentioned at the beginning of the chapter that a key assumption when we say we observe transference is that the therapist has done little or nothing to evoke the attitudes that have been "transferred." This assumption was originally tied to the idea of the psychotherapist as "mirror" or "blank screen." That is, if the therapist revealed nothing of him or herself, the client was assumed to be "transferring" from someone else any emotion which was felt about the therapist. Although many therapists do not consider themselves to be a "blank screen," it is still true that therapists do not routinely discuss their personal life; they do not say all their felt reactions to the client and his or her behavior; they do not talk about their reading habits, their preference for friends, or their preferred vacation spots; and they almost never express political preferences. Thus, the client will never know a therapist in the same way that he or she knows close friends; there will always be an element of mystery about who this person is. This mystery is addressed through fantasy—through a process whereby clients fill in the gaps of their knowledge with imagination based on their experiences with other people.

Therapist's role as authority.   Because therapists are people to whom others go to receive help in solving problems, their role, by definition, may be seen as involving the exercise of authority. Furthermore, the long dependency of childhood, during which one must count on parents and others to provide help and advice, seems to endow many in a more or less permanent fashion with an inclination to look to others for answers. This sort of inclination, which is sometimes called dependency, may be acted out toward the therapist because of the therapist's role as an authority figure. More generally, we might say that there is a *propensity* for clients to act toward the therapist in ways which are typical of how people in general behave toward authority figures within the culture. It is obvious that the client's dynamics ("personality" or whatever term you would like to use) will interact with this general propensity. However, when clients behave in a somewhat deferent manner, we think of this as being a more generalized transference (Weiner, 1975) and as being distinct from the transference attitudes which clients have that are based on the particular experiences of the client (discussed below).

Expression of clients' conflicts.   In defining transference, we said that one way to think of transference is to view it as a displacement of feelings from others (perhaps including generalized expectations about the world) onto the therapist. This inappropriate (or perhaps a better word would be *inaccurate*) generalization occurs in part because clients' emotional distresses make them less interpersonally flexible and more apt to engage in self-defeating behavior such as attacking the therapist with little or no provocation. For example, a female therapist may say to a male client, "You seem to have a hard time making a commitment to a job." The client replies, "You're just like my mother—always on my case." This is an example of transference, but it also reflects *why* transference occurs. Here the client has responded to the therapist not on any "reality" base (assuming the comment about commitment was not made in a critical tone and is not part of a larger pattern of criticism) but rather on the basis of strong feelings about his mother and how he felt he was treated by her. The assumption is that feelings are not transferred if they are not "in conflict," so to speak, with other feelings. Traditionally, the word *conflict* refers to the psychoanalytic idea of different drives or structures competing with each other. Perhaps another way of describing the above phenomenon (in a more generically clinical way) is that strong feelings which have not been integrated into the person's self-concept seem to "erupt" in situations which are similar in some ways to, but quite distinct from, the original situations in which the feelings were experienced.

As in so many other cases, therapists of different theoretical persuasions use different language to describe the same phenomenon. For example, a person-centered therapist might speak (concerning the above example) of "conditions of worth" experienced by the client, with the concomitant unacceptability to the client of angry feelings toward the mother. Therapists using a more cognitive approach might talk about the client's inaccurate generalization from mother to therapist and also about the client's (faulty) assumption that he is constantly being judged harshly by others. Such therapists also talk about helping the client modify his assumption that it is necessary for others to like him—an assumption which perhaps originated with his desire to please his mother. Thus, whatever theoretical perspective one takes, there is an assumption that transference, whatever one may call it, occurs in part because clients have had earlier experiences that predispose them to this sort of process. At times these earlier experiences may be described as involving conflicted feelings, unacceptable feelings, lack of integration of feelings, or early learning predisposing one to faulty assumptions or faulty generalizations.

Discussion of earlier emotional experiences.   Clients who are seen by therapists who do not emphasize earlier experiences when doing psychotherapy probably do not show transference to the degree that clients do when the therapist does emphasize these earlier experiences. Certainly, this is not to say that a focus on the present eliminates transference. As we said, even Carl Rogers acknowledged that many clients bring what he called "transference attitudes" to the therapeutic encounter—attitudes which cannot be eliminated immediately no matter what the therapist does or does not do. On the other hand, we think that Rogers was basically correct in suggesting that a primary focus on the present in psychotherapy tends to retard further development of basic transference attitudes. We are not suggesting that the therapist *should* focus on the present. We are merely underscoring the fact that one reason transference occurs is that therapists often *do* focus on earlier experiences.

Permissive and encouraging attitude of the therapist.   The accepting stance taken by the therapist encourages the expression of vulnerability and previously unacceptable ideas and feelings. Because the therapist is an integral part of the process whereby the client confronts such feelings, he or she may become a "handy target" for the client's strong feelings, whether they be feelings of relief or anger.

Importance of Using Transference

There are a number of reasons why, in our view, the therapist should not merely be aware of but also "use" transference. As we said earlier, one's ideas about transference certainly depend upon one's theoretical orientation. Nonetheless, many therapists agree that clients (like people in general) bring certain assumptions about and predispositions toward the other person to any interpersonal encounter. We will briefly mention three reasons why we think it is important to focus, at least to some degree, on these predispositions of the client.

Power of immediacy.   Most therapists agree that many clients, left to their own devices so to speak, often talk abstractly about their problems. Such abstract and emotionally removed discussions frequently do little to alleviate the client's suffering. Rogers, for example, talks about movement of the discussion from the "there and then" to the "here and now." Gestalt therapists emphasize the power of being "in the now," and cognitive therapists may ask questions like, "What is your thinking about suicide right this minute?" Each of these therapies, in its own way, is addressing the issue of immediacy. Because transference, by definition, is about current attitudes and feelings, a focus on this issue brings the client and therapist together "in the now." There is hardly anything more immediate than talking to another person about your current relationship with them.

Power of analyzing repeating themes.   We have said that in our view one of the most potent things a therapist does is to help the client understand the themes which seem to be repeated in his or her life. Because transference *is* a repeated attitude or feeling, it gives the therapist a uniquely potent opportunity to help the client look closely at a repetition. We say "uniquely potent" because transference combines the immediacy we discussed above with a repetition.

Power of interpersonal encounter.   In this book we have emphasized in numerous ways the importance of the relationship between the client and the therapist. To the client's vision of a disturbing universe, the therapist brings hope and perspective. The therapist also offers what may be the only nonexploitative relationship the client has ever known. One might say that this relationship offers the client the opportunity to straighten out the twists and kinks of previous relationships. So it is precisely when these "twists and kinks" make themselves manifest that a kind of maximum leverage has been created for change. We said above that transference combined the power of immediacy with the power of analyzing repeating themes. But to those two potent processes we now add a third—the power of an interpersonal encounter. In our view, it is certainly possible to help many clients without focusing on transference issues. However, a focus on transference combines at least three forces, each of which is seen by many therapists as often contributing to behavior change within the context of psychotherapy.

SUMMARY COMMENTS ON TRANSFERENCE

A number of processes involved in, and related to, transference have been discussed. Here we wish to emphasize three aspects of the discussion. First, transference, while it is sometimes described in rather mysterious terms, is perhaps best seen as an example of the larger process by which individuals come to have expectations and feelings about current interpersonal relationships based on previous interpersonal experiences. Second, there are a number of characteristics of typical therapeutic relationships which tend to make transference more likely to occur there than in other relationships. Third, we have emphasized that powerful forces are often involved in looking at transference. If these processes can be activated and used in a thoughtful manner, the possibility of behavior change is enhanced.

COUNTERTRANSFERENCE

Definitions

Countertransference as a reaction to transference.   Countertransference has been defined in a number of ways. The original definition was, of course, Freud's and emphasized that countertransference was a reaction to the transference of the client rather than a reaction based on the reality of the therapeutic situation. For example, if a male client became angry at the therapist because the therapist reminded him of his father and then the therapist became very upset because the client was angry, this would be an example of countertransference. Thus, the use of the word *countertransference,* using the original definition, was limited to those cases in which the client had engaged in transference.

Countertransference as general unconscious attitudes/behavior.   Another way in which countertransference is sometimes viewed is that it is any unconscious attitude or behavior on the part of the psychotherapist which is prompted by the needs of the therapist rather than by the needs of the client. For heuristic purposes it may be helpful to think of this process as involving either (a) a temporary need or (b) a longstanding need.

We will discuss first the case of a therapist need (or conflict or problem or whatever term you would like to use) which is temporary in nature. For example, a female therapist might be having serious conflict in her marriage and be sexually attracted to a male client and say to the client, "You seem to be attracted to me." This would be an example of projection in that the impulse (or feeling) experienced by the therapist was unacceptable and was then "projected" onto the client. Projection in this particular case might be considered countertransference because the behavior of the therapist was based on the needs of the therapist rather than on the needs of the client. Another example would be when the therapist displaces a feeling from someone else to the client. For example, if a therapist is angry with his wife and later that day angrily confronts the client about an issue, this might also be called countertransference. A third example would be of a therapist who has recently been given a speeding ticket by a police officer and fails to be empathic with the police officer he is currently seeing as a client. In each of these cases, we are emphasizing that the therapist may try unconsciously to solve a current problem by using the client. One of our jobs as therapists is to try to recognize (perhaps with the help of a supervisor) when we are doing this.

Therapists may also have longstanding character styles which reduce their effectiveness with particular types of clients or even all clients. For example, a therapist may have difficulty working with angry clients because she was punished severely as a child for being angry. Another therapist may have difficulty confronting *any* client because his parents were always very indirect with their children and merely dropped hints when they were upset about something. In his book, *Listening as a Way of Becoming,* Koile (1977) gives an example of a good way to become aware of the areas in which we may be vulnerable to countertransference. You are asked to imagine that a person (one could say client) is coming to visit you. You realize that you don't want to see this person, that you don't want to listen to what the person has to say. What is this person like that you don't want to see? What is it that this person will discuss and how will he or she discuss it that makes it difficult for you to listen?

More broadly, we might ask what types of strong feelings, preferences, assumptions, and expectations you bring to the therapeutic encounter which are likely to impede your effectiveness with clients. As we have suggested, these impediments may grow out of either a temporary situation in which we find ourselves or may be part of a longstanding personality style.

Countertransference as Temptation

One way we think of countertransference is that there are certain response styles which therapists frequently fall into as a reaction to clients about whom they have strong feelings. Certainly, any "error" on the part of the therapist potentially represents countertransference. However, we want to highlight four response styles which we think are especially tempting for therapists because these styles, in situations other than therapy, may be appropriate. We are making no assumption here about whether transference is or is not involved. We merely wish to mention four types of responses which therapists may fall back on when they have strong feelings about a client.

The all-knowing therapist.   One way we may deal with strong feelings about a client is to fall back on the dangerous assumption that we are an expert on this particular client. This assumption may in turn compound the problem by distancing us from the emotional experience of the client or leading us to give advice when it clearly is not needed.

Being bored.   Another way of controlling one's strong feelings about a client is to become bored during the therapy hour. It is certainly the case that clients may at times have their own unconscious reasons for wanting the therapist to be bored. Furthermore, some clients obviously are more interesting than others. Putting aside these issues for the moment, we are emphasizing that when therapists have strong feelings about their clients, one way to reduce the intensity of those feelings is to suddenly find that the client is not very interesting. Therefore, if you find yourself becoming bored with a client, one question you have to ask yourself is whether you have some strong feelings of which you have been unaware or only dimly aware.

Being especially nice.   Particularly if one has strong negative feelings about a client, a role which is very easy to fall back on is that of being very nice to the client. Psychoanalysts would label such a response as reaction formation. We are underscoring how therapists use "being nice" defensively because it is such a subtle process which often goes undetected for long periods of time. One reason therapists often do not realize what they are doing is that "being nice" is a culturally valued behavior. If you have a client to whom you are being especially nice, you should consider the possibility that you have strong negative feelings about the client but are dealing with these feelings by being nice. A related possibility is that by treating the client so gingerly, you are failing to acknowledge the client's coping skills.

Rescuing clients.   Just as some clients appear to be searching for someone who will solve their problems for them, so too are there some therapists who have difficulty refraining from becoming this rescuer. One example of when this process is likely to be activated is when therapists are not feeling good about themselves. When we are feeling ineffective in our personal or professional lives, it may become more and more important to us that we be able to help our clients. Clients who are "clearly in need of help" thus become the medium whereby therapists can elevate their self-esteem and renew their trust in themselves. In monitoring themselves for this type of countertransference, a danger signal therapists should look for is an opinion on their part that says, "The client has no one but me to turn to." In the first place, this conclusion is frequently (though certainly not always) inaccurate. In the second place, even if the client has no other social support, the job of the therapist is not to rescue the client but to help the client develop the internal and external resources needed to solve the problem.

Recognizing Countertransference

An ongoing series of similar therapeutic errors, especially if they have been discussed with a supervisor and a number of alternatives have been provided, may suggest countertransference. Another way of saying this is that simple lack of information about how to proceed with a client may certainly impede progress, but lack of information alone is not considered countertransference. When a mistake is repeated numerous times, particularly with multiple clients, however, countertransference is likely taking place. In such an instance we look for something a little more subtle than lack of information, something which is more basic to who the therapist is. We suggest that if you find yourself having the same difficulty over and over, even though you are receiving what seems to you to be good supervision, it will be helpful to consider how your feelings, assumptions, and expectations about the client may be getting in the way.

In addition to analyzing your therapeutic "errors," there are a number of other ways in which you can increase the likelihood of your recognizing a countertransference reaction before too much time has passed. One idea is to compare your feelings across different types of clients. If you are like most therapists, you will find that there are some types about whom you have stronger feelings, both negative and positive. If you can identify some of these types of clients, you can be ready to monitor yourself a little more closely when you begin seeing them. By "types of clients" we mean not merely personality style (e.g., aggressive, dependent, etc.) but also problem type (e.g., alcoholism, depression, etc.).

If you are seeing a client and are wondering whether some of your actions are motivated more by your own needs than by the needs of the client, you might ask yourself how another therapist whom you respect might handle the case. (It would obviously be important to select for comparison someone who had the same general theoretical orientation as you.)

Another thing you might do to recognize countertransference is to look for the presence of extreme emotions. We said above that therapists often devise ways, typically unconscious ones, to reduce strong feelings they have about their clients. On the other hand, these "reduction processes" don't always work immediately, and you may be able to catch yourself before your feelings "go underground," so to speak.

Lack of client progress is, of course, always a potential signal that one is acting more out of one's own needs than out of those of the client. However, there may be many other reasons for a lack of client progress, including a straightforward lack of skill on the part of the therapist, low client motivation, client characterological deficits, an environment which makes client change more problematic, or a poor match between client and therapist.

One last way to check for countertransference reactions is to think about ways in which the client is very much like you, or people close to you, and to think about how the client is very *unlike* you or someone close to you. The general assumption is that therapists are probably more prone to countertransference reactions if they identify very closely with the client or if they find it very difficult to identify with the client.

Countertransference as Diagnostic

Although the first view of countertransference was that it, like transference, represented an impediment to treatment, the view now taken by many therapists is that the therapist's emotional reactions to the client are a source for understanding the difficulties of the client. In this view, countertransference is not exactly something therapists want to have happen, but they see it as rather inevitable and then strive to understand how it can help them be better therapists. In this view, strong emotional reactions to the client are often a product both of one's own "issues" as well as of the client who is seen as helping to elicit such reactions.

If we become dissatisfied with a client's progress, we are interested in whether our standards may be too high or whether we are overidentifying with the client and demanding progress for *ourselves*. On the other hand, we should also wonder how it is that the client is able to set up a situation that involves our worrying so much about him or her. As another example, suppose that we realize that we have started giving the client repeated advice. While we should certainly wonder what about us had caused us to lapse into this role, we should also be interested in the traits of the client which made it easier for us to do this.

The client's role in helping to elicit countertransference (often involving emotional reactions) from us is important for at least three reasons. First, the client, whether consciously or unconsciously, may be reducing treatment effectiveness through these behaviors. Second, the kinds of reactions the client is getting from us very likely parallel the reactions he or she is receiving from many other people. If we seem routinely to become angry at the client, there is a good chance that a number of other people do also. In such a case (as an example) it becomes much more clear to us (and, we hope, subsequently to the client) how the client fails to achieve his or her interpersonal goals. In turn, this understanding sets the stage for the client to "recapture" some of the power which has been missing in his or her life. Finally, there may be instances in which our "failure" to hide our emotional reactions to clients, which in some very technical sense might be considered countertransference, may actually prove to be therapeutic in that clients may experience their power to evoke reactions from us. We are not suggesting this as a "technique" but are merely pointing out that the process may at times have positive consequences.

SUMMARY COMMENTS ON COUNTERTRANSFERENCE

We use the word *countertransference* to describe situations in which the psychotherapist acts toward the client on the basis of the therapist's needs rather than on the basis of the client's needs. This process may occur as the therapist attempts to solve a more or less temporary problem in his or her life, or it may occur as the therapist acts out longstanding problems which have become character traits. In order to deal with their strong feelings about clients, therapists may lapse into roles which are dysfunctional in terms of therapy but which do have the property of temporarily reducing the therapist's anxiety. There are a number of ways in which the therapist may recognize countertransference, including being aware of repeated therapeutic mistakes, comparing feelings across different types of clients, comparing one's responses to the responses of other therapists, being aware of extreme emotions, noting a lack of client progress, and being aware of similarities/dissimilarities between oneself and the client.

9

RESISTANCE

> If change were too easy and mental structures too fluid, the result would be greater instability, not quicker psychotherapy.
>
> —Harry Guntrip

"I just don't know what to do with her!" the student therapist told his supervisor, speaking about a client. "She says she wants my advice, but then she ignores it! She says she needs to see me, and then she arrives late! And in this last session, she said she didn't think she was making any progress with me. She's just so *resistant!*" In helping the therapist deal with his client and his feelings about the client, the supervisor in this case made an important distinction for the student between therapy and friendship. In a friendship, if the student were treated like this he might choose to withdraw, respond angrily, or use other distancing mechanisms, since such friendship behavior would seem irresponsible and unfair in its lack of reciprocity. Extreme annoyance would be an appropriate reaction. This client, however, was not paying for a friend; she was paying for a therapist, someone to help her, not punish her. What she needed from her therapist was for him to try to understand her, especially her fears, and to draw on the therapeutic alliance already in place so that together they could explore the client's behavior and what it meant. In this case, it turned out that the client had been feeling misunderstood and unsupported (in our view, a very common reason for "resistance"), but she was afraid to deal with the therapist directly. Getting her feelings out in the open was crucial for therapy to progress.

RESISTANCE

Resistance is a term used so loosely and often naively that it is difficult to know what others mean when they say it. Beginning therapists may use it ubiquitously to describe virtually anything the client does that makes them feel inadequate. Although behaviorists generally don't use the term, Davison (1973) mentions it as a substitute for "countercontrol," and it could describe, for example, a client who refused to do her assignment from the last session and is now crying rather than recommitting herself to the new behavior. Conversely, many therapists would view *not crying* as resistance and would assume that the client was unwilling to explore painful material. One neoanalyst (Hudson, 1978) sees resistance as identification by the client with the persona of the therapist. It depends, then, on what the definition of and goal for therapy is, to know what a given therapist means by saying a client is "resisting." (For a comprehensive review of some of the major contributions to the subject, see Strean, 1985.)

For the purpose of this book, we will define resistance as an intrapsychic process marked by ambivalence about exploring and claiming little known feelings and motivations within one's self. The ambivalence is rooted in the conflict between urges toward growth and completeness on the one hand and fear of pain or punishment on the other.

Consider a client one of the authors had, whom we will call "Ann." Ann had been an abused child, beaten regularly by her father and relatively ignored by her mother. She came for therapy because she wanted to be more assertive with her husband rather than continue to acquiesce through fear of his displeasure. As she worked to improve her assertion skills, she simultaneously began to explore her fears of standing up for herself. She acknowledged that she almost never felt angry with him, even when intellectually she knew her needs were being discounted. What happened to the anger? She didn't know. As nearly as she could tell, she had never assumed that her feelings and needs *should* be considered. She did, however, admit to behavior that seemed to be superficially passive-aggressive and traced it back to childhood. Even with her father, whom she greatly feared, she had exhibited such behavior. Believing that perhaps under such behavior might lurk some justifiable, self-affirming anger, the therapist encouraged Ann to "dig a little deeper." Surely, in addition to all the fear toward her dad, there had to have been some anger. Ann experienced enormous anxiety at such a notion—anger toward her father was simply unthinkable!—and missed the next session. Only over a period of months was she able to slowly accept her early rage as justifiable and healthy. Why the resistance to such an appropriate feeling.?

Consider what Ann must have been like at four or five years of age—

lonely, unsupported by her mother, and frightened of her father. Even when she tried very hard to second-guess her father and be "good," she received daily beatings. Simply thinking about expressing anger to him must have seemed terribly dangerous, especially since at that age admitting feelings is usually tantamount to acting on them. Small wonder, then, that Ann "resisted" experiencing anger as a child. By the time she entered therapy as an adult, she had been out of her parents' house for years, and her father had in fact died. Neither time nor death had been of much help, however, in erasing the old pattern of repressing anger—a pattern which had helped her survive as a child but which now was dysfunctional.

Ann's resistance exemplifies the way we see resistance operating generally. A pattern of coping with anxiety-provoking feelings—often originating in early childhood and an adaptive pattern at the time—continues into the present in a client's life and is demonstrated both in and out of the therapy session (Bauer and Kobos, 1987). Trying to strip away the resistance without dealing with the resulting fear can leave the client feeling overwhelmingly vulnerable and out of control. Good therapists do not assault resistance in an adversarial way; they "woo" the client, to use Roth's (1987) word, into trusting them enough to gradually expose the underlying feelings and motivations. That is a fearful process, for Ann, as it is for all of us, to venture into the hidden places within oneself. The Greek myth about Pandora's box captures the flavor of that apprehension.

In Ann's case, the fear was related to early associations of the expression of anger to the expectations of severe punishment. Similarly, someone shamed as a child for showing sadness or pain may be understandably reluctant to explore such feelings later in life. Other clients' fears may be less related to specific early episodes than to damage that they would incur on their self-image by admitting to what they would consider to be illegitimate feelings. In either case, the issue is often that the client does not feel *entitled* to certain feelings (Wile, 1984). Much of the therapeutic "working through" of resistance is thus dependent on the therapist's ability to help the client feel entitled to feelings and needs which the client had previously assumed must be denied.

Encouraging entitlement is not as simple as it sounds. The client is likely to sense the power of unexplored material and perhaps even overestimate such power (Langs, 1981) and look to you, the therapist, for reassurance that the fear will not be engulfing, the rage consuming, the pain shattering. Whether that reassurance is asked for overtly or not, your faith in the process will need to be somehow conveyed. Unless you have personally explored similar material within yourself, it is doubtful that you will be very persuasive with your client. We offer you the caution we have given our students: Never ask a client to do what you would not be willing to do yourself.

We want to underscore a point, which should be obvious by now. Clients do not demonstrate resistance out of irresponsibility, obstinacy, or dishonesty. They resist because they are ambivalent about change and self-exploration; they want greater freedom but fear the pain that might be necessary. As Singer (1970) indicated, "Resistance reflects both the patient's disbelief in an alternative way of life, reflects his desperate holding on to familiar self-esteem-furthering operations and at the same time his intense fear that any other approach to living would be self-esteem shattering" (p. 235).

Rather than personalize their clients' resistance or be annoyed by it, beginning therapists should realize that without resistance they would probably be out of a job. If every client were perfectly ready to change and able to do it, if it were really that easy, there would be little need for psychotherapists. When we view client resistance as a signal of fear, that thus deserves our support and empathy, rather than as some annoying obstacle we must batter down, it becomes easier for us to do our job of continuing to maintain the therapeutic alliance while encouraging client self-exploration.

Bugental's (1978) definition of the therapeutic alliance is worth noting. He refers to it as "a bond between what is best and most dedicated in the therapist and what is most health-seeking and courageous in the client" (p. 72). Your ability to offer the best of yourself rather than withdrawing or becoming adversarial when you sense resistance is what inspires clients to persevere even when they are fearful. If you become impatient, you add to clients' sense of unentitlement, since you have now communicated to them that they do not have the right to their own fear!

True resistance, in short, is a process that takes place *within* the client. As Taft (1933/1973) explains eloquently, it is a reflection of the inherent ambivalence of the human being toward growth and individuation. To quote more fully (Taft, 1933/1973):

> However speculative it may sound and however differently it may express itself in any particular case, the fact remains that always, at bottom, every serious blocking in a human life is the expression of an unsolved or rather unaccepted conflict between the will to become more and more individualized, to develop one's own quantum of life, and the reluctance to pursue wholeheartedly a course which is beyond control of the individual will and which inevitably leads to the annihilation of this dearly bought individuality. (pp. 284–285)

RELUCTANCE

There is a related process which is often mistaken for resistance. For lack of a better term, we will call this process *reluctance*. Reluctance, in contrast to resistance, has an interpersonal root. It arises not primarily out of ambivalence within the client but rather out of the interaction the client has with the therapist. Its origins are not so much fear of growth as fear/anger/distrust of the therapist. In both cases, the client balks at further therapeutic self-exploration, but the reasons behind the two processes vary.

The primary reason, we believe, that clients become reluctant (either temporarily or permanently) to continue with therapy is that from their perspective the therapeutic alliance has either been broken or was never satisfactorily forged in the first place. Clients who feel attacked or accused or unsupported are likely to "put on the brakes," less perhaps because they are unwilling to proceed than because they are unwilling to proceed with *this person*. Their trust in the therapist is at least temporarily shaken, and they feel unsafe and discounted. As Wile (1984) points out, in ordinary human discourse when people feel criticized, they often respond with anger and/or defensiveness. It should come as no great surprise that they respond similarly in therapy also. In effect, their balking is a protest. It is a way to say to the therapist, "Do not do to me what I do to myself. Do not attack and criticize me; I can do that at home, for free, by myself. I need your support and understanding."

Obviously, it makes little difference at this point whether the therapist intended to criticize or slight the client. It is the client's *perception* that matters, and until the client feels reassured and supported again, not much therapy will be taking place. We agree with the supervisor who told his supervisee when he heard a tape of a client becoming reluctant and balking, "This is an important process. Nothing else is more important. This is where you *stop* and *park your truck!*"

We underscore again that the relationship you offer is often what is healing to the client. To clients who have felt discounted and wounded, and who often discount and wound themselves, having a therapist listen to their protests— however inarticulately they may have been voiced—is indeed a corrective emotional experience. As one terminating client told her therapist after a year of therapy, "What you did that I remember most, what helped more than anything else, was when you listened to me that time I got so mad at you. You didn't get defensive or angry, although you didn't cave in either. You listened to me and even changed some of your behavior. I was amazed!" We agree with Stone (1981) that the possibility of therapist error needs to be consistently acknowledged and that (as in the above situation) a willingness to listen to client feedback and change behavior can *increase* the therapist's credibility.

Lewis and Evans (1986) suggest three reasons other than broken alliances for clients to balk at the interpersonal process inherent in therapy. First, they suggest that the client may be experiencing fear or anxiety, some of which may be what we earlier referred to as fear of individuation, but which they believe often has the clear interpersonal focus of fear of control by the therapist. Since we dealt rather extensively with this and other client fears in a previous chapter, we will not expand on this factor at this point.

The second reason Lewis and Evans suggest for client reluctance to proceed in therapy is that they may not believe the interactions the therapist is suggesting will be helpful. We think this may especially be operating with beginning therapists, who often do not take the time or do not know how to explain briefly to clients why they are recommending a course of action. If clients want to know *why* they should explore painful feelings, can you give a brief explanation in lay terms? If you wanted a client with an eating disorder to monitor food intake and she objected because of shame and embarrassment, could you explain convincingly why the benefits should outweigh the cost? When you suggest a role play, empty chair, or other interventions, do you understand the rationale and believe in it enough to explain it to clients, if that seems necessary? We are not suggesting that you always expect client opposition and offer lengthy explanations to fend off their possible questions. We do believe, however, that when you sense reluctance on the part of your clients you should be willing to explore the source of their reservations and if necessary be able to explain *briefly* why you think it would be helpful for them to do what you have suggested. (Again, to gain an appreciation of their perspective, it may help to imagine yourself going to a physician because you have what you believe is a sinus infection. You want an antibiotic. If the physician were to suggest an unexpected and possibly painful treatment instead, wouldn't you want an explanation? And if you asked for one and the physician couldn't or wouldn't give it, wouldn't you be offended?)

Finally, Lewis and Evans suggest that clients may appear uncooperative because they simply do not understand what the therapist expects of them. Unless they have been in therapy before, they may have only vague and misinformed ideas about how to proceed. Even if they have been in therapy, their first therapist's orientation and expectations may have been quite different. When our students complain that their clients are being too superficial, telling too many stories, changing the subject, etc., we often ask if they have bothered to indicate what they want the clients to do differently. Delineating roles and responsibilities is not always done directly, and clients can often pick up on fairly subtle clues, but some beginning therapists are unclear enough themselves about the roles that they offer few clues at all. So if clients seem to be doing the "wrong" things, our first suggestion is that therapists clarify for themselves and their clients what behavior would be more helpful. Our second suggestion is that they not expect one persuasive five-minute explanation to change a lifelong pattern of relating and that, instead, it should be assumed that clients' new behaviors, both in and out of therapy, will need to be encouraged and reinforced over time.

Before we leave this topic of client reluctance, we would like to suggest one more reason for the client's balking at the therapist's input. It might be that the therapist is simply wrong. As Singer (1970) noted with some irony:

> It must also be remembered that practitioners of psychotherapy are not necessarily oracles of wisdom, and therefore the patient's outright rejection of some interpretation or confrontational comment . . . is frequently a sign of remarkable well-being. Indeed it would indicate gross pathology were a patient to accept as gospel truth the therapist's misconceptions or inconsequential and irrelevant interpretations. (Or he would have to be very hostile to the therapist, because in accepting his silly pronouncements and pontifications, the patient would allow the therapist to live unchallenged in a fool's paradise.) (pp. 225–226)

TRANSFERENCE RESISTANCE

The third related process we wish to discuss that involves the client's balking is called by Freud (1926) "transference resistance." If resistance, as we defined it, is an intrapsychic phenomena and reluctance an interpersonal one, transference resistance is somewhere between the two. Or more succinctly, the resistance is in fact intrapsychic, but as the client manifests it, it *appears* interpersonal. Allen Wheelis (1973) described transference resistance when he said, "The trigger for anxiety is the giving of an account for which I may be judged" (p. 42). It is as if the client is so certain that what he or she is experiencing is unacceptable that the therapist is presumed to be unaccepting and critical, all evidence to the contrary. Thus, a simple empathic comment on the therapist's part, such as "That must have been really tough for you," can elicit an angry, "What? Do you think I'm such a baby I can't take it?" The process is transference in the sense that the client is transferring onto the therapist feelings that probably rightfully belong to an earlier relationship. In terms of present dynamics, however, the mechanism is a form of projection. The client's own self-judgments and worst fears about himself or herself are projected onto the therapist, with no awareness that the therapist may in actuality be feeling quite understanding and compassionate.

Clients exhibiting transference resistance often present themselves quite combatively; they require consistent support from their therapists as they sort out what they *fear* the therapist is feeling (or might feel) from what she or he actually is. If the therapist can remain emotionally available to the client and deal over and over with the immediacy of their relationship, gradually most clients will come to claim more readily their own fears, which can then be dealt with therapeutically. Prime requirements are the therapist's patience and ability to convey nondefensively "not guilty" when accused of being judgmental. The classical psychoanalytic way to deal with transference resistance was to remain emotionally neutral and to offer an interpretation of the process (Menninger, 1958). Therapy with a more supportive, interpersonal focus lends itself to a somewhat different approach. We believe that brief, supportive clarifications will work best: "Sounds like you felt judged just now. Actually, I was feeling pretty good about what you were saying." Or as one therapist said after a series of accusations, "You know, I don't *have* to feel about you the way you feel about yourself." Another therapist sometimes used humor: "Well, I agree that *someone* in this room might feel critical of you, but it isn't me. Who's left?" Whatever the style used, the goal is to help clients acknowledge and then deal with their projected self-judgments, after which the resisted material can be more easily explored.

RESISTANT OR RELUCTANT BEHAVIORS

As we briefly describe behaviors that therapists have come to recognize as potentially signaling resistance, reluctance, or transference resistance, we will not attempt to differentiate between the three processes. The behaviors could signify any of the three processes—or perhaps none. We list some of these, not so that in cookbook fashion you can identify them and then apply the appropriate remedy, but rather so that you can approach your clients with heightened awareness of processes that might profit from further exploration. Otani (1989) classifies resistant behaviors as response quantity resistance, response quality resistance, response style resistance, and logistic management resistance. For purposes of this discussion, however, we will categorize these client process behaviors in terms of how they affect most therapists; behaviors are categorized as disarming, innocuous, and provocative. We would like to repeat at this point that clients rarely use such behaviors as maneuvers to win at some imagined therapeutic chess game; they are not trying to outfox you.

As mentioned in other contexts throughout this book, it is the *pattern* of behavior that is important. Especially if therapy has been progressing fairly smoothly and suddenly the client behaves differently, it should become automatic for the therapist to pause to inquire what is causing the change.

Disarming behaviors.   Some of your clients will probably be charming, socially skilled, and very likable. They will be quite practiced at being engaging, and you may find yourself wishing that you had met them in another context so that you could be friends. The problem such clients have is that it is such second nature for them to read others' cues and be accommodating that they may have trouble exploring difficult feelings and motivations that may be less socially acceptable. They will need your encouragement and permission to give up their usual interactive style and be more transparent. You will do them no favors if you collude with them to stay "likable" and avoid such problematic issues.

Some behaviors that beginning therapists seem to find disarming that might perhaps signal resistance, reluctance, or transference resistance are

1. Humorous, charismatic storytelling.
2. Mild flirting.
3. Praising therapist's skills, wisdom, etc.
4. Asking about therapist's feelings, personal life, etc., especially when done with tact and concern.
5. Psychologically sophisticated "safe" self-disclosure (e.g., "I know I'm resisting, but . . .").

Whether your clients present with such styles or resort to them under pressure, it will be important for you to be empathically curious enough to invite them to explore the deeper issues that probably lie underneath. You will discover as you listen what the behaviors signified.

Innocuous behaviors.   There is another set of client behaviors that again may be either stylistic or situational. These behaviors are more clearly seen as defensive (i.e., self-protective) and less engaging than those in the above list and so are more clearly identified by beginning therapists as potentially needing attention. Our impression is that students feel less captivated by them than helpless. It can be frustrating for them to sense that there is something under the surface, ask the client, and be met by denial. What to do then? The frustration that arises is as often directed at themselves as the client, since they feel inadequate and directionless.

Some of these innocuous behaviors are

1. Changing the subject away from affect-ladened issues.
2. An unemotional recounting of powerful experiences.
3. Becoming helpless and passive.
4. Becoming confused.
5. Retreating into silence.

Provocative behaviors.   Finally, we want to describe behaviors which are alarming and provocative enough that "counterresistance" is somewhat likely. In our experience, these kinds of behaviors are most often evidenced by clients with personality disorders or more severe pathology. Since your typical reaction outside of therapy with such a person would very likely be to become punitive or to withdraw, neither of which is generally therapeutic, it is especially important that you be prepared to deal professionally with such behavior:

1. Punitive, withholding silence.
2. Accusations of therapist's unhelpfulness, biases, uncaring, etc.
3. Demands for closer, personal relationship.
4. Pattern of missed sessions, tardiness, emergency "midnight calls," etc.
5. Sexual overtures to therapist.

It should be obvious from this brief list that these behaviors tend not to elicit much therapist warmth and support. Nonetheless, although clients engaging in such actions need clear limit setting, they also need consistency, support, and patience from their therapists.

Working through resistance/reluctance.   Writers as theoretically diverse as Ellis (1985), Erickson (1964), Milman and Goldman (1987), and Wachtel (1982) suggest that the therapist's ability to properly handle client resistance is a crucial therapeutic skill. We will outline the process generally accepted by psychodynamic therapists to the working through of resistance. As Marshall (1982) points out, the crucial ingredient is to refuse to adopt an adversarial stance and instead to "join" with the client, thereby providing client support, lessening his or her fear, and encouraging the exploration of avoided material.

Bugental (1978) outlines this as a three-part process. First, the therapist draws the client's attention to the behavioral manifestation as nonthreateningly as possible. For example, the therapist may say noncritically, "You seem to be speaking more rapidly this session," or "For the last five minutes you've hardly looked at me," or "For a while you were always on time for our appointments, but lately I notice that you've been five to ten minutes late." Obviously, if the therapist is not annoyed but is instead interested in the process, it will be easier to convey warmth and support.

The second step, which may be combined with the first step, or with more fragile clients comes only after the first has been noted many times, puts the behavior in a specific context. For example, the therapist may note, "Just when your eyes well up and I think you might cry about your brother's death, you change the subject," or "You seem to withdraw and get quieter if I offer another point of view," or "It seems like when you leave a session angry, you tend to make contact before our next session by calling me at home." The more defensive/resistant/reluctant you expect the client to be, the more threatening you can infer that the hidden material is likely to be. It should seem appropriate to you by now to make your interventions quietly and supportively rather than to bludgeon the client to death with an accusative charge.

The final and most important step of this approach is to invite the clients to explore their process. Again, your own therapeutic curiosity and interest can be instrumental in conveying an open, noncritical attitude. This third step is often merged with the first two but may be quite separate. Examples of merged interventions are, "I notice that for the last couple of sessions you've seemed a little withdrawn, and I remember your being upset with me the session before. Are you still angry?" "You know, you've been in therapy for a year, and up until the last month, you'd never canceled a session. I'm wondering why you've canceled the last two. Are you feeling differently about coming here for some reason?" "Help me understand something. Whenever I ask about your daughter, you seem to shut down. Can you tell me what happens inside you when I bring her up?" "I wonder if you can do something. Can you hold a magnifying glass up to your feelings and tell me what your reactions are when I ask you how your job search is coming? You seem to brush aside the question."

The therapist, in order to invite such exploration, clearly needs to be willing to hear anything the client says—whether the material is intrapsychic or arises out of the client's feelings about the therapeutic relationship. The invitation to explore is thus done supportively, unapologetically, and nondefensively. If the issue is interpersonal, between the client and the therapist, we believe it is very important to be open to client feedback rather than to automatically chalk off the client's reactions as transference. If in fact the therapist erred in some way, he or she needs to be able to acknowledge the mishap nondefensively. This not only restrengthens the therapeutic alliance by legitimizing the client's feelings and by showing respect but also provides a good model for the client that being human and making mistakes does not have to destroy one's self-respect. If the issue explored turns out instead to be intrapsychic, helping the client understand *how* the process works and what alternative assumptions and behaviors there might be can be very therapeutic.

A final note: As mentioned earlier, "joining" with resistance does not mean you cannot set limits. Especially with clients with poor impulse control, your task will be to set limits nonpunitively and still remain emotionally supportive enough to encourage client self-exploration.

SUMMARY

In dealing with resistance, reluctance, or transference resistance, it is easy for the therapist to slip into an adversarial mode. From our framework, doing so jeopardizes the therapeutic alliance and thereby sabotages some of the most valuable aspects that therapy has to offer. As therapists come to view client's balking as a normal, expected component of the therapeutic process, they will find it increasingly easy to remain emotionally available while simultaneously encouraging the client to explore what is taking place. Paradoxically, the less a given therapist needs to fight resistance, the more therapeutic power she or he is likely to have.

It is sometimes far too easy to sit aside and wonder at clients' lack of "courage." Why don't they just jump feet first into the process and get on with it? It may help to remember that, from their perspective, you are asking them to question the bedrock of their lives, the foundation they have been standing on for years. None of us approaches such a task lightly. Louise White, as quoted by Fitts (1965), states a client's position succinctly:

> The gamble is a big one;
> All that I am,
> For all that I can be . . .
> I cannot hurry,
> For I have so much more at stake than you. (pp. 55–56)

10

TERMINATION

The best way out is always through.

—Robert Frost

If therapy could be easily divided into stages—with a clear beginning, middle, and end—it would probably be the final stage in which beginning therapists have the least training (Rice, Alonso, and Rutan, 1985). The stages or steps are never quite that clear-cut, of course. Sometimes the therapeutic alliance is never really forged in the beginning stage, and even with the most responsible clients, motivation will ebb and flow in the course of treatment, thereby making the middle stage hard to track. Still, most students seem to feel that they know intuitively when therapy is going well and in retrospect can often identify the turning points that marked a client's progress. Often, however, the ending of the relationship is not considered part of the process to be explored, with its own subgoals and issues, and instead therapy simply stops. The end of the semester comes, or the client announces this will be the final session, or perhaps there is a pattern of client cancellations and diminished energy. When it is over, the therapist (and probably the client also) is left feeling somehow incomplete but with little idea of what might have been done differently.

We believe that there are probably two main reasons for this awkwardness, from the therapist's perspective. First, many beginning therapists are still uncertain about their theoretical orientations and goals, so it is difficult for them to evaluate client progress. Not at all sure whether they should focus on relief of client symptoms, increased client insight, greater client spontaneity within the session, client self-report of feeling "helped," or perhaps something else altogether, they may disenfranchise themselves therapeutically when termination seems likely and defer entirely to the client. If the client does not feel like continuing, so they reason, they should respect her or his preference. Therapist passivity and lack of knowledge are thus rationalized as "respect."

A second and perhaps more powerful cause of awkwardness at termination is the therapist's own sense of loss and termination anxiety. Martin and Schurtman (1985) suggest five possible sources of such therapist anxiety: (1) termination dynamics independent of client reaction (i.e., difficulties with leave taking in general); (2) anxiety over loss of professional role; (3) therapist's reaction to client's termination anxiety (i.e., countertransference); (4) uneasiness over the implied importance of termination (i.e., performance anxiety about properly executing "the successful" termination); and (5) the literal loss of a meaningful relationship. The underlying assumption here is one that runs throughout this book. It is doubtful that a therapist can offer a client a relationship significantly healthier or more mature than the therapist is outside of therapy. If we as therapists have major unresolved issues regarding separation and loss, we will have few choices other than to let such issues leak out and contaminate the termination process or to defend massively against such a possibility. Neither approach is likely to work very well. To quote Martin and Schurtman (1985) more fully:

> Therapy, like life itself, ends. If as therapists we minimize the termination process or do not permit ourselves to be as emotionally available as we can be during the final sessions, what are we implying to the client about how to conduct one's waking activities during an experience that has a certain end? Might we not then be teaching the need to defend oneself against loss and death instead of the need to live life to its fullest? (p. 95)

As Kopp (1974) points out, staying emotionally available for the client during this last stage can be so painful that many therapists, unaware of what they are "teaching" clients, make sure to end therapy abruptly rather than risk ever going through the third stage at all.

If the therapy has been intense and has lasted for more than a few weeks, and especially if the interpersonal focus we have been suggesting has been implemented, the loss of the therapeutic relationship will likely evoke strong ambivalent feelings from your clients. If they, and you, however, can tolerate the pain enough to accept and explore the process, they will be able to go through a significant loss experience in a caring, affirming environment, perhaps for the first time. Further, they will have the opportunity to identify and work through with you their issues and conflicts associated with separation.

In some ways, we agree with Simonton's (1988) definition of therapy as "the short-term election of a surrogate parent." Giving up this wise, nurturing parent is usually painful, even if it was foreshadowed all along. Termination of therapy is thus an important step in the client's ongoing separation/individuation process. Accordingly, it can elicit a whole range of grief-related reactions. It is not unusual for clients to express sadness and/or anger that the therapy relationship is over, fear that they may not be able to make it on their own, perhaps disappointment that therapy did not result in a totally happy, problem-free existence (Kopp, 1977). Your task, as therapist, will be roughly what it was when the client discussed other painful issues: to remain emotionally available and supportive, to help him or her tease out feelings and meanings and choices, to avoid acting out countertransferential reactions, to help the client separate reality from illusion as best as the two of you can. The difference will be that the demands on you to accomplish these things during termination will be greater than before, since the client's feelings are aimed more directly at you. As you deal with this feeling, it will be important not just to analyze the transference but to aid the client (and yourself) in acknowledging and mourning the ending of the "real relationship" also.

GUIDELINES FOR TERMINATION

Each termination process is unique in that it grows out of the process between the two individuals involved and the issues that have been the therapeutic focus. The ending of a therapeutic relationship between a client with an eating disorder and her behavioral therapist will be quite different from the process between the same client and her analyst if she had instead chosen to enter long-term psychoanalysis. The guidelines we offer here are intended to be generic and transtheoretical, but we assume they will be most relevant for the therapist and client who have been working together for several weeks or months with an interpersonal focus.

In this section, we will suggest separate emphases for termination when the decision for that termination comes from three different loci—when the therapist makes the decision unilaterally, when the client makes the decision, and when the decision is mutually agreed upon. Before we discuss each situation separately, however, we would like to offer some general guidelines.

First, we agree with Kramer (1986) that termination needs to be discussed overtly, not just at the end of therapy, but from the early sessions on. Endings of relationships are so frequently nonverbal and/or impulsively acted out that, as Kramer says, there is much to be gained by bringing the termination process into the open where it can be discussed freely. There has been considerable controversy regarding the benefits of time-limited therapy with a termination date known from the beginning or agreed upon shortly thereafter. For a variety of reasons, some of them more economic than theoretical, the trend seems to be increasingly in this direction (Strupp and Binder, 1984). In such cases, it is especially important to keep the termination date in perspective as one of the limits built into the therapeutic relationship that serves to channel and focus the client's energy and attention. Lamb (1985) goes so far as to provide a model for the content of each of the last seven sessions so that termination issues are highlighted and virtually inescapable. Even if no specific termination date is set, however, the fact that therapy will not continue indefinitely should be in the client's awareness all along. No client, if it can possibly be avoided, should have to repeat earlier traumatic abandonment experiences by being subjected to an abrupt termination.

Another general guideline we offer for your consideration is that you maintain your therapeutic stance with the client right through the final moments of the last session, rather than dilute the experience by becoming "friends," even if the client is insistent. We are aware that there is some controversy over this issue, but we feel strongly that it is almost always in the client's best interest to follow the conservative "once a therapist, always a therapist" approach. It should be obvious that we are not proposing a rigid formality to your style that would preclude any warmth or self-disclosure. Rather, maintaining a therapeutic stance means that you honor your primary commitment to the client's growth and needs and do not allow yourself to slide into a social, chatty relationship simply because that makes you feel better. Most clients who ask for friendship probably do *not* mean that they want an equal, reciprocal relationship but instead secretly hope that the therapeutic alliance (which called for your offering the best of yourself in the service of their needs) can simply be continued indefinitely, for free. In our experience, it is almost inevitable that clients would feel disappointed and betrayed if you were to interact with them in a new social way that suggested you were no longer primarily focused on their growth, were sometimes distracted and irritable and bored, and in fact canceled or even forgot social engagements with them. In short, we feel that therapy and friendship have somewhat different foundations and that it is ill-advised and potentially damaging to the client to try to abruptly shift the structure from one set of goals and norms to another. (We are also aware that in small communities it can be quite difficult to keep relationship distinctions from getting blurred, but we feel that at least therapists in such situations can avoid the trap of naively assuming that all clients can be believed when they insist they can handle equality.)

The final general guideline we offer may seem at this juncture slightly contradictory after our heavy emphasis on termination as a meaningful, crucial stage in therapy. We suggest, nonetheless, that you not rule out the possibility of the client's returning to see you at some point. As the trend in the practice of psychotherapy seems to be shifting away from long-term work and moving in the direction of a shorter focus on situational and developmental issues (Strupp and Binder, 1984), the idea of having a "lifetime" therapist whom one can check in with from time to time (much as one might with a family physician or attorney) gains legitimacy. Even if, however, you as therapist have used a more traditional, long-term approach, it is usually not helpful to insist that the client never see you again. As Taft (1933/1973) says:

> The patient, like the rest of mankind, can learn to bear life only gradually. It is therefore no crime, but a sign of growth, that he is able to return in the face of fear, to experience more deeply and fully the life forces . . . and thus to acknowledge in turning to the therapist once more, not only his need for help but the new strength which enables him to take it. (pp. 294–295)

Regardless of the therapeutic approach, some post–therapy communications are likely to occur (Lamb, 1985). Sometimes clients ask if they can write; sometimes therapists express a desire to hear from the client. Occasional correspondence or even additional sessions are generally viewed as legitimate, especially after some time (perhaps a few months) has passed. At any rate, forbidding the client to communicate is likely *not* to be therapeutic.

We turn our attention now to a discussion of the various issues involved in termination when the locus of the decision to terminate is the client's, the therapist's, or reached jointly. In addition to the above general guidelines, we suggest one more—that regardless of who initiates the discussion, you consider termination to be a *mutual* concern. Both your input and the client's input should be considered and attended to thoughtfully, even if one or the other of you makes the final decision.

Client-initiated decision. *Premature termination* is a term with decidedly negative connotations. The use of it presupposes the therapist's objective assessment that the client is acting out his or her resistance to the exploration of important clinical material. Sometimes, of course, this is so unmistakable that even the client would not deny it. The substance abuser who resumes the use of drugs and misses his next session, the abused spouse who calls to cancel because she is moving back in with her husband, the anorexic who no-shows after losing three more pounds—these clients, if pressed, would probably acknowledge that they had made a choice that would be considered dysfunctional but that they preferred the immediate gratification of their present behavior to therapeutic exploration. Other clients, however, may terminate simply because they had different goals from their therapists. Wolberg (1988) found that most clients regard symptom relief as the best measure of positive gain, which, to say the least, is in contrast to the analyst's criterion of the resolution of transference (Levenson, 1976), the ego psychologist's expectations that the ego will be stronger (Blanck and Blanck, 1974), or Klein's (1950) hope that the patient will evidence an increased capacity to love. Symptom relief, from many clients' perspective, must seem considerably easier to attain! Other clients may terminate because they do not believe they are being helped, because of financial considerations, or for a variety of other reasons. In short, we urge you not to automatically make hasty, negative judgments regarding clients' motives for considering termination.

If clients simply cancel or fail to keep appointments and do not reschedule, you will be on safer grounds both ethically and legally (dissatisfied clients occasionally sue on malpractice grounds) if you communicate by letter or telephone to indicate your willingness to continue meeting with them and/or to refer them to another professional. Some therapists additionally offer a free session to help the client explore his or her reasons for terminating. The goal here is to offer continued professional help without in any way attempting to coerce the client into remaining in therapy.

Assuming you have the opportunity to discuss with the client her or his reasons for terminating, it will be important to avoid taking an adversarial stance. If, in fact, you want your clients to become more autonomous, you must be able to support their independence, even if that means they leave therapy against your advice. You may still, of course, offer your clinical opinion, but we suggest you do so as nondogmatically as possible. You may, for example, want to say something like, "My concern is that you have more work to do in the area of _____. I will respect your opinion, since you must make the decision, of course, but I'd like for you to consider what I've said. Can you tell me your reaction?" If clients insist on terminating after all, we believe you will have the most therapeutic impact if you back off at that point, review with them the progress you have seen them make, and then suggest that at some later date, if old or new issues arise, they may want to contact you or another professional. If you are quite worried about their well-being, one possibility is to say something along the lines of, "I really do hope things will go OK for you. I'd feel a lot better, though, if I knew that if your depression/anxiety/anger (or whatever) worsened, you'd contact me or another professional. Would you feel comfortable promising me that?"

Therapist-initiated decision.   There are two kinds of situations in which you as therapist may find it necessary to discontinue therapy with a client. We will consider these separately, since both your own motivations and the client's are likely to be quite different in the two scenarios.

In the first, more common situation, your decision has nothing to do with a particular client. The decision to terminate is demanded by your own situation. You are an intern, and it is time to rotate to another unit, or you work in an agency that has an eight-session limit, or you accept a new position somewhere else. Or perhaps you decide to retire or change careers. Whatever the precipitating cause, your clients' dynamics have not and cannot influence your decision. Depending on your clients' reactions to being helpless, they will find this either more or less easy to tolerate and understand than if your decision in fact had anything to do with them (as it does in the next scenario). You can assume that none of your clients will be very grateful for the disruption, but their relative helplessness will be a relief to some of them. For these individuals, knowing that at least they were not at fault will help them accept the situation. They will not need to wonder, as perhaps they have when experiencing other losses, what they could have done differently. Other clients, however, especially if they have been abused or neglected historically, may find their helplessness to influence your decision almost intolerable. It may provoke intense feelings of abandonment, rage, or despair.

Given these considerations, it should be obvious that your clients need to be given as much notice as possible about your plans. Preferably, you can tell them at the *beginning* of therapy, so they can pace themselves accordingly. We would also encourage you to allude periodically to the time frame during the course of therapy (as in, "Well, we're about halfway through our ten sessions. Are we on the right track as far as accomplishing your goals?" or "What did you want to focus on in our last four sessions?"). We also suggest that you ask specifically what your clients' reactions are to being terminated by you, that you listen nondefensively to any strong feelings they have, and that you demonstrate that you are somewhat affected by their reactions, even if you cannot change the final outcome. Expressing some regret, or your desire to hear from your clients, or any positive feelings you have for them can serve to lessen their sense of powerlessness. Obviously, you will also offer a referral and facilitate it as much as possible if the client wishes.

In the second scenario, you are not forced to end therapy with a client because of outside forces; instead, you *choose* to initiate termination because in your professional judgment that will enhance the client's growth. If clients were not grateful for the disruption in their lives in the above situation, you can be sure that in this instance they will be even less so. Some will react stoically, some will withdraw or terminate precipitously at the first hint of rejection, others may act out to the point of threatening suicide. (For a very thoughtful discussion of such a case, we refer you to chapter 4 in Irvin Yalom's excellent book, *Existential Psychotherapy*, 1980.) Before you make such a decision, it is crucial that you consult with your supervisor or, lacking a supervisor, with other professionals.

Your choice to initiate termination will probably be based on your view that the client is holding onto symptoms out of dependency on you and a desire to avoid termination. Sometimes this is overt and clearly manipulative on the client's part (although we encourage you to assume that the manipulation is based on fear rather than on spitefulness). At other times, the cues are subtle, and it is only gradually that you come to understand that the client may *never* choose to terminate if left to his or her own devices. As Allen Wheelis (1956) stated, "Knowledgeable moderns put their back to the couch and in so doing may occasionally fail to put their shoulders to the wheel." Whatever the specifics of the case, the judgment is made that further therapy is not in the best interest of the client. At this point, you will, with consultation, have to decide whether to encourage your client to let you make a referral or to suggest that she or he terminate therapy altogether. Clearly, decisions such as this are some of the most difficult ones therapists are called upon to make.

In most cases, you will be able to suggest termination as a possibility, discuss it with your clients, help them work through their reactions, and they will accept the suggestion over time. Occasionally, this may take place quite quickly, especially if the client was feeling "ready" but needed your permission to leave. At other times, several weeks may be required. Our point is that you will usually be able to avoid the power struggle that ensues when clients feel "kicked out" if you emphasize your clients' strengths and progress made and suggest that the time has arrived for them to try their wings. If that is too fearful for them to imagine, you may suggest that at least they try a "vacation" of several months away from you. Keeping your approach positive and supportive, as opposed to critical and impatient, is very important. No one, including clients, likes to leave important relationships feeling rejected.

Mutual decision. Ideally, and more frequently than you might imagine, you and your client will agree with each other that therapy has run its course. That does not mean that there will be no pain in its ending but rather that acceptance and a mutual acknowledgment of the meaningfulness of what has happened will be a predominant theme.

Various writers have suggested "cues" that signal the emergence of this third phase. Kramer (1986) concurs with the traditional view that transference issues tend to be replaced by a more egalitarian exchange between the therapist and client. Bugental (1978) looks for a recognition on the part of clients that growth is a continuous, never-completed process as a prelude to their readiness to move on without their therapist. Roth (1987) reports that themes regarding loss and separation, especially in patients' dreams, precede and coincide with termination. You may see similar cues, as well as others, such as an expressed desire on the part of the client to decrease the frequency of sessions, a lack of things to talk about, or clearly self-congratulatory client expressions of progress. Whether the therapy has been within a specific or open-ended time frame, such cues are signals that, if you have not already, it is time to begin the overt discussion of termination.

As in the previous discussions of more unilaterally initiated termination, much of your job will be to encourage and help the client explore the full range of his or her feelings—from gratitude and acceptance to anger and grief. The more "uncovering" the therapeutic work has been up until now (as opposed to strictly "supportive"), the more able the client will be to tolerate intense affect. Even so, do not be surprised if old issues and symptoms reemerge and if conflicts considered previously resolved resurface, especially around issues of loss. As Strupp and Binder (1984) state, "In the final analysis, termination, separation, and death are the bedrock of human existence, for which psychotherapy, whether it is time limited or unlimited, can offer no cure" (p. 264).

The ways that clients have typically coped with significant losses are likely to be reenacted with their therapists. Typical defensive modes of dealing with loss are devaluation of treatment, bargaining, therapist idealization, and regression (Roth, 1987), as well as those previously mentioned. As you help your clients recognize their feelings and coping styles and perhaps relate them to previous losses they have suffered, you will necessarily be helping them deal with *this* loss with increased awareness and potential for growth. At this final stage, perhaps more than at any earlier time, your faith in clients' process will be tested. If, in your urgency to rescue them from their reactions or hurry them so that they can reach the final session on cue, you inadvertently imply that their feelings are dangerous or illegitimate, you will likely undermine some of the hard-won gains they have made with you.

Final session.   We offer guidelines for the final session with some trepidation. Given the awkwardness and mixed feelings both you and your clients will likely be experiencing, it may be tempting to reach for an easy, systematic approach to bring therapy to a close. We urge you to remember that one of your primary responsibilities is to stay emotionally available to your clients, and hiding behind a set of procedures will hardly facilitate that. At the same time, it is generally not helpful to your clients to encourage them to explore new, difficult material in the last session.

Generally speaking, the last time you meet with a client will be a time for the two of you to say goodbye. As Lamb (1985) indicates, this can be accomplished in a variety of ways, including exchanging forwarding addresses, further expressions by therapist or client on the meaningfulness of therapy and leave-taking, or review of progress made by the client and an exploration of her or his future plans. Often clients, especially after long-term therapy, wish to give a gift to the therapist. While the acceptance of gifts, even during the last session, is somewhat controversial, it is our position that the ritual of gift giving is an important one for some clients and may help them accept the finality of the situation. We see the therapist's willingness to accept small gifts as a symbolic acknowledgment of the client's feelings, and in most cases we think it is more helpful to graciously accept a small gift than to encourage the client to explore the motivations behind the giving. (Expensive, valuable gifts are infrequently given and in our opinion should not be accepted.)

Another thing that therapists occasionally do, especially if they have routinely done this throughout the course of therapy, is to solicit their client's feedback. If a therapist has never done this with a given client, it would be inappropriate to shift the power balance of the final session by doing so. But if some mutual give-and-take and focus on the therapeutic relationship has been part of your style all along, then briefly asking the client what he or she found helpful or difficult in therapy may provide you with valuable feedback. If you ask, be prepared to live with some ambiguity, since what you get will be the client's very subjective assessment. Asking for in-depth clarification, even if you are bewildered by his or her answer, would be an unfair burden to a client in a final session and would probably increase the client's defensiveness.

Finally, we remind you again that in addition to acknowledging the range of your clients' feelings about you—including their gratitude for your help—you nonetheless should give them much of the credit for their progress. It may be tempting to let them idealize you and your therapeutic power, but they need to leave therapy in touch as much as possible with their own strengths and resources. Your acknowledging the value of their struggles and gains will help them further internalize your belief in their abilities.

SUMMARY

To underscore our main point: The final stage of therapy, as difficult as it may be for both therapist and client, is nonetheless an integral part of the therapeutic process. Your skills at helping the client during this phase are largely dependent on your overall ability to deal with losses and separations in general, since you can hardly offer the client an experiential understanding of a process that bewilders or overwhelms you personally.

Your clients will need your professionalism—which includes both your emotional availability and your commitment to their growth—right up through the end of the last session. Your helping them to understand their usual reactions to leave-taking, and perhaps to discover new ways to do it with you, is the last and one of the most important ways you can be of service to them. Not all clients will be able or willing to take advantage of the opportunity that termination offers, but those who do can leave therapy with an increased ability to embrace life more fully, in spite of the inevitable separations and losses.

11

MISTAKES THERAPISTS MAKE

A failure is not always a mistake; it may simply be the best one can do under the circumstances.

—B. F. Skinner

In this chapter we want to list and discuss a number of the mistakes which beginning therapists and counselors make. Earlier we both implicitly and explicitly discussed possible mistakes as we addressed various questions which beginning therapists ask. In a few cases there is partial overlap between the chapters due to the frequency of the behavior or importance of the issue.

The purpose of the chapter is not to provide an exhaustive list of mistakes. Neither do we claim that the worst possible, or even most frequent, mistakes are analyzed. Rather, we hope to stimulate your thinking about therapy by addressing some of the issues which we have confronted while providing supervision over a period of years. We do believe that the mistakes discussed are representative of those which beginning therapists make.

The first thing we want to say about mistakes is that we hope you will make a lot of them because they are the best way to learn. The second thing we will say is that you undoubtedly will. This is the good news—since you are expected to make mistakes, you have a license to fail. After you have your Ph.D., your license will not be as broad, and you will certainly put more pressure on yourself. So your years of training should be "the good old years." Perhaps more so than at any other time in your life, you will be rewarded for being able to recognize your shortcomings. So, we wish for you many mistakes, a good time talking about, them with your supervisor, and the healthy expectation on your part that you will commit, and are entitled to, a very large number of them.

MISTAKES AND THEORETICAL ORIENTATION

Let us roughly divide the behavior of therapists into three categories. In the first category, we have unanimous (or near unanimous) agreement on what should be done. For example, it is generally agreed that it is a mistake to have a sexual relationship with a client or to discuss one of your cases publicly at a cocktail party. In the second category, we have therapeutic interventions and behaviors about which the majority of therapists probably agree but which do elicit differing opinions among therapists. For example, touching clients, disclosing something about yourself, and expressing some of your feelings are things which the majority of therapists likely believe can be helpful at one time or the other but about which you will most certainly find some disagreement. In the third category are behaviors about which we assume we do *not* have a clear consensus among therapists. You may be surprised to learn that there are actually a large number of behaviors in this category. It is likely that the majority of such behaviors/interactions fall into the category of, "When should I intervene?" (timing) or "How should I intervene?" (style). The fact that experienced therapists may disagree on the best or ideal intervention at a given time does not, however, keep them from agreeing on many basics. So even though there are many interventions which fall into category three, there are still many that fall into category one or two. It is behaviors which we believe fall into these two categories that we will focus on in this chapter. Even though in the book we make an effort to discuss mainly "mistakes" on which there is general agreement, we recognize that when an intervention is labeled a mistake that judgment, and especially any elaboration of the judgment, will be strongly influenced by the theoretical orientation of the therapist. For example, a mistake in person-centered therapy might not be a mistake from Ellis's perspective. Although we try to discuss issues which transcend theoretical orientations, we realize that the extent to which you (and your supervisor) agree or disagree with our comments will be influenced by your theoretical orientation. It should also be noted that when we try to define mistakes we are forced to make assumptions about what is good mental health— assumptions that may have a very elusive character (Bugental, 1988).

We turn now to a discussion of various mistakes.

COMMON MISTAKES

Too Much of One Thing

In a prepracticum or in a first counseling methods course, students are often told, or may get the impression, that there are a number of rules of the form "don't do this" which guide therapeutic practice (this chapter might be viewed as one set of such rules). So, for example, you may be told, "Don't give advice," "Don't give too much reassurance," and "Don't ask too many questions." When it comes to such stereotypic interventions as advice, reassurance, asking questions, etc., the problem generally is not that you should not do it but rather (a) that the timing is bad or (b) that you may rely on it too much. We will delay for the moment the question of timing and discuss the issue of the "too much" mistake.

Here is an exercise you can try. After you have seen a few clients and audio- or videotaped the sessions, choose a few ten-minute segments at random. Before reviewing the segments, make a list of the stereotypic responses you believe are *generally* not good interventions. Add to this list any mistakes you fear you make too often. Then review a few segments of tapes from three or four clients and make a tally mark each time you hear yourself giving advice or whatever. After listening to eight or nine segments, you should be able to get a fairly good idea of the types of interventions on which you are overrelying. You should also begin to get a sense (this is more difficult) of the types of situations in which you are likely to rely on a particular form of intervention. For example, do you start to ask a lot of questions if the client becomes angry, do you tend to give advice when the client seems indecisive, etc.?

Each of us as therapists makes many mistakes. For some of us, one of the mistakes we make is to rely over and over on the same sort of response. One of your jobs in becoming a therapist is to identify the types of responses of which you make "too much" use, especially if one of these types falls into a category which we as therapists consider "suspect" anyway (for example, giving advice).

Social Behaviors Inappropriate to the Role

There is a "class" of behaviors, one might say, into which many beginning therapists fall from time to time. That is the group of social behaviors (within the session) which is clearly inappropriate to the role. Examples of this class include chatting, nervous laughter, and telling jokes with no therapeutic point.

"Chatting" is one of the social interactions which we all practice with our friends from time to time. It is generally not a form of interaction we should practice with our clients. What do we mean when we use the word *chatting*? Examples include giving detailed (and literal) answers when clients ask you a question about yourself or your interests and talking about things like the weather for the first few minutes of the session. If the client begins the session with, "Isn't today a lovely day?" there is nothing wrong with saying, "Yes, it certainly is." On the other hand, you need not, and should not, go on to comment on the possibility of whether this winter will be tougher than the last one, the unpredictability of the weather, etc.

Although most therapists tell very few jokes even to make a specific point, you will find that clients will from time to time tell you a joke. We are not suggesting that you should never laugh at a client's joke. However, we recognize that much humor is based on anxiety, subtle (or not so subtle) ridicule of various ethnic groups, and taboos. In such cases, laughing at the joke makes you a part of the ridicule, the rebellion, or whatever theme underlies the joke. Laughing communicates that you hold the values expressed by the joke. Since most clients realize they are not in therapy to "have a good time," they do not tell jokes; hence, when this norm is violated, the issue should be carefully noted by the therapist. In most cases the content of the joke should be carefully considered by the therapist, although the therapist may choose not to make any comments to the client. For example, one should ask oneself, "How is the theme in the joke related to the issues which the client brought to therapy or is now dealing with in therapy?"

There are at least two other issues which should be considered when clients tell a joke. The first is how the telling of the joke fits into the pattern of the session. Was it used to reduce anxiety about a subject? Did it follow your being confrontational about an issue, etc.? The second is what the telling of the joke suggests in terms of your relationship to the client. For example, might the client be attempting to make you a friend rather than a therapist?

Perhaps you are asking, "Well, what if they *do* tell a joke? Am I supposed to just look at them?" Certainly, there are many funny jokes which do not communicate a value to which we object. These jokes we tend to feel free to laugh at unless we believe that the joke is expressly designed to undermine therapeutic progress. Laughing at the joke does not mean you give up your right as a therapist to process it. At times you will laugh spontaneously at a joke, only to realize almost instantly that the joke subtly communicates a value to which you object or that makes a powerful statement about the difficulties of the client. In such cases we recommend that you say something like the following: "I find myself laughing at the joke you told, yet I'm realizing now how much *you* feel like that 'drunk' in the story." If the joke, for example, is racist, sexist, or in some other way does violence to our value system, we do not laugh. We do try very hard to understand what the client is trying to communicate. As we see our job, it is to understand (and help clients understand) why they ridicule others. Our job is not to tell clients that their values are wrong but rather to help them understand (if this is an issue in therapy) how their values and their distress are linked.

By definition, nervous laughter means that you are laughing because you are anxious and not because you are truly amused. Beginning therapists, however, often do find themselves laughing in response to something a client said and then realize in supervision that they laughed because they were uncomfortable with what the client said. Reviewing a few of your audio- or videotapes should be enough to help you ascertain whether you are prone to this sort of mistake. There are several reasons why nervous laughter is to be avoided. The first is that you are sending a mixed message to clients. You are verbally saying, "I thought that was funny," while in reality you did not think it was funny. If there is one thing clients don't need more of it is mixed messages. Of course, there are many other ways to send mixed messages, and these should also be avoided (for example, emotionally withdrawing from the client—for whatever reason—while in the same session saying, "Your lack of trust keeps you from making contact with people"). Mixed messages, including laughing when you are not amused, makes it very difficult for clients to learn to trust the environment (other people) because they can never be quite sure what the environment really *is*.

A second reason to avoid nervous laughter is that whatever is making you nervous is something you need to learn about. If you "laugh off" these situations, it is unlikely that you will ever discover what is making you anxious. If you do not become aware of what is making you anxious, you are operating with a blind spot with all your clients.

A third reason to avoid this type of laughter is that you could and should be making a more effective intervention than laughing. Laughing when you are nervous may help you to be less nervous, but it does not help clients explore their feelings or grapple with their problems. Fourth, laughing is often a form of reinforcement. Clients from time to time tell stories to avoid an issue. If you laugh (rather than help them go deeper into their feelings), they are more likely to tell more stories.

Finally, you should entertain the hypothesis that these situations may be produced by a kind of collusion between you and the client. Perhaps your laughing is in a sense encouraged by the client. Perhaps the client wants you to laugh rather than trying to help him or her go deeper into the problem. Some clients have become very adept at making others laugh to keep interactions on a superficial level. So even if you find yourself truly amused by some clients (as you most certainly will), appreciate and enjoy their humor but keep open the possibility that therapy can be held in check by this "strength" of the client.

Since we have raised the issue of nervous laughter and telling jokes, we want to emphasize that the use of humor in psychotherapy can be a very effective tool. If you view therapy as a grim procedure devoid of levity, you will probably not last long as a therapist. In the first place, it will be hard for you to find enough rewards to keep you doing therapy. In the second place, unless you are *very* good at what you are doing, your clients will be less than likely to return for very many sessions of this grim procedure.

Simply expressed, our philosophy is to have some fun at being a therapist. We also want to encourage our clients to use strengths, such as the ability to see humor in a situation, in order to deal with adversity. On the other hand, as therapists we must be alert to when we allow ourselves or our clients to use laughter as a way of avoiding that with which we must deal.

Setting the Client Up for Failure

All therapists presumably want the best for their clients. We want clients to be less anxious, to be creative, to have friends, to enjoy life, to be sensitive, caring people. In our exuberance to have this happen, we sometimes push clients, whether subtly or overtly, into behaviors for which they are not ready. Of course, part of our job is to encourage and support new behaviors for the client. Of course, there are judgment calls to be made as to when clients are ready to confront their mother, or invite a member of the opposite sex to dinner, or look for a new job. And, of course, it is possible to conspire with clients to help them avoid taking a slightly risky step for which they *are* ready. However, we emphasize here the necessity of not pushing clients into situations for which they are not prepared. We are sometimes prone to believe that we have easy answers to difficult problems. Most clients cannot and will not make dramatic changes quickly. If you push clients toward something for which they are not ready, and you are *lucky*, they will resist you, think you foolish and lacking in understanding, and will probably feel guilty because they are not living up to your expectations. If you are *unlucky*, these clients will perhaps either fail and regress or quit therapy altogether before being "forced" to do something they "know" they cannot do. It is very important to communicate to clients that therapy is a shared endeavor. If clients seek help in making behavioral changes, it is imperative that they receive the message from you that they will not be pushed into doing something for which they are not prepared. (Additional comments concerning this issue are found in the chapters "Client Fears," "Intake Interviewing," and "Listening.")

Perhaps you are asking, "What if the client has a great fear of failure and wants to be able to handle failure in a more satisfactory way?" For example, a female college student may say, "I want to be able to ask guys out for a date and not let it bother me when they say no." Your work with the client might then involve having her ask someone for a date when the probability for success is not particularly high. The critical issue here is ensuring that the client is ready to try this and that she is not just responding to subtle, or not so subtle, pressure from you. More generally, however, we would encourage you to take the time to ascertain in what way the reported symptom might be part of a larger issue—in this case, for example, perhaps ambivalence over leaving home and growing up. We discuss the issue of understanding the problem in the following section.

Trying to Solve the Problem Before You Understand the Problem

A few years ago one of us asked a well-known family therapist what the most frequent error was that she saw being made by beginning therapists. She answered, "Trying to solve the problem before they understand the problem." We agree that this is a frequent therapeutic mistake.

We discussed this issue briefly in the chapter on intake interviewing, noting that it takes some time to find out what the problem is—what its salient features are. Although we do not consider ourselves to be behavior therapists, we think it fair to point out that this is a system of psychotherapy which emphasizes careful analysis of the problem before trying to solve it. You may or may not believe in a "behavioral" approach to therapy, but thinking carefully about what the problem is and how best to approach the solution is an area in which most of us could use some improvement.

The above comments are not meant to suggest that therapy cannot begin until the client has answered hundreds of questions (the issue of questions is addressed below). Part of what we are saying is that problems are frequently very complex, with interlocking pieces. For example, consider the case of a woman who comes to a university counseling center and says, "I am depressed; I think it's because I'm flunking in one of my courses." In such a case you may begin to ask many questions about school. Perhaps the client acknowledges that school is very important—that she has never made less than a *C* before and that if she does now she thinks the world will end. You satisfy yourself that the client (as far as you can tell) has no unconscious wish to fail. You don't think she's trying to punish her parents. You don't think she's delaying "going into the real world." The figures she gives you suggest that many students do fail this particular course. She seems to be taking appropriate steps about her low grade. She has hired a tutor, she has talked to the instructor, she is studying for tests with friends, she has been to the study skills center. She reports that she is not particularly anxious during the tests. You don't see any additional behavioral steps that can be taken to help her improve her grade. Perhaps this area is just not her "cup of tea." You think, "If her grade went up, she would not be depressed." But you don't see how that's going to happen, and you don't think you have much to offer there. She reports that she has never been depressed before except once briefly when she made an *F* on a test. It seems that the depression is situation specific and reactive. If she does make a *D* in the course, she can't seem to think of anything that will happen that will be all that bad—she will just feel bad. You are ready as a therapist to deal with her high standards for herself. She is depressed, you think, because a failing grade in a course means *she* is a failure. She overidentifies with her achievements. Maybe her parents gave her subtle messages about how she needs to achieve for them. So you see the depression, and you think you understand the cause. You are ready to solve the problem with psychotherapy. You spend five sessions focusing on the issue of high standards. She admits that she is impatient with herself. She starts to understand, you think, that she does not have to be perfect. Therapy is progressing. She is still depressed, but you say to yourself, "These things take time." But wait. In the sixth week of therapy, *any* one of the following occurs:

Scenario #1:   Her mother calls and says, "I know Karen is seeing you. I'm very concerned because she seems to be getting more depressed, and last night on the phone she sort of hinted at suicide. I guess she told you about the fact that her fiancé died one year ago this week."

Scenario #2:   You client's roommate calls. "I know I probably shouldn't be calling you, but I was afraid that Karen hadn't told you that she's bulimic. I thought you should know."

Scenario #3:   At the end of the sixth session, your client says, "Well, I guess making a bad grade in calculus isn't so bad after all." She pauses. You say, "So you're not a failure even if your grade isn't all that hot." "Right," she says. "After all, even my older sister, who had a four-point in everything else, made a *B* in calculus."

Scenario #4:   At staffing that week a case is being presented. A female client has come seeking services. She is a lesbian who broke up with a lover two months ago. She wanted to tell the two sets of parents about the relationship. Her lover, who turns out to be your client, wasn't ready to "come out."

No therapist can always zero in on the key issue in the first session or two. (In fact, many cases turn out not to have a single *key* issue.) However, each of the scenarios above is likely a preventable surprise in that if the fictitious therapist had not been so intent on solving the problem of high standards, he or she perhaps would have learned something of the more pressing concern earlier. A good rule of thumb is to repeatedly ask yourself, "Is there something I might be missing here?" or "What cues do I seem to be minimizing?"

Focusing on Someone Other Than the Client

A mistake which is very easy to make when you are just starting out as a therapist is to allow yourself to be drawn into an extended (even repeated) discussion about someone in the client's life other than the client. Consider the following in which a client talks about his family, including his alcoholic mother:

CLIENT: I'm about to tell my brother that this time I am not going to be the one to rescue Mother.
THERAPIST: What do you think your brother will say?
CLIENT: Well, I don't know, but I think it's his turn. I've done it so much. I'm just sick of it. [Pause] It seems like somebody's got to do it; we can't leave her in that house by herself—she has almost died three times. But this time it's up to my brother.
THERAPIST: Will your brother do something about the situation?
CLIENT: Well, my brother is the kind of guy who . . .

In this example the therapist makes the almost immediate mistake of focusing on the brother rather than on the client. Perhaps the client's brother is indeed important in the client's dynamics. Certainly, we know that the family is. But that is not the issue. We emphasize here that the focus of individual therapy should be on the client and not on others. If the brother is a part of the picture, we should deal with that part by seeing how the client's distress is related to the brother. The place to start is with the client, not with the brother. So even if the brother is important in the client's distress, the focus must start with, and work through, the client. (Naturally, these comments are about individual therapy and do not apply if you are doing family therapy.)

Consider a second example in which a client talks about her parents who "treat me like a little girl":

CLIENT: I love them a lot, but I just can't be their little girl forever. They are just so hard to talk to about this.

THERAPIST: Parents can be difficult. Yet I also am guessing that something inside *you* makes this issue tough for you to handle.

CLIENT: Well, when someone says, "You're my little girl, and you always will be," what can you say?

THERAPIST: Perhaps it's tough to get clear in your mind about the kind of relationship you want.

CLIENT: What does it matter if I am clear? I just can't hurt their feelings by saying, "I'm not your little girl." They're going to treat me like that no matter what I do.

THERAPIST: Parents are human too. Do you think that maybe your parents are afraid of losing you completely?

CLIENT: I think you are probably right. They have always centered their life around us kids. I'm the last one, and they must be feeling sort of lonely.

THERAPIST: Well, for example, have your parents started any new activities since you moved to college—something to "fill the void"?

CLIENT: I don't think so. Maybe they could start having more friends over. I could mention that to my mom.

This example illustrates something which happens many times. In the first two interventions, the therapist keeps the focus on the client. However, the client repeatedly talks about her parents. In the third intervention, the therapist should have stayed with the client, perhaps addressing the client's sense of helplessness, her sense of responsibility, perhaps even her love and care for her parents. Instead, the therapist slips into talking about the parents. At first glance the intervention may seem fine. It is likely an accurate statement, and it communicates compassion for the parents. Notice that the client even "reinforces" the therapist for what the therapist has said. Having been reinforced, the therapist continues to focus on the parents, now expanding the focus to include an analysis of the *parents'* problem. The client's problem is now nonexistent. We are not saying that it is wrong to discuss with clients how someone else may be feeling or the motivation for someone else's action. We are saying that such an "educational procedure" should take a back seat to a focus on what is troubling the client.

Trying to Be a Friend

We will make just a few comments about this issue. Most beginning therapists know they should not be "just a friend" to a client. They know, for example, that you should not be having a beer with a client every Friday afternoon. There are a number of actions (innumerable, in fact) which, if taken, suggest that you are perhaps more a friend than a therapist. For example, you should not loan or give money to clients (such requests are most likely to be made in a hospital setting). Don't make a habit of "chatting" with them during the therapy session, don't try to rescue them from difficult situations, refrain from giving advice, and don't comment on the client's personal appearance unless this is an issue in therapy. There are some people with whom you will be very tempted to establish a friendship. For example, there will be those clients who have no friends. You may be tempted to just "let them talk since they have no one to listen to them." Although there are undoubtedly some cases in which the client's "just talking" is therapeutic, more often we view such an arrangement as the therapist selling him or herself short. You are not spending five or six years of your life training to be just "someone who listens," and most of your clients are asking for something more. Social listening may be a component of what you do, but do not allow it, except in very select cases, to define your function as a therapist.

Not Tolerating Silence

We discussed silence to some extent in the chapter "Questions Beginning Therapists Ask." We want to emphasize again that silence is not something bad. It is not a signal that you need to say something. One of the most common mistakes beginning therapists make is not being able to tolerate silence. If you are comfortable with therapeutic silence, the client is more likely to be also and thereby less likely to fill the airways with stories and tangential comments. One of our supervisees, in reflecting on his propensity to say *something* during silence, labeled what he was doing as "production therapy." In production therapy there is a limited amount of time, and products (words) must be produced at a high rate. It is often amazing when we consider the size of the "insight leap" we expect from our clients after only a few seconds of silence. So give your clients, and yourself, time to reflect on what has been said. We encourage you not to slip into "production therapy."

Asking Too Many Questions

We have previously broached this topic both when discussing intake interviewing and in the example of the case in which we provided several possible scenarios which might follow if a therapist fails to consider possible causes for a problem. Furthermore, we noted in the discussion of "too much" mistakes that questions were one example of a response on which we might rely too often. Because we believe that this response is used far too often (particularly after the initial interview), we emphasize here that you should refrain from subjecting the client to an ongoing barrage of questions. Beginning therapists know they shouldn't offer much advice, shouldn't give too much reassurance, shouldn't argue with clients, shouldn't "chat," etc. Having been left with a response repertoire seemingly limited in scope, they easily fall back on the old standby: a question. Yes, you have an ongoing need for information. You will find, however, that clients are much more interested in answering your questions if you provide a little variety. After all, this is an interchange between humans even if there are special ground rules. Consider the following example:

CLIENT: My ex-husband came in my house when he dropped the kids off this time.
THERAPIST: How did you feel about that?
CLIENT: I didn't like it. He won't let me in his house so why should I let him in mine?
THERAPIST: Why *did* you let him in?
CLIENT: I really didn't know what to say. Well, maybe I did want to talk to him.
THERAPIST: Why did you want to talk to him?
CLIENT: We have a lot of problems with the kids—we *do* need to talk.

In the above scenario, the therapist's repeated questions, although they are not necessarily bad ones, pushed the client toward feeling "on the spot." The result is a defensive maneuver in which the client answers the questions on a superficial level. Now consider the following version:

CLIENT: My ex-husband came in my house when he dropped the kids off this time.
THERAPIST: How did you feel about that? I get the impression that's not how it's been before.
CLIENT: You're right. It's a change. It made me angry. He won't let me in his house so why should I let him in?
THERAPIST: That's a good question.
CLIENT: Well, maybe I did want to talk to him.
THERAPIST: [Pause] I think part of what you are saying is that it's hard right now for you to be clear in your mind about how *you* want the relationship to be.
CLIENT: Well, it just seems like this house business is so much like our marriage was. It was always a question of him taking over and me giving in.

In this version the therapist, while still eliciting information, goes about it in a way that helps the client feel less defensive. Here the therapist takes more responsibility for actively trying to understand rather than merely rolling out a list of questions, however well crafted these questions may be.

Not Going into Deeper Levels

This mistake might also be called the "taking things at face value" mistake or the "failing to follow-up" mistake.

THERAPIST: Have you ever thought about seriously injuring yourself?
CLIENT: Sometimes I think I'd be better off dead. [Laughs] I was just kidding—I'd never do anything like that.
THERAPIST: Well, have you ever considered hurting anyone else?

Here the therapist makes a very serious mistake. The therapist seems to accept at face value, and without further exploration, a statement that denies suicidal thoughts just expressed by the client. Instead of going on to the issue of homicidal intent, the therapist should have said something like this: "Well, perhaps you *were* kidding. [Pause] Or maybe you were not. Maybe you were being honest about the way you really *do* feel sometimes. How often have you felt like that?"

As another example of not following up on an important issue, consider the following interchange:

THERAPIST: We talked last week about your mother and how critical of you she often is. How are you feeling about that?
MALE CLIENT: I just decided to ignore it. It doesn't bother me anymore.
THERAPIST: So things are OK now?
MALE CLIENT: Yea.
THERAPIST: Well, do you have some concerns other than your mother?

We are not saying that you should always disbelieve clients. On the other hand, there are many instances when clients do not go into detail and will not do so unless you ask them directly or assist them in exploring their deeper feelings, beliefs, hopes, etc. In the above example, after the client says, "It doesn't bother me anymore," the therapist should have sensed that the client had become anxious about his relationship with his mother and was ready to deny problems as a way of escaping the anxiety. The therapist, by his or her comments, makes it a little too easy for the client to continue the denial. A better response, for example, might have been: "I think what's coming through most clearly to me is that you would sure like to be able to 'ignore it.'" Perhaps you are wondering about what you should do if the client continues to deny the problem. Let's continue the example.

THERAPIST: I think what's coming through most clearly to me is that you would sure like to be able to "ignore it."
[Comment: At this point the therapist uses the language of the client—"ignore it"—rather than the more threatening "ignore your mother."]

CLIENT: That's what I've done this week, and it worked.

THERAPIST: It's tough, I gather, thinking about how *you* feel when she criticized you. Somehow it's tempting to block it all out.

[Comment: Since the client continues to deny the problem, the therapist again chooses a phrase, "block it all out," which is somewhat general in tone.]

CLIENT: Well, as they say, "if it works, do it."

THERAPIST: Would I be wrong in assuming that it's hard work to ignore your mother?

[Comment: Here the therapist picks up on the word *work* and uses it as a bridge to bring the issue of "mother" into the picture. The intervention is perhaps a little risky in that the client has been somewhat defensive about exploring his feelings. On the other hand, most people would agree that it's hard to ignore your mother. In this instance, such an agreement has the effect of focusing on a key element of the problem while simultaneously placing client and therapist together on the same side of the issue.]

CLIENT: Well, maybe a little bit. I just don't intend to let it destroy my life.

THERAPIST: I sense that in some ways your mother's criticism has felt destructive to you—that you really *would* like to ignore her because it hurts so much when she doesn't seem to approve of you.

In the above example, notice how the therapist refused to buy into the client's superficial explanation of "ignoring it works for me." Also, notice that the therapist doesn't say, "Why don't you stop denying that your mother is important to you?" Part of what the therapist is trying to do is talk about the issue in a way that allows the client to show a more vulnerable part of himself. In pursuing this goal, the therapist first addresses the hopes of the client ("want to ignore it"), then how the client feels when he thinks about being criticized, then addresses again the desire to "block it out," and finally makes the discussion more concrete by talking about the difficulty in ignoring mother. At this point the therapist "reaches" the client who opens the door by speaking about what he doesn't want ("to let it destroy my life") rather than continuing the platitude of "I'll ignore it." Notice that the therapist was not dissuaded by the repeated assertions ("I ignore it") of the client. Rather, the therapist continued a pattern of interventions which differed somewhat in their slants but which all continued the focus of client and mother. So in part, your ability to help the client go into deeper levels will depend on your willingness to trust your intuition about problem areas and also on your skill in selecting and using a variety of ways to approach a problem. Resist the temptation to accept from clients explanations that you do not believe. As we imply, you are not issued a license to bang people over the head with reality; rather, we are encouraging you to repeatedly pursue (with adroitness) any issue you feel is central to the client's problem. Additional material concerning this issue can be found in the chapter on resistance.

Poor Phrasing of Interventions

At first glance, the idea that the way we say things is important seems rather simple. After all, psychotherapy almost always involves verbal communication. The principle itself *is* simple. Every therapist would agree that how and when you say things has an impact on the kind of response you are going to receive (e.g., Dowd and Milne, 1986.) So there are various types of interventions which should be avoided because we know that their impact is to cause clients to withdraw, to distort, or to feel that we are not helpful. If any of these actions or feelings on the part of the client persist over time, therapy is likely to be ineffective at best and more likely than not will be terminated. First, the client should not be criticized or blamed. To criticize is not our role, and if we are critical, clients will tend to see us as a member of the large group of people who have already been nasty to them. Most therapists don't directly criticize their clients. However, clients feel criticized when, for example, we are impatient with them, or when we imply that they are not really interested in solving their problem, or when we imply that their behavior was lacking in some important way.

Suppose a client tells a story about the previous evening. He came home drunk, and his wife locked him out of the house. He is now very angry about it, he says. Perhaps you think, "I don't blame her." You are tempted to set him straight, to tell him that she was justified. Instead, depending on how long you have been seeing the client, you might say, "I can see you are very angry. I wonder if it seems easier for you to try to change her than to stop drinking," or "I can see you are very angry. I'm guessing that the helplessness you felt as you tried to get in the house was a little like the helplessness you feel when you think about trying to stop drinking."

There are some phrases you should typically avoid since within our culture they tend to set off defensiveness (not to mention the fact that they are vague). Examples include, "You are feeling sorry for yourself," "Complaining won't change things," and "You are a defensive person." You will find that you will make the mistake of poor phrasing only rarely if you are aware of what clients are feeling and thinking and act on the basis of having some appreciation for the predicaments in which they perceive themselves to be. This procedure does not mean that you support or condone all the activities of the client but rather that your *focus* is on clients' difficulties, not on correcting their values.

Not Finding Out How the Client Has Tried to Solve the Problem

As we discussed earlier, a thorough intake interview should include some idea about how the person has tried to solve the presenting problem. You might be surprised, however, to learn that many therapists plunge into trying to help the client solve the problem without ascertaining what solutions have, so to speak, been found wanting.

One thing which you can find out by pursuing this issue is some idea about how clients may be setting themselves up for failure. It will also give you some idea about what dimensions of the problem seem most central to the client, which aspects seem (to the client) resolvable and which do not, and how sophisticated and informed the client is or is not about therapy. By asking clients how they have tried to solve the problem, you begin the process of helping clients see themselves as able, within some (perhaps limited) area, to take action or make changes, which will help ameliorate the problem. Even if clients cannot at all see themselves in this light at the beginning of therapy, it may give them some "working hope" to hear such a question. Even in the difficult cases for which the question touches off feelings of helplessness and exhaustion, the process of therapy may be started by a discussion of these feelings.

As therapists we are prone to make this mistake because we may see ourselves as possessing special skills to solve problems. In this technocratic view of ourselves, we fail to remember that the client is a participant in the process and the central source of our data about the problem.

Allowing Too Limited a Time to Deal with Termination

Since we devote an entire chapter to the topic of termination, we will make only brief comments here. It is a very bad mistake to terminate therapy without giving the client ample opportunity to discuss and think about what the termination means. Weiner (1975) expresses well the importance of not terminating too hastily:

> Although the conduct of the psychotherapy is governed largely by relative rather than absolute principles, an absolute prescription can be written with respect to termination: never terminate psychotherapy with the session in which termination first comes up for discussion, regardless of how appropriate it is agreed to be. (p. 280)

There are numerous clinical issues involved in termination which we discuss in another chapter. Here, we chiefly emphasize that if you have seen someone several times try to avoid terminating abruptly. As an absolute minimum, try to contract for *at least* one or two more sessions if the client brings up termination abruptly. Of course, you can't force a client to return, and you should not place pressure on them to do so. Nonetheless, abrupt terminations are to be avoided if possible.

There are at least four reasons why therapists fail to allow enough time to deal with termination. One is that the therapist may be underestimating the client's dependency on therapy, in part because the therapist does not feel dependent on the client. A second reason is that the therapist may not want the therapy to end and may be expressing the desire unconsciously by not bringing up the subject. Third, the therapist may be a bit ignorant about generally expected client reactions. Fourth, the therapist may fear that the client will have a strong reaction to the subject of termination and be fearful of what the client might do when the subject is broached.

Not Setting Limits

In the chapter "Questions Beginning Therapists Ask," we addressed some of the potential events which may call for you to set appropriate limits. These include things like missing appointments, wanting to start early or late, and repeatedly calling you at home. In our efforts to be understanding and tolerant, we may occasionally lose sight of the fact that it does clients a great disservice to allow them to use (ultimately) dysfunctional strategies in pursuit of their goals in therapy. For example, let us say that a woman comes seeking help for her failing marriage. We recommend marital therapy. The husband comes, and treatment seems to be progressing. After eight to ten sessions the woman indicates that she wants to see the therapist for individual sessions also, in order for her to work on how to deal with her aging parents. The therapist assumes that there may be some connection between the request and how therapy is progressing, but the connection is unclear, and the idea of simultaneous marital and individual therapy is not at variance with the theoretical orientation of the therapist. The therapist and the woman agree that the individual sessions will not focus on her relationship with her husband. In the second individual session, the woman says, "It is so much easier to talk to you when my husband is not in the room. I just feel safer. Today I'd like to talk about why I don't seem to trust my husband." As in previous examples, there are many aspects to the client's statement on which we might focus. The central point we make here is that in such an instance you cannot allow yourself to be "seduced" into breaking your previous agreement. This is an example of a situation in which it is imperative that limits be set. If you are not strong enough to set and hold to limits, your clients cannot possibly trust you with their craziness.

Holding Too Much Back from the Client

As we have said previously, individuals who have chosen to be therapists generally have a very strong urge to protect and help others. This urge helps make you a good therapist because a caring attitude serves as both a motivator for you to help and as a personality feature to which your clients will be drawn. Unfortunately, this positive, caring attitude may at times lead us to make the therapeutic mistake of holding too much back from the client. If you are wondering whether saying a certain thing to a client would be helpful or not, you might ask yourself whether *you* would be strong enough to have a therapist say that to you without your becoming defensive. If the answer is yes, perhaps the client is stronger than you are giving him or her credit for. On the many occasions when we have asked our supervisees, "What would you like to say to the client?" we have found more often than not that the therapist's instincts were right on target and that the client would, we believed, benefit from the intervention contemplated by the therapist. What we are saying is not an excuse to blast the client with every raw insight you have. It is, instead, encouragement to see your clients as resilient, coping human beings who may not need as much protection as you might at first believe.

There is a second reason why therapists at times make the mistake of holding things back from the client. They may not trust themselves to handle the difficult situation which they fear will follow talking about an "unpleasant" or emotionally charged topic. For example, perhaps the therapist senses that therapy has become a "chore" for the client and that the client is "putting in time" more than actively participating in therapy. Naturally, there is the intellectual puzzle of trying to understand why this is happening. But there is also a very personal, emotional issue for the therapist when thinking about broaching a topic which may lead to a statement such as, "I no longer find your comments to be all that helpful," or "We just don't seem to be clicking anymore." Thus, holding back your thoughts may at times reflect your fears about yourself and how you are viewed by the client.

Discussing a Problem Only Once

One fear most therapists have is that they will "say the obvious," or perhaps more to the point, we as therapists fear that the *client* will say or imply that we are making a comment which is obvious (see chapter on therapists' fears). As a defense against this fear, we may make the mistake of discussing something once with the client and then assuming that the issue has been "dealt with." A number of years ago one of the authors heard a counselor describing a marital case in which one spouse had had an affair. The counselor, who had apparently been poorly trained, indicated that he had said something like the following to the couple: "We will discuss this affair thoroughly, but then we will put it behind us. We will not bring it up again. We will lay the issue to rest." This view of therapy is a naive one. The assumption that an issue can be talked about one time and then "laid to rest" is simply not true. Nonetheless, it is easy to fall into the trap of believing, for example, that if you discuss the client's angry feelings toward his or her mother once it would be redundant to talk about the issue again. Suppose a client is prone to being very self-critical. You point out that as a child he learned to criticize himself before his father could. The client agrees. He says, "So now that I'm an adult maybe I have no one to fear, but I still act as if I do." You say, "That's right. Now you need not be afraid. The only tyrant left is yourself." He says, "Well, I'm through being a tyrant. I'm going to give myself a long vacation.

It feels good to figure this out—to know I don't have to be afraid so I don't have to worry." Is this the end of the matter? Does the client live happily ever after? Probably not. Certainly, he has taken a first crucial step toward reducing a personal characteristic (self-criticism) that he finds very bothersome. But it would be a great mistake to assume that just because he has had this insight the issue of his self-criticism will not need to be discussed again. As behavioral scientists we do not completely understand why it is so, but there seem to be aspects of well-learned behavior that make it very difficult to change quickly, especially if the behavior involves strong emotions. It is important to remember that psychotherapy is a predominantly verbal interaction which has very real limits in terms of how quickly and the extent to which it can produce behavioral (including attitude and emotional) change. As one of the "substitutes" for the limits, we use a certain kind of repetitiveness. Going over the issue again and again with the client is typically necessary for several reasons. For example, those of us who are not behaviorists still recognize the powerful force the environment plays in eliciting and maintaining behavior. After we discuss an issue with clients, they go back out into the interpersonal world with which they had reached an accommodation based on neurotic behavior patterns. This interpersonal world is typically not as supportive and understanding of the changes being tried by clients as was the therapist. Often this interpersonal world fights back, and clients struggle to remain a part of their world yet make the changes they talked about in therapy. In such instances, the therapist and the healthy part of the client have one hour (or so) a week to influence the client whereas the environment has 167 hours a week of influence. The client is certainly a part of these other hours (and so is the therapist to the extent that the client identifies with the therapist), but it doesn't take a genius to figure out that a ratio of 167 to 1 is a bit unbalanced. One of our primary tools to offset this imbalance is that as therapists we help the client *focus, repeatedly* on an issue.

On the other hand, perhaps the environment is very supportive of the changes the client is making. Yet since the client has constructed an elaborate inner world to make sense of previous experience and get ready for new experiences, new perspectives tend to be short-lived at first. Thus, while in the powerfully supportive and limited time space of a therapeutic hour the old perspective may be temporarily swept away, it is not one insight that must be added or one idea that must be changed. It is an interlocking grid of assumptions, adaptations, and emotional reactions which make clients prisoners in their own houses. So even when the environment is very supportive, what we might call a "one discussion cure" is very rare. We must go over and over an issue with a client because it is only through this repetition that the underlying grid is slowly changed. In truth, we would not want it any other way. For if a large and lasting change in personality structure could be the result of a one-time discussion, our clients (and ourselves) would be the unwitting dupes of countless interpersonal con-artists. We know, of course, that some people are more easily duped than others.

But we also know that each of us has a constructed identity and belief world which by its interlocking nature is more suited to gradual evolution than to easy and quick transformation.

Moralizing or Passing Judgment on the Client's Problem

Psychotherapists, like all other human beings, do and should have moral standards. There is general agreement in the profession, however, that the role of the therapist is not to pass judgment. We perhaps adopt this role of being nonjudgmental in part because it seems to fit our personal values. Perhaps to an even greater degree, we adopt this role because passing moral judgment is thought, in the majority of cases, to decrease the probability of change. The stance we assume is one of trying to understand clients rather than to judge them. William Styron (1980), in his novel *Sophie's Choice*, describes an emotionally wrenching scene in which Sophie is brought to Auschwitz with her two children. In the "selection" line, the Nazi physician tells Sophie that she can keep one of her children but that she must *choose* which one is to live and which one is to die. One is tempted to label the physician as evil and stop at that point. The narrator, however, does what psychotherapists must do as they sit across from the client—he attempts to understand the forces which have set in motion this aberration, this terrible deed:

> I have always assumed that when he encountered Sophie, Dr. Jemand von Niemand was undergoing the crisis of his life: cracking apart like bamboo. . . . The renewed horror scraped like steel files at the doctor's soul, threatened to shred his reason. He began to drink, to acquire sloppy eating habits, and to miss God. *Wo, wo ist derr lebende Gott?* Where is the God of my fathers?
>
> But of course the answer finally dawned on him, and one day I suspect the revelation made him radiant with hope. It had to do with the matter of sin, or rather, it had to do with the absence of sin, and his own realization that the absence of sin and the absence of God were inseparably intertwined. No sin! He had suffered boredom and anxiety, and even revulsion, but no sense of sin from the bestial crimes he had been party to, nor had he felt that in sending thousands of the wretched innocent to oblivion he had transgressed against divine law. All had been unutterable monotony. All of his depravity had been enacted in a vacuum of sinless and businesslike godlessness, while his soul thirsted for beatitude.
>
> Was it not supremely simple, then, to restore his belief in God, and at the same time to affirm his human capacity for evil, by committing the most intolerable sin that he was able to conceive? Goodness could come later. But first a choice. After all, he had the power to take both. This is the only way I have been able to explain what Dr. Jemand von Niemand did to Sophie when she appeared with her two little children on April Fools' Day, while the wild tango beat of "La Cumparsita" drummed and rattled insistently off-key in the gathering dusk. (pp. 592–593)

We are not suggesting that the narrator has an accurate understanding of the physician's behavior and motivations. Rather, our emphasis is on the fact that the narrator *attempts to understand* the physician at a level that goes beyond merely making a moral judgment. Of course, to understand some of the forces propelling the physician in no way excuses him for his terrible deed. In our view, however, clients can seldom be helped by therapists who pass moral judgments to the exclusion of helping the client struggle toward an understanding of his or her needs, and this includes clients who have violated acceptable moral standards. This is a part of the special relationship we offer clients—we are committed to helping that part of the client which sought expression of a healthy need but which did so in an ill-chosen or regrettable form.

It is important to remember that cultural factors influence how we view the "acceptability" of a problem. Furthermore, many potential mistakes with ethnic minority clients may be avoided by the therapist being familiar with research and theorizing concerning racial/ethnic issues (Helmes, 1984; Parham, 1989).

SUMMARY

All therapists, whether experienced or inexperienced, make mistakes. We agree with Earl Koile (personal communication, 1974) that the issue is not whether one makes a mistake but rather how one recovers from it. The mistakes we make as therapists provide the foundation for an increasing sensitivity to the way people make sense of their world, the ways in which they may be caught by what they experience, and the high drama with which their struggles are played out. In turn, this increased sensitivity, coupled with developing technical skills, enables us to better respond to those who seek our assistance. When we make big mistakes as a therapist, we are reminded of our limits. Whatever other things are to be learned from a mistake, surely this reminder is a valuable one.

12

ETHICAL AND LEGAL ISSUES

Lodovico [*To Iago*]: O spartan dog,
More fell than anguish, hunger, or the sea.
Look on the tragic loading of this bed;
This is thy work . . .

　To you, lord governor,
Remains the censure of this hellish villain;
The time, the place, the torture,—O, enforce it.

　　　　　　　　　　　　　　　　　　—Othello

ETHICS

As we read Shakespeare's *Othello*, we perhaps assume that we need little reflection to know our feelings for Iago. He is false; his treachery is unbounded; and he seems to know nothing of kindness, decency, or commitment to others. We do not like this man. We can know some of our standards and values by experiencing our reactions to Iago. Our emotional reactions help us to define the kinds of principles in which we believe, to which we are committed, and on which we wish to act. Even though it may initially be helpful, this use of Iago is somewhat limited. For we must often struggle with questions such as, "What is the best way to be committed to another's welfare?" or "When does our trust in the one threaten the good of the many?"

There is a second way in which Iago can help us, and it is less limited than the first. If we can avoid defensiveness, Iago can perhaps help us recognize in ourselves the kinds of impulses which we are so quick to condemn in others. In turn, this recognition of our frailties helps us understand that people who violate ethical standards are human beings like us and that ethical principles, while often helpful, do not represent easy solutions to difficult problems. Good solutions to dilemmas are found in part by application of critical reasoning. Just as important, however, is that the person trying to apply ethical principles has a felt identity for the limitations of human beings. This idea is expressed well by George Eliot, as quoted by Carol Gilligan (1982):

> We have no master-key that will fit all cases [of moral decision] . . . general rules [will not lead people] to justice by a ready-made patent method, without the trouble of exerting patience, discrimination, impartiality, without any care to assure whether they have the insight that comes from a hardly-earned estimate of temptation or from a life vivid and intense enough to have created a wide, fellow feeling with all that is human. (p. 148)

The necessity of having this "wide, fellow feeling with all that is human" is easily seen when we consider many of the cases in which human beings have sought to stand in moral judgment of their fellow human beings. From the witch trials of Salem to the case of Salman Rushdie, one sees clearly the problems which arise when moral judgment is wielded in the absence of empathic identification. Perhaps the first ethical principle should be, "Remember that we are all human."

Ethical principles may be seen as arising from a number of sources and processes. One such source is moral reasoning. Among others, Hare (1981) and Kitchener (1984) have discussed two broad levels of moral reasoning. The first, called the Intuitive Level, is the "ordinary moral sense" we have as a result of living and interacting with others. The second level, called the "Critical-Evaluation Level," includes rules (e.g., professional codes), principles (e.g., autonomy, nonmalfeasance, beneficence, justice, and fidelity), and ethical theory. Kitchener suggests that these five principles just listed "constitute an initial foundation for the critical evaluation of ethical reasoning in the context of counseling and psychology." Put slightly differently, these principles may be seen as undergirding the *Ethical Principles of Psychologists.*

It is important to emphasize that true ethical codes are built on principles of behavior we value for itself and not on behavior which is mandated. That is, in the ideal, these codes are adopted voluntarily by members of a profession. It is perhaps also important to emphasize, however, that in the final analysis ethical codes are in fact tied to good practice in a very practical way. For example, when we say that clients should be able to discuss their problems without fear of our telling others what they have revealed (the principle of confidentiality), we adopt this stance, not just because "nice people don't tattle," but also because we fear we will not be able to help people unless they can trust us not to talk about them to others. Similarly, we say that a therapist should not engage in dual relationships in part because experience has shown that such relationships hinder therapy and run an inordinate risk of psychological damage to the client. In short, good ethics are good practice. In fact, there is some evidence to suggest that therapists' standards for good practice may even be more stringent than published ethical principles (Pope, Tabachnick, and Keith-Spiegel, 1988).

Resources

A number of resources are available to assist psychotherapists and counselors who are confronted with ethical dilemmas or who wish to be better informed about ethical principles. These include (but are not limited to) the *Ethical Principles of Psychologists* (American Psychological Association [APA], 1981), *Casebook on Ethical Principles of Psychologists* (APA, 1987), *Guidelines for Therapy with Women* (Task Force on Sex Bias and Sex Role Stereotyping in Psychotherapeutic Practice, 1978), and *General Guidelines for Providers of Psychological Services* (APA, 1987). The American Association for Counseling and Development and its various divisions have also published several related documents. Additionally, there have been many books and articles published about ethics in psychology in the last few years. For example, the APA Board of Professional Affairs (Committee on Professional Standards) and the APA Ethics Committee each have published a number of articles in the journal *American Psychologist*. Because there are so many resources available, this chapter will merely highlight a few of the ethical issues related to psychotherapy. The References/Selected Recommended Reading List at the end of the book includes several articles which, although not specifically cited in this chapter, may be helpful for the reader who wishes to read more widely about ethical and legal issues in psychotherapy. We especially recommend the *Casebook on Ethical Principles of Psychologists* (APA, 1987) and the book *Ethics in Psychology* (Keith-Spiegel and Koocher, 1985).

We will now comment briefly on parts of four of the ten principles listed in the *Ethical Principles of Psychologists*. The four principles on which we will comment are Competence, Confidentiality, Client Welfare, and Professional Relationships. We chose these four in part based on the types of questions raised by our students. All ten of the principles and all aspects of each principle are, of course, important, and psychotherapists have an ethical obligation to abide by the complete set of principles. We are choosing some aspects on which to comment, rather than others, as a matter of emphasis, not importance. (Note: As this book goes to press, the 1981 version of the *Ethical Principles of Psychologists* is under revision. It is likely that the revision will include many of the issues raised in the 1981 document.)

Competence

Accurately represent your training. In an earlier chapter, we noted that you should inform clients if you are a student in training. You also have an obligation to ensure that, for example, neither clients nor others "inadvertently" think you have a Ph.D. when you don't. Another example would be a case where one was trained as a clinical psychologist but, in an attempt to obtain a position at a university counseling center which was seeking a counseling psychologist, suggested in some explicit or implicit way that one was a counseling psychologist. APA has taken the position that you can claim a specialty area only if you were trained in that area, by a recognized program which publicly purports to train in the specialty area. (In our view, some of the APA definitions of specialty areas are in need of revision; however, under current APA ethical principles, there are some rather stringent limitations on how one can define her or his specialty area.) Furthermore, individuals who hold a master's degree should not, in the view of APA, refer to themselves as, for example, an industrial/organizational psychologist, a clinical psychologist, etc. This issue can be very confusing because some stage agencies have created job titles like "psychologist I" or "clinical psychologist" which do not, by job requirements, mandate a doctoral degree. Legally, individuals probably cannot be prevented from using their job title, but from an ethical perspective, such a presentation should never be used to represent one's credentials. It is important to emphasize that one's ethical responsibilities involve not just avoiding actually committing an overt unethical act but require one to correct misperceptions that have arisen due to no fault on the part of one's self.

Recognize the limits of your competence. At times a supervisor may assign you a case which you believe is outside your area of competence. If this should happen, you have an ethical responsibility to discuss the issue with your supervisor. Treatment procedures which you have "read about" but have not actually been trained to apply certainly demand close supervision. In particular, beginning therapists may assume that with a little reading they can institute a behavioral intervention like desensitization. We reject, and we assume other therapists do also, the idea that certain interventions are very simple ones with little training needed to implement them. As a minimum one needs to be able to conduct a very careful assessment of whether such an intervention is called for or not.

At times it may also be important to inform clients of the limits of your competency. For example, suppose that a client brings you pictures drawn by his five-year-old because the client is disturbed by the pictures. Suppose further that you have no training in child assessment. Whether the pictures do or don't look disturbing to you, it is your ethical responsibility to inform the client that you are not trained to interpret such material and that you will be happy to refer the client to someone who is.

Responsibility to seek and use supervision.   Most beginning therapists do not need too much encouragement to seek supervision because they experience it as helpful. In some cases, however, a supervisor may be perceived as not helpful. In such cases it is a very human reaction to withdraw and cease bringing up the more troubling aspects of one's interactions with clients. Before this gets very far, we strongly encourage you to process the issue with your supervisor, or if that does not seem workable, ask for another supervisor. Your clients have a right to be seen by someone who is being actively supervised by a competent supervisor with whom the therapist is working effectively. As we have previously suggested, when in doubt as to whether you need supervision concerning a development in therapy, the rule is unambiguous: seek supervision.

Responsibility to recognize differences among people.   Sensitivity to issues affected by gender, ethnicity, culture, sexual preference, age, etc., is an ethical responsibility. There are a number of resources available to help you in this regard. For example, the Office of Ethnic Minority Affairs of the American Psychological Association can make available the following (and other) resources: a bibliography on counseling and psychotherapy with Blacks, Asian Americans, and Hispanic Americans; a bibliography of texts on psychology, ethnicity, and culture; a directory of ethnic minority professionals in psychology; and a bibliography on the health of native Americans and Alaskan natives. We have already mentioned the *Guidelines for Therapy with Women.* Both Division 35 (Psychology of Women) and Division 17 (Counseling Psychology) of the American Psychological Association have made substantial contributions to our growing awareness of ethical issues as they relate to gender. For example, the January 1986 issue of *The Counseling Psychologist* (the journal of Division 17) contains the Division 17 Principles Concerning the Counseling/Psychotherapy of Women, together with comments on rationale and implementation.

Limits imposed by your personal problems.   You have an ethical responsibility to be aware of how your personal difficulties may be affecting your performance as a therapist. Such impact might take the form of a temporary general decline in your therapeutic skills or special difficulty with a particular client. If you are, for example, in the process of divorcing your spouse, it may be hard for you to ensure therapeutic objectivity with members of the opposite sex or with any client also in the process of a divorce. If you have just been denied a promotion, individuals who are particularly ambitious or conversely, who are underachievers may pose problems for you. Or if there has been a death in your family, you may fall victim to seeing death anxiety in many of your clients. Most therapists are at least somewhat aware of the potential for over- or underidentification with clients during personally troubled times. However, it is important to get in the habit of periodically thinking about how your personal life may be affecting your therapy. There is further discussion of this issue in the chapter "Transference/Countertransference."

Confidentiality

No part of the ethical code has been written about as much as has this principle. Confidentiality is certainly a keystone of psychotherapy. It is an ethical principle rather than a legal one. The parallel legal construct is privileged communication, and legal statutes spell out under what conditions a therapist can be compelled to break confidentiality—that is, under what conditions the communication between therapist and client is no longer "privileged" (DeKraai and Sales, 1982). Earlier we commented on the issue of talking to your clients about confidentiality. We also addressed the issue of when confidentiality can or should be broken. In a study of counselor trustworthiness, Merluzzi and Brischetto (1983) found that "counselors who breached confidentiality in cases involving highly serious problems were perceived as less trustworthy."

The repeated emphasis in the literature on the importance of confidentiality is there not only because confidentiality is so central to the process of therapy but perhaps also because there are so many ways in which we may inadvertently compromise this principle. Mythology (Warner, 1967) records what was perhaps the first case in which confidentiality was accidentally breached. The story involved Midas, who, following his predicament with the "golden touch," became embroiled in a dispute as to whether Pan or Apollo played better music:

> All agreed with the judgment of the mountain god—all except Midas, who kept disputing it and calling it unjust. Apollo then decided that he was unworthy to have human ears. He made them move from the base. In all other ways Midas was human: only as a punishment for his bad taste, he had the ears of an ass.
> Naturally he was ashamed of them and covered them up in a purple turban which he wore upon his head. But the servant who used to cut his hair discovered his secret. He dared not tell others what he had discovered, but he could not bear to keep the secret to himself. So he went out and dug a hole in the ground. Kneeling down he whispered into the hole: "King Midas has asses' ears." Then he carefully put back the earth and went away, relieved that he had spoken the words, even though no one had heard them. But a crop of whispering reeds sprang up in the place, and, when they were full-grown and swayed by the winds of the autumn, they repeated the words that were buried at their roots. "Midas has asses' ears," they said to every breeze, and the breezes carried on the news. (pp. 129–130)

One issue which can be particularly difficult is when clients are using a third party (such as an insurance company) to pay for treatment. Some companies require a periodic review of cases if they are to continue paying and may request information from the therapist. It is important for therapists to inform clients of these sorts of situations before they arise. Although we as therapists are not necessarily expected to be familiar with all companies and their policies, we are expected to inform clients of the range of requirements mandated by third-party payers. Of course, a signed release of information form is needed whenever information is to be provided companies, agencies, or other professionals.

Client Welfare

Dual relationships.   There is a growing body of literature which suggests that dual relationships, particularly sexual ones, are deleterious to those who engage in them (Bouhoutsos, Holroyd, Lerman, Forer, and Greenberg, 1983; Glaser and Thorpe, 1986; Pope and Bouhoutsos, 1986; Pope, Keith-Spiegel, and Tabachnick, 1986). The ethical principles state, "Sexual intimacies with clients are unethical." There is also a growing interest in the issue of therapists' relationships with former clients (Akamatsu, 1988; Gottlieb, Sell, and Schoenfeld, 1988). Gottlieb et al. have specifically proposed that the ethical principles be amended to say that sexual intimacies with former clients are unethical. Glaser and Thorpe (1986), as well as Robinson and Reid (1985), provided evidence that sexual relationships between graduate students and professors are often later perceived by the former students as harmful. Davenport (1983) has suggested that such relationships be considered clearly unethical.

The general principle concerning dual relationships is that professionals attempting to carry on relationships which involve conflicting or potentially conflicting roles are subjecting the other person to a set of unreasonable risks (they are also subjecting themselves, and at times other people as well, to a similar set of risks). The idea that dual relationships are to be avoided has a long history. For example, the military typically discourages intimate relationships between officers and enlisted personnel. Similarly, in the play *Becket* (Anouilh, 1960), King Henry II tells Thomas Becket that he wants Becket to be archbishop. Becket responds with several "excuses" but finally realizes that the king is serious:

> BECKET: My Lord, I see now that you weren't joking. Don't do this.
>   KING: Why not?
> BECKET: It frightens me.
>   KING: Becket, this is an order!
> BECKET: [*Gravely*] If I become Archbishop, I can no longer be your friend. (p. 72)

Thus, Becket recognizes the danger of dual relationships and attempts to warn Henry of one of the consequences. Of course, the king did not heed Becket, and tragedy followed.

The APA *Casebook on Ethical Principles of Psychologists* (1987) gives a number of good examples of dual relationships which should be avoided. These include seeing as a client someone you are supervising and agreeing to see someone as a client with whom you have had a friendship. Also, one should avoid serving as the instructor of a group process course, which is in reality psychotherapy for the participants, if there are students in the course with whom one would have additional relationships (such as serving on advisory committees). Each of the above examples constitutes a dual relationship and is to be avoided.

Termination when client is not benefiting from psychotherapy.   Our obligation is to terminate the therapy relationship when it becomes, in the words of the *Ethical Principles,* "reasonably clear" that the client is not benefiting from it. The point is also made that the therapist must offer to assist the client in locating alternative sources of help. Perhaps the slightly broader issue here is that the client's progress in, and satisfaction with, psychotherapy should be periodically discussed with the client. Unfortunately, clients often want to protect the feelings (or at least what they imagine to be the feelings) of the therapist and hence may be reluctant to articulate their dissatisfactions. At times the therapist may be subtly or unconsciously encouraging the client to be satisfied when he or she is not. Such unconscious needs on the part of the therapist are especially detrimental because they keep clients locked into a process which is not helpful while simultaneously communicating to them that they *ought* to be satisfied with what they are receiving. Unfortunately, this process is often a recapitulation of earlier interpersonal learning environments, so many clients may be especially vulnerable to a cycle in which their needs are *not* met, the psychotherapist communicates that their needs *are* being met, the clients feel guilty, blame themselves for lack of progress, and ultimately conclude that their needs are unimportant. This process is at complete variance with our intention to have clients reach a point where they can recognize, articulate, and act upon their fundamental needs. It is also at complete variance with our ethical responsibility to protect the welfare of our clients.

Informing clients of their rights.   Interestingly, the *Ethical Principles* do not specifically mention that clients in psychotherapy must be informed of their rights although the rights of research subjects are clearly spelled out. Principle six does state that "psychologists fully inform consumers as to the purpose and nature of an evaluative, treatment, educational, or training procedure, and they freely acknowledge that clients, students, or participants in research have freedom of choice with regard to participation." Principle five says, "Where appropriate, psychologists inform their clients of the legal limits of confidentiality." Principle three says, "In their professional roles, psychologists avoid any action that will violate or diminish the legal and civil rights of clients or of others who may be affected by their action."

Although the *Ethical Principles* do not make explicit the requirement that clients routinely be informed of their rights, this issue has received considerable attention (e.g., Everstine et al., 1980; Handelsman and Galvin, 1988; Handelsman, Kemper, Kesson-Craig, McLain, and Johnsrud, 1986; Hare-Mustin, Marecek, Kaplean, and Liss-Levinson, 1979; Talbert and Pipes, 1988). The Everstine et al. and Hare-Mustin et al. articles give good discussions of clients' rights and make specific proposals for the kind of written information a client should receive. Handelsman et al. and Talbert and Pipes concluded that clients typically do *not* receive extensive information about their rights. Based on a review of the literature, Talbert and Pipes identified 19 possible elements of an informed consent form, including (a) the right to switch therapists; (b) statement about referrals to other psychologists; (c) mention of community resources as an option; (d) right to end therapy; (e) statement concerning risks of unpleasant emotions; (f) statement concerning risks of change in relationships; (g) limits of confidentiality; and other risks, rights, and information. Handelsman and Galvin (1988) provided an excellent example of a document which might be given to clients to help them understand their rights. We think that this document is an especially good one because by listing questions a client might want to ask the therapist it encourages client-therapist interaction. The document is reproduced as the appendix to this chapter.

There are a number of reasons why therapists are reluctant to use extensive written descriptions of informed consent for therapy, but presumably one concern is how to describe all the various conditions under which confidentiality might be broken. The conditions vary by state but include such circumstances as child abuse, felonies, situations in which individuals make their mental health a legal issue, and others. Because this list can be rather long (e.g., DeKraai and Sales, 1982) and because each of the circumstances can be quite complicated, it is understandable why therapists might be reluctant to try to put all of this in writing. One idea is to say something to the effect that confidentiality will be protected to the limits of the law.

Commitment to the client.   It is very important that you be clear on who is your client and to whom you have primary responsibility. It is also important that you be clear with your client about what responsibilities you have to the agency if you are employed by one. Most therapists begin with the assumption that the person who is coming to see them is the person for whom they have responsibility. This is a good starting assumption; however, there may be complications. For example, what should you do if a client tells you that his or her mother is threatening suicide? What should you do if a person calls you on the telephone and says, "Your client is my roommate, and he is scaring me to death with all his talk about guns?" What should you do if a client says, "I'm going to take everything I can from my husband in the divorce settlement?" What if a client says, "My roommate treats me like dirt, so I'm going to get his girlfriend in bed?" Principles of good therapy aside, in each of these cases you must remember who is your client. It is not your job to save the client's mother from suicide, comfort a roommate who is frightened (although one would scarcely be blasé about such dangerous situations), ensure a fair divorce settlement, or uphold commonly accepted notions of decency and trust. Naturally, you may (and probably would like to) have some impact on these situations. But it is very important that you keep focused on the fact that the client who came to see you is where your loyalty, energy, and commitment must lie.

Marital and family therapy represent more difficult cases. A complete discussion of the perspective various therapists take on this issue is beyond the scope of this book. However, as we suggested earlier, it is advisable to set up the therapy situation so that you are as clear as you can be on your primary responsibilities and so that clients are clearly informed of your commitments.

Certainly, if other people are in danger from the client, you may need to take some action. But in the midst of action, you must never forget the welfare of your client.

Professional Relationships

Respect for other professionals. Unfortunately, the various helping professionals (e.g., psychology, counseling, psychiatry, and social work) do not always seem to respect each others' competencies. Nonetheless, we must take as our ideal the broad-minded recognition of both common and diverse strengths among these professions. Stereotyping and making caustic remarks about other professions do not advance our own profession. Certainly, there may be legitimate disagreements. However, and in particular where a client's interests are concretely involved, our ethical responsibility is to ensure that clients can benefit from the full range of available services.

We also have an ethical responsibility to show respect for other psychotherapists. Although the *Ethical Principles* (as of June 2, 1989) no longer prohibit offering psychotherapeutic services directly to a client who is being seen by another therapist, caution is still urged. Furthermore, prospective clients should be asked if they are currently being seen in treatment. Only in very unusual circumstances should you agree to see such a client before contacting the other therapist. An exception to the rule would be if the other therapist seems to be engaging in unethical behavior and the client asks that you not contact the therapist. Even in such a situation you would obviously try to deal with the client's anxieties and obtain permission to contact the other therapist. One reason you should do this is that the client's version of what happened in therapy may be at variance with the facts of the case. For example, we know of one situation in which a prospective client told a new therapist that the issue of termination was thoroughly discussed with a previous therapist. After seeing the client for several sessions, the therapist learned that in reality there had been no termination and that the client had in fact abruptly stopped coming in the middle of therapy, which was a recurrent pattern for him. Needless to say, the therapist who was now seeing the client was thus in a difficult position. Clearly, it is very important to "check the facts," especially if the client *says* that he or she is in therapy. The issue of being cautious about seeing clients who are currently being seen by other therapists is a good example of how *ethical* behavior goes hand in hand with good *psychotherapeutic* principles.

Conduct of colleagues. We assume that the reader is familiar with the requirement that when unethical behavior is observed one has an obligation to address the issue, whether by talking to the colleague and/or reporting her or him to the appropriate board or committee. Thus, the chief points we wish to emphasize here are the importance of (a) trusting your intuition when something bothers you and (b) seeking consultation from peers, supervisors, and/or the APA ethics committee if you are wondering if something is ethical. By "trusting your intuition," we mean simply that if something seems wrong it is inappropriate to shrug it off by saying something like, "Well, that person has a Ph.D. and I don't so they probably know what they are doing," or, "I guess there will always be differences," or, "I don't have all the facts," etc. Even though you should not ignore your intuition that something is unethical, neither should you completely trust your intuition when your "gut feeling" is that a behavior (either a colleague's or your own) is ethical. If you are unsure, no matter which way you are "leaning," you need to seek consultation.

As we earlier suggested, if a client complains of the behavior of a colleague, you have an obligation to try to get all the facts in the case. Certainly, any serious allegations should be thoroughly discussed with clients, and they should be informed fully as to their rights and the various options available to them. This is also a good example of the importance of being fully committed to your client's welfare. For example, your client might initially say, "I just want to write my previous therapist a letter." Under those conditions you should not pressure the client to file a lawsuit or take some other more drastic action. Conversely, if the client says, "I intend to sue," you certainly should not stand in his or her way but neither should you assume that a lawsuit is what the client really wants. Perhaps she or he just wants an opportunity to confront the other therapist. The key point is that after informing clients of all their options, you should work with them to help them select the option that is most likely to give them what they are looking for. Naturally, one's theoretical orientation, as well as one's personality, influences the degree to which one would want to be actively and continuously involved in the course of action chosen by a client who has been adversely affected by unethical behavior.

RECORD KEEPING AND LEGAL ISSUES

Record Keeping

In the chapter "Questions Beginning Therapists Ask," we commented briefly on some principles of record keeping, such as whether it is permissible to keep personal notes and what you should write in progress notes. For a good summary of issues involved in record keeping, we especially recommend the article by Soisson, VandeCreek, and Knapp (1987). Quoting the *Specialty Guidelines for Clinical Psychologists* (APA, 1981b), Soisson et al. note that in the absence of state or federal statutes a full record is to be kept for at least three years and the summary disposed of no sooner than 15 years. Interestingly, the *Specialty Guidelines for Counseling Psychologists* (APA, 1981c) stipulate that a full record must be kept for four years, with disposition of the summary allowed no sooner than seven years. We recommend that you follow the more conservative guideline in cases of doubt.

As each set of *Specialty Guidelines* and Soisson et al. point out, clients have a right to have access to the information in their files. The laws spelling out the exact nature of this right vary from state to state. The ethical responsibility is to allow clients to know *what* is in their files, although there is no *ethical* requirement to show the client every piece of paper in the file. In fact, showing clients notes or raw data might be considered unethical. Almost certainly, it would be considered unethical to hand a client his or her file containing extensive technical notes and then leave the room and not provide explanation. On the other hand, some states may require (in the legal sense) that a client be allowed to see all the contents of the file. Naturally, you should be familiar with the laws of your state concerning this matter, as well as any guidelines currently being used by the agency where you are working.

Finally, with regard to this issue of record keeping, we underscore the potential clinical significance of clients asking (or demanding) to see the contents of their file. As we said above, clients certainly have legal rights in this area. Nonetheless, it is important to try to understand in a nondefensive way what clients are concerned about when they make such a request. Some clients may be legitimately concerned about legal issues, wondering about the kind of information which may be available to their insurance company, or concerned about some other important aspect related to their records. Other clients may actually be more interested in hearing from you what your impressions are of them but may be afraid to ask or may be more comfortable with a "legal approach." In such instances, the nature of your relationship with the client is the real issue and should be processed. It is very important to remember that not every client request or demand represents a hidden challenge to, or implicit criticism of, the therapist. Clients will from time to time take positions with which we are in disagreement. This is as it should be, and clients who raise potential differences with us must be respected for their positions.

Malpractice

Malpractice in psychotherapy has been described by a number of writers (e.g., Cohen, 1979; Cavanaugh and Rogers, 1983; Harris, 1973; Deardorff, Cross, and Hupprich, 1984; VandeCreek, Knapp, and Herzog, 1988; Wright, 1981). To prove malpractice, the person filing the case must show four things: (a) that the defendant owed a "duty" to the plaintiff (this is normally established by pointing to the existence of the therapeutic relationship); (b) that the defendant failed to perform the duty (established by showing that the defendant failed to provide a standard of care expected of someone with similar training and experience); (c) that the plaintiff suffered harm (this might be either physical or psychological damage); and (d) that the defendant was the direct and proximate cause of the damage. In particular, the last of these four can be very difficult to prove since psychotherapists chiefly use words as their mode of intervention. A number of "grounds" for malpractice have been identified, including the following: (a) unauthorized release of information; (b) negligent treatment of suicidal or aggressive patients; (c) a sexual relationship between patient and therapist; (d) failure to diagnose properly; (e) improper hospitalization; (f) failure to keep adequate records; and (g) failure to treat properly (Deardorff et al., 1984; Soisson et al., 1987).

Duty to Warn and Protect

The most famous of all legal cases involving psychotherapy is commonly referred to as the *Tarasoff* case. In reality this case involved two different decisions which are called Tarasoff I and Tarasoff II (*Tarasoff* v. *Regents of the University of California,* 118 Cal. Rptr. 129, 529 P.2d533 [1974]; *Tarasoff* v. *Regents of the University of California,* 17 Cal.3d 425 551 P.2d334 [1976]). This case has been described and discussed frequently (e.g., Knapp and VandeCreek, 1982; Fulero, 1988; Winslade and Ross, 1983). Since the case has been so widely publicized, we will not review all the details. To summarize, we note that a client threatened (during a psychotherapy session) to kill his "girlfriend" and subsequently carried out the threat. Although the therapist informed the campus police of the threat, he did not warn the "intended victim." For this "failure to warn," the defendants were found negligent. From this first finding by the court, called Tarasoff I, a now rather famous quote came: "The protective privilege ends where the public peril begins." Informally, the court finding produced what came to be called the "duty to warn." Since 1974 countless counselors and therapists in training have undoubtedly been told that they have a legal responsibility to break confidentiality and to warn individuals whose lives have been threatened by a client. Actually one's duty may be much greater than merely "warning" the intended victim. Tarasoff II suggested that psychotherapists have a duty to *protect* intended victims. This duty presumably extends one's obligations to actions such as initiating commitment proceedings.

As Keith-Spiegel and Koocher (1985) point out, the decision about when to break confidentiality if danger to others seems possible is a very difficult one. Consultation with peers is highly recommended. Consultation with an attorney may also be appropriate. Clearly, every threat made by all clients cannot be acted upon by breaking confidentiality. Some issues which must be taken into consideration include the specificity of the threat (i.e., is the intended victim clearly identified or easily identified by logic); options available to the therapist (e.g., if the individual is psychotic, medication, or more medication if applicable, may be possible [Mills, 1985]); previous violent actions by the client; available means to carry out the threat (e.g., if the client threatens to use a gun, does he or she own one); and presence or absence of evidence as to whether the client's impulse control is deteriorating.

We emphasize that you should avoid being unduly influenced by the fact that the client has a history of threatening violence but not carrying it out. If the client has never acted on a threat, certainly he or she is less likely (statistically speaking) to carry out a threat now. But do not be "lulled" into the mistake of automatically thinking, "This is another bluff." Violence is very unpredictable, and this may be the occasion when all the necessary ingredients come together.

Fulero (1988) emphasized the importance of being familiar with the latest developments in handling violent patients (Roth, 1987) and evaluating dangerousness (Simon, 1987). He also emphasized the importance of good documentation (see also Soisson et al., 1987). If you are particularly interested in the duty to warn and protect, the Fulero article includes an appendix detailing a large number of cases involving this responsibility (cases reported as of June 1987; See also VandeCreek, and Knapp, 1989).

SUMMARY

We have commented on several of the ethical principles of psychologists and have also touched on some of the legal issues of interest to psychotherapists. A distinction can be drawn between ethical and legal behavior. An action may be ethical but illegal or, as is more frequently the case, legal but unethical. On the other hand, ethical and legal issues often become closely intertwined especially in psychotherapy. One example of how this can happen is when charges of malpractice raise the question, as they inevitably do, of whether the therapist has violated the standard of care—that is, whether the therapist did something other psychotherapists would *not* normally do or failed to do something other therapists normally *would* do. When these failures involve areas of ethical concern (such as in dual relationships), ethical and legal issues cannot be completely separated.

Ethical principles are important both because they represent a special set of values in which we believe deeply and also because they help lay the foundation for effective psychotherapy. We have emphasized the broadness of one's ethical responsibilities. One's duty is not merely to avoid making mistakes but also to be proactive. In particular, keeping up with new developments in the field and being sensitive to ethnic, gender, and life style issues as they may affect diagnoses and psychotherapy are examples of our responsibility to be proactive.

We have also emphasized the growing awareness of clients' rights and the concomitant responsibility of psychotherapists to provide clients with appropriate information about those rights. The potential risks and benefits of the therapeutic relationship should also be provided to clients. The extent to, and process by, which these rights, risks, and benefits should be spelled out by the therapist does not appear to be a settled issue among psychotherapists. However, a line of articles beginning in the late seventies seems to suggest that informed consent for psychotherapy is an idea whose time has come.

We encourage the reader to pursue the topic of ethical and legal issues in greater detail by consulting the many good resources now available.

APPENDIX
SAMPLE CLIENT INFORMATION FORM
INFORMATION YOU HAVE A RIGHT TO KNOW

When you come for therapy you are buying a service. Therefore, you need information to make a good decision. Below are some questions you might want to ask. We've talked about some of them. You are entitled to ask me any of these questions, if you want to know. If you don't understand my answers ask me again.

    I. Therapy
- A. How does your kind of therapy work?
- B. What are the possible risks involved? (like divorce, depression)
- C. What percentage of clients improve? In what ways?
- D. What percentage of clients get worse?
- E. What percentage of clients improve or get worse without this therapy?
- F. About how long will it take?
- G. What should I do if I feel therapy isn't working?
- H. Will I have to take any tests? What kind?

    II. Alternatives
- A. What other types of therapy or help are there? (like support groups)
- B. How often do they work?
- C. What are the risks of these other approaches?

III. Appointments

A.　How are appointments scheduled?

B.　How long are sessions? Do I have to pay more for ones that are longer?

C.　How can I reach you in an emergency?

D.　If you are not available, who is there I can talk to?

E.　What happens if the weather is bad, or I'm sick?

IV. Confidentiality

A.　What kind of records do you keep? Who has access to them? (insurance companies, supervisors)

B.　Under what conditions are you allowed to tell others about the things we discuss? (Suicidal or homicidal threats, child abuse, court cases, insurance companies, supervisors)

C.　Do other members of my family, or of the group, have access to information?

V. Money

A.　What is your fee?

B.　How do I need to pay? At the session, monthly, etc.?

C.　Do I need to pay for missed sessions?

D.　Do I need to pay for telephone calls or letters?

E.　What are your policies about raising fees? (for example, How many times have you raised them in the past two years?)

F.　If I lose my source of income, can my fee be lowered?

G.　If I do not pay my fee, will you take me to small claims court? Do you use a collection agency or lawyer? Under what circumstances?

VI. General

A.　What is your training and experience? Are you licensed? Supervised? Board certified?

B.　Who do I talk to if I have a complaint about therapy which we can't work out? (e.g., Supervisor, State Board of Psychologist Examiners, APA ethics committee)

The contract [or brochure, or our conversation] dealt with most of these questions. I will be happy to explain them, or to answer other questions you have. This will help you make your decision a good one. You can keep this information. Please read it carefully at home. We will also look this over from time to time.

(Reprinted from "Facilitating Informed Consent for Outpatient Psychotherapy: A Suggested Written Format," *Professional Psychology: Research and Practice*, 1988, *19*, pp. 223–225. Reprinted by permission of M. M. Handelsman and M. D. Galvin.)

OVERVIEW TO PART II

We conclude this book with two chapters, "Responsibility" and "Relationships." We have set them apart because books on psychotherapy typically do not use these topics as chapter headings (an exception would be Yalom, 1980), and yet, in our view, these are two ideas which are used repeatedly by a wide variety of psychotherapists. Whatever a therapist's theoretical orientation, we believe that she or he *thinks about* clients' relationships with others, and the clients' capacities to be responsible. Almost any typical definition of mental health includes, either explicitly or implicitly, these two constructs. Yalom suggested that psychotherapists "throw in something" in therapy which they don't (or perhaps can't) describe, which is a key ingredient in psychotherapy. To this we add that therapists, if you listen to them talk, slip into using certain constructs over and over, even if these constructs do not occupy a central role in their *stated* theory. Relationships and responsibility are two such constructs.

13

RESPONSIBILITY

I think one must finally take one's life in one's arms.

—Arthur Miller

"I'm getting sick of this," Judith Viorst (1986) quotes a seven-year-old boy as saying. "Everything I do you blame on me" (p. 153). Most of us have no trouble at all resonating to this child's annoyance. Learning to take responsibility for one's choices is usually a slow and fitful process, often cluttered with a concomitant willingness to accept responsibility for happenings (both good and bad) beyond one's control. It is not easy to sort out how and for what one must claim authorship. Nonetheless, this issue of responsibility is an undercurrent in most therapeutic work, for clients can make changes only in areas where they can claim responsibility (Frank, 1973).

In this chapter we will address some of the transtheoretical ways of thinking that therapists sometimes bring to client issues of responsibility. We will offer our own definition of responsibility for your consideration, and, since that definition draws heavily from three separate theoretical orientations, we will summarize those three approaches first. We will also offer some "common clinical wisdom" distinctions relevant to responsibility, as well as other therapeutic considerations you may find helpful in working with clients.

THEORETICAL CONTRIBUTIONS

The three therapeutic approaches that most specifically address client responsibility are existential psychotherapy, Gestalt therapy, and reality therapy. Let us briefly examine each of these in turn to see what their distinctive contributions are, as well as to delineate the underlying themes.

Existential psychotherapy.   With its proclamation that meaning in life could not be reached by looking to divine or ultimate sources, but was necessarily relative and individual, existentialism seemed to imply to some that there was no reason to do *anything*, since all values were arbitrary and relative and no action could be said to be ultimately more meaningful or worthwhile than another. Construed this way, it is reduced to little more than nihilism. The existential psychotherapists, notably Rollo May (1983) and Irvin Yalom (1980), however, bring a different perspective to this otherwise rather bleak picture of the human condition. Since we cannot attribute what happens to us to divine intervention, they suggest, and since others are only human and not capable of providing meaning to us or of "rescuing" us from our situations, we must rely ultimately only on ourselves. No one else is responsible for me; I make my own choices. Even if I derive a grim satisfaction from blaming someone else (my parents, for example) for failing me in major ways, only *I* can be responsible for making my life better. No one else can do it for me or tell me the "right" thing to do. I must live, in Sheldon Kopp's (1975) words, "within the ambiguity of partial freedom, partial power, and partial knowledge" (p. 32) and make the best decisions I can.

This focus on decisions and choices, and the need for the individual to accept responsibility for the consequences that ensue, is one of the cornerstones of existential psychotherapy. The therapist with such an approach would try to listen carefully to where his or her clients find meaning in their lives or, put another way, to what their deepest needs and goals are and would then aid them in learning to make conscious decisions that are meaningful and consonant with their values. The client who makes such conscious choices is considered "responsible"; the client who, conversely, adopts a passive attitude and simply waits hopefully (or hopelessly) for life to improve is "irresponsible."

Irvin Yalom's (1980) discussion of responsibility sums up the existential therapist's position: "Responsibility means authorship. To be aware of responsibility is to be aware of creating one's own self, destiny, life predicament, feelings, and if such be the case, one's own suffering. For the patient who will not accept such responsibility, no real therapy is possible" (p. 218).

Reality therapy.   William Glasser's *Reality Therapy* (1965) was in some ways similar to existential therapy. Although he has made major modifications in his theory in recent years, his early ideas have more sophistication and therapeutic validity than is generally recognized. Glasser defined responsibility as "the ability to fulfill one's needs and to do so in a way that does not deprive others of the ability to fulfill theirs." This presupposes the making of conscious choices that the existential therapists stressed. Glasser, however, felt that clients who are badly demoralized (or, in his terms, have a failure identity) cannot learn this responsible decision-making process without the active involvement of a responsible role model. Reality therapy, then, stated explicitly that the therapist must be responsible for himself or herself—as a personal life style, not as a mantle put on for an hour a week.

Reality therapy also defined what the basic human needs are (remember here that when we *need* something, we are likely to *value* it, which translates in existential terms to discovering what has *meaning* for us). According to reality therapy, all of us have two basic needs: to love and be loved and to feel worthwhile. The job of the reality therapist was to help the client learn to take responsibility for getting those needs met.

Although Glasser did not spell this out at length, learning how to love others and accept love in return is no small task for many clients. If he was right that the need for interpersonal contact and affirmation is innate but that one's ability to get that need fulfilled is a *learned* process, then we believe it follows that much therapeutic work must focus on intimacy skills. As Fromm (1956), Bowlby (1980), and others have pointed out, the simple forming of attachments is a fairly primitive process, but learning how to create and maintain those bonds in mature, fulfilling relationships is much more complex. Narcissism must be transcended enough to allow for empathic responsiveness; giving ourselves must become a creative, rewarding act, distinguished from depleting ourselves; we must be able to allow vulnerability in ourselves in order to be able to fully receive; and we must know how to protest and assert ourselves when necessary rather than acquiesce or dominate. Unfortunately, many clients have no idea that these are learned skills that are usually gained with struggle and determination, and hope instead that nourishing relationships will just "happen." For clients to take responsibility for getting their needs met to love and be loved, they must be willing to examine and probably change some of their behavior and attitudes.

Similarly, the reality therapist's goal of helping clients learn to assume responsibility for feeling worthwhile was also more difficult than it might appear. As Glasser pointed out, we cannot respect ourselves until we behave in ways that deserve respect. The client with a "failure identity" is one who expects failure and in fact often courts it. He or she must be confronted over and over with the "reality" that certain behaviors sabotage the possibility of attaining important goals and that different behavioral choices would be more successful.

Gestalt therapy.   Gestalt therapy's approach to responsibility is to break it down to "response-ability: the ability to respond, to have thoughts, reactions, emotions in a given situation" (Perls, 1969 p. 65). Being able to respond honestly is possible, according to Perls, only when we relinquish our defenses and allow ourselves to become aware of our true feelings and motivations, however inconsistent they may appear. Before we can take responsibility for ourselves, we must first make contact with and "own" all of our discrepant parts.

The ideally responsible person, from the Gestalt therapy perspective, is one who does not defend against his or her awareness of feelings and sensations and, in fact, welcomes them, one who can see others clearly and realistically without projecting disowned parts of the self onto them, and one who is self-supporting enough to risk the rejection of others by refusing to automatically acquiesce to their expectations. One's sense of identity comes from one's awareness of and experiences of one's self, rather than from others' feedback. What is painted here is an extreme portrait of the rugged individualist, strong and courageous and self-supporting, capable of making independent decisions in the face of others' expectations. The flip side of this total self-responsibility is the concurrent Gestalt insistence that we are not responsible for others. They, like us, must learn to become aware of and trust in themselves, and we do them no favors if we try to protect them from reality and take responsibility for making their decisions. The assumption is that each of us is equally strong—at least potentially—and that each must rely primarily on herself or himself. Perls's I-do-my-thing-and-you-do-your-thing "prayer" captures this spirit and is given as a directive for productive relationships. Needing or depending on someone else is thus seen as being suspiciously close to being irresponsible. The role of the Gestalt therapist is to aid clients in working through their blocks of defensive impasses by facilitating their awareness of their ongoing feelings and sensations. Therapeutic work is in the "here and now," with the assumption that increased awareness will lead to more responsible behavioral choices.

RESPONSIBILITY, NEWLY DEFINED

To underscore some of the key components of responsibility then, as derived from our overview of these three therapeutic systems: (1) Each of us is ultimately responsible for making his or her own decisions. No one, including a therapist, can "rescue" another from that responsibility. (2) Awareness of what one *wants* is crucial. Responsibility can then be taken for living one's life in a way that is most likely to achieve those goals. (3) Awareness of external reality is also crucial. We must give up our defenses of denial, avoidance, projection, etc., so that we may see others and our environment as realistically as possible. (4) We are as responsible for what we *don't* do as for what we *do*. Passivity and helplessness are no excuse. If we want something to be different, we must actively work for it to happen.

If you find one or more of the three approaches particularly relevant to your own experiences and ways of thinking, we encourage you to read more widely from the original works. Our brief summary obviously cannot begin to do justice to the complexity of the theories.

Let us turn now to a transtheoretical definition of responsibility. Drawing from these other definitions, we offer for your consideration our definition of responsibility as "the ability to be aware of one's own needs and those of others and the willingness to make proactive behavioral choices in accordance with that awareness." First, we want to underscore some of the points in this definition, after which we will examine some of the implications this definition might have for your work with clients.

As indicated by our choice of words, we see awareness as an *ability*, a learned process, that involves a committed refusal to be controlled by one's defenses. Defenses, as Freud indicated, are presumably in place to defend the ego against assault. Defenses are great coping devices; they allow us to continue to feel intact when our own motivations or external situations appear to be quite threatening. In some extreme situations (e.g., overwhelming loss, life-threatening catastrophes, etc.), defenses are necessary, at least until we have time to get our psychological feet back under us. But in most of our everyday activities, giving way to the desire to defensively distort reality costs us much more than we gain. There is some truth to the expanded biblical verse: "You shall know the truth, and the truth shall make you free—but first it shall make you uncomfortable as hell." When we tell ourselves that our boss is crazy about us, even though we were just passed up for the third time for a promotion, when we insist to ourselves that we very much want to maintain a relationship although we give it less and less time, when we nurse our resentment of the opposite sex and refuse to examine how the disowned parts of ourselves are remarkably similar to their most irritating qualities—when we engage in these forms of self-deception, we make it impossible for much improvement to occur.

Learning to "catch ourselves in the act" of being defensive (there are recognizable physiological and psychological cues which signal the sudden rigidity of defensiveness) and then stopping ourselves to examine the possible underlying feelings is a process we can practice, although never fully master. If I tell you your hair is red when in fact it is black, you are likely to deny the allegation fairly matter-of-factly (and maybe also with amazed amusement), but unless the color of hair carries some symbolic meaning for you, you will probably not get very defensive in your denial. If, on the other hand, I tell you the person you are falling in love with also elicits feelings of resentment and fear from you, you are likely to protest vigorously, especially if you have a variety of hopes already tied up in the relationship. That immediate protest, as opposed to the previous calm denial, is the hallmark of defensiveness. If, however, we truly believe that truth is a stronger ally than defensiveness, we may be willing to pause and ask ourselves, "Could it be true? Have I ever had even an inkling that this could be?" Often what we find is that, underneath the defensiveness, there is some basis of truth to the charge we want so badly to deny, but that admitting the truth—or more likely, the partial truth—is not nearly as devastating as we had feared.

Why is it then that so many clients have a phobic response to self-awareness? There are different reasons, of course. Some clients are afraid of discovering feelings that will contaminate their self-image. Others are more afraid that if they admit (especially out loud!) to an unwanted motivation, it will give it more power and permanence. Still others fear—perhaps with cause—that if they become aware of new things within them they will be called upon to make new changes, to disturb the status quo. And most frighteningly, some are reluctant to explore their deeper feelings because they sense a hollowness within themselves and fear that if they explore very deeply they will find nothing at all.

Exploring and owning one's feelings, of course, are just the first steps. In time, themes of meaning begin to emerge, and finally some of the core needs that make up one's identity can be inferred. This kind of in-depth awareness of one's needs is close to what most therapists are hoping clients can attain in the process of learning to take responsibility for how they lead their lives.

Let us return to the second part of our definition. Being aware of others' needs is a similar but more difficult challenge than being aware of our own. Most people are fairly good at letting us know, either overtly or covertly, what they want from us. They interact with us in patterns that are designed (often unconsciously) to elicit certain reactions from us that complement their own expectations and behaviors, and we find ourselves expressing the nurturance or anger or detachment, etc., that many others in their lives express. But what people indicate they *want* from us and what they really *need* are often two different things. As almost any parent can confirm, adolescents are prone to say that they want to make their own decisions with no parental interference, but what they usually need is continued guidance and limit setting (if of a different sort). Similarly, clients may insist that they want a mutual, perhaps sexual, relationship with their therapist, although considerable theory and research indicate that clients in fact need the reassurance of knowing that their therapist is nonseducible. Understanding what someone else needs, as opposed to wants, requires that we be able to deny meeting automatically his or her expectations and instead let ourselves respond to the whole three-dimensional human being before us—to the strengths as well as the weaknesses, to the hopes and fears and dreams, to her or his future development as well as to the present person. If in interacting with others we ask ourselves, "How can I best respond, so that their maximum potential can be tapped and facilitated?" then we are likely to be close to responding to their needs rather than to expectations or roles.

Once we know what we need and have at least a tentative guess about the needs of the other person(s) involved, then the challenge becomes one of orchestrating our behavior so that our choices are an attempt to meet both sets of needs. The more flexible we can be in terms of seeing that needs can often be met in several ways (as opposed to the assumption that there is a fixed, one-to-one ratio between what we need and how we must act), the more likely we will be able to behave in responsible ways that are fulfilling for both of us.

An example may help. Imagine the following scenario: A married couple, Wayne and Denise, come to you for counseling. As they begin to tell their story, they both affirm that they love each other very much but seem to be consistently disappointing each other. At some point, you ask them how they have shown their love for each other in the past week, and Wayne says, "Well, I washed her car for her," and Denise says, "Last night I stayed up late and baked his favorite pie for him." They look at each other for a moment, and then Denise blurts out, "But I don't need you to wash my car! I can wash my own car! What I need is for you to *tell* me that you love me!" And Wayne says, "Honey, thanks for the pie, but what I really wanted you to do for me last night was listen to me talk about my hassles at work." What becomes increasingly clear over time is that their desire to show love and affirmation of each other is genuine, but they are locked into preconceived ideas of the specific ways that that affirmation should be demonstrated. When they can begin to listen more deeply to each other and also increase their behavioral flexibility, it is likely that they will disappoint each other far less often. The challenge of trying to understand and meet each other's needs in ways that are consonant with their own becomes much less formidable if they can each stay open to a variety of optional responses. Once the concept of orchestrating themselves to meet *both* people's needs is internalized, the challenge of working out the specifics can be stimulating and fun.

Let us return now to the last part of our definition of responsibility. In addition to being aware of our own needs and those of others, we must have the willingness to make proactive behavioral choices in accordance with that awareness. A key word here is *proactive,* as distinguished from *reactive.* To be responsible requires a certain spirit of adventurousness. We must be willing to act, to consider our options and then take decisive action, rather than to wait passively for circumstances finally to force us into reacting. *If* we are aware of our needs and goals in life, they provide a magnet which gives direction and meaning to the taking of calculated risks. It helps to remind ourselves that "all important decisions must be made on the basis of insufficient data" (Kopp, 1975, p. 32). Knowing that there are no guarantees that our risk-taking behaviors will be successful, we nonetheless make the choices which seem most likely to meet our own and others' needs. Proactivity, then, is the major mechanism for giving ourselves some control over our lives. It is by behaving proactively that we are most able to control our destinies, to invite life to meet our needs by having first made self-affirming choices. The opposite of proactivity—passivity—tends to elicit predictable negative consequences. When we are unable or unwilling to throw the weight of our actions on the possibility of fulfilling our own needs, but instead simply sit and wait for things to improve, we set ourselves up for victimization. In its extreme forms, such passivity is evidenced by fear, paranoia, learned helplessness, and massive projection of responsibility.

A final word about our definition. The concept of "choices" implies the ability to renounce some alternatives. While it is true that frequently in life clients can find ways to compromise or negotiate enough to at least partially have two seemingly incompatible things, some avenues truly are mutually exclusive. Renunciation is always painful—occasionally so difficult that staying in limbo indefinitely seems preferable to the anguish of truly choosing one course and renouncing the other—but unfortunately life sometimes does involve saying yes to one thing and no to another. Allen Wheelis (1956) said it beautifully: "Some people sit at the crossroads, taking neither path because they cannot take both, cherishing the illusion that if they sit there long enough the two ways will resolve themselves into one and hence both be possible. A large part of maturity and courage is the ability to make such renunciations, and a large part of wisdom is the ability to find ways which will enable one to renounce as little as possible."

THERAPEUTIC DISTINCTIONS

In this next section, we will delineate some distinctions that many therapists find useful in working with clients. A word first about our terminology. In our discussion, we will imply or suggest outright that clients might be helped by "learning" certain things. We mean "learn" here not in the sense of accepting a logical explanation and perhaps being able to repeat it later—say, as in high school one memorized the factors leading to the Civil War. Nor are we referring simply to cognitive restructuring. We use the term *learn* in a much deeper sense to imply a new, richer understanding of one's self and one's relation to the rest of the world, a different stance to reality. In this respect, learning is a cumulative process that allows for new creative approaches to old problems. Something shifts deep inside the client that gives him or her a feeling of increased lightness and flexibility. Instead of being locked tightly into their former perceptions and assumptions, they see new possibilities. They begin to ask, "Why not?" Your role in "teaching" them is less to offer explanations—although that may occasionally be a well-timed part of the process—than to provide an atmosphere where your clients can *discover* new learnings. Only if the following distinctions make sense to you and are deeply internalized, only if you can live them out yourself, will you be in a position to "teach" them to your clients. Learning—in therapy as elsewhere—often takes place at an unconscious and nonverbal level, and the important lessons must usually be relearned over and over again.

Responsibility for versus responsibility to.   Although this is a somewhat overused and simplistic distinction, clients who are unfamiliar with it may find it freeing. When we feel responsible *for* others, we are likely to see them as an extension of ourselves. Thus, a mother who feels responsible for her six-year-old's rudeness will probably feel anger, humiliation, and embarrassment. She is blaming him for being rude but also herself for not having taught him to be more polite. If you ask her what her fantasies are, she is likely to say that she fears that others observing her son's behavior are thinking something like, "Oh, dear. Why hasn't that child's mother taught him how to behave?" If instead of feeling responsible *for* him, however, she felt responsible *to* him, she would probably feel more concern than embarrassment and would ask herself what experience she could provide that would encourage her son to be more sensitive to others' feelings. The focus would switch then from blame and punishment to a more constructive problem-solving mode.

This distinction between responsibility for and responsibility to can be a powerful one for someone who hears it for the first time, and the magic of it is not just semantic. The truth of the matter is that the mother in the above example is not in full control of her son's behavior, so it is unrealistic for her to feel full responsibility. At best, she can *influence* him to behave in certain ways; feeling enough responsibility to him that she uses her influence wisely is a much more realistic expectation of herself. Of course, the issue gets clouded because she may indeed be held legally responsible for his behavior, and observers may actually feel judgmental not only of her son but of her too. Nonetheless, she will probably be more effective in changing her son's behavior if she can adopt in large part this "responsible *to*" attitude. As a general rule, as individuals become chronologically and psychologically more adult, it is reasonable for us to feel less and less responsibility *for* their behavior and happiness and more responsibility *to* them so that ideally, with equals, we identify with them very little and see them as essentially responsible for their own choices. For example, the alcoholic's husband, with this ideal attitude, would feel little embarrassment or protectiveness for his wife's irresponsible behavior and would not feel obligated either to nag at her to change or to "cover" for her alcoholism with her acquaintances. He would ask himself what he could do in order to be responsible to her, and he would refuse to shield her from the consequences of her behavior.

Responsibility versus obligation. If you ask people off the street what their "responsibility" is, they will probably recount a lengthy list of obligations. They are responsible for going to their job, for rearing their children, for taking out the trash every second day, etc. From many of them you will get the impression that they simply go through the dreary motions of performing these endless obligations, and the only joy in their lives is a vague sense of virtue for having done what was "right." From others, you may get the feeling that they are driven by an anxious compulsion to meet another's expectations and demands and accordingly feel intense guilt for being "irresponsible" if they are unable or unwilling to comply. It is almost as if both of these groups are still children, trying hard to please a demanding parent so that they can "earn" approval or love.

This kind of empty or compulsive acquiescence to someone else's perceived demands is a long way from Perls' concept of response-ability. In contrast to a full, conscious choice that one's identity will be enhanced by responding to one's own or another's real need, automatic compliance smacks of subservience or cowardice. One is afraid not to comply, and hopes to forestall possible abandonment or punishment by acquiescing. In short, this act of "responsibility" is done from a position of weakness, not strength.

Trying to earn love by always doing what someone else demands or expects is futile. For one thing, love cannot be earned. But even if it could be, what is one supposed to do when *two* significant others make conflicting demands at the same time? In therapy, such compulsive pleasers need help in individuating more fully so that risking another's disapproval is less terrifying. One part of this process is aiding them in coping with their neurotic guilt at saying no; helping them to distinguish between a loved one's superficial demands and deeper needs can be another important step.

Self-responsibility versus selfishness.   A related misunderstanding is the assumption that accepting responsibility for trying to get one's own needs met somehow makes one "selfish." For someone who has been socialized—or may have even consciously chosen—to put oneself in a nurturing, care-taking role, even considering acting in one's own best interest can feel foreign or evil. Much meaning has been derived from actively giving to others (as opposed to the previous section which described one's giving out of obligation), and it can be very difficult to entertain the idea that one's own needs are also valid. Women may be especially immersed in this self-sacrificial attitude and often appear genuinely bewildered that their efforts are unappreciated or exploited by others (Lemkau and Landau, 1986). Why, they wonder, do others take for granted what is given and often give so little back? If you suggest that they might need to clarify what they need and actually ask for it, they tend to become acutely uncomfortable. That would make them selfish! They are caught in the bind of wanting others to validate needs that they themselves are ambivalent about.

Contrary to Norwood's (1985) belief, we feel that the issue here is not that they give or love too much. The problem is that they are not sure that they deserve to *receive*. Because they cannot truly affirm their own needs, they put themselves in a position where those needs can be ignored or exploited. As you work with them in therapy to begin the process of self-affirmation, what typically emerges is their fear that the pendulum will swing too far and that if they validate their own needs they might turn into selfish monsters. As indicated elsewhere (Davenport, 1982), such clients need help in understanding that their operating position does not have to swing from "you, not me" to "me, not you." A third possibility—"me *and* you"—is available to them if they can expand their awareness and responsiveness to include others' needs as well as their own. They must eventually believe that their needs to receive in reciprocal relationships are valid and in fact can contribute to deeper, richer interactions with others.

One way to begin this change in attitudinal sets is to suggest that they have *two* major responsibilities in healthy relationships—responsibilities to give and responsibilities to receive. Learning how to affirm their own needs and receive from others is not a luxury; it is a requirement if they hope to have mature, fulfilling relationships. Refusing to validate and assert their needs often has at least three negative consequences: (1) Their anger at being discounted builds, frequently leaking out in destructive ways or perhaps increasing to explosive proportions which can eventually destroy the relationship. (2) Their own self-respect suffers, since at some level they realize they are partners in the conspiracy to deny their own needs. (3) Significant others in their lives are placed in the position of having to guess what the client needs or, as one husband said, "playing twenty questions in the dark." This can get wearisome very quickly, and the client's self-denial can be perceived by others as less virtuous than manipulative.

At its core, self-denial is in fact often self-protective and manipulative. It is a shield from rejection. Eventually, most clients usually acknowledge that they know what they need but are afraid of asking and being refused. It feels safer, at least in the short run, not to ask. Besides, they may believe, as one woman told her therapist, "If I don't ask for very much, then when I *do* ask for something, I deserve to get it!"

Self-responsibility versus control.   At the other end of the continuum is the client who is psychologically sophisticated, skilled in self-assertive techniques, and sensitive to the cues of others. "Jim" comes to you because in spite of all he has learned about relationships, he is 35, unmarried, and beginning to feel desperate. He wants to know what he is doing wrong so he can take responsibility for himself and fix it. As you listen to Jim explain what he does and how he thinks in regard to women, you are at first impressed with his openness to feedback and his willingness to change. Here is a client to make up for the passive, resistant ones you work with! Gradually, however, you begin to get suspicious that somehow he is trying too hard. Although his communication skills are excellent and his openness is genuine, he seems to operate from the assumption that if he just learns enough he can be in control and will then find the perfect mate he longs for. In the meantime, his single-minded determination is frightening off the women he dates.

Jim is having difficulty distinguishing between taking responsibility for himself and trying to control others. His willingness to examine his own behavior and change it is admirable, but it is not enough. He must also accept his ultimate powerlessness to build a relationship unilaterally. All the assertive skills in the world will not compensate for his dates' lack of motivation, immaturity, or disinterest in marriage.

One of the perils in learning self-responsibility is that clients can get a lopsided view of the world and may forget that others have the right to say no to them. An important distinction for such clients, alluded to earlier in this chapter, is the difference between control and influence. We are rarely in full control, especially of other people; taking responsibility for ourselves affords no guarantees that others will respond as we want them to. If we are willing, however, to settle for *influencing* others and can give up our illusion of control, it will be easier for us to direct our efforts into responding spontaneously to the cues we pick up in the moment from ourselves and from those with whom we are interacting. When Jim can begin to see and appreciate his dates as complete, full individuals rather than as "potential wife" objects, then he will be better able to ascertain what the two of them might be capable of creating together in the way of a relationship.

A related confusion between responsibility and control is sometimes seen in clients who are extraordinarily self-disciplined. Well-trained athletes, for example, are accustomed to demanding a great deal from themselves both physically and psychologically. In return they are rewarded for this self-discipline by seeing their performance improve and by receiving honors and acclaim from others. The line between feeling responsible to their bodies and believing that they can *control* their bodies may grow dim, and their self-esteem may plummet when their bodies no longer function as well because of aging or illness. It may be very difficult for them to accept that they no longer have the same power to make their bodies "obey" them, particularly when they are bombarded by well-intentioned holistic health messages that imply that poor health might have been avoided if they had done everything right. Such clients may need help discovering what they can control and what they can't; eventually they, like the rest of us, need to understand that aging and death are not punishments for poor self-control, nor are they something one can choose to defer indefinitely. People age and get sick even if they don't smoke, always watch what they eat, and get regular checkups.

Self-responsibility versus self-blame.   A final similar distinction which therapists may need to help clients make is that accepting responsibility for their behavior is not the same as indulging in heavy self-blame. As clients become more aware of how their present behavior sabotages their attainment of present goals, they often go through a period of examining past choices and blaming themselves for having contributed to their own unhappiness. A certain amount of regret for one's past self-destructive behavior is appropriate. Some guilt, too, for the harm that one has caused others may be a necessary component of developing increased self-awareness and self-responsibility. But an inordinate and continued pattern of blaming oneself can easily become self-indulgent and frequently makes it *more* difficult to assume responsibility for making present changes in one's life.

If possible, learning self-responsible ways of behaving should be accompanied by learning to treat one's self with the same kind of compassion one would ideally try to offer others. The alcoholic who looks back over the last 20 years and sees the damage she caused her family, the father playing with children in the yard who looked away for just the instant it took for his three-year-old to dart into the street and get hit by a car, the daughter crying at the father's funeral because she hadn't told him she loved him—all of these people, in order to go on with their lives, must eventually move beyond total remorse over their past behavior to a more balanced perspective of their "true" responsibility in the situation. From there they may find at least partial self-forgiveness and a commitment to living out their futures in a way that indicates they have learned from their past experiences. Often, as Yalom (1980) points out, a part of this process involves separating one's neurotic guilt (emanating from *imagined* transgressions) from one's real guilt (which flows from an *actual* transgression against another) and then possibly attempting to make reparation for the actual damage caused. This reparation may be a concrete act or gift for the person harmed, or it may be a symbolic way of making amends. What is important is that such an act allows the person to accept responsibility and experience herself or himself as qualitatively *different* than the previously perceived irresponsible "guilty" self. The client is thus more fully freed from the past and can better respond to present and future potentialities.

THERAPEUTIC CONSIDERATIONS

In working with clients who are not "responsible" (please refer back to authors' definition), several considerations may be helpful.

Signals of Irresponsibility

First, it is important to be able to recognize those client attitudes and behaviors which signal an unwillingness/inability to accept responsibility. Some of these are obvious, but others are subtle enough to lead even quite experienced therapists off the track:

Helplessness.   The client who seems truly desperate and afraid of taking any action at all is likely to hook our rescuer tendencies. If the situation is truly critical (e.g., the client has just been raped, received devastating news, etc.), it may be necessary for the therapist or other outsider to be fairly directive and assume a certain amount of supportive responsibility that would ordinarily be the client's. The goal, however, should be for the client to reassume responsibility as quickly as possible for making as many decisions as he or she can. Clients who go from crisis to crisis or who have adopted a helpless life style are more likely to elicit our annoyance than our sympathy (unless they are in abusive situations), but they too need us to believe in and call forth the potential potency that lies beneath their helplessness.

Confusion.   A related symptom of unwillingness to take responsibility is exhibited by the client who regularly gets "confused" when a certain issue is addressed. She or he may be otherwise quite articulate and expressive but feel suddenly blocked or bewildered when asked questions about specific relevant areas. It is important for beginning therapists to keep in mind that clients are rarely deliberately evasive in order to spite their therapists. Rather, confusion is a defense employed presumably because the material feels too dangerous to the client to be explored. Stepping back a pace to try to understand with the client what is so potentially threatening about the topic is usually more effective than a frontal assault on the resistance. (For more on resistance, refer to that particular chapter.)

Displacement of responsibility.   Clients often wait, sometimes in subtle, barely perceivable ways, for their therapists or some other authority figure to make their important decisions for them. The responsibility of making crucial decisions, especially ones that involve renunciation, may seem too burdensome or fearful for them to accept. While is it appropriate with such clients to be wary of being led into taking too much responsibility, too many beginning therapists err in the other direction and disengage emotionally or react punitively whenever they sense client dependency. Clients who tend to displace responsibility for themselves onto others certainly need well-timed confrontation, but they also benefit from supportive exploration of their options. The client who asks, "What should I do?" may be helped by a response like, "That depends on what you want to accomplish. What is your *goal?*" The therapist's role here is to help the client clarify his or her needs and then to facilitate the development of an appropriate plan of action that is consistent with the client's values.

Compulsive action.   Although decisive activity is often equated with the assumption of responsibility, it may at times signal the opposite. "Burying oneself in work" is a common enough phenomenon that nonprofessionals are aware of it and understand that it is usually an attempt to avoid experiencing painful feelings. The therapist working with a compulsively active client will probably need to make a clinical assessment regarding the client's ego strength and ability to face what is currently being run from. Returning to our definition of "responsibility," until clients are *aware* of the avoided feelings, little progress can be made in assuming greater self-responsibility. Letting these negative feelings—usually shame, fear, or anger—into their awareness, however, will probably require trust in their therapists' support, as well as confidence in their own ability to maintain their equilibrium.

Client Change

A second consideration in working with clients lacking a strong sense of self-responsibility is that lectures and demands rarely work. As tempting as it may be to simply exhort, "Get a grip! Be more responsible, for God's sake!" these parental statements of exasperation/encouragement tend to be more therapeutic for the therapist than the client. The actual process of client assumption of responsibility is likely to be sporadic, slow, and ongoing.

Clients change because they become less afraid to. For most clients this requires a strong and supportive alliance with their therapist that will allow the examination of fears and assumptions that are currently hindering their development, the gradual replacement of these old dysfunctional ways of thinking and feeling with healthier ones, and increased confidence and ability to tolerate failures as they begin to acquire new skills to add to their repertoire. They change, not because someone tells them to, but because it now makes more sense to them experientially. They change because they have interacted with a therapist whose ways of thinking and making decisions—at both a personal and professional level—have provided a first-hand model of how to be responsible for oneself. As one client told his counselor, "You know, you leak out around the edges. It's not so much what you say, it's who you are that I listen to."

Acceptance of Ambiguity

A final note about therapeutic considerations: In spite of the distinctions made earlier, responsibility is a concept fraught with ambiguity. There will be many, many situations in therapy when it will be impossible for you or the client to have a clean, clear understanding of exactly what that client's responsibility to himself or herself should be. Exactly when should parents feel less responsible for their children's attitudes and behaviors? Is one as responsible for the *effects* of one's behavior on another as for the underlying *intent*? How much does a client's physical deterioration affect the amount of responsibility that client should feel for his or her psychological stability? For that matter, in what ways and for how long is a therapist responsible for/to a given client?

These questions, and many other similar ones, raise issues that clients and therapists struggle with continually. Hopefully, there will be no easy answers. Certainly, therapists should not fall into the trap of having to manufacture simple solutions just to make the client feel more comfortable. It is the very act of struggling with such questions that helps clients clarify their goals and values. Their eventual choices have more meaning exactly because they *have* struggled. The challenge for therapists should not be to perfectly understand responsibility but instead to help the client in his or her own attempts to find tentative answers. Omniscience is not a requirement for therapists; the willingness to struggle with ambiguity is.

SUMMARY

Encouraging clients to assume appropriate responsibility for their lives is one of the generally accepted meta-goals of psychotherapy. In this chapter we reviewed the concept of responsibility from three theoretical perspectives, and offered our own definition for consideration. Being able to make distinctions which help clients delineate responsibility from other less desirable processes can often be quite liberating for clients who have misunderstood what responsibility actually entails.

The therapist's own understanding, and her or his ability to serve as a responsible model, are crucial if consistent messages are to be communicated. As with other aspects of therapy, it is what the therapist does, as what he or she says that conveys the message.

14

RELATIONSHIPS

Human beings are afraid of love. And all the saccharine books to the contrary, there is reason to be afraid.

—Rollo May

Many of the problems which clients bring to therapy involve their relationships with others. While we do not agree with Sullivan (1954) that *all* client problems stem from relationship issues, we do feel that for many clients such issues tend to be a central focus. In this chapter we will provide you with some of the ways of thinking about relationships that many therapists find helpful, as well as some specific therapeutic considerations for you to keep in mind about relationships as you work with clients.

BASIC ASSUMPTIONS ABOUT RELATIONSHIPS

There are a few underlying assumptions about relationships which therapists from a variety of orientations adhere to, less out of theoretical loyalties than because they seem to be substantiated in their clinical work. As in other chapters, we offer a partial summary of these assumptions here, not as a group of constructs with an absolutely pure theoretical base and certainly not as a comprehensive analysis of all important views on the subject, but as a starting point for your own thinking. We encourage you to do your own in-depth reading of some of the primary current writers (Bowlby, 1988; Strean, 1980; Napier and Whitaker, 1978; Gilbert, 1987), to add to the ideas we will summarize here, and to be willing to tentatively modify your biases as your clinical experience increases.

Importance of Early Experiences

Freud (1933), of course, was especially adamant that childhood experiences affect adult behavior in profound, pervasive ways. As you probably know, there is considerable disagreement regarding his emphasis on several crucial issues, including his views on childhood sexuality, his insistence on the importance of *very* early experiences (to the exclusion of later ones), and the specifics of his stage theory. Nonetheless, many clinicians do accept his basic premise that many adult behaviors are rooted in childhood interpretations of events. The assumption here is that clients do not feel and behave the way they do arbitrarily; they respond to present events at least partially because of attitudes and responses developed at a much earlier age. In effect, life "taught" them to make certain assumptions and to react in specific ways, although much of this learning probably took place at an unconscious level.

Clarifying with the client what these unconscious "world views" are can be helpful in the therapeutic process in at least two ways. First, it helps counteract the sense of shame and hopelessness that many clients feel at not being able to will themselves to change more quickly. Having some of their reactions understood and validated helps them feel less "crazy." Second, once some of these assumptions are made conscious, responsible choices are more easily made by the client regarding whether or not to begin the process of formulating major new perceptions and making appropriate behavioral changes.

A case example may be illustrative, although it is far less complicated and subtle than most. The presenting problem of a client of one of the authors was shyness. "Larry" was a 21-year-old college male whose ambivalence about intimacy was demonstrated in his vacillating dating behavior: Either he was extremely fearful of rejection, to the point of almost total tongue-tied silence around women whom he found attractive, or he felt such a sense of entitlement that he retreated into a sulky silence if one of his rare dates failed to anticipate and meet his unspoken needs. After finally deciding that in either case silence was a somewhat shaky foundation for romance, he began working to make behavioral changes. He learned to initiate relationships more easily, to communicate more clearly some of his preferences, and to view women more realistically. Still, mistrust and cynicism permeated most of his interactions and were particularly evident in his continued testing of his female therapist. Did she still remember the dream he told her a month ago? Had that expression on her face at the end of the last session been a judgment of him? A turning point in therapy occurred when Larry mentioned his younger brother for the first time, with considerable annoyance. The story unfolded. It seemed that Larry, the first child of somewhat older parents, had been born with a heart murmur and his parents had been instructed not to let him cry. Accordingly, for the first five years of his life, he was cuddled and pampered. When he was five, two things happened within three months of each other—he had successful corrective heart surgery, and his brother was born. As he said bitterly, "Everything was downhill after that." His parents' sudden willingness to ignore his crying and to set limits was painful and bewildering and in marked contrast to the attention the new interloper was receiving. It must have felt like a long, hard fall from grace. In simplified "world view" terms, it seems likely that for his first five years Larry felt:

> I am much loved, very important to my parents, and clearly entitled to have my every whim granted. What a nice world! I can trust others to cater to me and please me, and very little is expected of me in return.

Then abruptly, and to his mind without explanation, the world changed. His subsequent "world view" thus must have become (and continued to be until he came to therapy) something like:

> People are not to be trusted. While I am *entitled* to be treated very well, even people who love me can change without warning, and there is nothing I can do about it. To avoid being hurt, I must be hypervigilant and withdraw at the first sign of rejection.

Making at least partial sense of Larry's childhood experiences and his interpretations of them thus allowed him to understand some of his continued vacillating behavior and made it more possible for him to make conscious choices about further changes he wanted to make.

Larry's childhood situation was more dramatic than most in that it involved a clear change in early circumstances. With your help, however, many clients, like Larry, can benefit from identifying their early assumptions and then perhaps beginning the work of modifying them. There are two points that may be important to remember. First, there is general agreement among clinicians that what shapes a person's belief system is less what happened to her or him than the sense the person made of the events. Our current state of knowledge does not provide a complete understanding for us of how it is that the same event early in life can have radically different impacts on different children. On the other hand, strongly negative events have a typical impact on children. That is, for children who are subjected to more and more negative events, it becomes increasingly unlikely that they will be left unaffected by these events. For example, overt abuse or negligence leave typical wounds on almost any child. It is important to remember that your work is not to judge the accuracy or morality of the client's story nor to decide whether an event should or should not have affected the client but to help him or her understand the impact it did have and continues to have on present patterns.

Second, the deeper, more pervasive, and unconscious the beliefs, the longer it will take the client to change them. This "working through" process is addressed in part through "therapeutic repetition" and in part through focus on affect. We mention it here to remind you that consistent, compassionate patience is an important part of what you offer in therapy.

Implications of Persistent Patterns

A usual assumption that therapists make, and that clients very much *resist* making, is that persistent patterns of behavior (e.g., marrying substance abusers, losing jobs, getting manipulated by others, etc.) are at least partially the result of the client's choices and expectations. It is probably not just fate, bad luck, or unfairness that explains why a pattern of bad things keeps happening. We emphasize the word *pattern*. Isolated problems that have very little to do with clients' choices can arise in relationships, and some recurring events happen (miscarriages and racial discrimination, as examples) that dramatically affect clients' quality of life but seem to be almost entirely outside of their control. But as a general rule, at least most of the patterns in relationships that clients discuss are partially "courted" by the clients themselves.

> . . . at bottom, no subject is naive. Every deceived lover, every betrayed friend, every subject of writing knows on some level what is in store for him, and remains in the relationship anyway, impelled by something stronger than his reason. (p. 39)

Almost always, such structuring of unfortunate patterns takes place unconsciously, which helps explain, of course, clients' angry resistance when confronted with the possibility that they are partially responsible. They do not *feel* responsible. They feel, in fact, helpless and often ashamed that sheer force of will is insufficient to extricate themselves. As Malcolm (1989) indicated.

The client who insists she wants her grown child out of the house but cannot find a way to get her to move is usually quite conscious of her anger and resentment but much less aware of how and why she refuses to set limits. Nor is she aware that this difficulty has probably been evidenced in other relationships. The first approach used by some therapists with such a client in individual therapy will be educational and behavioral—helping her clarify her position relative to her daughter, teaching her assertive skills, etc. But if that approach doesn't work, many times the therapist and client will step back a pace to examine what expectations, fears, guilt, and hopes keep her "stuck" in this and other relationships. Perhaps she will discover that, like many women, her identity seems to be at stake when important relationships feel threatened and that setting limits is perceived as threatening rather than enhancing relationships

(Gilligan, 1982). Or perhaps she will uncover promises she made to herself as a child about the way she would treat her children. Regardless, discovering some of the less conscious roots to her present behavior may aid her in feeling freer to take decisive action.

As noted above, you can expect a strong defensive reaction if you suggest outright that the client has had a part in structuring the pattern that is being bemoaned. Any confrontations or interpretations you make will need to be phrased as empathically and tactfully as possible to enhance the likelihood that they will be heard. (For more on this topic, see the chapter "Resistance.")

Complementary expectations.   An easy trap for beginning therapists to fall into is taking sides. (This is especially likely to happen if they hear only one point of view but is not uncommon when working with couples.) Typically, they will side with whomever they see as the underdog. It seems so clearly unfair and unjust what the client is having to go through that they may focus exclusively on how the environment is blocking the client's progress. They may work very hard to help the client be more assertive, more proactive, more self-affirming—only to see that again and again he or she chooses to stay in relationships that appear totally unpromising. After this happens with a few hundred clients, many therapists become jaundiced and cynical. Why bother to help, they wonder, when clients keep sabotaging their best efforts?

The alternative either to naively buying into the client's point of view or to feeling angry and disillusioned if immediate change is not forthcoming is to understand from the beginning that the client is part of a *system*. We will not at this point review the complicated and often very insightful literature on systems therapy, except to remind you of a key proposition—that people gravitate toward others with similar or complementary expectations. It is uncanny how predictably a person who takes a victim position can find an abuser for a mate. Or, conversely, how someone who expects to be treated with respect, and will tolerate nothing less, frequently has a variety of rich and fulfilling relationships.

The issue, as we see it, is not that clients in destructive relationships do not feel that they need more. With few exceptions, they *feel* angry, hurt, or bewildered. The problem is that they do not *believe* they can get more. Their assumption, their "world view," is that they must settle for what they can get if they want to have any relationships at all, and to insist on mutuality and reciprocity will drive everyone away. That assumption, unsurprisingly, sets them up for exploitation.

We think you will find that your therapy is more effective if you resist the temptation to think of clients in terms of "games" they are playing. We also suggest that you not be overly infatuated with the concept of "secondary gains." The amount of human pain some clients experience is staggering. Many (though not all) of these clients would not tolerate such pain if they truly believed that there were other options. It will probably be more helpful if you see your task, as one therapist (Bown, 1979) said, as getting them to the point where they can "believe in the impossible." Until they can begin to believe that they can have reciprocal, rich relationships, they will probably continue to structure the same patterns and norms as before, albeit with new partners. (We note again at this point a consideration that threads throughout this book—that the relationship you offer clients can be crucial in this process of helping them to experience and thus believe in the "impossible." Your relationship with them is not equal or reciprocal in the usual use of the term, but the essential quality ingredients of respect and empathy and clear limits should be undeniable.)

Ambivalence about intimacy.   A final assumption about relationships is that people seem both to fear and to long for intimacy. While there has been recent speculation that women consider relationships "safer" and more identity-enhancing than men (Gilligan, 1982; Chodorow, 1974; Miller, 1976), this seems to be a matter of degree, not sharp distinction. Our impression is that part of the human condition is the strong, sometimes overpowering, need for affirmation from others and the concurrent vulnerability one feels if that affirmation is not forthcoming.

Clearly, some people let their need for affirmation show more transparently than others—for example, the hypochondriac, the dependent personality, the bereaved. In working with these clients, you will sense an almost tangible longing. But those who try to deny their need (avoidant personalities, acting-out adolescents, abusive partners, etc.) are also transparent in their obsession with relationships. Their need to avoid pain and humiliation is simply the flip side of their need for intimacy.

Most student therapists are so relationship-oriented by nature that it comes as no great surprise to them that clients need human attachments. What is sometimes harder for them to understand is that the same clients who work so hard to attain intimacy sometimes also work very hard to sabotage their own efforts. Eventually, most therapists come to appreciate the power and potential danger of loving, and it begins to make more sense to them why clients are so ambivalent about intimacy. Person (1988) said it well: "While it is true that love can be an agent for personal growth and change, it is also a loose cannon on the deck of human affairs."

What are humans afraid of, in relation to intimacy? The answer to that seems to be that we are usually afraid of two things—engulfment and/or abandonment. People who are afraid of engulfment are likely to be quite consciously wary of being trapped, of making commitments prematurely, or giving up their freedom. (While it makes sense that this kind of fear would have its roots in early experiences of being controlled or smothered, that explanation does not always seem to apply.) Abandonment fears, conversely, are excruciatingly painful but for the opposite reason; the terror, as one client described it, is similar to being "lost in space, forever, all by myself." Our experience is that most people have both sets of fears, to a greater or lesser extent, but that one set usually predominates in a given individual (and that, predictably, such fears will be part of what the client brings into therapy). As you might guess, two people with complementary sets of fears often manage to find each other with considerable regularity and then set up a painful and enmeshed "dance" of approach/avoidance.

DYSFUNCTIONAL STYLES

The risk in categorizing and describing typical dysfunctional styles is that the categories will necessarily be somewhat arbitrary and will thus lend themselves to superficial treatment. We believe that the potential benefits of describing for you some of the styles you will need to understand and deal with as a therapist will outweigh these risks, but we encourage you to see each client as a complex and multidimensional human being whom you will never fully understand. We offer the following descriptions in the hope that you will find them useful as you try to understand and help your clients, rather than simply relating to them as others in their lives do by reacting to the dysfunctional styles. Your task is to make sure you have more to offer them than automatic reactions and to maintain your therapeutic position of "compassionate dispassion."

We believe that, at base, dysfunctional relationship styles derive from an attempt to control others so that one's needs for affirmation can be met and that such a style was usually forged early in life. Given the vulnerability clients feel when their needs for acknowledgment and affirmation are unmet, there is a certain logic to their trying to control the ones in their lives whom they perceive as potential need satisfiers. Regardless of your personal feelings about such a "control" issue, this is perhaps less a moral issue than a practical one: Control rarely works in interpersonal relationships, and when it does, there is almost always a big cost. (For a theoretical discussion of behavior as a "control of perception" mechanism, we refer you to Powers [1973]. Hyland [1987] specifically applies control theory to depression.)

The controlling styles and underlying dynamics that are simplest to identify are those that rely on overt domination, such as physical or verbal abuse. The typical abusive spouse, for example, is frequently "hooked" by jealousy and defiance—behaviors that make him or her feel inadequate and out of control. Their strong needs for attachment and their fears of abandonment lead them to defend against painful feelings of vulnerability by becoming abusive, in hopes that the offending spouse will be bullied back into line. They may be relatively unaware of either the increasing resentment they engender or the damage they do to the trust in the relationship each time they resort to such tactics. Like other controllers—only perhaps more dramatically—they end up "winning the battle and losing the war." They succeed in getting their way in the short run, but they irreparably damage the relationship over time. At a bare minimum, such clients need help in learning new behaviors that are more functional, in understanding the long-term effects of their behavior, and in facing the reality of their helplessness to make others love them.

Only slightly less obvious in their attempts to dominate are what Bergman (1985) calls the "bulldozers." These people are less overtly abusive than they are strong-willed and self-righteous. It simply does not often occur to them to treat others' needs and ideas with much respect; they operate in life as if their integrity depends on never being influenced by someone else. Often they bear some of the marks of the "detached personality" (Bowlby, 1973). Listening to others and accommodating their needs is thus quite difficult for them, and they tend to wear out both their friendships and work relationships quickly. Such clients have little experiential understanding of the creative give-and-take that leads to mutuality and reciprocity. If they cannot dilute their compulsive need to control others enough to acknowledge and respect others' separateness, they are likely to continue to sacrifice intimacy for dominance.

Another controlling style, often manifested by clients with narcissistic personality disorders, is one based on subtle, manipulative deception. The client who consciously pretends to be sick or helpless in order to gain her family's attention, the "Joe Cool" who relies on false protestations of love to seduce his dates, the employee who lies about sick relatives to gain his boss's sympathy—individuals who make life styles of such tactics seem to do so because they do not trust their personal power to elicit affirmation from others. Rather than simply asking for what they want, they rely on untruthfulness to justify their requests. The ones who have well-developed styles you may never see in your office, for they are getting reinforced enough by others to make changing seem too risky. It is the ones who have gotten "caught" in the dishonesty or are in enough pain that they cannot deny their vulnerability who may be open enough to explore what they are up to and make some changes. As the first two groups substituted dominance for affirmation, so this group seems to substitute attention. At best, they have learned something about drawing others toward them but little about maintaining attachments in nonexploitative ways.

At the other side of the continuum from these overt controllers are the dependent individuals who attempt to control relationships by pleasing. Frightened by the possibility of being abandoned or rejected, they become quite practiced at picking up on others' cues and trying to accommodate them. Their own preferences and needs are often ignored by both themselves and the other party as they focus on being pleasant, undemanding, and, as one client said, "irresistible." The resulting pain, anger, and diminishing self-respect frequently do lead many of these folks into therapy, where they need to learn to affirm their own needs more and to allow exploitation less. It is unlikely that they are consciously aware that their self-denial is a form of control and that they, like other controllers, are defending against feelings of vulnerability by sacrificing true intimacy for, in this case, the hope of a permanently harmonious relationship.

The group that is least likely to be viewed as exercising much control interpersonally is the one made up of passive victims. Certainly, there are many situations when relatively powerless people are abused and dominated. Especially when these are the very young, or ill, or elderly, or the victims of violent crimes like rape or murder, their choices are so limited as to be almost negligible. It is unconscionable to hold someone accountable when he or she has no power; such "blaming the victim" is both unfair and dishonest, and it contributes to clients' guilt (Ryan, 1971). Nonetheless, therapists who automatically champion the underdog in less extreme situations may be blinding themselves to the reality that some victims at least theoretically *could* make changes or extricate themselves from destructive relationships. As Perls (1969) reminds us, underdogs or "martyrs" often have more power than is immediately apparent. Part of your job as therapist will be to help your clients feel more empowered, when possible, and to encourage them to use that power wisely. You will discover that some victims seem so addicted to simple contact with their exploiters that they return again and again, at times behaving in ways that clearly elicit the abuse. In a sense, they may be assuming a one-down role to gain a very empty sense of control, for the reassurance of attachment to another, even toxic attachment, may seem preferable to them to being ignored or abandoned.

The final group of controllers we wish to mention is one that attempts to maintain contact with others by adopting a combative style. They want engagement that is relatively equal—but without the vulnerability of intimacy. And so they fight, not just occasionally, but as a relationship habit. Staying available to each other, but as adversaries, they do succeed in forging attachment, but the bond is predicated upon conflict rather than cooperative relating.

RELATIONSHIP SKILLS

Many of the clients you will see will be very unhappy in some of their relationships, will ask for help in improving them, but will nonetheless feel quite sure that good relationships are more contingent on luck or chemistry than on aspects they can directly influence. They will ask for new ideas, but their underlying beliefs may keep them from implementing those ideas consistently. As indicated earlier, our belief is that helping them explore some of their early problematic attachments can be very helpful, but it is also possible to work almost entirely in the present. We believe you will be more likely to help such clients if you do *both* and if the suggestions you offer for present changes are not isolated into unrelated behaviors but instead fit into a contextual understanding of qualities and skills that tend to lead to deeper, richer relationships. You will discover as you read through the next section that the skills mentioned not only overlap but are somewhat arbitrarily defined. They reflect the qualities of a mature, healthy adult who is relatively free of some of the control issues just discussed.

Self-respect.   Without a belief that what they have to offer others is valuable and that they themselves are lovable, clients will continue to structure relationships that are unfulfilling, if not destructive. To build good relationships with others requires at least a marginal respect for oneself.

We prefer the worlds *self-respect* or *self-affirmation,* old-fashioned as they may be, to the ubiquitous term *self-esteem.* Esteeming oneself is difficult to do if one has long ago internalized negative ways of relating to oneself and especially if one is behaving in ways that are nonestimable. Respecting oneself and affirming one's strengths and potential, conversely, are closer to conscious choices one can make in an ongoing way. As clients make new choices and refuse to collude with others in allowing themselves to be treated in ways that lack respect and affirmation, their relationships and views of themselves are likely to improve substantially. In a sense, they create their own "self-esteem," not by giving themselves empty pep talks, but by experiencing the rewards of making different choices.

Honoring one's needs.   People who build healthy relationships tend to be relatively unapologetic about what they need and expect from others (Branden, 1985). Rather than ruminating about whether or not they have the "right" to need something, they behave in ways that suggest that reciprocity and mutuality are the only real options they will consider. They are more likely to see their needs as a contribution to the relationship—something that allows for their receptiveness to others' caring—and not simply as an inroad for possible injury and exploitation. Knowing and affirming what one needs from another is not, of course, a license to make childish demands to be rescued from self-responsibility. One must still be willing to grow up. But grown-ups, as well as children, have legitimate needs for deep, enhancing, mutual relationships, and your clients may benefit from your help in believing and acting on this concept.

Setting limits.   A related skill that enhances relationships is the ability to set limits. Actually, this ties in closely with both respecting oneself and honoring one's needs; we should set limits or say no when, for example, someone purposefully or inadvertently treats us in unacceptable ways. Many of your dependent clients will be quite fearful of saying no. It will probably be necessary for you to recouch this kind of "limit setting" for them in such a way that it is seen as part of the responsibility they have to define for another how they want and do not want to relate, rather than making the other person guess.

Setting limits does, in fact, involve some risks. Someone may like them less because of a stand they take. On the other hand, not setting limits often involves higher risks in the long term, since the usual consequence is increased resentment and the gradual erosion of identity. For your clients to have more successful relationships, they will need to believe that the more clearly they define themselves and the various roles from which they operate the more likely others will be to respect them. They will discover that limits are not, after all, just reflected by their no's; they can affirm, or say yes, more freely also when they can differentiate what they value and are willing to tolerate from what they cannot.

Listening and responding.   As was discussed in the chapter "Responsibility," healthy relationships require that both parties have the ability to understand and respond with some consistency to each other's needs. Listening in the relationship thus becomes part of the ongoing process, since one's own and the other's needs and feelings are often in flux. One does not accomplish much by listening once and then stopping. The commitment to listen works best when it is directed to the continual exploration/discovery of the evolving issues relevant to the relationship. As Gilbert and Rachlin (1987) point out, such listening and nurturing have traditionally been more expected of women than of men but, especially among dual-career couples, need to be reciprocal for the relationship to thrive. Many of our clients will explain that they like to be needed, just not *too much* (perhaps because that would require them to set limits). As they work through some of their own dependency and responsibility issues, they will find it easier and more fun to listen and respond to others. With your help, they may even discover that listening and responding can be creative acts, from which they emerge more fulfilled and enhanced.

Tolerating ambiguity and conflict.   Healthy relationships tend to be characterized by harmony, cooperation, and pleasure. Conflict, nonetheless, is inevitable, since no two people have identical identities. Fearful as many of your clients will be of it, it is not the conflict of desires or preferences or values that is so destructive; it is the way the individuals deal with those conflicts that largely determines the prognosis of a relationship.

Conflict is a test of one's ability to remain separate but still in a relationship. For your clients to do that, they will have to have a strong enough sense of their self that they can manage without the other's affirmation for a while. They will need to rely on their own resources without panicking until the conflict can be resolved. In major disagreements, this may take weeks or months. The same principle applies, however, with the common, small irritations that ensue when any two people spend extended periods of time together. As two people in conflict learn to expand their viewpoint to include the other's perspective, they will find that conflict resolution can be based optimally on a win-win approach (Campbell, 1984).

Committing Oneself.   The last quality we will mention which we see as an essential ingredient in healthy relationships is the ability to commit oneself to the relationship process. Although some of your clients may associate commitment with entrapment, we see commitment less as an eternally binding promise than as a willingness and desire to fully invest oneself. Commitment is not loyalty to the status quo (the name for that phenomenon is often "insecurity"), nor is it a sense of duty to the fulfilling of joyless responsibilities and obligations. Duty may well be virtuous and at times required, but it is usually more closely related to resignation and resentment than to the wholehearted investment in a life-enhancing process.

Ideally, people make commitments from a position of strength, not weakness, and they do it because they believe such commitment will allow them an opportunity to nurture and enhance their self. The clients you work with who are afraid of commitment may need your help in understanding that psychologically healthy people do not make commitments because they feel certain that no one "better" will come along; they make them because the interaction between them and the other person is so enhancing they do not want to live without it. If, after many relationships, clients still insist that the "right person" has just not crossed their path, it may be more accurate and helpful to suggest that the problem instead might be that they have not invested enough in any of the interactions to feel challenged and fulfilled (Yalom, 1980).

THERAPEUTIC CONSIDERATIONS

There are several suggestions we offer for your consideration to help you as you work with clients on relationship issues. Some of these have been alluded to previously.

Monitor countertransference.   For a further exploration of this topic, refer to the specific chapter "Countertransference." At this point, we would only underscore two related issues: (1) The client's interactional patterns with you often provide valuable clues regarding his or her style with others, and (2) part of your responsibility to your clients involves your refraining from impulsively acting out your nontherapeutic reactions to them and instead consistently offering them a relationship which to some extent models those skills and qualities described in the previous section.

Encourage empathy.   Many of your clients will be experiencing relationship difficulties as a result of becoming polarized from their associates. In an attempt to defend their position and protect themselves from hurt or criticism, they may have quit listening to others or considering alternative perceptions. (It is difficult, after all, to prove to someone else that you are right and still listen.) Part of your task may be to simultaneously provide support and empathy for your clients and also help them broaden their understanding of what may be happening in a given situation. Asking occasional well-timed questions like, "How does your wife feel about that?" or "What do you suppose was going on with him when he said that?" or "How did she feel differently after you made your point?" can begin to sensitize them to others' feelings. More dramatically, you may want to set up role plays or use imagery or a modified empty-chair technique to encourage a client to take on the role of someone he or she is in conflict with or does not understand. Similarly, well-timed self-disclosure, when blended with empathy, can serve to open a client to unexplored alternative perspectives. When working with couples, a role reversal role play is sometimes beneficial if the conflict is not too pronounced.

The timing of such interventions is crucial. Remember that from your clients' perspective your challenging their point of view may seem as if you have broken the alliance and are now "against" them instead of "for" them. This is particularly likely if you are encouraging them to understand the position of someone with whom they are in a power struggle. As one client told her therapist in such a situation, "It felt like it used to when I would tell my mother what my brother had done to hurt me and she would try to explain his side."

Investigate overt behavior.   In much of this book, we have suggested you focus heavily on the client's intra- and interpersonal dynamics. We would like to suggest at this point that you not forget to ask about *what* and *how* they communicate to others. Most therapists have been in the position from time to time of "stumbling on" a piece of client behavior that suddenly clarifies many of that client's difficulties (for example, finding out that in arguments the client withdraws and sulks). Accordingly, many of us have trained ourselves to routinely inquire about behavior, even if our orientation is far from behaviorist. We think you will understand your clients' relationships much more fully if you can get an idea of how they express anger, fear, vulnerability, affection, regret, etc.

Asking specifically, "What did you *do* when you were feeling that?" is certainly one way to get such information. Other ways include asking related questions such as, "How would an objective observer have described you at that point?" or, with humor, "If I talked to your teacher, what would *she* tell me you had done?" Again, setting up a role play, either for the client to demonstrate how an event transpired or to rehearse new ways of coping, can give you valuable insights into your client's style.

Certainly, the most direct way to learn about clients' interactions with others is to observe them, as in couples, family, or group therapy. One of the authors was astonished to discover, for example, that the reserved, middle-40s British male she had been seeing individually for a year, and had understood to be somewhat fearful and subservient with his lover, was quite different when his partner came to the session. The fear and passivity he had alluded to in therapy were cloaked in a heavy veneer of defensiveness, and even when his lover reached out, he tended to respond with suspicion and veiled attacks. Being able to *see* how the system worked was enormously enlightening and offered new direction for therapeutic focus.

Discuss others discreetly.   In discussing with a client his or her relationship with another, it may be tempting for you to speculate on this absent third person's behavior or motives. We suggest professional restraint. Remember that your clients are not bound by confidentiality, although you are. Remember also that their styles in these outside relationships may be dysfunctional, and in a conflict they may be tempted to quote you. One of our students, for example, received an irate phone call at 11:00 P.M. from the boyfriend of a client, demanding to know if in fact she had called him a "jerk." (As it turned out, it was true that she had said, "He sounds like a real jerk," and she admitted in supervision that she had been tempted originally to use a more colloquial anatomical term than jerk.) The guideline we offer is that you exercise great caution in your speculations and that you never say anything about a third person unless you would be willing to say it if she or he were present.

Know referral sources.   Not everything that is helpful or therapeutic for a client takes place during the psychotherapy hour. If you can recommend to clients appropriate outside forms of help, you may be able to help them structure their "nontherapy" hours in ways that support the work the two of you are doing regarding relationships.

Often therapists recommend relevant self-help books to clients who enjoy reading. Similarly, referrals are often made to such self-help groups as AA, Al-Anon, Emotions Anonymous, Compassionate Friends, etc., to give clients further support and insight as they struggle with relationship issues. Get familiar with the ones in your area so that you can make knowledgeable suggestions. Finally, it will be important to become familiar with other community policies and procedures, such as psychiatric hospitalization procedures, police interventions, etc., since some of your clients' relationship and personal issues may escalate to crisis proportions.

SUMMARY

Many of your clients will want your help with their relationship difficulties. Some of them may be haunted by past experiences of abuse, neglect, or abandonment; others will be struggling with how to improve or extricate themselves from present relationships. As you attempt to help such individuals, a solid understanding of the interpersonal dynamics that lead to both healthy and dysfunctional relationships will be very important. We encourage you to listen carefully to the patterns your clients describe—and especially to attend to their habitual ways of interacting with you—so that you can help them resolve some of their pain from the past and create more fulfilling relationships in the present.

REFERENCES AND SELECTED RECOMMENDED READING

ADLER, A. (1933). *What life should mean to you.* Boston: Little.

AINSWORTH, M.D.S., BLEHAR, M.C., WATERS, E., & WALL, S. (1978). *Patterns of attachment.* Hillsdale, NJ: Erlbaum.

AKAMATSU, T.J. (1988). Intimate relationships with former clients: National survey of attitudes and behavior among practitioners. *Professional Psychology: Research and Practice, 19,* 454–458.

AMERICAN PSYCHIATRIC ASSOCIATION. (1987). *Diagnostic and statistical manual of mental disorders* (3rd ed., rev.). Washington, DC: American Psychiatric Press.

AMERICAN PSYCHOLOGICAL ASSOCIATION. (1981a). *Ethical Principles of Psychologists* (rev. ed.). Washington, DC: Author.

AMERICAN PSYCHOLOGICAL ASSOCIATION. (1981b). Specialty guidelines for the delivery of services by clinical psychologists. *American Psychologist, 36,* 640–651.

AMERICAN PSYCHOLOGICAL ASSOCIATION. (1981c). Specialty guidelines for the delivery of services by counseling psychologists. *American Psychologist, 36,* 652–663.

AMERICAN PSYCHOLOGICAL ASSOCIATION. (1987a). *Casebook on ethical principles of psychologists* (rev. ed.). Washington, DC: Author.

AMERICAN PSYCHOLOGICAL ASSOCIATION. (1987b). *General guidelines for providers of psychological services.* Washington, DC: Author.

AMERICAN PSYCHOLOGICAL ASSOCIATION, COMMITTEE ON WOMEN IN PSYCHOLOGY. (1989). If sex enters into the psychotherapy relationship. *Professional Psychology: Research and Practice, 20,* 112–115. (Also available as a brochure.)

AMERICAN PSYCHOLOGICAL ASSOCIATION, ETHICS COMMITTEE. (1985). Rules and procedures. *American Psychologist, 40,* 685–694.

AMERICAN PSYCHOLOGICAL ASSOCIATION, TASK FORCE ON SEX BIAS AND SEX ROLE STEREOTYPING IN PSYCHOTHERAPEUTIC PRACTICE. (1978). Guidelines on therapy with women. *American Psychologist, 33,* 1122–1123.

ANCHIN, J.C., & KIESLER, D.J. (EDS.). (1982). *Handbook of interpersonal psychotherapy.* New York: Pergamon.

ANDREWS, J.D.W.   (1989). Integrating visions of reality: Interpersonal diagnosis and the existential vision. *American Psychologist, 44*, 803–817.

ANOUILH, J.   (1960). *Becket.* New York: New American Library.

ARKOWITZ, H., & MESSER, S. (EDS.).   (1984). *Psychoanalytic and behavior therapy: Is integration possible?* New York: Plenum.

ATKINSON, D.R., & GIM, R.H.   (1989). Asian-American cultural identity and attitudes toward mental health services. *Journal of Counseling Psychology, 36*, 209–212.

ATKINSON, D.R., POSTON, W.C., FURLONG, M.J., & MERCADO, P.   Ethnic group preferences for counselor characteristics. *Journal of Counseling Psychology, 36*, 68–72.

BACHELOR, A.   (1988). How clients perceive therapist empathy: A content analysis of "received" empathy. *Psychotherapy, 25*, 227–240.

BACORN, C.N., & DIXON, D.N.   (1984). The effects of touch on depressed and vocationally undecided clients. *Journal of Counseling Psychology, 31*, 488–496.

BANDURA, A.   (1978). The self system in reciprocal determinism. *American Psychologist, 33*, 344–358.

BANDURA, A.   (1982). The psychology of chance encounters and life paths. *American Psychologist, 37*, 747–755.

BARLOW, D. (ED.).   (1981). *Behavioral assessment of adult disorders.* New York: Guilford.

BARROWS, P.A., & HALGIN, R.P.   (1988). Current issues in psychotherapy with gay men: Impact of the AIDS phenomenon. *Professional Psychology: Research and Practice, 19*, 395–401.

BAUER, G.P., & KOBOS, J.C.   (1987). Brief Therapy: Short term psychodynamic intervention. Northvale, N.J.: Aronson.

BAUMEISTER, R.F.   (1982). A self-presentational view of social phenomena. *Psychological Bulletin, 91*, 3–26.

BEANE, J.   (1981). "I'd rather be dead than gay": Counseling gay men who are coming out. *Personnel and Guidance Journal, 60*, 222–226.

BELLACK, A.S., & HERSEN, M. (EDS.).   (1988). *Behavioral assessment: A practical handbook* (3rd. ed.). New York: Pergamon.

BERGER, D.   (1987). *Clinical empathy.* Northvale, NJ: Aronson.

BERGIN, A.E.   (1980). Psychotherapy and religious values. *Journal of Consulting and Clinical Psychology, 48*, 95–105.

BERGIN, A.E.   (1985). Proposed values for guiding and evaluating counseling and psychotherapy. *Counseling and Values, 29*, 99–116.

BERGMAN, J.   (1985). *Fishing for barracuda: Pragmatics of brief system therapy.* New York: W.W. Norton.

BEUTLER, L.E.   (1981). Convergence in counseling and psychotherapy: A current look. *Clinical Psychology Review, 1*, 79–101.

BEUTLER, L.E.   (1983). *Eclectic psychotherapy: A systematic approach.* New York: Pergamon.

BLANCK, G., & BLANCK, R.   (1974). *Ego psychology, theory, and practice.* New York: Columbia University Press.

BOUHOUTSOS, J., HOLROYD, J., LERMAN, H., FORER, B., & GREENBERG, M.   (1983). Sexual intimacy between psychotherapists and patients. *Professional Psychology: Research and Practice, 14*, 185–196.

BOWLBY, J.   (1969). *Attachment and loss: Vol. 1. Attachment.* New York: Basic Books.

BOWLBY, J.   (1973). *Attachment and loss: Vol. 2. Separation: Anxiety and anger.* New York: Basic Books.

BOWLBY, J.   (1980). *Attachment and loss: Vol. 3. Loss: Sadness and depression.* London: Hogarth Press.

BOWLBY, J.   (1988). Attachment, communication, and the therapeutic process. In J. Bowlby, *A secure base: Clinical application of attachment theory.* London: Routledge.

BOY, A., & PINE, G.   (1982) *Client-centered counseling: A renewal.* Boston: Allyn & Bacon.

BRANDEN, N.   (1985). *Honoring the self.* New York: Bantam Books.

BRAUN, J.A.   (1982) Ethical issues in the treatment of religious persons. In M. Rosenbaum (Ed.)., *Ethics and values in psychotherapy* (pp. 131–160). New York: Free Press.

BRODY, E.M., & FARBER, B.A.   (1989). Effects of psychotherapy on significant others. *Professional Psychology: Research and Practice, 20*, 116–122.

BROVERMAN, I.D., BROVERMAN, D.M., CLARKSON, F.E., ROSENKRANTZ, P.S., & VOGEL, S.R.   (1970). Sex-role stereotypes and clinical judgments of mental health. *Journal of Consulting and Clinical Psychology, 34*, 1–7.

BUCK, R.   (1985). Prime theory: An integrated view of motivation and emotion. *Psychological Review, 92*, 389–413.

BUGENTAL, J.   (1978). *Psychotherapy and process.* Reading, MA: Addison–Wesley.

BUGENTAL, J.F. (1987). *The art of the psychotherapist.* New York: W.W. Norton.

BUGENTAL, J.F.T. (1988). What is "failure" in psychotherapy? *Psychotherapy, 25,* 532–535.

BUTLER, M. (1985). Guidelines for feminist therapy. In L. Rosewater & L. Walker (Eds.), *Handbook of feminist therapy: Women's issues in psychotherapy* (pp. 32–38). New York: Springer.

BYRNE, D. (1971). *The attraction paradigm.* New York: Academic Press.

CADDY, G.R. (1985). Alcoholism. In M. Hersen & S.M. Turner (Eds.), *Diagnostic interviewing* (pp. 161–182). New York: Plenum.

CAMPBELL, S. (1984). *Beyond the power struggle.* San Luis Obispo, CA: Impact Publishers.

CAPLAN, P.J. (1984). The myth of women's masochism. *American Psychologist, 39,* 130–139.

CARKHUFF, R., & ANTHONY, W. (1979). *The skills of helping.* Amherst, MA: Human Resource Development Press.

CASAS, J.M. (1984). Policy, training, and research in counseling psychology. The racial/ethnic minority perspective. In S. Brown & R. Lent (Eds.), *Handbook of counseling psychology* (pp. 785–831). New York: Wiley.

CASAS, J.M., PONTEROTTO, J.G., & GUTIERREZ, J.M. (1986). An ethical indictment of counseling research and training: The cross-cultural perspective. *Journal of Counseling and Development, 64,* 347–349.

CAVANAUGH, J.L., JR., & ROGERS, R. (EDS.). (1983). Informed consent [Special issue]. *Behavioral Sciences and the Law, 2,* (3).

CAYLEFF, S.E. (1986). Ethical issues in counseling gender, race, and culturally distinct groups. *Journal of Counseling and Development, 64,* 345–347.

CHEKHOV, A. (1959). Misery. In D.H. Green (Ed.) and C. Garnett (Trans.), *Great stories by Chekhov* (pp. 11–24). New York: Dell. (Reprinted from *The schoolmistress and other stories,* 1918. New York: Macmillan.)

CHODOROW, N. (1974). The Reproduction of Mothering. Berkely, C.A. University of California Press.

CLAIBORN, C.D. (1982). Interpretation and change in counseling. *Journal of Counseling Psychology, 29,* 439–453.

CLAIBORN, C.D., & LICHTENBERG, J.W. (1989). Interactional counseling. *The Counseling Psychologist, 17,* 355–453.

CLAIBORN, C.D., WARD, S.R., & STRONG, S. (1981). Effect of congruence between counselor interpretations and client beliefs. *Journal of Counseling Psychology, 28,* 101–109.

CLANCE, P.R., & IMES, S.A. (1979). The impostor phenomenon in high achieving women: Dynamics and therapeutic intervention. *Psychotherapy: Theory, Research, and Practice, 15,* 241–247.

COHEN, R.J. (1979). *Malpractice: A guide for mental health professionals.* New York: Free Press.

COMAZ-DIAZ, L., & GRIFFITH, E.A. (1988). *Clinical guidelines in cross-cultural mental health.* New York: Wiley.

COMMITTEE FOR PROTECTION OF HUMAN PARTICIPANTS IN RESEARCH IN COOPERATION WITH THE COMMITTEE ON GAY CONCERNS. (1986). Ethical issues in psychological research on AIDS. *Journal of Homosexuality, 13,* 109–116.

CONOLEY, C.W., CONOLEY, J.C., McCONNELL, J.A., & KIMZEY, C.E. (1983). The effect of the ABCs of rational emotive therapy and the empty-chair technique of gestalt therapy on anger reduction. *Psychotherapy: Theory, Research, and Practice, 20,* 112–117.

CONOLEY, C.W. & GARBER, R.A. (1985). Effects of reframing and self-control directives on loneliness, depression, and controllability. *Journal of Counseling Psychology, 32,* 139–142.

COREY, G., COREY, M.S., & CALLANAN, P. (1988). *Issues and ethics in the helping professions* (3rd ed.). Belmont, CA: Wadsworth.

CORMIER, L.S., & BERNARD, J.M. (1982). Ethical and legal responsibilities of clinical supervisors. *Personnel and Guidance Journal, 60,* 486–491.

COURTOIS, C. (1988). *Healing the incest wound.* New York: W.W. Norton.

COWEN, E.L. (1982). Help is where you find it: Four informal helping groups. *American Psychologist, 37,* 385–395.

CROWNE, D.P., & MARLOWE, D. (1960). A new scale of social desirability independent of psychopathology. *Journal of Consulting Psychology, 24,* 349–354.

CUMMINGS, N.A. (1988). Emergence of the mental health complex: Adaptive and maladaptive responses. *Professional Psychology: Research and Practice, 19,* 308–315.

DAVENPORT, D. (1982). Women and the daimonic. *The Counseling Psychologist, 10*(3), 76–78.

DAVENPORT, D. (1983). A redefinition of the professor's role: From transparency to responsibility.

Paper presented at the annual meeting of the American Psychological Association, Washington, DC.

DAVISON, G.   (1973). Counter-control in behavior modification. In L. Hamerlyncy & E. Mash (Eds.). *Behavioral change: Methodology, concepts, and practice.* Champaign, IL: Research Press.

DEARDORFF, W.W., CROSS, H.J., & HUPPRICH, W.R.   (1984). Malpractice liability in psychotherapy: Client and practitioner perspectives. *Professional Psychology: Research and Practice, 15,* 590–600.

DEKRAAI, M.B., & SALES, B.D.   (1982). Privileged communications of psychologists. *Professional Psychology, 13,* 372–388.

DEKRAAI, M.B., & SALES, B.D.   (1984). Confidential communications of psychotherapists. *Psychotherapy, 21,* 293–318.

DELEON, P.H., VANDENBOS, G.R., & CUMMINGS, N.A.   (1983). Psychotherapy—Is it safe, effective, and appropriate? The beginning of an evolutionary dialogue. *American Psychologist, 38,* 907–911.

DORN, F.J. (ED.).   (1986). *The social influence process in counseling and psychotherapy.* Springfield, IL: C.C. Thomas.

DOWD, E.T., HUGHES, S.L., BROCKBANK, L., HALPAIN, D., SEIBEL, C., & SEIBEL, P.   (1988). Compliance-based and defiance-based intervention strategies and psychological reactance in the treatment of free and unfree behavior. *Journal of Counseling Psychology, 35,* 370–376.

DOWD, E.T., & MILNE, C.R.   (1986). Paradoxical interventions in counseling psychology. *The Counseling Psychologist, 14,* 237–282.

DRYDEN, W. (ED.).   (1987). *Therapists' dilemmas.* Cambridge, England: Hemisphere.

EAGLE, M.   (1987). Theoretical and clinical shifts in psychoanalysis. *American Journal of Orthopsychiatry, 57,* 175–185.

EDWARDS, A.L.   (1957). *The social desirability variable in personality assessment and research.* New York: Dryden.

EGAN, G.   (1986). *The skilled helper* (3rd ed.). Monterey, CA: Brooks/Cole.

ELLIS, A.   (1985). Expanding the ABC's of rational emotive therapy. In M.J. Mahoney & A. Freeman (Eds.), *Cognition and Psychotherapy* (pp. 313–323). New York: Plenum.

ELLIS, A.   (1985). *Overcoming resistance: Rational-emotive therapy with difficult clients.* New York: Springer.

EPPERSON, D.L., & LEWIS, K.N.   (1987). Issues of informed entry into counseling: Perceptions and preferences resulting from different types and amounts of pretherapy information. *Journal of Counseling Psychology, 34,* 266–275.

ERICKSON, M.H.   (1964). A hypnotic technique for resistant patients: The patient, the technique, and its rationale and field experiments. *The American Journal of Clinical Hypnosis, 7,* 8–32.

EVERSTINE, L., EVERSTINE, D.S., HEYMANN, G.M., TRUE, R.H., FREY, D.H., JOHNSON, H.G., & SEIDEN, R.H.   (1980). Privacy and confidentiality in psychotherapy. *American Psychologist, 35,* 828–840.

FAUSTMAN, W.O.   (1982). Legal and ethical issues in debt collection strategies of professional psychologists. *Professional Psychology, 13,* 208–214.

FISHER, J.D., RYTTING, M., & HESLIN, R.   (1976). Affective and evaluative effects of an interpersonal touch. *Sociometry, 39,* 419–421.

FITTING, M.D.   (1986). Ethical dilemmas in counseling elderly adults. *Journal of Counseling and Development, 64,* 325–327.

FITTS, W.H.   (1965). *The experience of psychotherapy.* Princeton, NJ: Van Nostrand.

FITZGERALD, L.F., & NUTT, R.   (1986). The Division 17 principles concerning counseling/psychotherapy of women: Rationale and implementation. *The Counseling Psychologist, 14,* 180–216.

FORD, M.R., & WIDIGER, T.A.   (1989). Sex bias in the diagnosis of histrionic and antisocial personality disorders. *Journal of Consulting and Clinical Psychology, 57,* 301–305.

FOREYT, J.P., & KONDO, A.T.   (1985). Eating disorders. In M. Hersen & S.M. Turner (Eds.)., *Diagnostic interviewing* (pp. 243–260). New York: Plenum.

FRANK, J.D.   (1973). *Persuasion and healing* (rev. ed.). Baltimore: Johns Hopkins University Press.

FRANK, J.D.   (1985). Therapeutic components shared by all psychotherapists. In M.J. Mahoney & A. Freeman (Eds.), *Cognition and psychotherapy* (pp. 49–79). New York: Plenum.

FREUD, S.   (1926/1961). Inhibitions, symptoms, and anxiety. *Standard edition* (Vol. 20). London: Hogarth Press.

FRIED, E.   (1980). *The courage to change.* New York: Brunner/Mazel.

FRIEDLANDER, M.L., & WARD, L.G.   (1984). Development and validation of the supervisory styles inventory. *Journal of counseling psychology, 31*, 541–557.

FRIEDMAN, R.C.   (1988). *Male homosexuality: A contemporary psychoanalytic perspective.* New Haven: Yale University Press.

FROMM, E.   (1956). *The art of loving.* New York: Harper & Row.

FULERO, S.M.   (1988). Tarasoff: 10 years later. *Professional Psychology: Research and Practice, 19*, 184–190.

GARFIELD, S.L.   (1980). *Psychotherapy: An eclectic approach.* New York: Wiley.

GARFIELD, S.L., & BERGIN, A.E. (EDS.).   (1986). *Handbook of psychotherapy and behavior change* (3rd ed.). New York: Wiley.

GELSO, C.J., & CARTER, J.A.   (1985). The relationship in counseling and psychotherapy. *The Counseling Psychologist, 13*, 155–244.

GILBERT, L.A.   (1980). Feminist therapy. In A.M. Brodsky & R.T. Hare-Muston (Eds.), *Women and psychotherapy* (pp. 245–266). New York: Guilford.

GILBERT, L.A.   (1987). Female and male emotional dependency and its implications for the therapist-client relationship. *Professional Psychology: Research and Practice, 18*, 555–561.

GILBERT, L.A., & RACHLIN, V.   (1987). Mental health and psychological functioning of dual-career families. *The Counseling Psychologist, 15*, 7–49.

GILLIGAN, C.   (1982). *In a different voice.* Cambridge, MA: Harvard University Press.

GILLILAND, B.E., & JAMES, R.K.   (1988). *Crisis intervention strategies.* Pacific Grove, CA: Brooks/Cole.

GIOVACCHINI, P.L.   (1988). *Countertransference: Triumphs and catastrophes.* New York: Aronson.

GLASER, R.D., & THORPE, J.S.   (1986). Unethical intimacy: A survey of sexual contact and advances between psychology educators and female graduate students. *American Psychologist, 41*, 43–51.

GLASS, G.V., & KLIEGL, R.M.   (1983). An apology for research integration in the study of psychotherapy. *Journal of Consulting and Clinical Psychology, 51*, 28–41.

GLASSER, W.   (1965). *Reality therapy: A new approach to psychiatry.* New York: Harper & Row.

GLIDDEN, C.E., & TRACEY, T.J.   (1989). Women's perceptions of personal versus sociocultural counseling interventions. *Journal of Counseling Psychology, 36*, 54–62.

GOLDFRIED, M.R.   (1980). Toward the delineation of therapeutic change principles. *American Psychologist, 35*, 991–999.

GOODMAN, M., & TEICHER, A.   (1988). To touch or not to touch. *Psychotherapy, 25*, 492–500.

GOODMAN, T.A.   (1985). From Tarasoff to Hopper: The evaluation of the therapist's duty to protect third parties. *Behavioral Sciences and the Law, 3*, 195–225.

GOODYEAR, R.K., & BRADLEY, F.O.   (1983). Theories of counselor supervision: Points of convergence and divergence. *The Counseling Psychologist, 11*(1), 59–67.

GORKIN, M.   (1987). *The uses of countertransference: Working with the therapist's response.* Northvale, NJ: Aronson.

GOTTLIEB, M.C., SELL, J.M., & SCHOENFIELD, L.S.   (1988). Social/romantic relationships with present and former clients: State licensing board actions. *Professional Psychology: Research and Practice, 19*, 459–462.

GREEN, S.L., & HANSEN, J.C.   (1986). Ethical dilemmas in family therapy. *Journal of Marital and Family Therapy, 12*, 225–230.

GREENBERG, J.R., & MITCHELL, S.A.   (1983). *Object relations in psychoanalytic theory.* Cambridge, MA: Harvard University Press.

GREENBERG, L.S., & SAFRAN, J.D.   (1987). *Emotion in psychotherapy: Affect, cognition, and the process of change.* New York: Guilford.

GREENBERG, L.S., & SAFRAN, J.D.   (1989). Emotion in psychotherapy. *American Psychologist, 44*, 19–29.

GUIDANO, V.F., & LIOTTI, G.   (1985). A constructivistic foundation for cognitive therapy. In M.J. Mahoney and A. Freeman (Eds.), *Cognition and psychotherapy* (pp. 101–142). New York: Plenum.

GURMAN, A.S., KNISKERN, D.P., & PINSOF, W.M.   (1986). Research on the process and outcome of marital and family therapy. In S.L. Garfield & A.S. Bergin (Eds.), *Handbook of psychotherapy and behavior change* (3rd ed.) (pp. 565–624). New York: Wiley.

GYNTHER, M.D., LACHAR, D., & DAHLSTRON, W.G.   (1978). Are special norms for minorities needed? Development of an MMPI *F* scale for Blacks. *Journal of Consulting and Clinical Psychology, 46*, 1403–1408.

HAAS, L.J., & FENNIMORE, D.   (1983). Ethical and legal issues in professional psychology: Selected works, 1970–1982. *Professional Psychology: Research and Practice, 14*, 771–779.

HAAS, L.J., FENNIMORE, D., & WARBURTON, J.R.   (1983). A bibliography on ethical and legal issues in psychotherapy, 1970–1982. *Professional Psychology: Research and Practice, 14,* 771–779.

HALL, J.E., & HARE-MUSTIN, R.T.   (1983). Sanctions and the diversity of ethical complaints against psychologists. *American Psychologist, 38,* 714–729.

HAMMOND, C., HEPWORTH, D., & SMITH, V.   (1978). *Improving therapeutic communication.* San Francisco: Jossey-Bass.

HANDELSMAN, M.M., & GALVIN, M.D.   (1988). Facilitating informed consent for outpatient psychotherapy: A suggested written format. *Professional Psychology: Research and Practice, 19,* 223–225.

HANDELSMAN, M.M., KEMPER, M.B., KESSON-CRAIG, P., & JOHNSRUD, C.   (1986). Use, content, readability of written informed consent forms for treatment. *Professional Psychology: Research and Practice, 17,* 514–518.

HARDIN, S.I., SUBICH, L.M., & TICHENOR, V.   (1988). Expectancies for counseling in relation to premature termination. *Journal of Counseling Psychology, 35,* 37–40.

HARE-MUSTIN, R.T. & MARECEK, J.   (1988). The meaning of difference: Gender, theory, postmodernism, and psychology. *American Psychologist, 43,* 455–464.

HARRIS, M.   (1973). Tort liability of the psychotherapist. *University of San Francisco Law Review, 8,* 405–436.

HARRIS, T.   (1979). *I'm o.k.—you're o.k.* New York: Harper & Row.

HAUT, M.W., & MUEHLEMAN, Y.   (1986). Informed consent: The effects of clarity and specificity on disclosure in a clinical interview. *Psychotherapy, 23,* 93–101.

HEITLER, J.B.   (1976). Preparatory techniques in initiating expressive psychotherapy with lower-class, unsophisticated patients. *Psychological Bulletin, 83,* 339–352.

HELMS, J.E.   (1984). Towards a theoretical explanation of the effects of race on counseling: A Black and White Model. *The Counseling Psychologist, 12(4),* 153–165.

HEPPNER, P.P., & KRAUSKOPF, C.J.   (1987). An information-processing approach to personal problem solving. *The Counseling Psychologist, 15,* 371–447.

HEPPNER, P.P., & CLAIBORN, C.D.   (1989). Social influence research in counseling: A review and critique. [Monograph]. *Journal of Counseling Psychology, 36,* 365–387.

HERSEN, M., & TURNER, S.M. (EDS.).   (1985). *Diagnostic interviewing.* New York: Plenum.

HILL, C.E., & O'GRADY, K.E.   (1985). List of therapist intentions illustrated in a case study with therapists of varying orientations. *Journal of Counseling Psychology, 32,* 3–22.

HINKELDEY, N.S., & SPOKANE, A.R.   (1985). Effects of pressure and legal guideline clarity on counselor decision making in legal and ethical conflict situations. *Journal of Counseling and Development, 64,* 240–245.

HOBBS, N.   (1962). Sources of gain in psychotherapy. *American Psychologist, 17,* 741–747.

HOPKINS, B.R., & ANDERSON, B.S.   (1985). *The counselor and the law* (rev. ed). Alexandria, VA: American Association for Counseling and Development.

HOWARD, G.S., NANCE, D.W., & MYERS, P.   (1986). Adaptive counseling and therapy: An integrative, eclectic model. *The Counseling Psychologist, 14,* 363–442.

HOWARD, K.I., KOPTA, S.M., KRAUSE, M.S., & ORLINSKY, D.E.   (1986). The dose-effect relationship in psychotherapy. *American Psychologist, 41,* 159–164.

HUDSON, W.   (1978). Persona and defense mechanisms. *Journal of Analytic Psychology, 23,* 54–62.

HYLAND, M.E.   (1987). Control theory interpretation of psychological defense mechanisms of depression: Comparison and integration of several theories. *Psychological Bulletin, 102,* 109–121.

HYMER, S.   (1987). Respect in psychotherapy. *Journal of Contemporary Psychotherapy, 17,* 6–21.

JANOFF-BULMAN, R.   (1979). Characterological versus behavioral self-blame: Inquiries into depression and rape. *Journal of Personality and Social Psychology, 37,* 1798–1809.

JENSEN, J.P., & BERGIN, A.E.   (1988). Mental health values of professional therapists: A national interdisciplinary survey. *Professional Psychology: Research and Practice, 19,* 290–297.

JENSEN, J.V.   (1982). Perspective on non-verbal intercultural communication. In L.A. Samovar & R.E. Porter (Eds.), *Intercultural communication: A reader* Belmont, CA: Wadsworth.

JONES, E.E.   (1964). *Ingratiation.* New York: Appleton-Century-Crofts.

JONES, E.E., CUMMING, J.D., & HOROWITZ, M.J.   (1988). Another look at the nonspecific hypothesis of therapeutic effectiveness. *Journal of Consulting and Clinical Psychology, 56,* 48–55.

KAPLAN, M.   (1983a). A woman's view of DSM-III. *American Psychologist, 38,* 786–792.

KAPLAN, M.   (1983b). The issue of sex bias in DSM-III: Comments on the articles by Spitzer, Williams, and Kass. *American Psychologist, 38,* 802–803.

KASS, F., SPITZER, R.L., & WILLIAMS, J.B.W.   (1983). An empirical study of the issue of sex bias in the diagnostic criteria of DSM-III Axis II personality disorders. *American Psychologist, 38,* 799–801.

KEGAN, R.   (1982). *The evolving self:* Problem and process in human development. Cambridge, MA: Harvard University Press.

KEITH-SPIEGEL, P., & KOOCHER, G.P.   (1985). *Ethics in psychology: Professional standards and cases.* New York: Random House.

KIESLER, C.A.   (1985). Meta-analysis, clinical psychology, and social policy. *Clinical Psychology Review, 5,* 3–12.

KIESLER, D.J.   (1982). Interpersonal theory for personality and psychotherapy. In J.C. Anchin & D.J. Kiesler (Eds.), *Handbook of interpersonal psychotherapy* (pp. 3–24). New York: Pergamon.

KILBURG, R.R., NATHAN, P.E., & THORENSON, R.W. (EDS.).   (1986). Professionals in distress: Issues, syndromes, and solutions in psychology. Washington, DC: American Psychological Association.

KITCHENER, K.S.   (1984). Intuition, critical evaluation and ethical principles: The foundation for ethical decisions in counseling psychology. *The Counseling Psychologist, 12,* 43–55.

KLEIN, M.   (1950). On the criteria for termination of psychoanalysis. *International Journal of Psychoanalysis, 31,* 78–80.

KNAPP, S., & VANDECREEK, L.   (1982). Tarasoff: Five years later. *Professional Psychology, 13,* 511–516.

KNAPP, S., & VANDECREEK, L.   (1983). Privileged communications and the counselor. *Personnel and Guidance Journal, 62,* 83–85.

KNAPP, S., VANDECREEK, L., & ZIRKEL, P.A.   (1985). Legal research techniques: What the psychologist needs to know. *Professional Psychology: Research and Practice, 16,* 363–372.

KOHUT, H.   (1977). *The restoration of the self.* New York: International Universities Press.

KOHUT, H.   (1984). *How does analysis cure?* Chicago: University of Chicago Press.

KOILE, E.   (1977). *Listening as a way of becoming.* Waco, TX: Regency Books.

KOILE, E.   (1988). Workshop on "Marital and Divorce Therapy." Austin, TX.

KOKOTOVIC, A.M., & TRACEY, T.J.   (1987). Premature termination at a university counseling center. *Journal of Counseling Psychology, 34,* 80–82.

KOPP, S.B.   (1972). *If your meet the Buddha on the road, kill him!* New York: Bantam Books.

KOPP, S.   (1974). *The hanged man.* Palo Alto, CA: Science and Behavior Books.

KOPP, S.   (1975). *No hidden meanings.* Palo Alto, CA: Science and Behavior Books.

KOPP, S.   (1977). *Back to one.* Palo Alto, CA: Science and Behavior Books.

KOTTLER, J.A., & BLAU, D.S.   (1989). *The imperfect therapist: Learning from failure in therapeutic practice.* San Francisco: Jossey-Bass.

KRAJESKI, J.P.   (1986). Psychotherapy with gay men and lesbians: A history of controversy. In T.S. Stein & C.J. Cohen (Eds.), *Contemporary perspectives on psychotherapy with lesbians and gay men* (pp. 9–25). New York: Plenum Medical.

KRAMER, S.   (1986). The termination process in open-ended psychotherapy: Guidelines for clinical practice. *Psychotherapy, 23,* 526–531.

LAMB, D.   (1985). A time-frame model of termination in psychotherapy. *Psychotherapy, 22,* 604–609.

LANGS, R.   (1978). *The listening process.* New York: Aronson.

LANGS, R.   (1981). *Resistance and interventions.* New York: Aronson.

LAZARUS, A.   (1971). *Behavior therapy and beyond.* New York: McGraw-Hill.

LAZARUS, A.   (1976). *Multimodal behavior therapy.* New York: Springer.

LEMKAU, J., & LANDAU, C.   (1986). The selfless syndrome: Assessment and treatment considerations. *Psychotherapy, 23,* 243–249.

LEVENSON, E.   (1976). Problems in terminating psychoanalysis (a symposium): The aesthetics of termination. *Contemporary Psychoanalysis, 12,* 338–342.

LEWIS, W., & EVANS, J.   (1986). Resistance: A reconceptualization. *Psychotherapy, 23,* 426–433.

LITTLE, M.I.   (1981). *Transference neurosis and transference psychosis.* New York: Aronson.

LONDON, P.   (1986). *The modes and moral of psychotherapy* (2nd ed.). New York: W.W. Norton.

LONNER, W.J.   (1985). Issues in testing and assessment in cross-cultural counseling. *The Counseling Psychologist, 13,* 599–614.

LUBIN, B., LARSEN, R.M., & MATARAZZO, J.D.   (1984). Patterns of psychological test usage in the United States: 1935–1982. *American Psychologist, 39,* 451–454.

LUBIN, B., LARSEN, R.M., MATARAZZO, J.D., & SEEVER, M.   (1985). Psychological test usage patterns in five professional settings. *American Psychologist, 40,* 857–861.

LUBORSKY, L., SINGER, B., & LUBORSKY, L.   (1975). Comparative studies of psychotherapies. Is it true that "Everyone has won and all must have prizes"? *Archives of General Psychiatry, 32,* 995–1008.

MAGNUSSON, D. (ED.).   (1981). *Toward a psychology of situations: An interactional perspective.* Hillsdale, NJ: Erlbaum.

MAHONEY, M.J.   (1985). Psychotherapy and human change processes. In M.J. Mahoney & A. Freeman (Eds.), *Cognition and psychotherapy* (pp. 3–48). New York: Plenum.

MAHONEY, M.J., & FREEMAN, A. (EDS.).   (1985). *Cognition and psychotherapy.* New York: Plenum.

MALCOLM, J.   (1989, March 13). Reflections: The journalist and the murderer. *The New Yorker,* 38–73.

MAPPES, D.C., ROBB, G.P., & ENGELS, D.W.   (1985). Conflicts between ethics and law in counseling and psychotherapy. *Journal of Counseling and Development, 64,* 246–252.

MARKUS, H., & NURIUS, P.   (1986). Possible selves. *American Psychologist, 41,* 954–969.

MARSHALL, R.   (1982). *Resistant interactions: Child, family, and psychotherapist.* New York: Human Sciences Press.

MARTIN, A.   (1982). Some issues in the treatment of gay and lesbian patients. *Psychotherapy: Theory, Research, and Practice, 19,* 341–348.

MARTIN, E., & SCHURTMAN, R.   (1985). Termination anxiety as it affects the therapist. *Psychotherapy, 22,* 92–96.

MAXMEN, J.   (1986). *Essential psychopathology.* New York: W.W. Norton.

MAY, R.   (1969). *Love and will.* New York: W.W. Norton.

MAY, R.   (1981). *Freedom and destiny.* New York: W.W. Norton.

MAY, R.   (1983). *The discovery of being.* New York: W.W. Norton.

McCANN, I.L., SAKHEIM, D.K., & ABRAHAMSON, D.J.   (1988). Trauma and victimization: A model of psychological adaptation. *The Counseling Psychologist, 16,* 531–594.

McNEILL, B.W., MAY, R.J., & LEE, V.E.   (1987). Perceptions of counselor source characteristics by premature and successful terminators. *Journal of Counseling Psychology, 34,* 86–89.

MEARA, N., PEPINSKY, H.B., SHANNON, J., & MURRAY, W.A.   (1981). Semantic communication and expectations for counseling across three theoretical orientations. *Journal of Counseling Psychology, 28,* 110–118.

MEDEIROS, M.E., & PROCHASKA, J.O.   (1988). Coping strategies that psychotherapists use in working with stressful clients. *Professional Psychology: Research and Practice, 19,* 112–114.

MELVILLE, H.   (1930). *Moby dick.* New York: Random.

MENNINGER, K.   (1958). *Theory of psychoanalytic technique.* New York: Basic Books.

MERLUZZI, T.V., & BRISCHETTO, C.S.   (1983). Breach of confidentiality and perceived trustworthiness of counselors. *Journal of Counseling Psychology, 30,* 245–251.

MESSER, S.B., & WINOKUR, M.   (1980). Some limits to the integration of psychoanalytic and behavior therapy. *American Psychologist, 35,* 818–827.

MILBY, J.B., & RICE, J.A.   (1985). Drug abuse. In M. Hersen & S.M. Turner (Eds.), *Diagnostic interviewing* (pp. 183–204). New York: Plenum.

MILLER, J.B.   (1976). *Toward a new psychology of women.* Boston: Beacon Press.

MILLS, M.   (1985). Expanding the duties to protect third parties from violent acts. In S. Rachlin (Ed.), *Legal encroachment on psychiatric practice* (pp. 61–68). San Francisco: Jossey-Bass.

MILLS, M.J.   (1984). The so-called duty to warn: The psychotherapeutic duty to protect third parties from patients' violent acts. *Behavioral Sciences and the Law, 2,* 237–257.

MILLS, M., SULLIVAN, G., & ETH, S.   (1987). Protecting third parties: A decade after *Tarasoff. American Journal of Psychiatry, 144,* 68–74.

MILMAN, D.S., & GOLDMAN, G.D. (EDS.).   (1987). *Techniques of working with resistance.* Northvale, NJ: Aronson.

MUEHLEMAN, T., PICKENS, B.K., & ROBINSON, F.   (1985). Informing clients about the limits of confidentiality, risks, and their rights: Is self-disclosure inhibited? *Professional Psychology: Research and Practice, 16,* 385–397.

NAPIER, A., & WHITAKER, C.   (1978). *The family crucible.* New York: Harper & Row.

NELSON, A.A., & WILSON, W.P.   (1984). The ethics of sharing religious faith in psychotherapy. *Journal of Psychology and Theology, 12,* 15–23.

NICHOLS, S.E.   (1986). Psychotherapy and AIDS. In T.S. Stein & C.J. Cohen (Eds.), *Contemporary perspectives of psychotherapy with lesbians and gay men* (pp. 209–239). New York: Plenum Medical.

NORCROSS, J.C. (ED.).   (1986). *Handbook of eclectic psychotherapy.* New York: Brunner/Mazel.

NORCROSS, J.C., & PROCHASKA, J.O.   (1988). A study of eclectic (and integrative) views revisited. *Professional Psychology: Research and Practice, 19,* 170–174.

NORWOOD, R.   (1985). *Women who love too much.* New York: Pocket Books.

NOVAK, M.   (1970). *The experience of nothingness.* New York: Harper & Row.

OFFICE OF TECHNOLOGY ASSESSMENT.   (1980). *The cost implications of cost-effectiveness analysis of medi-*

cal technology. Background paper #3: The efficacy and cost-effectiveness of psychotherapy. (Stock No. 052-003-00783-5). Washington, DC: U.S. Government Printing Office.

OTANI, A. (1989). Client resistance in counseling: Its theoretical rational and taxonomic classification. *Journal of Counseling & Development, 67,* 458–461.

OTHMER, E., & OTHMER, S.C. (1989). *The clinical interview using DSM-III-R.* Washington, DC: American Psychiatric Press.

PARHAM, T.A. (1989). Cycles of psychological nigrescence. *The Counseling Psychologist, 17,* 187–226.

PARLOFF, M.B. (1976, February 21). Shopping for the right therapy. *Saturday Review,* pp. 14–16.

PARLOFF, M.B. (1984). Psychotherapy research and its incredible credibility crisis. *Clinical Psychology Review, 4,* 95–109.

PASCAL, G.R. (1983). *The practical art of diagnostic interviewing.* Homewood, IL: Dow Jones-Irwin.

PEDERSEN, P.B., & MARSELLA, A.J. (1982). The ethical crisis for cross-cultural counseling and therapy. *Professional Psychology, 13,* 492–500.

PEDERSEN, P.B., SARTORIUS, N., & MARSELLA, A. (EDS.). (1984). *Mental health services: The cultural context.* Beverly Hills, CA: Sage.

PERLS, F. (1969). *Gestalt therapy verbatim.* Lafayette, CA: Real People Press.

PERSON, E.S. (1988). *Dreams of love and fateful encounters.* New York: W.W. Norton.

PIPES, R.B., SCHWARZ, R., AND CROUCH, P. (1985). Measuring client fears. *Journal of Consulting and Clinical Psychology, 53,* 933–934.

PONCE, F.Q., & ATKINSON, D.R. (1989). Mexican-American acculturation, counselor ethnicity, counseling style, and perceived counselor credibility. *Journal of Counseling Psychology, 36,* 203–208.

POPE, B. (1979). *The mental health interview: Research and application.* New York: Pergamon.

POPE, K.S. (1986). Research and laws regarding therapist-patient sexual involvement: Implications for therapists. *American Journal of Psychotherapy, 40,* 564–571.

POPE, K.S., & BOUHOUTSOS, J.C. (1986). *Sexual intimacy between therapists and patients.* New York: Praeger.

POPE, K.S., KEITH-SPIEGEL, P.C., & TABACHNICK, B. (1986). Sexual attraction to clients: The human therapist and the (sometimes) inhuman training system. *American Psychologist, 41,* 147–158.

POPE, K.S., TABACHNICK, B.G., & KEITH-SPIEGEL, P. (1988). Good and poor practices in psychotherapy: National survey of beliefs of psychologists. *Professional Psychology: Research and Practice, 19,* 547–552.

POWERS, W.T. (1973). *Behavior: The control of perception.* Chicago: Aldine.

PRESSER, N.R., & PFOST, K.S. (1985). A format for individual psychotherapy session notes. *Professional Psychology: Research and Practice, 16,* 11–16.

PRICE, R.E., OMIZO, M.M., & HAMMELL, U.L. (1986). Counseling clients with AIDS. *Journal of Counseling and Development, 65,* 96–97.

PROCHASKA, J.O., & DiCLEMENTE, C.C. (1984). *The transtheoretical approach: Crossing traditional boundaries of therapy.* Homewood, IL: Dow Jones-Irwin.

REID, W.H., & WISE, M.G. (1989). *DSM-III-R training guide.* New York: Brunner/Mazel.

RICE, C., ALONSO, A., & RUTAN, J. (1985). The fights of spring: Separation, individuation, and grief in training centers. *Psychotherapy, 22,* 97–100.

ROBERTIELLO, R.C., & SCHOENEWOLF, G. (1987). *101 common therapeutic blunders: Countertransference and counterresistance in psychotherapy.* Northvale, NJ: Aronson.

ROBINSON, W.L., & REID, P.T. (1985). Sexual intimacies in psychology revisited. *Professional Psychology: Research and Practice, 16,* 512–520.

RODOLFA, E.R., KRAFT, W.A., & REILLEY, R.R. (1988). Stressors of professionals and trainees at APA-approved counseling and VA medical center internship sites. *Professional Psychology: Research and Practice, 19,* 43–49.

ROGERS, C.R. (1951). *Client-centered therapy: Its current practice, implications, and theory.* Boston: Houghton Mifflin.

ROGERS, C.R., & DYMOND, R. (EDS.). (1954). *Psychotherapy and personality change.* Chicago: University of Chicago Press.

ROGERS, C.R. (1961). *On becoming a person.* Boston: Houghton Mifflin.

ROGERS, R. (ED.). (1988). *Clinical assessment of malingering and deception.* New York: Guilford.

ROSENTHAL, R.H., & AKISKAL, H.S.   (1985). Mental status examination. In M. Hersen & S.M. Turner (Eds.), *Diagnostic interviewing* (pp. 25–54). New York: Plenum.

ROSENTHAL, V.   (1971). Transcending the role of psychotherapist. *Voices, 7*(3), 2–7.

ROSEWATER, L.B.   (1984). Feminist therapy: Implications for practitioners. In L. Walker (Ed.), *Women and mental health policy* (pp. 267–279) (*Women and policy series, Vol. 9*). Beverly Hills, CA: Sage.

ROSEWATER, L.B., & WALKER, L.E.A. (EDS.).   (1985). *Handbook of feminist therapy: Women's issues in psychotherapy.* New York: Springer.

ROSS, L., GREENE, D., & HOUSE, P.   (1977). The false consensus effect: An egocentric bias in social perception and attribution processes. *Journal of Experimental Social Psychology, 13,* 57–70.

ROTH, L.H. (ED.).   (1987). *Clinical treatment of the violent person.* New York: Guilford.

ROTH, S.R.   (1987). *Psychotherapy: The art of wooing nature.* Northvale, NJ: Aronson.

ROWE, C.J.   (1984). *An outline of psychiatry* (8th ed.). Dubuque, IA: Brown.

RUSS, S.W., & GROSSMAN-MCKEE, A.   (1985). The persisting concept of masochism in women. *American Psychologist, 40,* 571.

RYAN, W.   (1971). *Blaming the victim.* New York: Vintage.

SAMPSON, E.E.   (1985). The decentralization of identity: Toward a revised concept of personal and social order. *American Psychologist, 40,* 1203–1211.

SANDE, G.N., GOETHALS, G.R., AND RADLOFF, C.E.   (1988). Perceiving one's own traits and others: The multifaceted self. *Journal of Personality and Social Psychology, 54,* 13–20.

SCHACHT, T.E.   (1985). DSM-III and the politics of truth. *American Psychologist, 40,* 513–521.

SCHAFER, R.   (1954). *Psychoanalytic interpretation in Rorschach testing.* New York: Grune & Stratton.

SCHMIDT, L., & MEARA, N.   (1984). Ethical, professional, and legal issues in counseling psychology. In S.D. Brown & R.W. Lent (Eds.), *Handbook of counseling psychology* (pp. 56–96). New York: Wiley.

SCHOENER, G., MILGROM, J.H., & GONSIOREK, J.   (1984). Sexual exploitation of clients by therapists. *Women and Therapy, 3,* 63–69.

SCHUTZ, B.M.   (1982). *Legal liability in psychotherapy.* New York: Jossey-Bass.

SELL, J.M., GOTTLIEB, M.C., & SCHOENFELD, L.   (1986). Ethical considerations of social/romantic relationships with present and former clients. *Professional Psychology: Research and Practice, 17,* 504–508.

SHAPIRO, D.A., & SHAPIRO, D.   (1982). Meta-analysis of comparative therapy outcome studies: A replication and refinement. *Psychological Bulletin, 92,* 581–604.

SHERIDAN, K.   (1982). Sex bias in therapy: Are counselors immune? *Personnel and Guidance Journal, 61,* 81–83.

SIMON, R.   (1987). *Clinical psychiatry and the law.* Washington, DC: American Psychiatric Press.

SIMONTON, S.   (1988). Workshop on *Psychotherapy with the cancer patient.* Little Rock, AR.

SINGER, E.   (1970). *Key concepts in psychotherapy* (2nd ed.). New York: Basic Books.

SLAIKEU, K.A.   (1984). *Crisis intervention: A handbook for practice and research.* Boston: Allyn & Bacon.

SLATER, B.R.   (1988). Essential issues in working with lesbians and gay male youths. *Professional Psychology: Research and Practice, 99,* 226–232.

SLOANE, R.B., STAPLES, F.R., CRISTOL, A.H., YORKSTON, N.J., & WHIPPLE, K.   (1975). *Psychotherapy versus behavior therapy.* Cambridge, MA: Harvard University Press.

SMITH, E.M.J., & VASQUEZ, M.J.T.   (1985). Introduction: Special issue on cross-cultural counseling. *The Counseling Psychologist, 13,* 531–536.

SMITH, N.L., GLASS, G.V., & MILLER, T.I.   (1980). *Benefits of psychotherapy.* Baltimore: Johns Hopkins University Press.

SNYDER, C.R., & INGRAM, R.E.   (1983). "Company motivates the miserable": The impact of consensus information on help seeking for psychological problems. *Journal of Personality and Social Psychology, 45,* 1118–1126.

SNYDER, D.K., & WILLS, R.M.   (1989). Behavioral versus insight-oriented marital therapy: Effects on individual and interspousal functioning. *Journal of Consulting and Clinical Psychology, 57,* 39–46.

SOISSON, E.L., VANDECREEK, L., & KNAPP, S.   (1987). Thorough record keeping: A good defense in a litigious era. *Professional Psychology: Research and Practice, 18,* 498–502.

SORENSON, R.L., GORSUCH, R.L., & MINTZ, J.   (1985). Moving targets: Patients' changing complaints during psychotherapy. *Journal of Consulting and Clinical Psychology, 53,* 49–54.

SPITZER, R.L.   (1985). DSM-III and the politics-science dichotomy syndrome: A response to Thomas E. Schacht's "DSM-III and the politics of truth." *American Psychologist, 40,* 522–526.

SPITZER, R.L., GIBBON, M., SKODOL, A.E., WILLIAMS, J.B.W., & FIRST, M.B.   (1989). *DSM-III-R Casebook: A learning companion to the diagnostic and statistical manual of mental disorders, third edition, revised.* Washington, DC: American Psychiatric Press.

STEIN, T.S., & COHEN, C.J. (EDS.).   (1986). *Contemporary perspectives on psychotherapy with lesbians and gay men.* New York: Plenum Medical.

STEINER, C.   (1974). *Scripts people live.* New York: Bantam Books.

STEWART, A.J., & HEALY, J.M., JR.   (1989). Linking individual development and social changes. *American Psychologist, 44,* 30–42.

STILES, W.B., SHAPIRO, D.A., & ELLIOT, R.   (1986). "Are all psychotherapies equivalent?" *American Psychologist, 41,* 165–180.

STILES, W.B., SHAPIRO, D.A., & FIRTH-COZENS, J.A.   (1988). Do sessions of different treatments have different impacts? *Journal of Counseling Psychology, 35,* 391–396.

STONE, L.   (1981). Notes on the noninterpretive elements in the psychoanalytic situation and process. *Journal of the American Psychoanalytic Association, 29,* 89–118.

STREAN, H.   (1980). *The extramarital affair.* New York: Free Press.

STREAN, H.   (1985). *Resolving resistance in psychotherapy.* New York: Wiley.

STRONG, S.R.   (1968). Counseling: An interpersonal influence process. *Journal of Counseling Psychology, 15,* 215–224.

STRONG, S., & CLAIBURN, C.   (1982). *Change through interaction: Social Psychological processes of counseling and psychology.* New York: Wiley.

STRUPP, H., & BINDER, J.   (1984). *Psychotherapy in a new key.* New York: Basic Books.

STYRON, W.   (1976). *Sophie's choice.* New York: Bantam.

SULLIVAN, H.S.   (1954). *The psychiatric interview.* New York: W.W. Norton.

SURREY, J.   (1985). The "self-in-relation": A theory of women's development. *Work in Progress (No. 13)* Wellesley, MA: Stone Center for Developmental Services and Studies.

SULS, J., & WAN, C.K.   (1987). In search of the false-uniqueness phenomenon: Fear and estimates of social consensus. *Journal of Personality and Social Psychology, 52,* 211–217.

TAFT, J.   (1933/1973). *The dynamics of therapy in a controlled relationship.* Gloucester, MA: Peter Smith.

TALBERT, F.S., & PIPES, R.B.   (1988). Informed consent for psychotherapy: Content analysis of selected forms. *Professional Psychology: Research and Practice, 19,* 131–132.

TARACHOW, S.   (1963). *An introduction to psychotherapy.* New York: International Universities Press.

TARASOFF V. REGENTS OF THE UNIVERSITY OF CALIFORNIA,   118 Cal. Reptr. 129, 529 P.2d 533 (1974). (Tarasoff I).

TARASOFF V. REGENTS OF THE UNIVERSITY OF CALIFORNIA,   17 Cal.3d 425, 551 P.2d 334 (1976). (Tarasoff II).

TEYBER, E.   (1988). *Interpersonal process in psychotherapy: A guide for clinical training.* Chicago: Dorsey.

TINSLEY, H.E.A., BOWMAN, S.L., & RAY, S.B.   (1988). Manipulation of expectancies about counseling and psychotherapy: Review and analysis of expectancy manipulation strategies and results. *Journal of Counseling Psychology, 35,* 99–108.

TOLKIEN, J.R.R.   (1965). *The lord of the rings: Part 1. The fellowship of the ring.* New York: Ballantine Books.

TRACEY, T.J.   (1986). The stages of influence in counseling and psychotherapy. In F.J. Dorn (Ed.), *The social influence process in counseling and counseling psychotherapy* (pp. 105–114). Springfield, IL: Thomas.

TRACEY, T.J., & DUNDON, M.   (1988). Role anticipations and preferences over the course of counseling. *Journal of Counseling Psychology, 35,* 3–13.

TRACEY, T.J., HECK, E.J., & LICHTENBERG, J.W.   (1981). Role expectations and complementary/symmetrical therapeutic relationships. *Psychotherapy: Theory, Research, and Practice, 18,* 338–344.

TURNER, S.M., & HERSEN, M.   (1985). The interviewing process. In M. Hersen & S.M. Turner (Eds.), *Diagnostic interviewing* (pp. 3–24). New York: Plenum.

VANDECREEK, L., & KNAPP, S.   (1989). *Tarasoff and beyond: Legal and clinical considerations in the treatment of life-endangering patients.* Sarasota, FL: Practitioner's Resource Series.

VANDECREEK, L., KNAPP, S., & HERZOG, C.   (in press). Malpractice risks in the treatment of dangerous patients. *Psychotherapy: Theory, Research, and Practice.*

VanHoose, W.H., & Kottler, J.A.   (1985). *Ethical and legal issues in counseling and psychotherapy* (2nd ed.). San Francisco: Jossey-Bass.

Wachtel, P.L. (Ed.).   (1982). *Resistance: Psychodynamic and behavioral approaches.* New York: Plenum.

Warner, R.   (1967). *The stories of the Greeks.* New York: Farrar, Straus, & Giroux.

Watkins, C.E., Jr., & Terrell, F.   (1988). Mistrust level and its effects on counseling expectations in black client–white counselor relationships: An analogue study. *Journal of Counseling Psychology, 35,* 194–197.

Weed, L.   (1968). Medical records that guide and teach. *New England Journal of Medicine, 278,* 593–600, 652–657.

Weinberg, G.   (1984). *The heart of psychotherapy: A journey into the mind and office of the therapist at work.* New York: St. Martin's.

Weiner, I.B.   (1975). *Principles of psychotherapy.* New York: Wiley.

Werrbach, J., & Gilbert, L.A.   (1987). Men, gender stereotyping, and psychotherapy: Therapists' perceptions of male clients. *Professional Psychology: Research and Practice, 18,* 562–566.

Westefeld, J.S., & Furr, S.R.   (1987). Suicide and depression among college students. *Professional Psychology: Research and Practice, 18,* 119–123.

Westefeld, J.A., & Patillo, C.M.   (1987). College and university student suicide record-keeping procedures: The case for a national clearinghouse. *Journal of College Student Personnel, 28,* 34–38.

Wheelis, A.   (1956). Will and psychoanalysis. *Journal of the Psychoanalytic Association, 4,* 285–303.

Wheelis, A.   (1973). *How people change.* New York: Harper Colophon Books.

Widiger, T.A., & Rorer, L.G.   (1984). The responsible psychotherapist. *American Psychologist, 39,* 503–515.

Wile, D.   (1984). Kohut, Kernberg, and accusatory interpretations. *Psychotherapy, 21,* 353–364.

Williams, J.B.W., & Spitzer, R.L.   (1983). The issue of sex in DSM-III: A critique of "A woman's view of DSM-III" by Marcie Kaplan. *American Psychologist, 38,* 793–798.

Winslade, W., & Ross, J.   (1983). *The insanity defense.* New York: Scribner's.

Wolberg, L.R.   (1988). *The technique of psychotherapy* (4th ed., Parts 1 & 2). New York: Grune & Stratton.

Wollersheim, J.P., McFall, M.E., Hamilton, S.B., Hickey, C.S., & Bordewick, M.C.   (1980). Effects of treatment rationale and problem severity on perceptions of psychological problems and counseling approaches. *Journal of Counseling Psychology, 27,* 225–231.

Worthington, E.L., Jr.   (1986). Religious counseling: A review of empirical research. *Journal of Counseling and Development, 64,* 421–431.

Worthington, E.L., Jr.   (1988). Understanding the values of religious clients: A model and its application to counseling. *Journal of Counseling Psychology, 35,* 166–174.

Wright, R.H.   (1981). Psychologists and professional liability (malpractice) insurance: A retrospective review. *American Psychologist, 36,* 1485–1493.

Wright, R.H.   (1981). What to do until the malpractice lawyer comes: A survivor's manual. *American Psychologist, 36,* 1535–1541.

Yalom, I.D.   (1975). *Theory and practice of group psychotherapy* (2nd ed.). New York: Basic Books.

Yalom, I.D.   (1980). *Existential psychotherapy.* New York: Basic Books.

Zuniga, M.E.   (1988). Assessment issues with Chicanos: Practice implications. *Psychotherapy, 25,* 288–293.

SELECTED BIBLIOGRAPHY ON SHORT-TERM/TIME-LIMITED PSYCHOTHERAPY (BOOKS AND ARTICLES PUBLISHED IN 1980 AND AFTERWARD)

These references are provided as a resource because of the increasing interest in short-term therapy (e.g., Cummings, 1988).

Short-term therapy has been variously defined. In these various definitions the number of sessions has ranged from 1 to 25. Koss and Butcher (1986) have presented a comprehensive review of the research in this area. Mandel (1981) published an extensive, annotated bibliography of publications through April of 1980.

This list of books and articles is not exhaustive but is assumed to include a good sampling of published material after 1980 concerning short-term and time-limited (primarily individual) psychotherapy with outpatient adults. Unpublished manuscripts and articles published in regional journals are not included. Also, generally excluded are publications concerning chemical dependency as well as specialized techniques used in short-term psychotherapy. Examples of omitted material include behavioral techniques, hypnotherapy, and crisis intervention.

BAUER, G., & KOBOS, J. (1984). Short-term psychodynamic psychotherapy. *Psychotherapy, 21*, 153–170.

BENNETT, M. (1984). Brief psychotherapy and adult development. *Psychotherapy, 21*, 171–177.

BERGMAN, J.S. (1985). *Fishing for barracuda: Pragmatics of brief systematic therapy.* New York: W.W. Norton.

BINDER, J.L., HENRY, W.P., & STRUPP, H.H. (1987). An appraisal of selection criteria for dynamic psychotherapies and implications for setting time limits. *Psychiatry, 50*, 154–166.

BINDER, J.L., STRUPP, H.H., & SCHACHT, T.E.   (1983). Countertransference in time-limited dynamic psychotherapy. *Contemporary Psychoanalysis, 19,* 605–623.

BLOOM, B.L.   (1981). Focused single-session therapy: Initial development and evaluation. In S.L. Budman (Ed.), *Forms of brief therapy* (pp. 167–218). New York: Guilford.

BROWN, S.L.   (1980). Dynamic family therapy. In H. Davanloo (Ed.), *Short-term dynamic psychotherapy* (pp. 193–206). New York: Aronson.

BROWN, S.L.   (1980). The family crisis. In H. Davanloo (Ed.), *Short-term dynamic psychotherapy* (pp. 207–220). New York: Aronson.

BUDMAN, S.H. (ED.).   (1981). *Forms of brief therapy.* New York: Guilford.

BUDMAN, S.H.   (1981). Introduction. In S.H. Budman (Ed.), *Forms of brief therapy* (pp. 1–5). New York: Guilford.

BUDMAN, S.H., DEMBY, A., REDONDO, J.P., HANRAN, M., FELDSTEIN, M., RING, J., & SPRINGER, T.   (1988). Comparative outcome in time-limited individual and group psychotherapy. *International Journal of Group Psychotherapy, 38,* 63–86.

BUDMAN, S., & GURMAN, A.   (1983). The practice of brief therapy. *Professional Psychology: Research and Practice, 14,* 277–292.

BUDMAN, S.H., & GURMPOAN, A.S.   (1988). *Theory and practice of brief therapy.* New York: Guilford.

BUDMAN, S.H., & SPRINGER, T.   (1987). Treatment delay, outcome, and satisfaction in time-limited group and individual psychotherapy. *Professional Psychology: Research and Practice, 18,* 647–649.

BUDMAN, S.H., & STONE, J.   (1983). Advances in brief psychotherapy: A review of recent literature. *Hospital and Community Psychiatry, 34,* 939–946.

BURLINGAME, G.M., & BEHRMAN, J.A.   (1987). Clinician attitudes toward time-limited and time-unlimited therapy. *Professional Psychology: Research and Practice, 18,* 61–65.

BURLINGAME, G.M., & FUHRIMAN, A.   (1987). Conceptualizing short-term treatment: A comparative review. *The Counseling Psychologist, 15,* 557–595.

BURLINGAME, G., FUHRIMAN, A., & PAUL, S.   (1987). An eclectic, time-limited therapy perspective. In J.C. Norcross (Ed.), *Casebook of eclectic psychotherapy* (pp. 96–131). New York: Brunner/Mazel.

CLARKIN, J.F., & FRANCES, A.   (1982). Selection criteria for brief psychotherapies. *American Journal of Psychotherapy, 36,* 166–180.

CLARKIN, J.F., & FRANCES, A.   (1983). Brief psychotherapies. In B. Wolman (Ed.), *The therapist handbook* (2nd ed.). New York: Van Nostrand Reinhold.

COYNE, J.C., & SEGAL, L.   (1982). A brief, strategic interactional approach to psychotherapy. In J. Anthony & D. Kiesler (Eds.), *Handbook of interpersonal psychotherapy* (pp. 248–261). New York: Pergamon.

CROSS, D.G., SHEEHAN, P.W., & KHAN, J.A.   (1982). Short- and long-term follow-up of clients receiving insight-oriented therapy and behavior therapy. *Journal of Consulting and Clinical Psychology, 50,* 103–112.

CUMMINGS, N.A.   (1986). The dismantling of our health system: Strategies for the survival of psychological practice. *American Psychologist, 41,* 426–431.

CUMMINGS, N.   (1988). Emergence of the mental health complex: Adaptive and maladaptive responses. *Professional Psychology: Research and Practice, 19,* 308–315.

DAVANLOO, H.   (1980). A method of short-term dynamic psychotherapy. In H. Davanloo (Ed.), *Short-term dynamic psychotherapy* (pp. 43–74). New York: Aronson.

DAVANLOO, H.   (1980). Response to interpretation. In H. Davanloo (Ed.), *Short-term dynamic psychotherapy* (pp. 75–92). New York: Aronson.

DAVANLOO, H. (ED.).   (1980). *Short-term dynamic psychotherapy* (Vol. 1). New York: Aronson.

DAVANLOO, H.   (1980). Trial therapy. In H. Davanloo (Ed.), *Short-term dynamic psychotherapy* (pp. 99–128). New York: Aronson.

DeLaCOUR, A.T.   (1986). Use of the focus in brief dynamic psychotherapy. *Psychotherapy, 23,* 133–139.

DIAMOND, M.J., & WAGGONER, M.L.   (1986). The effects of short-term psychotherapy on cardiac clients and their families. *International Journal of Eclectic Psychotherapy, 5,* 167–178.

DONOVAN, J.M.   (1987). Brief dynamic psychotherapy: Toward a more comprehensive model. *Psychiatry, 50,* 167–183.

EISENSTEIN, S.   (1980). The contributions of Franz Alexander. In H. Davanloo (Ed.), *Short-term dynamic psychotherapy* (pp. 25–42). New York: Aronson.

ELLIOTT, R.   (1985). Helpful and nonhelpful events in brief counseling interviews: An empirical taxonomy. *Journal of Consulting and Clinical Psychology, 32,* 307–321.

FAIRBURN, C.G., KIRK, J., O'CONNOR, M., & COOPER, P.J. (1986). A comparison of two psychological treatments for bulimia nervosa. *Behavior Research and Therapy, 24,* 629–643.

FISCH, R., WEAKLAND, J.H., & SEGAL, L. (1982). *The tactics of change: Doing therapy briefly.* San Francisco: Jossey-Bass.

FLEGENHEIMER, W.V. (1982). *Techniques of brief psychotherapy.* Northvale, NJ: Aronson.

FUHRIMAN, A., PAUL, S., & BURLINGAME, G. (1986). Eclectic time-limited therapy. In J. Norcross (Ed.), *Handbook of eclectic psychotherapy* (pp. 226–259). New York: Brunner/Mazel.

GARFIELD, S.L. (1989). *The practice of brief psychotherapy.* New York: Pergamon.

GELSO, C., & JOHNSON, D. (1983). *Explorations in time-limited counseling and psychotherapy.* New York: Teachers College Press.

GOLDRING, J. (1980). *Quick response therapy: A time-limited treatment approach.* New York: Human Services Press.

GRAND, S. (1985). *Transference in brief psychotherapy: An approach to the study of psychoanalytic process.* Hillsdale, NJ: Analytic Press.

GUSTAFSON, J. (1984). An integration of brief dynamic psychotherapy. *American Journal of Psychiatry, 141,* 935–944.

HARTLEY, D.E., & STRUPP, H.H. (1983). The therapeutic alliance: Its relationship to outcome in brief psychotherapy. In J. Masling (Ed.), *Empirical studies of psychoanalytical theories* (Vol. 1, pp. 1–38). Hillsdale, NJ: Analytic Press.

HAWTON, K., REIBSTEIN, J., FIELDSEND, R., & WHALLEY, M. (1982). Content analysis of brief psychotherapy sessions. *British Journal of Medical Psychology, 55,* 167–176.

HILL, C., CARTER, J., & O'FARRELL, M. (1983). A case study of the process and outcome of time-limited counseling. *Journal of Counseling Psychology, 30,* 3–18.

HILL, C.E. (1989). Therapist techniques and client outcome: *Eight cases of brief psychotherapy.* Newberry Park, CA: Sage.

HILL, C.E., HELMS, J.E., TICHENOR, V., SPIEGEL, S.B., O'GRADY, K.E., & PERRY, E.S. (1988). Effects of therapist response modes in brief psychotherapy. *Journal of Counseling Psychology, 35,* 222–233.

HILL, C.E., O'FARRELL, M.K., & CARTER, J.A. (1983). Reply to Howard and Lambert: Case study methodology. *Journal of Counseling Psychology, 30,* 26–30.

HOROWITZ, M.J., ET AL. (1986). Comprehensive analysis of change after brief dynamic psychotherapy. *American Journal of Psychiatry, 143,* 582–589.

HOROWITZ, M., MARMAR, C., KRUPNICK, J., WILNER, N., KALTREIDER, N., & WALLERSTEIN, R. (1984). *Personality styles and brief psychotherapy.* New York: Basic Books.

HOYT, M.F. (1985). Therapist resistances to short-term dynamic psychotherapy. *Journal of the American Academy of Psychoanalysis, 13,* 93–112.

HOYT, M.F. (1987). Resistance to brief therapy. *American Psychologist, 42,* 408–409.

HOYT, M.F., & FARRELL, D. (1985). Countertransference difficulties in a time-limited psychotherapy. *International Journal of Psychoanalytic Psychotherapy, 10,* 191–203.

JANIS, I.L. (1982). *Counseling on personal decisions: Theory and research on short-term helping relationships.* New Haven: Yale University Press.

JANIS, I. (1983). *Short-term counseling.* New Haven: Yale University Press.

JOHNSON, H., & GELSO, C. (1980). The effectiveness of time limits in counseling and psychotherapy. *The Counseling Psychologist, 9,* 70–83.

JONES, E.E., KRUPNICK, J.L., & KERIG, P.K. (1987). Some gender effects in a brief psychotherapy. *Psychotherapy, 24,* 336–352.

KIRSHNER, L.A. (1988). Implications of Loevinger's theory of ego development for time-limited psychotherapy. *Psychotherapy, 25,* 220–226.

KOSS, M., & BUTCHER, J. (1986). Research on brief psychotherapies. In S. Garfield and A. Bergin (Eds.), *Handbook of psychotherapy and behavior change* (pp. 627–670). New York: Wiley.

KOSS, M., BUTCHER, J., & STRUPP, H. (1986). Brief psychotherapy methods in clinical research. *Journal of Consulting and Clinical Psychology, 54,* 60–67.

LAMBERT, M.J. (1983). Comments on "A case study of the process and outcome of time-limited counseling." *Journal of Counseling Psychology, 30,* 22–25.

LEON, I.G. (1987). Short-term psychotherapy for perinatal loss. *Psychotherapy, 24,* 186–195.

MACKENZIE, K.R., & LIVESLEY, W.J. (1986). Outcome and process measures in brief group psychotherapy. *Psychiatric Annals, 16,* 715–720.

MALAN, D.H. (1980). Basic principles and technique of the follow-up interview. In H. Davanloo (Ed.), *Short-term dynamic psychotherapy* (pp. 349–378). New York: Aronson.

MALAN, D.H.   (1980). Criteria for selection. In H. Davanloo (Ed.), *Short-term dynamic psychotherapy* (pp. 169–192). New York: Aronson.

MALAN, D.H.   (1980). The most important development since the discovery of the unconscious. In H. Davanloo (Ed.), *Short-term dynamic psychotherapy* (pp. 13–24). New York: Aronson.

MALAN, D.H.   (1980). The nature of science and the validity of psychotherapy. In H. Davanloo (Ed.), *Short-term dynamic psychotherapy* (pp. 319–348). New York: Aronson.

MANDEL, H.   (1981). *Short-term psychotherapy and brief treatment techniques: An annotated bibliography 1920–1980.* New York: Plenum.

MANN, J.   (1981). The core of time-limited psychotherapy: Time and the central issue. In S. Budman (Ed.), *Forms of brief therapy* (pp. 25–42). New York: Guilford.

MANN, J.   (1985). The management of countertransference in time-limited psychotherapy: The role of the central issue. *International Journal of Psychoanalytic Psychotherapy, 10,* 205–214.

MANN, J., & GOLDMAN, R.   (1982). *A casebook in time-limited psychotherapy.* New York: McGraw-Hill.

MARMOR, J.   (1980). Evaluation and selection. In H. Davanloo (Ed.), *Short-term dynamic psychotherapy* (pp. 149–168). New York: Aronson.

MARMOR, J.   (1980). Historical roots. In H. Davanloo (Ed.), *Short-term dynamic psychotherapy* (pp. 3–12). New York: Aronson.

MARZIALI, E.A., & SULLIVAN, J.M.   (1980). Methodological issues in the content analysis of brief psychotherapy. *British Journal of Medical Psychology, 53,* 19–27.

MOLEY, V.A.   (1987). Brief therapy and eating disorders. *Family Therapy Collections, 20,* 40–54.

MORAS, K., & STRUPP, H.H.   (1982). Pretherapy interpersonal relations, patients' alliance and outcome in brief therapy. *Archives of General Psychiatry, 39,* 405–409.

MORAWETZ, A.   (1984). *Brief therapy with single-parent families.* New York: Brunner/Mazel.

O'DOWD, W.T.   (1986). Otto Rank and time-limited psychotherapy. *Psychotherapy, 23,* 140–149.

PEAKE, T.H., BORDUIN, C.M., & ARCHER, R.P.   (1988). *Brief psychotherapies: Changing frames of mind.* Beverly Hills, CA: Sage.

PHILLIPS, E.L.   (1985). *A guide for therapists and patients to short-term psychotherapy.* Springfield, IL: C.C. Thomas.

PHILLIPS, E.L.   (1988). Length of psychotherapy and outcome: Observations stimulated by Howard, Kopta, Krause, and Orlinsky. *American Psychologist, 43,* 669–670.

PIPER, W.E., DEBBANE, E.G., BIENVENUE, J.P., & GARANT, J.   (1984). A comparative study of four forms of psychotherapy. *Journal of Consulting and Clinical Psychology, 52,* 268–279.

RASMUSSEN, A., & MESSER, S.B.   (1986). A comparison and critique of Mann's time-limited psychotherapy and Davanloo's short-term dynamic psychotherapy. *Bulletin of the Menninger Clinic, 50* 163–184.

REICH, J., & NEENAN, P.   (1986). Principles common to different short-term psychotherapies. *American Journal of Psychotherapy, 40,* 62–69.

ROBBINS, S.B., & ZINN, V.R.   (1988). Implementing a time-limited treatment model: Issues and solutions. *Professional Psychology: Research and Practice, 19,* 53–57.

ROSENBAUM, M.   (1983). *Handbook of short-term therapy groups.* New York: McGraw-Hill.

RUSH, A.J. (ED.).   (1982). *Short-term psychotherapies for depression: Behavioral, interpersonal, cognitive, and psychodynamic approaches.* New York: Guilford.

SACHS, J.S.   (1983). Negative factors in brief psychotherapy: An empirical assessment. *Journal of Consulting and Clinical Psychology, 51,* 557–564.

SCHNEIDER, W.J., & PINKERTON, R.S.   (1986). Short-term psychotherapy and graduate training in psychology. *Professional Psychology: Research and Practice, 17,* 574–579.

SCHWARTZ, A.J., & BERNARD, H.S.   (1981). Comparison of patient and therapist evaluations of time-limited psychotherapy. *Psychotherapy: Theory, Research, and Practice, 18,* 101–108.

SEGAL, L., & KAHN, J.   (1986). Brief family therapy. *Individual Psychology: Journal of Adlerian Theory, Research, and Practice, 42,* 545–555.

SHAPIRO, L.E.   (1984). *The new short-term therapies for children: A guide for the helping professions and parents.* Englewood Cliffs, NJ: Prentice-Hall.

SIFNEOS, P.   (1980). Motivation for change. In H. Davanloo (Ed.), *Short-term dynamic psychotherapy* (pp. 93–98). New York: Aronson.

SIFNEOS, P.   (1980). Short-term anxiety-provoking psychotherapy. In H. Davanloo (Ed.), *Short-term dynamic psychotherapy* (pp. 129–168). New York: Aronson.

SIFNEOS, P.   (1984). The current status of individual short-term dynamic psychotherapy and its future. *American Journal of Psychotherapy, 38,* 472–483.

SIFNEOS, P.E. (1987). *Short-term dynamic psychotherapy: Evaluation and treatment* (2nd ed.). New York: Plenum.

SILVER, R.J. (1982). Brief dynamic psychotherapy: A critical look at the state of the art. *Psychiatric Quarterly, 53,* 275–282.

STRUPP, H.H. (1980). Problems of research. In H. Davanloo (Ed.), *Short-term dynamic psychotherapy* (pp. 379–392). New York: Aronson.

STRUPP, H.H. (1980). Success and failure in time-limited psychotherapy: A systematic comparison of two cases. Comparison I. *Archives of General Psychiatry, 37,* 595–603.

STRUPP, H.H. (1980). Success and failure in time-limited psychotherapy: A systematic comparison of two cases. Comparison II. *Archives of General Psychiatry, 37,* 708–717.

STRUPP, H.H. (1980). Success and failure in time-limited psychotherapy: Further evidence. Comparison IV. *Archives of General Psychiatry, 37,* 947–954.

STRUPP, H.H. (1980). Success and failure in time-limited psychotherapy: With special reference to the performance of a lay counselor. *Archives of General Psychiatry, 37,* 831–841.

STRUPP, H.H. (1981). Toward the refinement of time-limited dynamic psychotherapy. In S.L. Budman (Ed.), *Forms of brief therapy* (pp. 219–240). New York: Guilford.

STRUPP, H., & BINDER, J. (1984). *Psychotherapy in a new key.* New York: Basic Books.

TRACEY, T., & RAY, P. (1984). Stages of successful time-limited counseling: An interactional examination. *Journal of Counseling Psychology, 31,* 13–27.

TRUJILLO, M. (1986). Short-term dynamic psychotherapy. In I. Kutash and A. Wolf (Eds.), *Psychotherapist's casebook.* San Francisco: Jossey-Bass.

VASLAMATZIS, G., & VERVENIOTIS, S. (1986). Early dropouts in brief dynamic psychotherapy. *Psychotherapy and Psychosomatics, 44,* 205–210.

VICKERS, R.L. (1987). A reply to Cummings. *American Psychologist, 42,* 408.

WELLS, R.A. (1982). *Planned short-term treatment.* New York: Free Press.

WESTON, D. (1986). What changes in short-term psychodynamic psychotherapy? *Psychotherapy, 23,* 501–512.

WHITE, H.S., BURKE, J.D., & HAVENS, L.L. (1981). Choosing a method of short-term therapy: A developmental approach. In S. Budman (Ed.), *Forms of brief therapy* (pp. 243–269). New York: Guilford.

WILSON, G.T. (1981). Behavior therapy as a short-term therapeutic approach. In S.H. Budman (Ed.), *Forms of brief therapy* (pp. 131–166). New York: Guilford.

WINSTON, A. (1985). *Clinical and research issues in short-term dynamic psychotherapy.* Washington, DC: American Psychiatric Press.

WOLBERG, L.R. (1980). *Handbook of short-term psychotherapy.* New York: Thieme-Stratton.

YALOM, I.D. (1983). *Inpatient group psychotherapy.* New York: Basic Books.

SELECTED BIBLIOGRAPHY OF BOOKS ABOUT PSYCHOTHERAPY

These books represent a variety of perspectives on psychotherapy. There is no attempt to include books focusing on specific client populations or on specific diagnoses.

ANCHIN, J.C., & KIESLER, D.J. (EDS.). (1982). *Handbook of interpersonal psychotherapy.* New York: Pergamon.

BALSAM, M.B., & BALSAM, A. (1984). *Becoming a psychotherapist: A clinical primer* (2nd ed.). Chicago: University of Chicago Press.

BECK, A.T. (1976). *Cognitive therapy and the emotional disorders.* New York: International Universities Press.

BRAMMER, L.M., SHOSTROM, E.L., & ABREGO, P.J. (1989). *Therapeutic psychology: Fundamentals of counseling and psychotherapy* (5th ed.). Englewood Cliffs, NJ: Prentice-Hall.

BRENNER, D. (1982). *The effective psychotherapist: Conclusions from practice and research.* New York: Pergamon.

BRODSKY, A.M., & HARE-MUSTIN, R. (EDS.) (1980). *Women and psychotherapy: An assessment of research and practice.* New York: Guilford.

BRUCH, H. (1974). *Learning psychotherapy: Rationale and ground rules.* Cambridge, MA: Harvard University Press.

BUGENTAL, J.F.T. (1987). *The art of the psychotherapist.* New York: W.W. Norton.

CASHDAN, S. (1988). *Object relations therapy: Using the relationship.* New York: W.W. Norton.

CHOCA, J. (1988). *Manual for clinical psychology practicums* (2nd ed.). New York: Brunner/Mazel.

ERSKINE, R.G., & MOURSUND, J.P. (1988). *Integrative psychotherapy in action.* Beverly Hills, CA: Sage.

FLACH, F. (ED.). (1989). *Psychotherapy.* New York: W.W. Norton.

FRIED, E. (1981). *The courage to change: From insight to self-innovation.* New York: Grove.

FROMM-REICHMAN, F. (1960). *Principles of intensive psychotherapy.* Chicago: University of Chicago Press.

HIGGINBOTHAM, H.N., WEST, S.G., & FORSYTH, D.R.   (1988). *Psychotherapy and behavior change: Social, cultural, and methodological perspectives.* New York: Pergamon.

IVEY, A.E.   (1986). *Developmental therapy.* San Francisco: Jossey-Bass.

JOHNSON, S.M.   (1985). *Characterological transformation.* New York: W.W. Norton.

KELL, B.L., & MUELLER, W.J.   (1966). *Impact and change: A study of counseling relationships.* Englewood Cliffs, NJ: Prentice-Hall.

KOTTLER, J.A., & BLAU, D.S.   (1989). *The imperfect therapist: Learning from failure in therapeutic practice.* San Francisco: Jossey-Bass.

LAZARUS, A.A.   (1971). *Behavior therapy and beyond.* New York: McGraw-Hill.

LUBORSKY, L.   (1989). *Principles of psychoanalytic psychotherapy: A manual for supportive/expressive treatment.* New York: Basic Books.

MALAN, D.H.   (1979). *Individual psychotherapy and the science of psychodynamics.* Boston: Butterworths.

MEIER, S.T.   (1989). *The elements of counseling.* Pacific Grove, CA: Brooks/Cole.

MOURSUND, J.P.   (1985). *The process of counseling and therapy.* Englewood Cliffs, NJ: Prentice-Hall.

NEAHAUS, E.C., & ASTWOOD, W.   (1980). *Practicing psychotherapy: Basic techniques and practical issues.* New York: Human Sciences.

O'HANLON, W.H., & WEINER-DAVIS, M.   (1988). *In search of solutions: A new direction in psychotherapy.* New York: W.W. Norton.

PROCHASKA, J.D., & DiCLEMENTE, C.C.   (1984). *The transtheoretical approach: Crossing traditional boundaries of therapy.* Chicago: Dorsey.

ROSEWATER, L.B., & WALKER, L.E.A. (EDS.).   (1985). *Handbook of feminist therapy: Women's issues in psychotherapy.* New York: Springer.

ROTH, S.R.   (1987). *Psychotherapy: The art of wooing nature.* Northvale, NJ: Aronson.

SINGER, E.   (1970). *Key concepts in psychotherapy* (2nd ed.). New York: Basic Books.

STORR, A.   (1979). *The art of psychotherapy.* New York: Metheun.

STREAN, H.   (1972). *The experience of psychotherapy: A practitioner's manual.* Metuchen, NJ: Scarecrow.

STREAN, H.S.   (1985). *Therapeutic principles in practice.* Beverly Hills, CA: Sage.

STRONG, S., & CLAIBURN, C.   (1982). *Change through interaction: Social psychological processes of counseling and psychology.* New York: Wiley.

TARACHOW, S.   (1963). *An introduction to psychotherapy.* New York: International Universities Press.

TEYBER, E.   (1983). *Interpersonal process in psychotherapy: A guide for clinical training.* Chicago: Dorsey.

THORESEN, C.E., & MAHONEY, M.J.   (1974). *Self-control: Power to the person.* Monterey, CA: Brooks/Cole.

U'REN, R.C.   (1980). *The practice of psychotherapy.* New York: Grune & Stratton.

WEINBERG, G.   (1984). *The heart of psychotherapy: A journey into the mind and office of the therapist at work.* New York: St. Martin's.

WEINER, I.B.   (1975). *Principles of psychotherapy.* New York: Wiley.

WEINER, M.F.   (1986). *Practical psychotherapy.* New York: Brunner/Mazel.

YALOM, I.D.   (1980). *Existential psychotherapy.* New York: Basic Books.

ZARO, J.S., BARACH, R., NEDELMAN, D.J., & DREIBLATT, I.S.   (1977). *A guide for beginning psychotherapists.* London: Cambridge.

THE AUTHORS

RANDOLPH B. PIPES teaches in the Department of Counseling and Counseling Psychology at Auburn University. He received his Ph.D. in Counseling Psychology from the University of Texas at Austin in 1977. His primary teaching responsibilities include supervising practicum students and teaching professional, ethical, and legal issues in counseling psychology.

DONNA S. DAVENPORT teaches in the Counseling Psychology program at Texas A & M University in College Station, Texas. She received her Ph.D. in Counseling Psychology from The University of Texas at Austin in 1978, and has taught and supervised graduate students in individual, marriage, and group counseling. She engages in private practice and consultation in psychotherapy.

NAME INDEX

Adler, A., 146
Ainsworth, M. D. S., 8
Akamatsu, T. J., 214
Akiskal, H. S., 90
Alonso, A., 178
Anouilh, J., 214
Anthony, W., 132, 137

Bachelor, A., 129
Bacorn, C. N., 32
Bandura, A., 2, 3
Barlow, D., 90
Barrows, P. A., 33
Bauer, G. P., 169
Baumeister, R. F., 76, 77
Beane, J., 32
Beck, A., 119
Becket, T., 214
Bellack, A. S., 90
Berger, D., 137, 143
Bergin, A. E., 23, 67
Bergman, J., 249
Beutler, L. E., 67

Binder, J., 180, 181, 185
Blanck, G., 182
Blanck, R., 182
Bordewick, M. C., 104
Bouhoutsos, J., 214
Bowlby, J., 8, 126, 130, 229, 243, 249
Bowman, S. L., 91
Bown, O., 37, 127, 136, 246
Boy, A., 137
Bradley, F. O., 40
Branden, N., 251
Brischetto, C. S., 213
Brody, E. M., 86
Broverman, D. M., 101
Broverman, I. D., 101
Buck, R., 6
Bugental, J., 67, 125, 170, 175, 185, 189
Butler, M., 67, 68
Byrne, D., 67

Caddy, G. R., 108
Campbell, S., 252
Caplan, P. J., 102

Carkhuff, R., 132, 137
Carter, J. A., 126
Cavanaugh, J. L. Jr., 219
Chekhov, A., 98
Chodorow, N., 247
Claiborn, C. D., 9, 68
Clance, P. R., 82
Clarkson, F. E., 101
Cohen, C. J., 32
Cohen, R. J., 219
Comaz-Diaz, L., 102
Conoley, C. W., 11
Courtois, C., 109
Cowen, E. L., 3
Cristol, A. H., 5
Cross, H. J., 219
Crouch, P., 65
Crowne, D. P., 77
Cummings, N. A., 5

Dahlstrom, W. G., 102
Davenport, D., 214, 236
David, 201
Davison, G., 168
Deardof, W. W., 219, 220
DeKraai, M. B., 213, 216
DeLeon, P. H., 5
Dixon, D. N., 32
Dundon, M., 91, 133
Dymond, R., 77
Dryden, W., 4

Eagle, M., 4
Edwards, A. L., 77
Egan, G., 132, 137
Eliot, G., 209
Elliott, R., 5
Ellis, A., 84, 119, 175, 189
Epperson, D. L., 67
Erickson, M. H., 175
Eth, S., 107
Evans, J., 171, 172
Everstine, L., 215

Farber, B. A., 86
First, M. B., 90
Fitts, W. H., 177
Fisher, J. D., 32
Forer, B., 214
Foreyt, J. P., 108

Frank, J. D., 5, 99, 133, 227
Freeman, A., 8
Freud, S., 7, 21, 71, 152, 161, 172, 243
Fried, E., 132
Friedlander, M. L., 40
Friedman, R. C., 32
Fromm, E., 229
Fulero, S. M., 107, 220, 221
Furr, S. R., 114

Galvin, M. D., 215, 216, 221
Garber, R. A., 11
Garfield, S. L., 5
Gelso, C. J., 126
Gibbon, M., 90
Gilbert, L. A., 9, 68, 101, 102, 243, 252
Gilligan, C., 209, 246
Gilliland, B. E., 92
Glaser, R. D., 214
Glass, G. V., 5
Glasser, W., 8, 228, 229
Goethals, G. R., 83
Goldman, G. D., 175
Goldfried, M. R., 5
Goodman, M., 32
Goodyear, R. K., 40
Gorsuch, R. L., 110
Gottlieb, M. C., 214
Greenberg, J. D., 6
Greenberg, J. R., 71
Greenberg, M., 214
Greene, D., 82
Griffith, E. H., 102
Guidano, V. F., 7, 8
Gurman, A. S., 5
Gynther, M. D., 102

Halgin, R. P., 33
Hamilton, S. B., 104
Hammell, U. L., 33
Hammond, C., 134
Handelsman, M. M., 215, 216, 221
Hardin, S. I., 91
Hare, R., 209
Hare-Muston, R. T., 215
Harris, M., 219
Harris, T., 147
Healy, J. M., Jr., 9
Heck, E. J., 91
Heitler, J. B., 104
Helms, J., 207

Heppner, P. P., 68
Hepworth, D., 134
Hersen, M., 90
Heslin, R., 32
Herzog, C., 219
Hickey, C. S., 104
Hobbs, N., 5
Holroyd, J., 214
House, P., 82
Howard, G. S., 11
Hudson, W., 168
Hupprich, W. R., 219
Hyland, M. E., 248
Hymer, S., 96

Iago, 208, 209
Imes, S. A., 82
Ingram, R. E., 82

James, R. K., 92
Jensen, J. P., 67
Jensen, J. V., 102
Janoff-Bulman, R., 45
Johnsrud, C., 215
Jones, E. E., 77

Kaplan, M., 102
Kass, F., 102
Kegan, R., 47, 98
Keith-Spiegel, P., 210, 214, 220
Kemper, M. B., 215
Kesson-Craig, P., 215
Kiesler, D. J., 5, 6
Kilburg, R. R., 42
Kitchener, K. S., 209
Klein, M., 182
Kliegl, R. M., 5
Knapp, S., 16, 218, 219, 220, 221
Kniskern, D. P., 5
Kobos, J. C., 169
Kohut, H., 6, 137
Koile, E., 136, 137, 145, 162, 207
Kokotivic, A. M., 68
Kondo, A. T., 108
Koocher, G. P., 210, 220
Kopp, S., 96, 179, 180, 228, 233
Kraft, W. A., 42
Krajaski, J. P., 32
Kramer, S., 180, 185

Lachar, D., 102
Lamb, D., 181, 182, 186
Landau, C., 236
Langs, R., 137, 169
Lazarus, A., 21, 137
Lemkau, J., 236
Levenson, E., 182
Lee, V. E., 69
Lerman, H., 214
Lewis, K. N., 67
Lewis, P., 9
Lewis, W., 171, 172
Lichtenberg, J. W., 9, 91
Liotti, G., 7, 8
Liss-Levinson, N., 215
London, P., 67
Lonner, W. J., 102
Lubin, B., 120
Luborsky, L., 5

Magnusson, D., 9
Mahoney, M. J., 6, 8
Malcolm, J., 245
Marecek, J., 215
Markus, H., 70
Marlowe, D., 77
Marsella, A., 102
Marshall, R., 175
Martin, A., 32
Martin, E., 179
Maxmen, J., 90
May, R., 132, 149, 228
May, R. J., 69
McFall, M. E., 104
McNeill, B. W., 69
Medeiros, M. E., 42
Menninger, K., 173
Messer, S. B., 3
Meehl, P., 69
Melville, H., 152
Merluzzi, T. V., 213
Meyers, P., 11
Miller, J. B., 247
Miller, T. I., 5
Mills, M., 107, 220
Milman, D. S., 175
Milne, 201
Mintz, J., 110
Mitchell, S. A., 71

Nance, D. W., 11

Napier, A., 243
Nathan, P. E., 42
Nichols, S. E., 33
Norcross, J. C., 11
Norwood, R., 236
Novak, M., 146
Nurius, P., 70

Omizo, M. M., 33
Otani, A., 174

Parham, T. A., 207
Parloff, M. B., 5
Parrino, 104
Pascal, G. R., 90
Pearls, F., 21
Pedersen, P. B., 102
Perls, F., 229, 230, 250
Person, E. S., 247
Pfost, K. S., 16
Pine, G., 137
Pinsof, W. M., 5
Pipes, R. B., 65, 215
Pope, B., 90
Pope, K. S., 210, 214
Powers, W. T., 248
Presser, N. R., 16
Price, R. E., 33
Prochaska, J. O., 42

Rachlin, V., 252
Radloff, C. E., 83
Ray, S. B., 91
Reid, P. T., 214
Reid, W. H., 90
Reik, T., 129, 137
Reilley, R. R., 42
Rice, C., 178
Robinson, W. L., 214
Rodolfa, E. R., 42
Rogers, C. R., 8, 77, 127, 137, 143, 153, 156, 159,
    160
Rogers, R., 91, 219
Rosenkrantz, P. S., 101
Rosenthal, R. H., 90, 143
Rosewater, L. B., 9
Ross, J., 220
Ross, L., 82
Roth, L. H., 92, 221
Roth, S. R., 8, 137, 139, 169, 185

Rowe, C. J., 90
Russ, S. W., 102
Ryan, W., 250
Rutan, J., 178
Rytting, M., 32

Safran, J. D., 6
Sales, B. D., 213, 216
Sampson, E. E., 9
Sande, G. N., 83
Schacht, T. E., 101
Schafer, R., 121, 122
Schoenfield, L. S., 214
Schurtman, R., 179
Schwarz, R., 65
Sell, J. M., 214
Shakespeare, W., 208
Shapiro, D. A., 5
Simon, R., 221
Simonton, S., 179
Singer, B., 5
Singer, E., 169, 172
Skodol, A. E., 90
Slaikeu, K. A., 92
Slater, B. R., 33
Sloane, R. B., 5
Smith, E. M. J., 102
Smith, N. L., 5
Smith, V., 134
Snyder, D. K., 5
Snyder, C. R., 82
Soisson, E. L., 16, 218, 219, 220, 221
Sorenson, R. L., 110
Spitzer, R. L., 90, 101, 102
Staples, F. R., 5
Stein, T. S., 32
Steiner, C., 146
Stewart, A. J., 9
Stiles, W. B., 5
Storr, A., 152
Strean, H., 168, 243
Strong, S. R., 19, 68
Strupp, H., 180, 181, 185
Styron, W., 202
Subich, L. M., 91
Sullivan, G., 107
Sullivan, H. S., 6, 242
Suls, J., 82
Surrey, J., 6

Tabachnick, B. G., 210, 214

Taft, J., 170, 181
Talbert, F. S., 215
Tarachow, S., 97, 99–101
Teicher, A., 32
Teyber, E., 10
Thorpe, J. S., 214
Thoreson, R. W., 42
Tichenor, V., 91
Tinsley, H. E. A., 91
Tolkien, J. R. R., 1
Tracey, T. J., 68, 91, 133
Turner, S. M., 90

VandenBos, G. R., 5
Viorst, J., 227
VandeCreek, L., 16, 218, 219, 220, 221
Vasquez, M. J. T., 102
Vogel, S. R., 101

Wachtel, P. L., 175
Walker, L. E. A., 9
Wan, C. K., 82
Ward, L. G., 40
Warner, R., 213

Weed, L., 16
Weinberg, G., 3, 64, 75, 76
Weiner, I. B., 151, 154, 155, 158, 202
Werrbach, J., 102
Westefeld, J. S., 114
Wheelis, A., 173, 184, 234
Whitaker, C., 243
White, L., 177
Wile, D., 169
Williams, J. B. W., 90, 102
Wills, R. M., 5
Winokur, M., 3
Winslade, W., 220
Wipple, K., 5
Wise, M. G., 90
Wolberg, L. R., 13, 90, 154, 182
Wollersheim, J. P., 104
Worthington, E. L., Jr., 24
Wright, R. H., 219

Yalom, I., 66, 95, 125, 127, 157, 184, 225, 238, 253
Yorkston, N. J., 5

Zuniga, M. E., 102

SUBJECT INDEX

Abuse/Battering, 5, 81, 82, 91, 102, 108, 109, 183, 248, 249–250
Affect/Emotion, 4–6, 8, 71, 132, 140, 164, 165, 205, 245
AIDS, 33–34
Alliance (Therapeutic), 8, 126, 134, 136, 138, 155, 156, 170, 171, 176, 254
Ambiguity In Responsibility, 239
Anger (Toward Client), 22, 49, 55
Anger (Toward Therapist), 49, 51, 52, 73
Anxiety, 119, 141
Attachment, 7, 8, 126, 128, 142, 248, 250
Awareness, 130, 228–232, 240

Balance Between Therapist Involvement/Distance, 61
Bartenders, 3

Chance, 3
Childhood, 4, 7, 8, 10, 153, 158, 168, 169, 243, 244
Client Fears, 63–88, 95, 96, 100, 101, 104, 167, 169, 170, 171, 173, 180

Client Relationships, 119, 147, 148, 157
Client Requests, 94
Client Strengths, 97, 112, 136
Client Vulnerability, 95–96, 128
Cognitive Errors, 81
Common Clinical Wisdom, 3, 4, 9, 10
Compulsive Action, 239
Conditions of Worth, 70, 77, 159
Confusion (Client), 50, 239
Confusion (Therapist), 50, 52
Corrective Emotional Experience, 171
Countertransference, 81, 117, 120, 136, 142, 161–166, 179, 180, 253
Culture/Cultural, 2, 3, 9, 10, 23, 64, 68, 77, 81, 83, 102, 154, 156, 157, 201, 207
Curiosity, 139

Death, 3
Dependency, 7, 15, 46–48, 70–72, 74, 82, 87, 88, 141, 142, 143, 155, 158, 249
Depression, 113, 135
Development/Developmental, 7, 8
Diagnostic Categories, 90

Drugs/Alcohol, 91
DSM III-R, 90, 93
Dual Relationships, 210, 214
Duty To Warn And Protect, 220–221

Elves, 1
Empathy, 7, 64, 129, 133–135, 137, 139, 140
Empowerment, 250
Environment, 2, 3, 9, 10, 11, 81, 147, 205
Ethics, 130, 141, 208–218, 219
Ethnic/Racial Issues, 55, 56, 68, 81, 94, 102, 113, 191, 207, 212
Expectations (Client), 71, 77–78, 79–81, 91, 97, 99, 104, 110, 131, 133, 153, 161, 164, 169, 172
Expectations (Therapist), 53, 125, 136
Expletives (Therapist Use Of), 32

False Self, 66
False Consensus Effect, 82
Family, 10, 111, 112, 216
Free/Freedom, 3, 4, 132
Functional Psychosis, 93

Gender, 50, 86, 94, 101, 102, 113, 212, 236
Grief, 5, 130, 142, 180, 185
Groups, 94, 95

Hairdressers, 3
Hallucinations, 92
Help-Rejecting Complainer, 75
Homicide/Violence, 92, 95, 106, 107, 220–221
Hope/Encouragement, 5, 8, 86, 99, 101, 133, 134, 140, 174
Hospitalization, 19–20, 34, 35, 255

Impostor, 82, 85
Informed Consent, 215–216, 222–223
Insurance, 15, 213, 219
Irresponsibility, 239–240

Listening, 98, 119, 129, 132–133, 135, 137–150, 197, 252
    For Content, 144–145
    For Feelings, 145–146
    For Themes, 119, 146–150

Malingering, 91

Malpractice, 219–220
Medical Psychology, 111
Medication, 95, 220
Mental Status Exam, 92, 105–109, 124
Ministers, 3

Need for Client Approval, 56–57
Neurotic Guilt, 238
No-Shows, 30–31

Organic Psychosis, 93

Physical Illness/Disease, 111, 112
Presenting Complaint, 64, 66, 90, 91, 109–110, 126
Previous Psychotherapy, 72–74, 112
Projection, 66, 71, 173
Psychosis, 92, 93, 95
Psychotherapy
    Boredom In, 163
    Common Elements In, 4, 5, 77, 79
    Confidentiality In, 14, 64, 75, 76, 209, 213, 216, 220
    Crying In, 59
    Effects Of, 85–88
    Feminist, 9, 67, 68
    Friendship In, 47, 67, 181, 191, 196–197
    Gifts In, 31–32, 186
    Giving Clients Credit, 97, 186, 204
    Identification With Client, 55, 56, 60, 61, 68, 96, 138, 139, 164, 165, 168, 212
    Impact Of, 67, 86–88
    Interpersonal Experience, 1, 4, 6, 8, 10, 78, 160, 170, 171, 179
    Limitations Of, 2, 4, 46, 53, 54, 205
    Mistakes, 188–207
        Too Much Of One Thing, 189–190
        Social Behaviors Inappropriate To The Role, 190–192
        Setting The Client Up For Failure, 192–193
        Trying To Solve The Problem Prematurely, 193–195
        Focusing On Someone Other Than The Client, 195–196
        Trying To Be A Friend, 196–197
        Not Tolerating Silence, 197
        Asking Too Many Questions, 197–198
        Not Going Into Deeper Levels, 199–200
        Poor Phrasing Of Interventions, 201
        Not Finding Out How The Client Has Tried To Solve The Problem, 201–202

Allowing Too Limited A Time To Deal With
   Termination, 202–203
Not Setting Limits, 203
Holding Too Much Back From The Client,
   203–204
Discussing A Problem Only Once, 204–206
Moralizing Or Passing Judgment, 206–207
Records/Notes, 15–17, 50, 218–219, 221
Relationship, 9, 11, 38, 39, 57, 60, 65, 69–72, 78,
   79, 84, 126–128, 134, 136, 142, 155, 171,
   179, 247
Rescuing Clients, 127, 142, 156, 163, 197
Setting Limits In, 17, 18, 20, 29, 30, 35, 36, 127,
   135, 148, 176, 203
Sexual Attraction/Behavior, 28–31, 58
Silence In, 37, 38, 197
Therapist Disclosure, 22, 49
Third Party Payers, 213
Touching In, 32
Priests, 3

Rabbis, 3
Racism, 68, 130, 191
Reactive Psychosis, 93
Real Guilt, 238
Referral, 95, 110, 184, 255
Relationships, 65, 69, 77–79, 87, 119, 242–255
   Importance Of Early Experiences, 243–245
   Implications Of Persistent Patterns, 245–248
      Complementary Expectations, 246–247
      Ambivalence About Intimacy, 247–248
   Dysfunctional Styles, 248–250
Religion, 23–25, 81, 94
Reluctance, 170–172
Resistance, 26, 38, 39, 70, 83, 101, 131, 145, 155,
   167–177, 193
Respect (For Client), 54, 66, 67, 75, 96, 97, 99, 104,
   130, 134, 136, 154, 179, 219
Respect for Other Professionals, 217
Responsibility, 99, 227–241
Responsibility (Client), 131, 132
   Openness to help, 131
   Exploration of Affective Issues, 132
   Willingness to make behavioral changes, 132
Responsibility (Therapist), 128–130, 216
   Clear Therapeutic Priorities, 129
   Emotional Availability, 129
   Objective Assessment, 129
   Therapeutic Knowledge and Skill, 129–130
   Self-Understanding, 130
Responsibility For Versus Responsibility To, 234–235
Responsibility Versus Obligation, 235–236

Self, 4–6, 10, 11, 49, 66, 70, 75, 78, 79, 85, 87, 238
Self-Affirmation, 236, 251
Self-Deception, 231
Self-Presentation, 66, 76–78, 85, 119
Self-Responsibility
   Versus Selfishness, 236–237
   Versus Control, 237–238
   Versus Self-Blame, 238–239
Sexism/Sex Bias, 9, 10, 68, 130, 191, 210
Sexual Preference/Gay/Lesbian, 17, 32–34, 212
Short-Term/Time-Limited Psychotherapy, 48, 74,
   85, 94, 101, 180
Social Influence, 19, 68, 72
Stress In Psychotherapists, 42
Suicide, 16, 92, 95, 106, 107, 113–117, 124, 199
Supervision, 22, 26, 27, 34, 39–42, 45, 48, 54, 56,
   57, 61, 62, 211, 212

Tarasoff, 220–221
Termination, 20, 56, 69, 72, 131, 178–187, 202–
   203, 215
   Client-Initiated Decision, 182–183
   Therapist-Initiated Decision, 183–185
   Mutual Decision, 185–186
   Final Session, 186
Testing, 120–122
Therapists Fears
   Clients Getting Too Close, 46–48
   "Making A Fool Of Oneself", 48–53
   Not Being Competent To Help, 53, 54
   Making The Client Worse, 54, 55
   Not Liking The Client, 55, 56
   Client Not Liking The Therapist, 56, 57
   Losing Control Of The Session, 57–60
   Losing Control Of Emotions, 60, 61
   Making A Difference, 61
   Supervisors Evaluation, 61, 62
Transference, 79, 81, 151–161
   Factors Producing, 157–159
   Importance of Using, 160
   Limits Of Using In Psychotherapy, 157
   Positive And Negative, 154–155
Transference Resistance, 172–173
True Self, 85

Unconscious, 125, 127, 161, 215, 243, 245

Working Alliance, 156

Values, 5, 23, 67, 68, 191, 201, 206, 221, 241